POWER, POLITICS AND IDENTITY IN SOUTH AFRICAN MEDIA
SELECTED SEMINAR PAPERS

EDITED BY ADRIAN HADLAND, ERIC LOUW, SIMPHIWE SESANTI & HERMAN WASSERMAN

Published by HSRC Press
Private Bag X9182, Cape Town, 8000, South Africa
www.hsrcpress.ac.za

First published 2008

ISBN 978-0-7969-2202-1

© 2008 Human Sciences Research Council

The views expressed in this publication are those of the authors. They do not necessarily reflect the views or policies of the Human Sciences Research Council ('the Council') or indicate that the Council endorses the views of the authors. In quoting from this publication, readers are advised to attribute the source of the information to the individual author concerned and not to the Council.

Copyedited by Lisa Compton and Karen Press
Typeset by Jenny Wheeldon
Cover design by Fuel Design
Print management by comPress

Distributed in Africa by Blue Weaver
Tel: +27 (0) 21 701 4477; Fax: +27 (0) 21 701 7302
www.oneworldbooks.com

Distributed in Europe and the United Kingdom by Eurospan Distribution Services (EDS)
Tel: +44 (0) 20 7240 0856; Fax: +44 (0) 20 7379 0609
www.eurospanbookstore.com

Distributed in North America by Independent Publishers Group (IPG)
Call toll-free: (800) 888 4741; Fax: +1 (312) 337 5985
www.ipgbook.com

POWER, POLITICS AND IDENTITY IN SOUTH AFRICAN MEDIA

Contents

Abbreviations and acronyms   vii

1   Introduction   1
    Adrian Hadland, Eric Louw, Simphiwe Sesanti and Herman Wasserman

Identity in theory

2   Media, youth, violence and identity in South Africa: A theoretical approach   17
    Abebe Zegeye

3   Essentialism in a South African discussion of language and culture   52
    Kees van der Waal

4   'National' public service broadcasting: Contradictions and dilemmas   73
    Ruth Teer-Tomaselli

5   Field theory and tabloids   104
    Ian Glenn and Angie Knaggs

6   Identity in post-apartheid South Africa: 'Learning to belong' through the (commercial) media   124
    Sonja Narunsky-Laden

Media restructuring and identity formation after apartheid

7   Finding a home in Afrikaans radio   151
    Johannes Froneman

8   The rise of the *Daily Sun* and its contribution to the creation of post-apartheid identity   167
    Nicola Jones, Yves Vanderhaeghen and Dee Viney

9   Online coloured identities: A virtual ethnography   184
    Tanja Bosch

10   The mass subject in Antjie Krog's *Country of My Skull*   204
      Anthea Garman

Expressing identities

11   Crime reporting: Meaning and identity making in the South African press   223
      Marguerite J Moritz

12   Afrikaner identity in post-apartheid South Africa: The Self in terms of the Other   239
      Wiida Fourie

13   Foreign policy, identity and the media: Contestation over Zimbabwe   290
      Anita Howarth

14   Masculine ideals in post-apartheid South Africa: The rise of men's glossies   312
      Stella Viljoen

15   Tsotsis, Coconuts and Wiggers: Black masculinity and contemporary South African media   343
      Jane Stadler

16   The media and the Zuma/Zulu culture: An Afrocentric perspective   364
      Simphiwe Sesanti

17   Black masculinity and the tyranny of authenticity in South African popular culture   378
      Adam Haupt

Contributors   399

Abbreviations and acronyms

AMPS	All Media and Products Survey
ANC	African National Congress
BBC	British Broadcasting Corporation
CODESA	Congress for a Democratic South Africa
COSATU	Congress of South African Trade Unions
CP	Conservative Party
DA	Democratic Alliance
DSTV	digital satellite television
IBA	Independent Broadcasting Authority
ICASA	Independent Communication Authority of South Africa
LSM	Living Standards Measure
MDC	Movement for Democratic Change (Zimbabwe)
NP	National Party
RSG	radiosondergrense
SABC	South African Broadcasting Corporation
SACP	South African Communist Party
SANEF	South African National Editors Forum
TRC	Truth and Reconciliation Commission

1 Introduction

Adrian Hadland, Eric Louw, Simphiwe Sesanti and Herman Wasserman

The second decade of democracy in South Africa has created a sufficient distance for media scholars to look back on what has been achieved and to begin to understand and critique the trends and developments that have transpired in the years since the abolishment of apartheid in 1994. It is true that the media, like South African society itself, have undergone massive changes in this period. The liberalisation of the broadcast sector, the arrival of the tabloids, the growth of the Internet and significant shifts in the ownership patterns of media organisations are sufficient evidence of the predominance of change. But, again as in society itself, there are some areas of the media where change has been lacking or minimal. Some of these areas are the participation of women in the media, where the status quo has remained stubbornly resistant, as well as the terms on which the voices of black youth are heard in mainstream media. A study of the South African media post-1994 must therefore tread carefully so as to explore the interesting and often unpredictable ways in which change has been taking place while at the same time not be so celebratory of change that persisting challenges and problems get overlooked.

This 'double moment' of change and continuity can also be noted in studies of South African identity post-1994. Alexander (2006: 13) refers to two opposing views of South African identity after apartheid. The one view is that the social landscape of South Africa has changed to such an extent that identities have become fluid, changing and hybrid. On the other hand, as Alexander shows, scholars like Zegeye (2001) maintain 'a primary concern with political identity' after apartheid (Alexander 2006: 14). This dualism becomes clear in the ways in which specifically the category of 'race' in post-apartheid society has been studied. Nuttall (2006) identifies two streams of race studies. The first, and dominant, stream consists of work 'paying renewed attention to racism and identity'. This work, exemplified by Wasserman and Jacobs (2003) and Zegeye (2001), 'focuses on hidden, invisible forms of racist expression and well-established patterns of racist exclusion that remain unaddressed and uncompensated for, structurally marking opportunities and access, patterns of income and wealth, privilege and relative power' (Nuttall 2006: 271). The second stream of race studies, into which Nuttall categorises the work of Achille Mbembe (2004) and others, draws on discourses of 'multiculturalism' that simultaneously acknowledge the history of 'race thinking' and attempt to move beyond it. The latter type of study aims to highlight the agency exercised by actors in reshaping their identities, especially in assuming a role as consumers in the market economy. The increasing emergence of consumer identity, especially among young South Africans, is also a development identified by Alexander (2006: 60).

The renegotiation of identity in the contemporary South African context, whether in terms of a re-emergence of old identities (Alexander 2006: 39) or as part of 'new ways of imagining' (Nuttall & Michael 2000), takes place at the intersection of the local and the global. On the one hand, the influence of 'supranational forces' (Alexander 2006: 37) on the formation of identity has been marked; on the other hand, shifts in local discourses have led to different notions of citizenship, nationhood and cultural identity emerging in the post-apartheid period. These two sources of influence on identity formation should not be seen as separate – rather, the global and the local often overlap or feed off each other. While the consolidation of local identities frequently takes place in reaction against the perceived threat of 'McDonaldisation', discourses such as the 'African Renaissance' also position the construction of South African identity within a broader pan-African sphere of influence. The latter discourse, supported by President Thabo Mbeki, can be seen as a reassertion of African identity that represents a move away from the conception of the 'rainbow nation' that was the 'leitmotif of Nelson Mandela's presidency' (Alexander 2006: 40).

From the above overview it becomes clear that the study of identity and culture in post-apartheid South Africa has yielded multiple and often divergent insights. These concerns remain important for scholarship aimed at understanding the rapid and often complex shifts taking place in South African society, political life and cultural formations. However, while the media have emerged as important role-players in all these areas, they are still often relegated to a marginal position in identity studies as well as within the broader terrain of cultural studies. When the media do enter the discussion, they are mostly treated as textual artefacts containing representations of identity categories such as gender or race, rather than in terms of their implication in broader social, political and economic processes.

If identity studies have diverged, as shown above, into a study of the emergence of new hybrid forms on the one hand and a study of the continuity of structural impediments mitigating against them on the other, the study of journalism and the media has equally been divided between structure and agency. Scholarly debates around the media's position in post-apartheid society have tended to focus either on structural shifts and continuities (by studying, for example, the media's place in the political economy of the transition; ownership and editorial changes; and the media's relationship with civil society); professional issues (usually taking the form of reiterations of functional orthodoxy, such as the media's role as 'watchdog of government' or protector of the 'public interest'); or symbolic dimensions (of which the representation of race and gender has enjoyed particular attention). These different aspects have until now seldom been connected. This collection of essays is intended as an exploration of these intersections. It brings together perspectives on the media's role in the transition that interrogate the relationships between identity discourses and political power, between new subjectivities and persisting legacies of apartheid, and between new narratives of nationhood and the increased commercialisation and privatisation of the public sphere. While this exploration takes the local specificity of South Africa as its point of departure, it remains aware of the acceleration of globalisation facilitated largely through the media. While the focus falls on the era after apartheid, it strives towards understanding contemporary developments against a wider historical backdrop. In doing so, the collection aims to investigate how the media's construction of identity in post-apartheid South Africa is inextricably linked with the politics of the transition in all its multifarious dimensions.

This collection of essays – many of which were presented at an international conference in Stellenbosch on the same theme in July 2006 – came about as a project to excavate the space between media and identity. The media, of course, have many forms, just as identity has many variations. Their interrelationship is a complex, shifting matrix as difficult to narrow down as it is important to the people who find their meaning within it. The media do generate, corroborate and accelerate identity formation, just as they diminish, overshadow and negate it. The variety of essays included in this volume reflects the various forms this process has taken during the first decade and more of democracy in South Africa.

South Africa offers a rich context for the study of the interrelationship between media and identity because its recent emergence as a democracy out of the quagmire of profound racial conflict, as well as the history of that conflict, has been closely tied to the role of its sophisticated media sector. During apartheid, large sections of the media were complicit in the legitimation of the ruling class's logic of separateness, or what Zegeye (2001: 1) has called 'imposed ethnicity'. Some media, however, also played a role in the resistance against apartheid. With the shift to democracy, the South African media have had to reposition themselves ideologically, politically and culturally. The influence this repositioning has had on the shaping of new identities in this period is investigated from various angles in this volume.

The essays are organised into three sections. In the first section, 'Identity in theory', contemporary theories relating to media and identity are interrogated and applied to the South African context. In his chapter 'Media, youth, violence and identity in South Africa', Abebe Zegeye draws on notions of the 'subaltern' in postcolonial theory, especially as it has been developed by Gayatri Spivak, to show how the legacy of the youth protests against apartheid led to their silencing in scholarship. Challenging what he calls 'elitist sociology', Zegeye investigates a number of structural conditions within which the identities of the youth of South Africa today are formed.

In his discussion of essentialism, Kees van der Waal emphasises the challenge to studies of identity, culture and language to 'probe for the assumptions underlying the discourses that form part of the encounters in this field' and to pay attention to human interactions and the context of events. Van der Waal's injunction against essentialism is a vital warning that fittingly frames the chapters to follow, given the dangerous tendency to homogenise and lapse into binary thinking when investigating identity issues in a context marked by a history of systemic polarisation, as was the case in South Africa. Van der Waal reminds us that '[a]ll forms of essentialism need to be questioned and seen as political attempts to frame constructions in a specific way, based on a set of interests and relationships'.

The normative theoretical concept of the 'public sphere' developed by Jürgen Habermas has become one of the standard theories by which the role of the media in contemporary society has come to be described. Ruth Teer-Tomaselli, in her study of the relationship between the public broadcaster, the public, the nation and the state, problematises the way that this concept 'has been applied to media with an almost canonical reverence'. She points out how the confluence of South Africa's democratising process and accelerated globalisation has put the South African public broadcaster in a precarious position. It has to balance the demands to reconstruct national identity after apartheid with the imperatives of a postmodern, globalised media market in which older notions of the public broadcaster – and therefore also the 'public sphere' – are forced to undergo revision. Public broadcasting in South Africa has thus become a terrain where the media's role in constructing identity has become severely contested.

In the following chapter, the Habermasian concept of the 'public sphere', as well as Benedict Anderson's well-known notion of the nation as an 'imagined community', is again found not to be suitable for an understanding of developments in the South African media. In their study of a Cape Town tabloid, the *Daily Voice*, Ian Glenn and Angie Knaggs suggest that the field theory of Pierre Bourdieu provides a better way of understanding the issues of media and identity in general and the tabloids in particular.

Sonja Narunsky-Laden also draws on the work of Bourdieu to develop a theory of cultural economy in South African media. Narunsky-Laden points to the salience of consumer culture in post-apartheid South Africa as a discourse through which new identities are forged, even as old racialised identities are reactivated in the context of consumption. She argues for a more dynamic approach to the formation of identity through media use than that entailed in theories of political economy or race. She sees the discourses of consumption, consumer culture and promotional culture as 'the dominant register of public debate in post-apartheid South Africa today'. These discourses are important to study because of their influence on social conduct, aspiration and cultural identity.

The overall impression left by the contributors to the first section of the volume is that, while investigations of the relationship between media and identity in post-apartheid South African society should take cognisance of theoretical approaches that seek to explain this relationship, these approaches should also be contextualised to fit the imperatives of the local and the contemporary.

The second section of the volume, 'Media restructuring and identity formation after apartheid', explores in more detail this contemporary local context. South Africa's media system underwent massive change in the wake of the country's political transition from apartheid to democracy in the early 1990s. Broadcast was the first sphere to experience dramatic transformation with the deregulation of the state monopoly in the run-up to the 1994 election. This process was fuelled by political concerns, principally from a liberation movement and broadcast-rights community hitherto excluded from access to state-dominated airwaves. The Independent Broadcasting Authority (IBA)

Act No. 153 of 1993 was the outcome of broad multi-party negotiations and established an independent regulatory authority to administer the newly liberalised airwaves. Within 10 years, almost 100 community radio stations had been granted licences by the IBA and its successor, the Independent Communication Authority of South Africa.

In addition, the introduction of a free-to-air television channel (e.tv), the privatisation of several radio stations that had once fallen under the ambit of the state-owned South African Broadcasting Corporation, and the arrival of satellite broadcasting propelled South Africa from a narrow, closely controlled broadcast sphere into a diverse and largely liberalised zone. This opening of the airwaves, and the appearance of the voices, languages and agendas therein, inevitably impacted on the articulation and development of South African identities. In the first chapter of this section, 'Finding a home in Afrikaans radio', Johannes Froneman provides an overview of the development of the South African broadcast media together with case studies of two Afrikaans radio stations, radiosondergrense (RSG) and Radio Pretoria. He asks how these two very different stations have become sites of struggle in the creation of meaning for an ethnic and language group stripped of its political power. Both stations, he finds, are entrenched in their ideological positions vis-à-vis the new political dispensation. RSG provides a home for an increasingly mixed racial grouping of Afrikaans speakers who broadly accept the non-racial imperative of the 1996 Constitution and who recognise the need for cultural and linguistic diversity. Radio Pretoria, on the other hand, 'insists on the right to reject the dominant political paradigm, while pragmatically seeking to find some minimum accommodation and ensure cultural and economic survival'. The existence of both stations, and the manner and direction of change in their audiences, demonstrate the diversity of identity within the Afrikaans community as well as the challenges and opportunities that this presents to a responsive broadcast media.

In the print media sector, similarly powerful developments were experienced with equally important consequences for the manner in which South Africa's many communities were represented. The country's small but influential alternative press, starved of foreign funds and with little appeal to commercial advertisers, struggled on into the mid-1990s before collapsing. Only the *Mail & Guardian* continues, now with foreign owners rather than overseas funders. Foreign capital also made its mark on the mainstream print media with the arrival of Tony O'Reilly's Independent Newspapers group just before the democratic election of 1994. With African National Congress (ANC) approval, O'Reilly bought the Argus newspaper group, formerly the country's largest collection of print media titles. Nigerian investment also saw the launch of a new daily in South Africa in 2003, *ThisDay*. The paper lasted just under a year.

One of the most significant trends of the post-1994 period in the South African print media was the arrival of tabloid newspapers. In 1994, the biggest selling daily newspaper – which sold an average of 191 322 copies per day in the first half of 1994 – was *The Star* of Johannesburg. By 2006, the *Daily Sun* was selling over 450 000 copies a day and had a daily readership of 3.44 million. The arrival of the tabloids, as the authors of the second chapter in this section point out, sparked fierce controversy among media analysts. At first, commentators bemoaned the apparently poor journalism of the tabloids seemingly founded on dodgy ethics and pandering to the lowest common denominator. Since then, according to Nicola Jones, Yves Vanderhaeghen and Dee Viney, more critical thought is being given to the impact and importance of the tabloid phenomenon.

In their chapter on the rise of South Africa's biggest tabloid, the *Daily Sun*, these authors argue 'while tabloid journalism may have many faults, it can also be seen as an alternative arena for public discourse'. Within this domain, new possibilities have been created for the provision of access and for the representation of citizens previously excluded from mainstream print media discourse. The authors suggest that the concomitant rise in literacy, in levels of participation and in the frequency and verisimilitude of self-identification necessarily supports a deepening of the quality of democracy. They also explore the relationship between cultural consumption and questions of cultural identity and investigate, in particular, how the *Daily Sun* has acted as a mechanism for identity change by offering 'tools of identity making' to its millions of daily readers.

Racial identity has never had more currency than in the post-apartheid era, argues Tanja Bosch in her chapter on online coloured identities. And with the Internet, new possibilities have been created for the exploration and articulation of these identities. Conducting a virtual ethnography of the Internet portal Bruin-ou.com, Bosch examines how the meaning of 'coloured' is explored on the Internet and how identity is constructed and contested via the site. She finds that coloured identity is linked more to global notions of blackness than to a South African black identity: 'coloured identity is still more than a dated apartheid label; it has been invented and reinvented'. She argues that the creation of virtual communities in cyberspace facilitates cultural empowerment as minority groups are able to consolidate their cultural identities despite geographic borders or other constraints.

An important trend in South African journalism, as well as in the world at large, has been the shift toward convergence. This process implies both the presentation of the same or similar content on a range of platforms as well as the concentration of those platforms into multi-use devices. Examples include the development of information and news websites by newspaper companies and the increasing multifunctionality of cellphones. Both trends are characteristic of the South African media sector in the post-1994 period. Both also demonstrate how the restructuring of the media has not been simply about changing ownership patterns, new media platforms or increased diversity. It has also been underpinned by shifting relationships between media forms and the manner in which these forms are accessed. In her chapter on Antjie Krog's account of her experience of reporting on the Truth and Reconciliation Commission (TRC), *Country of My Skull*, Anthea Garman illustrates exactly this notion and contemplates its implications for identity formation.

The TRC was the most important of the new South African state's attempts to deal with the past, Garman writes. Krog's book combines her own witnessing of the TRC's work with personal testimony from perpetrators and victims, and reportage of behind-the-scenes events and discussions. The product, argues Garman, is a work of journalism that the traditional journalistic outlets of radio, television and print could not convey equally well. The book allowed Krog to combine her skills as a poet with her insights as a reporter to present an understanding of what happened at the TRC and what it meant for South Africa.

Writer Andre Brink has argued that trying to contemplate the importance of the TRC would be 'irresponsible' without reference to Krog's text. In her chapter, which again leans on developments in public-sphere theory, Garman claims the text of *Country of My Skull* enables readers to participate in a 'mass subjectivity' that allows for an imaginary but demonstrable notion of national unity: '[I]t is this very construction of public-private subjectivity in relation to texts that allows for participation in an imagined, public and unknowably large community.' The chapter is a reminder that new forms of media are in the process of being created all the time and with them new avenues for the articulation, or subjugation, of identities. We therefore need to re-evaluate constantly the restructuring of the media matrix and of the place of identity within it.

Since 1994 South Africa has experienced a significant transformation of its political and media landscapes. Not surprisingly, these transformations have impacted on both collective and individual identities of South Africans. On the one hand, those identities that had emerged and grown under apartheid were destabilised by post-1994 hegemonic shifts. On the other hand, the reconfiguration of the country's socio-political and media landscape created the conditions for – and promoted – the emergence of new individual and collective identities. A complex process of identity construction, deconstruction and reconstruction has effectively characterised post-apartheid South Africa. Section three of this volume, 'Expressing identities', examines some of these processes through discussions of various media examples.

The authors contributing to section three have all focused on different identity formations. Only one author, Simphiwe Sesanti, deploys a form of perennialism to understand identity, while the other six authors contributing to this section share a common understanding of the phenomenon of identity. These six implicitly use constructivism, wherein identity is viewed as the outcome of a construction process. Sesanti's chapter thereby offers an interesting counterpoint to the way the other authors have viewed South African identity.

Overall, section three offers a series of case studies depicting the tensions and struggles associated with the birth of new and the mutation of old identities in contemporary South Africa. The case studies show how old identities have been reconstructed (or, alternatively, have resisted reconstruction), how new identities have been constructed out of the resources made available by a transformed media environment, and how new identities have grown from appropriating and/or reconfiguring media constructions imported from America via an increasingly globalised media system. The case studies also highlight the role of the post-1994 state in constructing new ideologies and identities, and the relationship of the news media to aspects of South African identity formation.

The result has been a dynamic environment for the birth of new identities and the mutation of old identities. If one examines the resultant process of identity formation and mutation through the case studies in section three, one is struck by the importance of:
- the role played by new (post-1994) media genres which function within the logic of neo-liberal globalised economics;
- the way in which identities emerge both 'organically' (from grass-roots

engagements with the world) and through the 'organised' labour of media professionals;
- how individuals construct their identities from the stories and images carried in the media, as well as from how they choose to relate to people around them;
- the impact of television and film images imported from America;
- the contradictions between, on the one hand, the preferred discourses of progressive media producers and ANC leaders and, on the other, realities on the ground (these contradictions get encoded into media products which then impact on identity formation);
- the resilience of old identities and ideologies;
- the local context which sets the parameters within which identity formation ultimately takes place; and
- the contradictions inherent in the contemporary nation-building and hegemony-building exercise that South Africa is grappling with, and how these contradictions impact on identity formation.

When reading these case studies, one is reminded of Karl Marx's observation that humans make their own history but are not free to make it as they please. Humans may be active builders of their worlds and their identities, but they are simultaneously constrained by existing social, economic and political conditions and by the weight of the past that is always already encoded into existing conditions and existing identities. Post-1994 South Africa illustrates all too well how the world is not a tabula rasa upon which the new can be inscribed afresh.

Wiida Fourie's analysis of letters to the *Beeld* newspaper is revealing of how Afrikaners, in adjusting to the post-apartheid environment, have reconstructed a number of key elements of their self-identity. Equally significant, Fourie shows how some core features of Afrikaner identity have remained resistant to change. In particular, letters to *Beeld* suggest that Afrikaner perceptions of 'the other', as well as attitudes about how Afrikaners should relate to 'others' (i.e. group boundary maintenance), have remained resistant to change. This mixture of change and resistance is revealing of the complexity that is identity construction.

Adam Haupt's analysis of the construction of South African black masculinity tells us much about the impact of popular culture on identity construction. In particular, we see the way in which black males are influenced by media images of African Americans and how these American media-made identities are both incorporated and reconfigured by South Africans as they construct their own identities.

Significantly, both Fourie's and Haupt's work reveals how the processes of post-apartheid identity reconstruction can be painful – and not only for white Afrikaners as might have been expected, but also for members of the emergent black middle class.

Both Haupt and Jane Stadler reveal the significance of images delivered by a globalised media, and how these global images are appropriated and localised in a South African context. Stadler's work unpacks how film images have simultaneously served to reproduce old identities, construct new identities, and disseminate and popularise American identities (especially African American identities) in a South African context. But, most significantly, Stadler's work on 'Coconuts' and 'Wiggers' shows us how South Africans have also subverted, deconstructed and reconfigured (that is, localised) these identities imported from America.

Stella Viljoen's work on South African men's magazines shows us something similar: when commercialised global media genres were imported into South Africa after 1994, they encountered a local context that demanded modifications. Viljoen's analysis suggests that identity construction among Afrikaner and black males requires a significant localisation of the content of media products. Again we see that, although American-derived media content is a resource South Africans do use in constructing their identities, it is an appropriation that often localises and modifies such content.

Anita Howarth's approach to identity is different from the other contributions insofar as it focuses on the government's attempts to manufacture a state identity. Howarth argues that South Africa's collective identity constructed and popularised since 1994 is now under threat due to a struggle over how South Africa should respond to the Zimbabwean crisis. This crisis is undermining some elements of the 'self-vision' South Africans have constructed of themselves. If Howarth is correct, South Africans may end up reconceptualising their collective vision, which would reconstruct key elements of their collective identity.

Marguerite Moritz and Sesanti both focus on the relationship between the news media and aspects of South African identity. Moritz examines how the discourses and practices of crime reporting generate a particular genre of news story which, in turn, helps construct a particular understanding of South Africa. Of interest is how these discourses and practices vary little from pre-1994 journalistic practices. Another point brought home in Moritz's chapter is that while journalists cherish criticising others, many journalists are themselves very sensitive to criticism. There is often a refusal to turn the mirror. Moritz observes that 'South African journalists acknowledge that the impact of their approach to crime reporting has been largely unexamined by journalists and by the media organisations they work for'. The question is, why? Is it the avoidance of deeper probing that may unearth the existence of inadequacies in the process of carrying out their duties? Or is it the refusal to acknowledge the bitter truth that journalists are not as 'independent' as they often claim to be or want to be – that more often than not they have to bow down to companies' newsroom culture that is often driven by profit imperatives as opposed to the often bandied-about 'public interest'?

In many ways both Moritz and Sesanti are concerned with the resilience of the sorts of journalistic practices and discourses that would have been familiar during the apartheid era. Through an examination of the reporting of incidents involving Jacob Zuma, Sesanti develops a full-blown critique of contemporary South African journalism. Sesanti's chapter is timely because it addresses the conflicting narratives of a Western-inspired liberalism underpinning the professional ideologies of South African journalism on the one hand, and a (largely state-sponsored) narrative of the 'African Renaissance' on the other. The discourse of Africanness is pervasive in post-apartheid society (for instance, one university has declared itself a 'World Class African University'; a newspaper has declared itself 'Distinctly African'; and former South African president FW de Klerk, in response to President Thabo Mbeki's 'I am an African' speech, declared that 'I am an African too'). Yet Sesanti criticises mainstream South African journalism for failing to understand African identity (which he sees as rooted in a perennial African culture) due to the resilience of Eurocentricism in South Africa's newsrooms.

Ultimately, each of the case studies in section three reveals that a struggle over South African discourses, practices and identity continues.

The essays in this collection show, from a range of perspectives and approaches, that South African identity formation remains an intriguing work in progress – and one worthy of ongoing analysis. We hope that this volume will make a lasting contribution to finding new ways of thinking about this complex, multi-layered and fascinating process.

The Editors
February 2007

References

Alexander P (2006) Globalisation and new social identities: A jigsaw puzzle from Johannesburg. In P Alexander, MC Dawson and M Ichharam (eds) *Globalisation and new identities: A view from the middle*, pp. 13–65. Johannesburg: Jacana

Mbembe A (2004) Faces of freedom: Jewish and black experiences. *WISER Review* 1(1): 4–5

Nuttall S (2006) A politics of the emergent: Cultural studies in South Africa. *Theory, Culture and Society* 23(7–8): 263–278

Nuttall S & Michael C (eds) (2000) *Senses of culture.* Cape Town: Oxford University Press

Wasserman H & Jacobs S (eds) (2003) *Shifting selves: Post-apartheid essays on mass media, culture and identity.* Cape Town: Kwela Books and SA History Online

Zegeye A (2001) Introduction: Imposed ethnicity. In A Zegeye (ed.) *Social identities in the new South Africa*, pp. 1–23. Cape Town: Kwela Books and SA History Online

Identity in theory

2 Media, youth, violence and identity in South Africa: A theoretical approach

Abebe Zegeye

There has been a tendency in analyses of the links between media and identity formation to concentrate on representation, that is, on how culture, people and events are represented in the media within different contexts and how that influences the formation of their identities. Often, the more structural aspects of the societies within which those identities are formed, and the effect they have on identity formation, have been neglected. In the present chapter, this lacuna is partially addressed, without attempting systematic analysis or completeness, by discussing a number of arbitrarily chosen structural conditions in South African society which may be utilised as the basis of a theoretical approach to such analyses.

In broad terms the conditions on which this chapter focuses are: youth and ethnicity, race and class structures, gender and HIV/AIDS, violence, poverty and unemployment, and education and globalisation. Before discussing these, however, I need to assert what I mean by identity, a broad concept variously defined in recent times.

What is identity?

Identity can be understood as the sense and continuity of 'self' that first develops as the child differentiates from parents and family and takes up an individualised place in society (Jary & Jary 2000: 285). In South Africa, during the uprisings that began in 1976 and continued into the 1980s, this differentiation appears to have assumed the character of a sharp rupture. Black adolescents turned against their parents in the struggle to liberate South Africa from apartheid, on the presumed grounds that their parents were too placid and inactive in the struggle. Many young people during that time then assumed the identity of revolutionaries. Erikson proposes that there is a crisis of identity during adolescence (Erikson 1968). At this stage of development the young person searches for an identity, trying out different friendship groups, different lifestyles and different career plans. Ideally, though, by the end of adolescence the identity has stabilised and the young person accepts him- or herself, feeling at ease with this identity. Because of the momentous and politically effective consequences of the youthful revolutionaries' actions in South Africa, this identity, formed under conditions of such stress, may even have been carried forward well into adulthood.

Furthermore, identity can be interpreted as people's source of meaning and experience (Castells 1999: 6–7). Identity, as it applies to social actors, refers to the process whereby social actors construct meaning on the basis of a cultural attribute or related set of cultural attributes. These attributes are assigned priority over other sources of meaning by the social actor. For a given individual or collective actor, there may be a plurality of identities, although such a plurality may be a source of stress and self-contradiction in both self-representation and social action. This is because identity must be distinguished from what sociologists have traditionally called roles. Roles (for example mother, neighbour, churchgoer, smoker, socialist militant) are defined by norms structured by the institutions and organisations of society. Their relative weight in influencing people's behaviour depends upon negotiations and arrangements between individuals and these institutions and organisations. Identities, on the other hand, are sources of meaning for the actors themselves and by themselves, constructed through a process of individuation. Although identities can be initiated from within dominant institutions, they become identities only when and if social actors internalise them and construct their meaning around this institutionalisation. There can be little doubt that the revolutionary black youth of South Africa internalised their identity largely through their experience of an oppressive society and in organisations and institutions resisting that oppression.

The concept of identity has become the primary medium for understanding the relationships between the personal (subjective) and the social, the individual and the group, the cultural and the political, and the group and the state. Within the discourse on identity there has been considerable divergence and debate. Whereas some academics have focused on the macro-level struggles through which identities are forged, constructed or imposed, others have investigated micro-level processes through which individual identities are formed and developed and collective ties are asserted and ascribed. Yet, despite disagreements and opposing viewpoints, most academics agree that questions regarding identity are fundamental to an understanding of the processes that link the individual and personal experience to large-scale cultural, social and political processes.

At the individual level, identity as a definition of personhood refers to *sameness* or *continuity* of the self over space and time, as well as to a *uniqueness* that is to be differentiated from other people or humankind (Baumeister 1986; Erikson 1968). However, contemporary use of the term 'identity' does not refer only to forms of personhood (either individual or social) but also to qualities of collectivities or groups. In this sense the term has been used to refer to the *sameness* among people belonging to the same collectivity or group and the *differences* between groups and collectivities – it forms part of the discourse on sameness and difference. These understandings of identity are used in association with a wide spectrum of perspectives in political and social theory.

The discourse on identity has also increasingly been associated with a variety of social struggles. Thus the politics of identity have spread from academic discourse to the centre of public conversation. The pursuits labelled 'identity politics' are consequently collective rather than merely individual, and are also public, not only private. As will become clear from this discussion, this response is of critical importance in understanding the recent social history of conflict and change in South Africa.

South African society is, even after the change brought about by the demise of apartheid in the 1990s, characterised by deep segmentation not only on the basis of culture, race, historical background, language and religion, but also on the grounds of economic status and class. South Africa has a centuries-long history of enforced racial segregation and domination, by the British and then by the apartheid government. Although this segmentation was not always institutionalised in the strictest sense of the word as legally enshrined practices, it entrenched racial differences in life chances and wealth. The country's history has also been characterised by numerous instances of political mobilisation buttressed by identity struggles. The mobilisation of Afrikaners after the South African War (1899–1902) that culminated in the seizure of political power in 1948 and the struggle of black people against the apartheid system are only two obvious examples (Adam & Giliomee 1978; Bekker 1996).

Despite the complex system of differentiation and segmentation, there are several examples of overarching identities. Thus African, 'coloured' (people of mixed racial descent) and Indian people united in the struggle against apartheid, and coloured and Indian people are now, in most scholarly works, included under the umbrella term 'black', signifying an identification with the aim of overthrowing the apartheid government. This intricate system of group categorisation and segmentation makes it almost inevitable that group identities, whether overarching or selective, will play a major role in the formation of self-concepts among South Africans.

Youth

Youth identities in South Africa assume a special significance in the analysis of recent structural aspects of this society. Although much has been written on the development of youth subcultures, in South Africa the black youth subculture and black culture in general came together as the youth of South Africa took the lead in the revolt during the 1970s, 1980s and 1990s.[1] Those momentous events led to greater equality between black and white South Africans, as well as democratisation of the government in South Africa, which began with the first free elections in 1994. Thus youth culture appears to have played a more dominant role in the recent history of South Africa than was the case in many other societies.

Another characteristic of South African society serves as further justification for inclusion of youth and youth culture in analyses of the structural conditions contributing to the formation of South African identities in general. The chronological age distribution of South African society is broadly similar to that of developing countries in the sense that it is basically a 'young' nation; more than 50 per cent of the population are below the age of 24 (*Umrabulo* 2006).

When analysed in terms of race, the age distribution patterns resemble those of developing and developed countries, with the two extremes being the African and white populations (*Umrabulo* 2006). Although the population aged slightly (reflecting lower fertility rates) between 1996 and 2001, the overall pattern has remained the same. The conclusion that can be drawn from this is that in general, because the majority of the population resembles that of developing nations, the overall dynamic is that of a developing nation. This undoubtedly plays a significant role in identity formation in South Africa.

Although divisions between youth and adults are evident, youth culture itself is not uniform (Jary & Jary 2000: 684). Youth culture is divided by gender, ethnicity, class, education and many competing cultural styles. The rise of distinctive youth cultures in modern societies is associated with the central role of mass communications media and increasing affluence. As South African society (of which the youth are an integral part) becomes more affluent, greater proportions of the population can be expected to have access to mass media, with a resulting increase in the influence of the media (and the representation of youthful events) on identity formation.

Ethnicity and black identity in South Africa

Ethnicity contributes to the collective sense of identity of black and white South Africans alike. The ethnic identity of South Africans, in terms of this approach, is to be understood as partially an ethnic and partially an African identity. Ethnicity in Africa is often misunderstood (Appiah 1999). Many people assume that virtually all the contemporary ethnic groups in modern Africa are descended from 'tribes', which are thought of as groups of people descended from common ancestors, ruled by a hereditary 'chief' and sharing a single culture, in particular a language and a religion. Although some pre-colonial African societies, such as some of the small Akan states in south-western Ghana and south-eastern Côte d'Ivoire, did approximate such a model, most did not. Even where they have come close to this model, this has usually been quite a recent development. Consequently, it is generally misleading to speak of modern ethnic groups as 'tribes'.

In spite of this, many Africans, when speaking of their identities, speak of their 'tribe' (Appiah 1999). African social and political life cannot be understood unless one understands what Africans mean when they refer to their 'tribe'. Tribal identities understood in this manner were not the only, or even the most important, of the identities recognised in pre-colonial Africa. People also belonged to clans or lineages, both groups defined by shared ancestry. Also, a group of modern ethnonyms refers to groups that have related languages and often share important cultural practices, but were not necessarily ever members of a single political community. The broadest such term is 'Bantu', which refers to hundreds of groups in east, central and southern Africa.

Ultimately, the conception of ethnicity adhered to in this chapter is consistent with the 'floating' concept of ethnicity which has been utilised by many researchers. In terms of this concept, ethnicity need not necessarily strongly influence people's actions or attitudes, but may become activated in different social conditions. However, once ethnic identities become politically significant, people who previously thought of themselves as belonging first and foremost to a small local group may decide to identify with a larger, more widely distributed group that appears to be more successful at winning resources (Appiah 1999). The size and boundaries of ethnic groups may shift with shifting political fortunes.

Some anthropologists, such as the Norwegian Frederick Barth, have indeed argued that the very idea of ethnicity exists only where there are boundaries between 'us' and 'them' within a shared social context (Appiah 1999). As a result, one may speak of ethnicity only in the context of many groups, defined by real or imagined shared ancestry, either living together within a single political system or at least in regular contact.

'Tribalism' has, according to Appiah (1999), come to be interpreted as one of modern Africa's major problems. However, by 'tribalism' people usually mean the *illegitimate* appeal to ethnic loyalty. When people speak of 'tribalism' they really assume that to act on the basis of ethnic loyalty is always wrong. This is because appeals to ethnic loyalty often occur in contexts of national-level competition between 'us' and 'them', resulting in ethnicity becoming a divisive factor. This interpretation of ethnicity probably explains to a large degree the ethnic conflict between Zulus and Xhosas in KwaZulu-Natal (with its inevitable consequences for identity formation in that region) after the first democratic elections in South Africa in 1994. However, Appiah points out that ethnic loyalty in Africa and elsewhere can also lead people to do good things for fellow members of their 'tribe', and that this is not necessarily at the expense of others.

Race and class as reflected in post-apartheid South African identities

The manner in which race and class simultaneously affect citizenship and democratisation, and thereby also identity formation among South Africans, needs to be considered. The South Africa of the past can be viewed as a society which was incontrovertibly dominated by a racist ideology. One may conclude from the societal changes that have taken place in South Africa, resulting in the demise of discriminatory apartheid, that in this country, as in the USA, class is assuming greater significance relative to race in determining stratification structures and black identities. At the same time, this may be the appropriate place to warn, as does Wolpe (1989), against the dangers of both race and class reductionism in social analyses in South Africa.

It is undeniable that inequality and widespread poverty among the black population is one of the most crucial legacies of apartheid. As measured by the gini coefficient in 2000 (six years into democracy), South Africa ranked as the third most unequal society in the world (Zegeye & Maxted 2002: 13). The desperately poor black people of Alexandra, for example, live cheek by jowl with the affluent white residents of nearby Sandton and this marked correspondence between race and class is poignantly captured in a poem by a young black person, wa Mogale, who writes:

> alexandra
> my home town
> of ramshackle shelters built from sacking
>
> cardboard
> scraps of wood
> and rusting corrugated iron...
>
> rust
> wretchedness
> and want
> in the milk-white teeth
> of sandton
> (wa Mogale 1992: 1; cited in Zegeye & Maxted 2002: 14)

Three conceptual obstacles have in the past tended to impede an analysis of the South African political system (Wolpe 1989: 5). These are, first, a particular simplistic variant of the idea of continuity in South African history, overemphasising the continuity of racial domination and imputing to people invariant, primordial racial motivations. Second, reductionist views of race and class were prevalent. Third, there is the overwhelming priority that was assigned in the analysis of the state and politics to the terrain and conduct of struggles, while little or no attention was given to the *structural* conditions and context of such struggles. These impediments were found singly or in combination in analyses of South African social formation which were informed by different theoretical perspectives. The effect of these obstacles was that significant questions on the character and trajectory of political struggles could not be posed and investigated.

The class struggle for socialism found organised expression in the South African Communist Party in 1921 (Wolpe 1989). In the struggle against the system in South Africa, the class struggle and the national struggle were often represented as being separate modes of political intervention, each with its own distinctive objectives and different social constituencies. However, according to Wolpe (1989: 11) a different theory of the South African revolution was developed in which the convergence of the class and the national struggles was emphasised. In terms of this theory, the liberation movement headed by the ANC is a multi-class alliance and draws inspiration from both nationalism and socialism. The growth and stabilisation of black trade unions in the 1970s tended to confirm the convergence in South Africa of nationalism and socialism, especially as the organised black working class later emerged as the dominant political actor in the country.

In exploring whether class analysis has utility in understanding identity formation among the black youth and adult population in South Africa, the sociological researcher is confronted by a number of pertinent questions. What, one wonders, is the best way to define 'class' in South Africa given that our society is complex, diverse and interdependent? What is the identity of the people who fall into the rising new black 'middle class'? How influential is this 'new middle class' in South Africa and what are its values and attitudes? We also need to enquire about the nature of the class structure of South Africa and whether all class structures can be investigated in the same way. To what extent does class, rather than race, motivate South Africans' behaviour? Is class a useful construct to use in analysing social relations in South Africa, and is South Africa a semi-industrial capitalist society or just a semi-industrial one? And finally, it is important to examine whether ascriptive or achievement-related markers of class and stratification are more acceptable in contemporary South Africa.

None of these questions has been adequately researched in South Africa to date. Within the limitations imposed by the provisos detailed above, it appears safe to assume that class has also come to play a decisive role in establishing the identity of South Africans.

Black identity in South Africa: a new approach

In any investigation focusing on group dynamics, the first requirement is to know who it is one is studying. Who do we include if we speak of the 'youth'? Youth is a category only in the most general sense (Slabbert et al. 1994: 12). The category of people designated to be the 'youthful' is positioned somewhere between one status – that of childhood – and another, adulthood. Both childhood and adulthood are socially constructed and are defined within institutional frameworks. All cultures distinguish between children and adults, but differ widely on their definitions and the ways in which they handle the transition from childhood to adulthood. Those who straddle the transition are known as the youth. In one community a person is a child until he or she marries, so that adulthood may be achieved between the ages of 12 and 24. In another community, a person may remain a child in terms of dependence until education is completed, which age may also be approximately between 12 and 24.

Because youth lies on a continuum between childhood and adulthood and is socially and institutionally defined, no absolute designations are possible. All designations of youthfulness are in fact arbitrary and dependent on the social and institutional contexts within which they occur. For South Africa, Slabbert et al. (1994: 13) favour the broadest possible definition of youth, namely people between the ages of 15 and 30 years. Taking cognisance of the dramatic recent developments in South Africa, this appears to be sensible. People between the ages of roughly 14 or 15 and approximately 30 did indeed play a crucial role in the changeover to majority rule with the election of the ANC to govern the country in 1994. It is generally accepted that the uprisings of 1976 (and the culmination of the liberation process in 1994) were youth-led from the outset, with many people in that age category being martyred. It is also recognised that the changeover brought about (potentially at least) fundamental societal change in South Africa, with attendant changes in identity and specifically youth identity.

It can be safely assumed that the identities of the black youth are an integral part, a subset, of the identity of black people as a whole in this country. Approaches to investigating black identities and culture have changed in recent times, however. For instance, Hall (1999) has suggested that two moments in black cultural politics have emerged, one tied to the past and another to the present. Both are rooted in history and the politics of anti-racism.

The first was the moment when the term 'black' was first used to refer to the common experience of racism and marginalisation in Britain. The term 'black' then became the organising category of a new politics of resistance among groups and communities with, in fact, widely differing histories, traditions and ethnic identities. In this moment, the 'black experience' as a singular and unifying context became dominant over other racial and ethnic identities although the latter did not disappear. In this manner, black people were positioned as the unspoken and invisible 'Other' in predominantly white aesthetic and cultural discourses.

In the most recent period, a second and new moment has arisen (Hall 1999). Here, the recognition of the extraordinary diversity of subjective positions, social experiences and cultural identities comprising the category of 'blackness' is at issue. 'Blackness' is viewed as essentially a politically and culturally constructed category, which cannot be based on a fixed set of trans-cultural or transcendental racial categories. The idea that race, or some composite of race relating to blackness, will guarantee the effectiveness of any cultural practice or determine in any final sense its aesthetic value, therefore loses ground.

The rub is that the end of the politics of blackness brings about a continuous, turbulent mass of political argument and debate: a critical politics, and a politics of criticism (Hall 1999). Black politics can no longer be conducted by simply replacing the bad old essentially white subject with the new and essentially good black subject. Rather, it requires ridding oneself of the fiction that all black people are good, or indeed the same. The black subject can also no longer be represented without reference to such dimensions as class, gender, sexuality and ethnicity. The mutual political accommodation of the essentially human characteristics (identities) of the various categories of black South Africans may accordingly prove to be one of the crucial aspects determining the future of South Africa.

The implication of such a new approach to investigating identity and culture in South Africa is that there are no longer any guarantees in black culture and debate. This lack of guaranteed identities and patterns of social relations in South Africa was, in theory, heightened in the fundamental rupture and subsequent rebuilding of society which followed the youth revolt and led to the first democratic election in 1994 in South Africa. At the same time, new pressures to remain committed to the perpetuation of black politics were introduced as the new, black-majority government strove to redress the injustices committed against black people under the apartheid system. These are the guiding principles of the investigation undertaken here.

Sharpeville, Black Consciousness and youth revolt in South Africa

State policy after 1950 was to apply rigid segregation along racial lines in every possible sphere. As influx control tightened its grip on black people there was an outburst of defiance and pass burning that escalated into the Sharpeville shootings of 1960. Demonstrators were mowed down by gunfire, the majority shot in the back as they rushed away. This brutal action awakened international shock, horror and serious talk of imposing economic sanctions on the Pretoria regime. The apartheid government's reaction to the heightened tempo of black resistance, initiated by the Pan-Africanist Congress under Robert Sobukwe and the newly formed Congress Alliance (formed by the major anti-apartheid movements, of which the ANC was the most significant), was supremely predictable – increasingly stringent repression.

Sharpeville and its aftermath, as Worden (1994: 107) puts it, was for many blacks the final straw: the situation 'revealed the failure of non-violent resistance and forced a new approach from opponents of apartheid'. In this new wave of more assertive action against apartheid, one of the most influential organisations initiated by the youth was the Black Consciousness Movement, inspired and led by a young medical student, Stephen Bantu (Steve) Biko. Martyred for his convictions in 1977, he was still in his early twenties when his ideas on black assertion and self-esteem began to find wide acceptance. Black people, he said, should rid themselves of their debilitating 'slave mentality' and claim their rightful place in society. This emergent attitude was a crucial stage in the process of identity change among the youth. It motivated young people to move away from passive acceptance of the injustices of apartheid to active involvement in an attempt to change this oppressive political system (Magubane 2006: 18).

The dynamics of this new assertive attitude adopted by the black youth, and the volatile roles they began to assume, have been subjected to close analysis in a recent study by Hjalte Tin (2001). Tin's research leaves us in little doubt that the black youth of South Africa were, prior to 1976, both unheard and suppressed and that 1976 marked a watershed in their emancipation as well as their identification with a broad spectrum of civil society interests. He argues that studies of the Soweto uprising have not tried to understand the role of the children 'in their own right' (Tin 2001: 128). He uncovers some of the contradictory and many-layered relations between children, parents and the state that have, to this day, remained enigmatic. He also addresses the central question of the children as *attackers*: how, he asks, could the youth hope to force the strong and seemingly well-entrenched apartheid state to defend itself against *children*? What, I now ask, were the dynamics of this remarkable new role that the children of Soweto assumed?

By virtue of traditional initiation rites at puberty, black youth are admitted to adulthood and become emotionally empowered. In an apartheid society where inequality of opportunity and a shockingly deficient education system kept black youth locked into poverty and rendered them materially vulnerable, the scene was set for the youth to burst into the political arena. Bundy (1987: 310) goes so far as to say that in grappling with a distinct set of social and historic problems, a generation may develop an awareness and common identity that is analogous with class consciousness and national consciousness.

The children of Soweto, says Tin, confronted the state in three clearly defined but overlapping spaces (Tin 2001: 128). First, they challenged the state as *minors* at a time when the state ruled the nation because it had unquestioned power over the *fathers* and therefore over the family in a patriarchal society. Family life, Tin argues, was defined by descent, conjugality and patriarchal authority (although this was sometimes vested in a female) and family life had captured and preserved a private space different from public space. This private space he calls 'house space'. By its laws and practices the South African state at the time recognised house space to be beyond its direct reach. *Minors* were the responsibility of fathers; there was no necessity for the state to control them. The state possessed no instruments to rule children as children. If parental rule broke down in an emergency, the state could only treat children as adults.

Second, the children defied the state as *pupils* in the schools, that is, the functionally defined 'town space'. In schools, the children were confronted with state rule as applied by the teacher, who was servant of the state and an instrument of the notoriously inadequate 'Bantu education' system (Tin 2001: 129). Here, however, they were not ruled as daughters and sons of the father, but as pupils, or in more modern parlance, as *learners*. The lessons provided had functional rationality; learners had to learn whatever the state thought it necessary to teach them to fill a functional role in the future. This state aim was not, however, necessarily in sync with functionality as seen by the pupils; they had ambitions of their own to gain an education and secure paid employment.

Third, the children tackled the state at the frontiers of the *ethnic/racial space* (Tin 2001: 129). On the street the state confronted the children in the figure of the unremitting police officer (and even, as happened ever more frequently as the decade progressed, the armed soldier) who was there to enforce racial segregation.

On all three of these fronts there was generational conflict; the children were inevitably pitted against adults, rendered powerless by the confines of the spaces in which they moved, unable to create individual roles and identities for themselves or to exercise any agency (Tin 2001: 129). Tin's central argument is that the three children–adult structures of rule relied upon and supported one another. When one collapsed, the others became extremely vulnerable. The intricate interplay of generational conflict, of patriarchs versus minors, of state functional requirements (as vested in teachers) versus the ambitions of pupils, of the racist (ethnic) conflict of black teenagers versus the white police officer on the street – all this culminated in the explosion of youthful emotions that boiled over on 16 June 1976.

To defend the white town from the threat of the enormous concentration of poverty-stricken, oppressed black people, the state went to great lengths to segregate such townships, walling them in or using physical barriers like highways, railroads and industrial areas. One of the biggest and most populous of these black townships was sprawling Soweto on the outskirts of Johannesburg, the wealthy gold-mining centre of South Africa – developed, ironically, on the labour of the black proletariat. It was here in Soweto that the black youth took their defiant and unprecedented stand in 1976. The trigger, but by no means the only reason for this outburst and the unrest which followed, was the apartheid regime's insistence that black schoolchildren be taught in Afrikaans, the language of their oppressors (Ndlovu 2006: 324–325).

There was no industry at all in Soweto in the 1970s and the few shops provided only the most basic necessities. The law forbade black people to own property, but homes were rented from the municipality. There were no paved streets and most houses lacked electricity and piped water. Furthermore, there were no formal public spaces such as town squares, parks, main avenues or a city centre – these amenities, including department stores, industry, offices and public institutions from universities to gaols were in the 'white' town. According to Tin this rather peculiar township terrain impacted upon the children of Soweto and 'generated a highly specific mixture of violence'. He identifies five different forms of violence that were prevalent, all of which were created by the children themselves 'in response to the different terrains and adversaries they encountered' (Tin 2001: 132). These include fighting inside the township, contesting the township border, enforcing stay-aways from the white town, attacking the white town and ruling the parents. These issues are directly relevant to this study of the black youth and their changing roles and identities in the 1970s, and are discussed briefly below.

Fighting inside the township

The uprising unfolded when the children met on the morning of 16 June 1976 and marched non-violently with placards expressing their grievances on the use of Afrikaans in the schools. But their inner turmoil was much more deep-seated than the authorities realised and soon, when the children were face to face with stubborn rejection of their pleas, street battles erupted. Stones, glass bottles and bricks were thrown at the police; cars and commercial vehicles were stoned and burnt. Matters soon escalated beyond control (Ndlovu 2006: 341–342; Tin 2001: 132). The police were reinforced by border troops; they baton-charged, tear-gassed, shot and killed the frenzied children. By the evening of 16 June the authorities had already reached a maximum level of force and this was to be sustained during the next few months (Ndlovu 2006: 344–347).

The children were determined to counter the draconian white control of schools. School buildings were burnt down indiscriminately and in the following days no less than 50 Transvaal schools were damaged by fire as arson spread from the cities to outlying areas, including even the smallest towns (Tin 2001: 133). Indeed, burning schools became the primary transmitter of unconventional action from the metropolitan to the rural areas, including the homelands. The schools remained empty for the rest of the year and even, in some areas, into the year that followed (Ndlovu 2006: 350).

Contesting the township border

Nor was the youth-led unrest restricted to the townships. When the street battles pushed the armed bureaucratic forces to the boundaries of the townships, the confrontations immediately overflowed from the public space inside the township to the border areas that lay between the black and the white residential areas. Within 24 hours of the beginning of the uprising, youths had erected barricades in order to keep the police out and prevent commercial vehicles from entering Soweto. The state retaliated by halting all commuter trains and buses, preventing people from going to and fro from Johannesburg and Soweto (Tin 2001: 133–134).

Enforcing stay-aways from the white town

According to Tin, stay-aways were 'the first major step beyond the street battle and introduced the first direct child-patriarch confrontation' (2001: 134). Early on 4 August the children called for the first stay-away. What is remarkable about this is that in a traditionally patriarchal society where each household was headed by the father, it was the *children* that picketed stations and bus terminals, using all manner of coercion to persuade *adults* to stay at home in a form of resistance that was more politically sophisticated than street violence.

Attacking the white town

The first youth-inspired attack on white people that took place outside the township was a stoning incident on 20 July 1976, when at least 20 whites were injured on the main thoroughfare between Pretoria and Witbank, a coal-mining town to the east (Tin 2001: 134). There was also a dramatic escalation of the black–white struggle in early September when black schoolchildren travelled by train into Cape Town city centre and successfully staged large demonstrations. Later, similar attacks were repeated in the Johannesburg area, culminating in a march of black youngsters into the central city. Fierce clashes followed and for some hours the children held sway in the financial capital of Johannesburg, the very heart of metropolitan South Africa.

Ruling the parents

Finally, and arguably the most remarkable youthful transformation, Tin shows how children challenged their parents head-on in the heart of their family homes (2001: 135). Sifiso Ndlovu reports that on the eve of the Soweto uprising 'most parents were unaware of the plans for the demonstration' and goes on to quote the evidence of the father of 16-year-old Hastings Ndlovu, who was subsequently killed in the uprising: 'On 16 June I woke up as usual. I did not know anything, these kids were too secretive' (Ndlovu 2006: 341).

In a desperate attempt to forestall this takeover of authority and reinstate patriarchal control over the rebellious schoolchildren, the government held meetings with *makgotlas* (black vigilante groups consisting of older males) in September 1976, and granted the *makgotlas* legal recognition by the police (Tin 2001: 135). This was to no avail; in the Soweto uprising and over the decades that followed the children proved far stronger and more resilient than their parents. Indeed, in an ultimate show of defiance towards their parents – whom they perceived to be passively submitting to apartheid – many black teenagers fled from South Africa to join the ANC military wing, Umkhonto we Sizwe. The conflict had 'escalated into an all-out attack on the racist foundation of apartheid South Africa' – and one in which black children exercised primary agency (Tin 2001). In the coming decades the youth grew increasingly powerful and played a major role in the liberation struggle.

The influence of the conflict between state and the youth in South Africa on the youth's identity in the absence of the usual social and parental control cannot be overestimated and indeed appears to have thrust the youth into a leadership role in changing the structure of their society. This changed youth identity is assumed in the present discussion to have had a crucial and lasting effect on social and identity formation among black South Africans in general and the youth in particular. It is clear that the youth played a crucial role at many different levels in changing the structure of South African society and that violence was a basic ingredient of these changes.

It is also true, however, that the nature of violence and the identity of the youth have changed drastically in recent times in South Africa, especially since the transition to a democratic political dispensation in 1994. Whereas the youth-led uprising was the spark that ignited the liberation struggle and led to a new political dispensation in South Africa, it was clearly politically motivated and aimed at a more just and equitable society in South Africa. In contrast, the violence that still plagues South Africa has become more gender, crime and poverty related. In addition, a number of youth-linked phenomena have assumed greater prominence in South African society, chiefly the scourge of HIV/AIDS. These changes have been well documented in two significant studies by Pumla Gqola (2007) and Nthabiseng Motsemme (2007), whose work I discuss below.

A gender-sensitive approach to studying HIV/AIDS in conditions of poverty

Before I embark on a discussion of the work of Gqola and Motsemme, some remarks on gender in Africa are needed. Traditional African pre-colonial societies were patriarchal, closely linked to the bride-wealth system, and evidenced a marked sexual division of labour. Under colonialism and particularly during the apartheid era when many of the menfolk were swallowed into the migrant labour system, rural women, left to cope without their husbands, became the 'most overburdened sector of the labour force and the product of an enduring chauvinist tradition'. Furthermore, 'unorganised and low-paid black women were increasingly used to undercut higher-paid male labour' (Zegeye & Maxted 2002: 37).

It is clear that gender plays a more important role in African communities than was previously thought, and that the nature of the influence of gender is also changing. Since the first democratic elections in 1994 women have gained a great deal of agency in the sense that there is now a range of legislation of specific concern to women as well as relatively more women-sensitive legislation. In spite of this, race, class and gender continue to determine access to economic privilege.

The occurrence of HIV/AIDS, especially among the youth, has become one of the dominant phenomena in South African society. The number of children orphaned by HIV/AIDS is increasing at an alarming rate and this has given rise to enormous social problems. It is undeniable that the scourge is largely a post-apartheid dilemma. Furthermore, HIV/AIDS has had its most devastating toll on those – the poverty-stricken black majority – who were arguably entitled to have the highest expectations of the new democracy. The outlook on this front is grim and the ANC government came under heavy fire in 2000–2001 for its alleged lack of foresight in dealing with the pandemic; eventually, in late 2003, there was a decision to begin a rollout of antiretroviral drugs. Other endeavours to curb HIV/AIDS have also been stepped up, largely comprising education on the use of condoms and the dangers of indulging in unprotected sex.

Many of the youthful responses relating to HIV/AIDS, violence, the breakdown of parental authority, poverty and unemployment, the exposure to repeated experiences of death and the necessity to formulate survival strategies, are analysed below with reference to the ground-breaking work of Nthabiseng Motsemme. In the course of her research she conducted a number of conversational interviews with young black women and her findings indicate that the socio-cultural environment in which these young people are re-imagining their identities and having to redefine what constitutes 'risky and normative intimacy' and what 'remains joyous about relationships, sex and love in an age of HIV/AIDS', is indeed 'highly contradictory and complex' (Motsemme 2007: 61–62).

Motsemme argues convincingly that:
- Many of the current investigations of HIV/AIDS are too closely focused on specific high-risk behaviours found among what she calls 'groups who occupy the margins of society – homosexuals, prostitutes, blacks' (2007: 63–64). Other studies have erred in that they have concentrated on personality variables such as low self-esteem and low internal locus of control. Although knowledge of these issues is necessary, most of these studies have failed to explain why transmissions of the virus continue despite the absence of some or all of these factors. She argues that one of the major reasons for indulging in unsafe sex is love; this involves 'risk-taking, giving and trusting' – yet very little research has been done in this area. Motsemme's own research has shown that despite strong messages on the dangers of HIV/AIDS and publication of the very high infection rates in South Africa, unprotected sex remains the norm (2007: 64).
- Other studies have searched for individual personal deficiencies among those who engage in unsafe sex. This emphasis on the individual determinants of sexual behaviour and HIV/AIDS has tended to ignore the widely diverse social, cultural, economic and political circumstances that have the potential to influence sexual experience to varying degrees (Motsemme 2007: 65).
- The dominant use of survey research methods and psychological models of behaviour change have proved inadequate as they do not provide 'multi-dimensional insight into sexual accounts and the experience of suffering' (Motsemme 2007). There is a need to go beyond the routine witnessing, recording and dispassionate analysis of the problem – a liberal measure of 'outrage and compassion', says Motsemme, is needed. *Emotion* and *commitment* then become central to the researchers' work. A new language to describe intangible elements such as pain, suffering and recovery may even be needed.
- Part of human sexuality is about the search for pleasure, abandoning and surrendering oneself to another (Motsemme 2007: 65). This basic human need, she argues, cannot simply be pushed aside because a dangerous epidemic lurks. At the same time, the youth should not blindly compromise themselves by acting irresponsibly just because they have to satisfy a basic sexual instinct. Motsemme arrives at the nub of the study when she poses the challenging question: 'What is it like to try to love in a time of hopelessness?' (2007: 65).
- It is undeniable that the HIV/AIDS pandemic has become feminised and racialised. It now has the face of a black woman. More than that, it has the

face of a *young* black woman. Researchers need to be constantly on guard against reinforcing stereotypes of this kind.

Motsemme's analysis leaves no doubt that young black people in South Africa face serious challenges in view of poverty and HIV/AIDS. However, it is when the occurrence of HIV/AIDS is linked to other noteworthy phenomena that are embedded in the very fabric of South African society – such as violence, the breakdown of parental authority, poverty and unemployment, repeated exposure to HIV/AIDS deaths and the necessity of devising survival strategies – that the seriousness of the burgeoning HIV/AIDS dilemma begins to emerge. The issue of HIV/AIDS and violence is one that needs to be addressed.

HIV/AIDS and violence

By international standards and more particularly by African standards, South Africa has a relatively sound economy but there are still huge imbalances in poverty levels and inequality. The bald fact is that while there is a rising black middle class, some of whom have accumulated great wealth, the majority of the population, the black people, are poor. Despite government initiatives, unemployment rates are high and many homes still have no access to basic services. Added to this, the HIV/AIDS pandemic continues to have a huge detrimental impact not only on the social fabric of South Africa but also on the rapidly globalising economy.

Ari Sitas (2007) has given depth to this debate in a recent study of what he calls 'disabled systems and disabling social actions' in South Africa. He points out that in its path to democracy the country has 'followed a unique trajectory' but this process, as far as the well-being of the masses is concerned, has not been without flaws. It is unique in that it was 'neither a transition from a crisis in the fiscal state of the welfare democracies of the West, nor…a transition from a crisis in state socialism and the command of economies of Eastern Europe' (Sitas 2007: 33). South Africa's economic boom of the late nineteenth-century mineral revolution blossomed in the 1920s and progress followed apace until the 1970s, by which time the black youth (soon to be followed by the significant, and unionised, black working class) stepped in to precipitate the social and political crises that led to a democratic dispensation. However exceptional this transformation was, writes Sitas, the reality is that South Africa 'shares with the rest of the world and the rest of the African continent in particular, profound institutional configurations that flow from the conundrum of a globalising world' (2007: 34). Social existence is still fraught by issues of poverty and inequality and, argues Sitas in his title, there are still, more than 10 years into democracy, 'disabling social actions' in evidence.

When the close interconnection between HIV/AIDS, violence, the breakdown of parental authority (see the work by Tin [2001] discussed above), poverty and unemployment, and the continual need to devise survival strategies is investigated, a frightening picture emerges. Violence and crime of different proportions have long been characteristic of South Africa. We need to understand the dynamics of these socio-economic issues before they can be addressed.

Apartheid violence targeted the family, in particular African-centred cultural resources that formed the backbone of black communities and maintained their essence and continuity. Local moral worlds were shattered, especially during the terror of high apartheid and the internal conflict among black people during the 1980s. However, in many accounts of the violence of apartheid and colonisation these aspects have been omitted. Few accounts give resonance to apartheid's ruthless onslaught on the home and how this translated into a violation of the community's ability to nurture relations and regenerate itself (Motsemme 2007: 66). This attack on homes emphasises for her the need to obtain a more complete perspective of the lived effects of such fundamental violations as the right to sanctuary.

Many of Motsemme's (2007) young black interviewees referred to the fact that they regularly witnessed brutal killings, burning of their homes and other violent crimes. This cannot be separated from their views of what constitutes a 'good' life and what makes a 'bad' or threatened way of life. It also influenced their subsequent choices and how to cope with their everyday experiences. In this manner the past continues to have an 'ominous presence' in their lives. It thus becomes crucial to understand the role of memory and violence on the identities that these young women developed because, says Motsemme, memory is a particularly 'strong element in shaping and reconfiguring our identities'. A major aspect of memory in South Africa is the history of real and symbolic violence (Motsemme 2007: 69).

The breakdown of parental authority

Motsemme's interviewees were adamant that the breakdown of parental authority that began in the 1970s and intensified during the turmoil of the 1980s, continues to this day. They all contended that the children rapidly destroyed the authority that parents had previously enjoyed (Motsemme 2007: 69). Citing Tin (2001), Motsemme claims that despite the traditional societal structure inherent in pre-colonial black communities, the position of the patriarch in the apartheid townships was tenuous, as he was torn between the demands made upon him by his radical children and by the repressive state. Many children lost respect for what they saw as the 'pitiful survival strategies of their fathers', which indeed often involved 'leaving the hassles of the overcrowded house, drinking beer in some shebeen and leaving the family to its own devices' (Motsemme 2007: 69–70).

Faced by the threat that there would be an ethical breakdown of the family (and, by extension, of the community), black women carefully promoted the rapidly receding myth of the man as the supporter, protector, provider and decision-maker on the home front (Motsemme 2007: 70). When, as Tin (2001: 135–136) explains, the children of the 1970s threw off the mantle of parental control, the reorganisation of the family structure tended to extend women's role as principal providers and disciplinarians, which remains a heavy burden on mothers. The current breakdown of parental authority is convincingly attributed by Motsemme's interviewees to the emerging rights-based culture in South Africa and prompts Motsemme to contend that black parents in contemporary South Africa play a 'watching' role rather than the traditional 'intervening' or 'disciplining' role of pre-apartheid days.

Poverty and unemployment

Many of Motsemme's interviewees answered that they were 'sitting' when she enquired about their lifestyle and the focus of their lives. This meant that they were unemployed, a situation which was widespread. Almost all the respondents explained that they had been 'sitting' for years and that this was a serious challenge for many urban youths. They contended that many '*kwere-kwere*' (foreigners from other parts of Africa) were often hired to do work they felt they should have secured. 'The politics of "race", unfair labour practices, complex expressions of xenophobia and what was felt to be a deeply racist employment context' were also part of the young women's narrations (Motsemme 2007: 72). While Motsemme's research was undertaken among young women in a small town situated in a poverty-stricken rural area, there is convincing evidence that unemployment among the youth is causing resentment and dissatisfaction of far wider scope.

Frequent exposure to HIV/AIDS deaths

Frequent exposure to death has become an embedded, inescapable reality in black South African communities. Recent experiences of so-called political deaths have not received due attention from South African social researchers. During the apartheid years, many black people were deprived of the opportunity to mourn their dead and, as Motsemme points out, 'death without mourning constitutes death without reflexivity' (2007: 73). In the 1980s there were many mass political funerals – the burials of young men murdered by the state and/ or vigilante groups. This once again forced women to extend their already severely stretched roles and to take on additional responsibilities that involved providing care and compassion; they became weary of burying their dead. And this ongoing experience of death has continued, inviting analysts to interpret how those living in HIV/AIDS-ridden communities handle an everyday life that is structured by death rather than by life.

Refusal to confront the existence of HIV/AIDS – by seeing themselves in effect as invincible and declaring 'this will not happen to me' – is also part of the avoidance mechanism used by young people in attempts to avoid thinking about HIV/AIDS all the time or allowing it to dominate conversations – a typical reaction that can be linked to the adventurous spirit of youthful identity. Moreover, there appears to be a fear of actually enunciating the words 'HIV/AIDS', as if saying them will actually invoke the disease's destructive power (Motsemme 2007: 74).

Survival strategies (*ukuphanta*)

Some of the young women interviewed by Motsemme admitted that they 'had men on the side' specifically for the purposes of eking out day-to-day survival, or what is popularly known as *ukuphanta* (surviving each day). *Ukuphanta* can be defined as a philosophy and a practice of 'getting by' or 'making ends meet'; in a poverty-stricken township it implies doing anything that brings in money. These survival techniques may include (and frequently do) illegal or unconventional ways of acquiring cash, food or other goods (Motsemme 2007: 80–81). Whether these items are acquired legally or not, *ukuphanta* is an accepted way of surviving in the townships. Mothers of unemployed youngsters complain that their children still depend on them for support when they could well go out and *phanta* to help the family survive. Young women do not readily seek a relationship with a boyfriend who is still dependent on his parents; he is expected to go out and *phanta*, to 'try something' to provide for his partner in some way. This can mean 'housebreaking, pick-pocketing, stealing cars or general theft' from stores in the city centre, white people's homes and/or the homes of wealthy black people, but not from neighbours who are themselves struggling, as this is seen as 'theft' (Motsemme 2007: 80–81).

Furthermore, there is an unspoken rule in township households that a young woman who spends a night out with her boyfriend will not return home without a contribution of some sort towards the household economy (Motsemme 2007: 82). Where a woman cannot meet her family's needs because her male partner is unemployed, she may decide to strike up a liaison with another man, one who will be more able to make a suitable difference to the survival of the girl's family. She will not be seen as 'loose' in her community; indeed, she may well feel empowered because she has the ability to contribute to her family's earnings. This transactional sex certainly contributes to increased HIV infection in that it encourages multiple partnering; it also limits women's sexual autonomy and curtails their capacity to negotiate healthy sexual preferences (Motsemme 2007: 83). But Motsemme also makes the point that in current times of despair and hopelessness transactional sex (despite its dangers and limitations) may go some way towards giving young black people from poor communities some sense of intimacy and meaning in their otherwise drab lives. Sex, as the young women in this survey explained, can provide a sense of well-being and empowerment where there is ostensibly only an all-pervasive hopelessness.

Motsemme's detailed interviews of a group of South African youths are a useful window through which one can assess the dynamic politics of identity formation in the country. However, her cultural–anthropological approach runs the risk of fudging certain issues. For example, without providing sufficient background to the reasons why she focuses on her particular cohort, it is difficult to accept her argument when she suggests that South African youth are negatively uniform in their response to the issues of sex and loving in a situation where there is a high prevalence of HIV/AIDS.

Furthermore, Motsemme writes as an impartial observer and declines to comment on the thoughts and opinions of her interviewees. As the critic that she is, she should be prepared to engage in these debates. The effect is that her work will interest those who see in South African youth undifferentiated strata at both the collective as well as the individual level. This is how she tends to interpret the responses from her sample group. Motsemme's concept of 'flawed' agency is particularly suspect for use in critical discourse, because although she implies that she knows what 'unflawed' agency is, she does not spell this out. The idea of 'flawed' agency also gives the erroneous impression that human behaviour can be measured against a certain template – and that those who do not measure up to this norm have flawed (and thus limited) agency. Instead of using this particular term, it would be more fruitful to discuss the contradictory behaviour and convictions of her interviewees as paradoxical – in the sense that a paradox implies unity in disunity of a single entity. This complex understanding of the agency of South African black youth is what Pumla Gqola grapples with in her analysis of youth identities in the South African context.

Changing structures in South Africa

It is clear that despite the freedoms fought for and won in 1994, there is no room for political complacency in South Africa. As Pumla Gqola puts it, '…many freedoms still need to be attained and defended' (2007: 113). At the same time the structures within which violence is perpetrated in South Africa have taken on radically different forms; violence is less decriminalised or at least more devoid of moral justification. Gqola (2007) provides us with fresh insights on the new societal structures that have arisen in South Africa since the transitions of 1994.

Although Gqola's work does not focus exclusively on young South Africans, it is as well to remember here that the youth is a significant sub-sector of the larger society. Moreover, progress towards a more just and equitable society depends to a large extent on the identities that young people develop in assuming their positions and roles within their society. What is then the nature of the society within which the roles, attitudes and identities of present-day South African youth are formed? It is this question that Gqola addresses.

For Gqola, 'fighting and the presence of violence' links many of the recent events in South Africa (2007: 113). In the years of the liberation struggle right through until the first democratic election in 1994, as Africans took up arms against colonialism, self-defence found expression not only in South Africa, but throughout the African diaspora. Apartheid capitalised on this through militaristic control and the structural violence of an economy that denied life chances to the majority of the population.

A close reading of Gqola reveals that the nature of violence in South Africa has changed. Whereas it was predominantly political until 1994, in the post-apartheid period state violence towards black people has taken on an increasingly gender-oriented character. Thus for Gqola, throughout the apartheid era brutalisation by dominant men in the family unit – a patriarchal structure – was rigidly maintained in both black and white communities in South Africa. Ross adds to this when he claims that when violence reached an all-time high in the 1980s, 'the boundaries between criminality and political action became blurred...and young men grasped the opportunity to impose themselves on their surroundings...to re-establish...the relationship between the generations...which had been destroyed by the dehumanisation of township life, and thus indirectly by apartheid' (Ross 1999: 153–154). Militarisation took on a variety of gendered forms; children were socialised into a society that was violent at its very core. Even the playground was not free of violence and militarism, as evidenced in the popularity of Boy Scout and Girl Guide movements in both English-speaking and black communities, and *Veld and Vlei* (nature oriented) holidays for Afrikaans-speaking schoolchildren (Gqola 2007: 113–114).

Significantly, Gqola argues that it is the failure to dismantle this 'ideology of militarism' that underlies much of what ails post-apartheid South Africa today (2007: 114). Silence surrounds the connections between acceptance of violence as a given and potential discussion of how it affects South African society. It is this silence that continues to trouble South Africa. She goes on to explain that dismantling this militaristic ideology requires a great deal of rigour; silence and denial are not a solution. The Truth and Reconciliation Commission (TRC) offered useful insights into the interaction between silence and violence through 'discipline', highlighting what was said, sayable and difficult to articulate. Motsemme (2004) concurs. In her work on women's testimonies and voices at the TRC, she shows that ultimately 'the mute always speak', so that silence and trying to wish away what cannot be spoken are simply not the answer.

The South Africa of today has a Constitution that affirms women's dignity and rights, but there are still significant silences and gaps on the gender dimensions of its past. To solve this anomalous situation 'requires that we explore what it is that South Africans have spoken about' (Gqola 2007: 114) and then continue to discuss it publicly until the impasse is resolved. The anti-apartheid struggle was articulated as a struggle for a constitutional society free of oppression and discrimination on the grounds of race, class, gender, sexual orientation, religion, language, geographical location and ability – Gqola insists that there should be no compromise, in any form whatsoever, in pursuing the realisation of these goals.

It is clear that Gqola sees a number of glaring weaknesses in the present situation as far as the empowerment of women in South Africa is concerned. She writes:

> This talk of 'the empowerment of women', as currently employed and aired in South Africa, rests on the assumption that ensuring that *some* women have access to wealth, positions in government and corporate office is enough gender-progressive work for our society. This assumption is flawed on various levels, even if increased representation of women across all sectors of our society is a worthwhile and necessary project. (2007: 115–116)

She explains that while significant strides have been made to give some women (more particularly those in state structures and comparatively less so in the business sector) access to high office, this is of little significance to the vast majority of women because class, homophobia, race and xenophobia still mediate women's access to power. Her second point is that talk of the 'empowerment of women' requires women to *adapt to the present system*, rather than transforming the workplace into a space more receptive to women's contributions, needs and wants.

The third basic flaw that she highlights in talk of women's empowerment is linked to the second. Here Gqola argues that greater equity for women requires more than the increased representation of women in the state (Gqola 2007: 116). Increased and assertive representation of poor women in the state and a strong feminist movement outside the state are also needed. In other words, it is necessary that empowerment should also cut across *class* if there is to be meaningful gender transformation.

The fourth flaw becomes evident upon consideration that the conservative debate on the empowerment of women applies to women only when they are in an official 'public space': the workplace. There is a different set of rules that directly contradicts the women's empowerment discourse; this continues to regulate the 'private' world of the home and other spaces in between, such as public transport, the streets, clubs, restaurants and shebeens. In these private spaces, she claims, very limiting notions of femininity apply.

The current women's empowerment hype is not transformative and is thus a mere red herring, a sop and a sham. This is because – and this is Gqola's major point:

> It...assumes that women are the only ones who need empowerment, as limited as routes to such empowerment are. It leaves the cult of 'femininity' intact and violent masculinities untouched. Gender-transformation work requires that masculinities – black, white, straight, queer – be radically revisited and transformed in the interest of a country that is not just gender-equitable on paper. (Gqola 2007: 117)

Gqola claims that gender-based violence will continue as long as silence is maintained on the long histories that gave rise to these untenable behaviours. She urges women to speak out rather than pretend, as millions of women do, that denial of these inequities will protect them.

Gqola's analysis leaves one in little doubt that South African society still has a long way to go before real gender equity can be fostered among the youth, society's future leaders. The conclusion is inevitably that it is the youth that are the vanguard of change; they will have to 'unlearn' the stereotypes of violent masculine aggression and submissive, feminine passivity. It is they who have the responsibility to shape a more just and equitable society. This will have to take place primarily in the private spheres in which young people are socialised and develop their identities.

Gqola's major thrust is to mainstream the role of women in the current burgeoning of black youth identities in South Africa. But her major challenge – one she has been unable to transcend – is a conceptual one. There is an element of lack of clarity in her argument; she sometimes assumes that 'gender' is synonymous with 'women'. In the reality of today's South Africa, there are some South African male youths who are virtually powerless – and young females who are both rich and powerful. In other words, she shows an uncritical urge to rope feminist theory into all her work; this has led to an oversimplification of the politics of black South African youth identities. She tends to forget that these emerging identities are articulated through the social construct, the interaction, of the roles played by both men and women in society.

Education and globalisation

A matter of the utmost importance in the formation of youth identities – in South Africa and elsewhere – is education. According to Grimond (2001), 29 per cent of government spending for the year 2000–2001 was on education, equating to 5.7 per cent of the gross domestic product. Spending alone cannot, however, be considered a measure of educational success. By way of comparison the apartheid government spent 20 per cent of its budget on education – but 85 per cent of this money went towards educating white learners (Grimond 2001: 6). As a result, South Africa had some of the best state schools in the world but also, undeniably, some of the very worst.

In the past 10 years the education playing field, in a manner of speaking, has been levelled, but the nationwide percentage pass rate in the final school examination is still disappointingly low. And there is also a plethora of problems in the schools, all of which need to be addressed, including those of mother-tongue education; increasing crime, drugs and violence at state schools; and the dilemma of how to react to the escalating number of school pregnancies. In his Budget speech of February 2007, Trevor Manuel announced a huge increase in the allocation for the Ministry of Education, and added, with a wry smile, that under the circumstances young learners would be expected to 'deliver' in the form of improved final results.

Currently, post-apartheid black youth are experiencing a disheartening unemployment crisis. Young people with a sound education have a far better chance of finding employment in the formal sector but because of the low pass rate and the inherent problems outlined above many young people are undereducated for such positions. The new post-apartheid government, despite the huge education backlog it inherited, cannot justifiably (after 12 years of democracy) put *all* the blame on the apartheid regime's hopelessly deficient 'Bantu education' system.

Mgobozi (2004) adds a theoretical dimension to the debate on racial inequalities in the South African education system. He utilises human capital theory and the theory of credentialism to explain these inherent inequities and shows how these are eventually also transferred to the labour market, with black South Africans remaining the most disadvantaged. Human capital theory may well be a useful tool; however, it fails to explain some economic phenomena such as differences in skill, inequalities in the occupational structure, differences in knowledge, racial disparities in wages in South Africa and the segmented labour market in South Africa (Mgobozi 2004: 776).

Emphasising that the labour market is a social institution, Mgobozi claims that in the labour market the powers of capitalism versus those of the workers, management versus the workers, racial and gender discrimination and the organisational or administrative imperatives of the labour market all work together to determine the wages people receive (2004: 778). Human capital theory recognises that educated workers generally earn more than workers who are poorly educated (Mgobozi 2004: 779). However, in South Africa's segmented, socially constructed labour market, white people have become credentialled in the labour market to the detriment of their black fellow-South Africans, who occupy devalued positions in the labour market.

Kader Asmal, a previous minister of education, said in 2000 that 30 per cent of the country's schools were unfit for use, 40 per cent did not have water and 50 per cent did not have electricity (Grimond 2001). In spite of this, Grimond feels that very good results could be obtained even in the worst circumstances – and often were. South Africa, in his view, compares very well with other countries in many educational respects. The general picture is of good primary education, a much more mixed secondary education and troubled universities. Formerly white institutions such as the University of the Witwatersrand and the University of Cape Town are still judged to be excellent, while he is far more critical of several of the historically black universities, calling them 'atrocious'. He claims that universities are abused by the South African youth who interpret higher education as an end in itself. University life brings with it a 'comfortable' existence, largely at the taxpayer's expense. In Grimond's view, many students spin out the process of studying, whether or not fees are paid or exams passed. This is hardly the ideal training needed for a globalised economy.

In view of the unique significance of the nation-building project in South Africa, in which education of the youth can be expected to play a major role, South Africans need to recognise that globalisation can have seriously detrimental effects on sections of the nation's population. Prioritisation of education could suffer in view of other global demands. However, the nation state can use its regulatory powers against multinational companies by declaring that it will not hesitate to use such instruments as public ownership should the companies in question act in a manner contrary to the national interest. This is highly unlikely in a South Africa set on a course of change through growth and investment, but can be considered as a last resort. There are also many fiscal, monetary and exchange rate policies that could enable the nation state to challenge the adverse effects of globalisation. The stage may have been reached for South Africa to consider legislating for itself instead of for the demands of global capitalism. In the meantime, a variety of identities, not all conducive to nation building, will continue to be formed in this country.

Thus historical precedents call into question the appropriateness of meeting the demands of globalised information technology-led economic development in South Africa in an inflexible manner. The masses of the South African population are poverty-stricken and ill-educated and South Africa is a country crying out for job creation – not only highly skilled, technology-based jobs, but employment as a means for independence and survival. It is not that the benefits of information technology-led globalisation are being denied here. It is more a case of a nation in need of a new nationhood because its masses are badly educated and unemployed; there appears to be a need for a different set of priorities. In such circumstances, legislation aimed at meeting the needs of South Africans, rather than of global capitalists, is required. Few analysts could in any case dispute on moral grounds the legitimacy of a government that legislates in order to meet more adequately the needs of its own people.

Crime

Since the introduction of the new political dispensation in South Africa in 1994, the country as a whole has often been described as a crime-ridden society. The influence of this on the identity formation of the youth in many parts of the country should be considered. The number of crimes committed, especially rape, carjacking, serious assault, housebreaking and common robbery, has been increasing since 1996 (Grimond 2001: 7) and appears to have been climbing particularly sharply (by as much as 9% for violent crimes) since 1998. Although the murder rate has been falling, thanks to a reduction in political thuggery, the rate for all other types of violent crime has been rising: in 1999 about a third of all the reported crimes were violent. South Africa has thus become one of the most violent countries in the world. One answer to the question 'why?' is that it was always violent. Apartheid was a system based on violence, whether it was a matter of forcibly uprooting people, herding migrant labourers into hostels or beating confessions out of those suspected of 'crimes against the state'. Much of the violence is also alcohol-related.

Furthermore, black men were systematically humiliated by apartheid. The system kept them subordinate and undermined their role as protectors, as their wives and children were often dumped in distant 'homelands'. Moreover, apartheid frequently prevented them from providing for their families. Because they were ill-educated, many men were too proud to do menial jobs, leaving the women to act as breadwinners. The net effect was that many men felt robbed of their very manhood. Today, the only escape, in their view, is through the control they exercise over African women and children and 'empowering' themselves through crime.

It is within these social parameters of poverty and violence that the identities of the youth have been formed in our contemporary society. Ontological commitments to racialised, ethnic and class identities have developed and have served to blur the distinction between crime and political and/or labour action. The theoretical and practical issue is whether there is sufficient commonality in South Africans' sufferings and hopes, the modes and sources of their oppressions and expressions, and in the creation of a social order to eliminate destructive divisions and forge a concrete unity in diversity. When all is said and done, this involves commitment to the ideal of maintaining own integrities without encroaching on the integrity and well-being of others, both at the individual and the collective level.

Conclusion

In conclusion it is important to invoke the authority of Stuart Hall's provocative essay titled 'New Ethnicities', which helps us to situate the challenges of constructing new identities by and for the South African youth, particularly in the post-1994 era. Hall describes the subjectivities of blacks in terms of the 'end of innocence, or the end of the innocent notion of the essential black subject' (Hall 1996: 443). This description aptly fits the challenges that face the South African youth in the aftermath of the struggle and the dawn of democracy. South African youth are confronted by poverty. This is a phenomenon that cuts across the class, race, gender and generational configuration of young people in post-apartheid South Africa. The view that we have reached the 'end of the innocent' notion of the essential black subject also implies an infinite disappearance of the signifier 'black'. This is true in the South African context where some black youth who come from rich families have not escaped involvement in the plagues of violent crime, HIV/AIDS and a general breakdown of the moral order; these are issues that preoccupy the youth in both black and white communities. Besides, the aspirations of black and white youth do not always coincide. It is also true that the visions of the black youth and of their parents can be plotted on a continuum that recognises conflict of interests as well as confluence of vision. This is hardly surprising given the chequered political history of South Africa that is openly defined by the extent to which youth revolted against the authority of their parents in order to accelerate the speed of the train of freedom.

Hall, however, has a different understanding of the notion that the innocence of the essential black subject has come to an end. This alternative conception is lodged in the ways in which black South African youth contest their representation by their parents and sometimes by other young South Africans. Here it is worth noting that there is 'contestation of the marginality, the stereotypical quality and the fetishized nature of images, by the counter-position of a "positive" black imagery' (Hall 1996: 442). In the South African context we noted that identities such as *ukuphanta* that would normally be associated with degraded forms of life such as prostitution and crime, are inverted and new content infused in them so that black identities previously positioned as negative acquire positive attributes or are valorised. It is true that the youth do not always succeed in constructing their identities in affirmative terms. Sometimes they are themselves implicated in crimes such as hijacking, murder and abuse of drugs. These aspects should not be swept under the carpet. In South Africa, black youth have a visible presence and a meaningful representation in the political arena. This will almost certainly play an important role in the progress of the new democracy.

As I have demonstrated in this chapter, to interrogate South African youth identities forces us to come face to face with questions related to Mamdani's (1996) notion of citizen and subject. In the South African context the youth are citizens with assumed full democratic rights; 'assumed' because these rights are constantly under siege from the imperatives of capital. South African youths are 'subjects' in the sense that they are ruled over by their own government – composed of their parents with whom they do not have a totally consensual political relationship. Youths are therefore subjected to the governing policies of those in power; they also possess 'subjectivities' and they have learnt to bargain politically with the ruling elites. The youths' main issues of concern relate to the effects of poverty on the development of their identities. They also demand accountability and want their government to deliver on social services. This accounts for the massive surge of youthful demonstrations sweeping through Soweto and Mamelodi in the month of July 2007 as I write.

An important issue that was discussed in this chapter is the problem of the occurrence of crime and HIV/AIDS among the youth of South Africa and the effects of these, both social and psychological, on society in general. A major investigation into the links between HIV/AIDS, violence, the breakdown of parental authority, poverty and unemployment, is long overdue. It would help if that study was undertaken by the youth themselves because, as argued in this chapter, the parents' politics of the 1970s constantly clashed with the immediate challenges of the youth. They suffer from and simultaneously perpetrate this violence in expressing their need for quality education, water, electricity, jobs and, more importantly, the need to own and participate meaningfully in evolving the ethos of a robust democratic culture.

An overwhelming proportion of young black South Africans appear to feel that voting during national election time is just a single step towards transforming the unequal relations of class, race and gender in the new South Africa. These expectations are underpinned by an understanding among the youth that they are well placed to make a contribution to the political, social and economic life of the country in spite of limited opportunities for cultural affiliation. To reiterate Lukalo's (2006) observation, the restlessness of the South African youth in search of change suggests that new democracies in Africa have emerged from colonialism and apartheid; these can only survive if they recognise the power of the youth to change the course of African history. Should this be so, the case of building the South African nation would be well served.

Note

1   As indicated above, 'black' in this context refers collectively to the African, Indian and coloured population groups.

References

Adam H & Giliomee H (1978) *Ethnic power mobilised.* New Haven, CT: Yale University Press

Appiah KA (1999) Ethnicity and identity in Africa: An interpretation. In KA Appiah and HL Gates (eds) *Africana: The encyclopedia of the African and African American experience.* New York: Basic Books

Baumeister A (1986) *Identity, cultural change and the struggle for the self.* Oxford: Oxford University Press

Bekker S (1996) Conflict, ethnicity and democratisation in contemporary South Africa. In S Bekker and D Carlton (eds) *Racism, xenophobia and ethnic conflict.* Durban: Indicator Press

Bundy C (1987) Street sociology and pavement politics: Aspects of youth and student resistance in Cape Town. *Journal of Southern African Studies* 5(3): 303–330

Castells M (1999) *The information age: Economy, society and culture.* Vol. 2, *The power of identity.* Oxford: Blackwell Publishers

Erikson EH (1968) *Identity: Youth and crisis*. New York: Norton

Gqola PD (2007) How the 'cult of femininity' and violent masculinities support endemic gender-based violence in contemporary South Africa. *African Identities* 5(1): 111–124

Grimond J (2001) Africa's great black hope. *The Economist: A survey of South Africa.* 24 February

Hall S (1996) New ethnicities. In D Morley and C Kuan-Hsing (eds) *Critical dialogues in cultural studies*. London: Routledge

Hall S (1999) Ethnicity and politics: An interpretation. In KA Appiah and HL Gates (eds) *Africana: The encyclopedia of the African and African American experience*. New York: Basic Books

Jary D & Jary J (2000) *Collins dictionary of sociology*. Glasgow: HarperCollins

Lukalo FK (2006) 'Consuming my loyalty': Youth, popular culture and gender contestations in Kenya. *Muziki* 3(1): 97–113

Magubane B (2006) Introduction to the 1970s: The social and political context. In South African Democratic Education Trust *The road to democracy in South Africa, Volume 2 (1970–1980)*. Pretoria: UNISA Press

Mamdani M (1996) *Citizen and subject: Contemporary Africa and the legacy of late capitalism*. Cape Town: David Philip

Mgobozi I (2004) Human capital and credentialism: The sociological explanation of racial inequalities in South Africa. *Current Sociology* 52(5): 775–783

Motsemme N (2007) Loving in a time of hopelessness: On township women's subjectivities in a time of HIV/AIDS. *African Identities* 5(1): 61–87

Ndlovu S (2006) The Soweto uprising. In South African Democratic Education Trust *The road to democracy in South Africa, Volume 2 (1970–1980)*. Pretoria: UNISA Press

Ross R (1999) *A concise history of South Africa*. Cambridge: Cambridge University Press

Sitas A (2007) Disabled systems and disabling social actions in South Africa. *African Identities* 5(1): 33–37

Slabbert F van Z, Malan C, Marais H, Olivier J & Riordan R (1994) *Youth in the new South Africa*. Pretoria: HSRC

Tin H (2001) Children in violent spaces: A reinterpretation of the 1976 Soweto uprising. In A Zegeye (ed.) *Social identities in the new South Africa*. Vol. 1 of *After apartheid*. Cape Town: Kwela Books and SA History Online

Umrabulo (2006) A nation in the making: Macro-social trends in South Africa. *Umrabulo* No. 27. Accessed 22 January 2007, http://www.anc.org.za/ancdocs/pubs/umrabulo/umrabulo27/art6.html November

wa Mogale D (1992) *Prison poems*. Johannesburg: AD Donker

Wolpe H (1989) *Race, class and the apartheid state*. Oxford: James Currey, OAU and UNESCO Press

Worden N (1994) *The making of modern South Africa: Conquest, segregation and apartheid*. Oxford: Blackwell

Zegeye A & Maxted J (2002) *Our dream deferred: The poor in South Africa*. Pretoria: SA History Online and UNISA Press

3 Essentialism in a South African discussion of language and culture

Kees van der Waal

The central aim of this volume is to investigate and interpret the close connection between the media and the (de)construction of identities in post-apartheid South Africa. This chapter approaches the discussion by looking at the role of culture and language in the making of a social identity – the process of social identification – first theoretically and then by means of a case study.

The main focus here is on the notion of 'essentialism' and the process of essentialising as these can be traced in the 'Stellenbosch language debate' case study. Core questions that are addressed in this chapter concern the meanings of 'essentialism', 'language' and 'culture' and how a critical and constructivist understanding of these notions can contribute to the interpretation of the process of neo-Afrikaner identification. The role of the media in these processes is also highlighted.

My point of departure is the anthropological approach in which prominence is given to a grounded understanding of socio-cultural meanings, relationships, processes and contexts, based on ethnographic fieldwork. I frame this chapter with the notion of 'essentialism', a term originating from the same class as other notions with negative connotations, such as 'positivism'. These are terms of abuse usually ascribed to 'the other'. But this notion is indeed useful for understanding dominant ideas about language and culture that one usually comes across in their unreflexive use. We should ask whether the terms 'culture' and 'language' have not perhaps been overrated in the eagerness accompanying a process of identity construction and, furthermore, what the implications of this tendency could be. Maybe there is not even a basis for using the terms 'culture' and 'language' in the bounded sense in which they are mostly understood. It is especially pertinent for an understanding of public debate, as reflected in the media, that these questions be posed.

Essentialism

Essentialism has emerged as a notion in the fields of philosophy and cultural studies, from where it moved into feminist writing, anthropology and other social sciences. First then: what is essentialism? It is an understanding of a phenomenon in terms of a set of characteristics that overgeneralise and thereby overdetermine that phenomenon. It is a belief in the real, true essence of things, the perceived properties that define the 'whatness' of an entity, for example that gender is biologically given as a fixed human essence (Morton 2003: 73). The sociologist Stephen Fuchs, in his book *Against Essentialism* (2001: 12), asserts: 'Essentialism searches for the intrinsic "nature" of things as they are, in and of themselves. The opposite strategy is relationalism.' Also: 'In essentialism, the preferred mode of operation is static typologies and rigid classifications, whose grids separate things that are everywhere, and under all circumstances, really separate' (Fuchs 2001: 15). Essentialism therefore expresses a dualistic cosmology, with deep distinctions and polar opposites. 'Operationally, essentialism is the failure to allow for variation. Where nothing is allowed to vary, nothing can be explained' (Fuchs 2001: 15). A very insightful remark by Fuchs is that essentialism is clearly evident in how a social network operates when it protects its foundations (Fuchs 2001: 16). Social networks under pressure do not allow the questioning of their basic understandings. Therefore, essentialism is quite unscientific in its negation of critique. The media, as interpretative and political mechanisms in modern society and falling outside the demands for rigour of scientific argumentation, are very prone to the use of uncritical essentialist understandings current in a given social formation of which they are the mouthpiece. Having said that, it needs to be pointed out that essentialism can also often be found in uncritical social science.

Essentialism assumes that things are as they are perceived to be, which raises the question of whether one can ultimately do without generalisation and classification. Of course we need to generalise and classify; these are activities which seem to be basic to human understanding and human logic, especially in situations where our knowledge is slim and where we need a conceptual handle (a first working definition) on what we experience. Generalisation is useful when supported by sufficient evidence on the level at which it is used. Generalisations need to be explained, however, and not to be taken for granted. There is always the danger of glossing over those variations that do make a difference. Essentialism as applied to human cultural and social life, therefore, risks underplaying the continuities and internal variations that are of importance. The problematic aspect of essentialism is that it does not yield to insight about complexity, process and differentiation. It therefore cannot be a heuristic tool leading to new understanding. It is an ontological claim, often in the service of ideological contestation and identity politics played out in arenas such as the public media.

A good example of essentialism, as an interpretative strategy, is the opposition that is thought to exist between African and Western ways of thinking, assumed to encompass homogeneous entities. The idea of the 'clash of civilisations' in the work of Huntington (1997), through its seductive and elegant simplification, is similarly based on this type of essentialism. This notion has been influential in many discussions in the media on the supposed incompatibility of an Asian or African world-view with a Westen world-view (seen as grand systems). Edward Said's (1991) work on orientalism exposes the myths of such ideological generalisations. In our post-9/11 world these issues remain highly relevant, for example with regard to the common-sense polarisation of Christianity and Islam, easily spoken and written about in the media.

Stephen Fuchs (2001: 12) argues further that science has to advance from common-sense understandings, that is, essentialism, otherwise it reproduces knowledge that already exists on the level of everyday understanding. Against essentialism, he identifies relationalism as a superior strategy for understanding, as things are better understood in terms of their location and movement in a network of forces (Fuchs 2001: 16). His strategy for the practice of social science is summed up when he says: 'What matters is relations, and variations among them, not kinds, essences, things as such, intrinsic properties, or the like' (Fuchs 2001: 51).

In the 1980s a shift was made in the social sciences towards an anti-essentialist position, involving the rejection of all stable categories of identity (Morton 2003: 73). This occurred in the theoretical context of neo-Marxism, postmodernism and postcolonial studies. Postcolonial work has, for instance, strongly argued against the reduction of people to an essential idea, for example in terms of what it means to be African, Muslim, etc. Interestingly, nationalists opposing the hegemony of colonial reductionism have written back against these identity-destroying essentialisms, but then paradoxically also defined themselves in essentialist terms. In Mahatma Gandhi's work one finds such a reactive essentialism in the form of the positive mystification of Indian nationalism. This was a form of cultural and political resistance against European orientalism, in which many negative stereotypes of the East dominated.

An interesting turn in the development of the term is the use of 'strategic essentialism' by the feminist and postcolonialist writer Spivak (1996). She coined the term to refer to the need for temporary solidarity for purposes of social action in specific cases. Her approach is to see the need among oppressed social categories or 'subaltern groups' as a justified emphasis on their separateness, but only as a short-term strategy in their search for recognition and social influence (Morton 2003: 75). According to Spivak, this approach can, for example, be justified as use of an ethnic identity to affirm minority-group status, but only as a context-specific strategy adopted by a dominated social category and not as a long-term political solution to end oppression, nor as a theory. In any event, it seems as if we cannot easily escape essentialism (understood as unjustified generalisation) in constructing our interpretations of social life, as we have to represent and select aspects of that life. Therefore, one could probably best speak of degrees of essentialism that have important consequences for both social analysis and practical action. Reflexivity is needed to discern instances of essentialism that undermine a view of the social as differentiated and process-oriented on the one hand, and that prevent questioning privilege and inequality in social identities on the other. In this regard, a discussion of essentialism in language and culture, referring to the role of the media as well, is useful before we turn to the details of our case study.

Language

In most cases the media use and promote mainly one standard form of a language. They target specific segments of the population as their audience, thereby influencing and reflecting a specific view of what a language is or, normatively, what it should be. This is a political process, contributing to identity formation and the creation of a set of common points of reference among the readers, listeners or viewers, and is part of a broader set of relationships and identity-formation processes in society. The now common (but mistaken) understanding of a language as an essentialised unitary phenomenon, something structured, closed and bounded, has been promoted by the growth of standard forms of language. One encounters these standardised forms of language in print (books and newspapers) and in education, especially since the spread of 'print capitalism' (Anderson 1983) and the nation state in the nineteenth century. These standard forms of language are not mere reflections of speech actions, but are ideological identity constructions, symbols of 'imagined communities' and tools for control by the state and its social partners. The emphasis on the standard language form (invariably of urban origin), as developed especially in Europe by elites in order to create assimilated nation states, overrules the many dialectal forms that continue to exist on the ground. It also overrules the continuum of language interactions in the multilingual speech communities that exist before the state starts to simplify this complexity.

The media are useful tools in the hands of the ruling elites, or of contesting elites, to promote a specific set of assumptions about social identity categories and their place in the world. Specifically, the idea of one unitary language for a state, or for a population segment within it, provides a basis for political mobilisation, especially where ethnic and nationalist identities are already strongly manifested. Typically, political parties and newspapers have been aligned in their common causes and in their quest for reaching large numbers of the public they have often promoted a single language variant and contributed to the idea of a unitary social identity. In language planning, typically a function of the state, one privileged variety of language is often imposed by an authority on the rest of the population; it is standardised and fixed with the aim of converging the varieties of language in use (Wright 2004: 97). With the increasing influence of supranational processes, the weakening of states and increased multilingualism, however, the distinct linguistic mosaic of the national era may significantly change or even disappear in future (Wright 2004: 11, 14).

Taking the constructed nature of language entities into account, one could ask whether languages do in fact exist in the world of practical experience in the form of the exact entities into which they are usually organised and by which they are known. These entities are assumed to have a high measure of order and uniformity. Sociolinguists and linguistic anthropologists, however, indicate that the use of language in communication is much more complex than an image of a world of neatly bounded languages would suggest. Sue Wright indicates, for instance, that '[l]anguage is behaviour and has no existence outside the speaker, writer, listener or reader who uses it' (2004: 12). Duranti (1997: 45) emphasises that a language exists as a linguistic habitus, a set of practices that display considerable variation. As the difference between 'a language' and 'a dialect' may be due to political circumstance or stigma and does not reflect a taxonomic truth, it is preferable to use the notion of 'a variety of language' rather than 'language' (Duranti 1997: 70). Similarly, the often used term 'language communities' is difficult to define as there is enormous complexity of social interaction flowing from multilingualism, internal variation in languages and individual 'linguistic repertoires' (Grillo 1989: 10; Webb 2002: 159). As there seems to be an overemphasis on the systematic nature of language, Foley (1997: 27) proposes that '[i]t may be better to abandon the reifying term "language", which tends to connote a closed discrete system, in favor of linguistic practices, which recognize talking as an activity in structural coupling, one with porous borders with other cultural practices, or even "languaging" ... ' This view is very far removed from the way in which formalised institutions (those involved in education, media and the state generally) tend to use languages as given and precisely defined entities in their practices. Human life, thinking and communication are much more complex than is suggested by these neatly bounded entities.

Humans engage their life-world through the unique features of the embodied mind, not all of which are conscious, cultural or linguistic. Culture refers to the richness of shared ideas, of which language is perhaps the most important aspect. However, in the study of culture the analogy with languages as relatively fixed systems has often been used in structural approaches, especially on the basis of the Saussurean distinction between *langue* (language as a system) and *parole* (the spoken variety of language). In these approaches language as a system serves as a model for understanding culture, viewed as a symbolic system similar to a language system. One of the most influential anthropologists of the twentieth century, Claude Lévi-Strauss, developed structuralism as a theoretical approach that elaborates on this close association between culture and language as structured systems. It understands the working of the human mind in terms of structures of opposition, through which we may understand universal and specific features of cultural classification and symbolism. While this approach is elegant and provides many unique insights into structures of symbolism, it is also one-sided. The problem, of course, in focusing on language and culture as structures and formal systems, is that this underrates the importance of agency, creativity, contradiction and change. This is also the problem with the approach to language taken in the work of the renowned linguist Noam Chomsky, as his generative analysis delinks language from the user and the social situation, focusing instead on homogeneous human competence rather than on the specificities of performance (Duranti 1997: 15, 51).

Language and culture, seen as abstract formal systems, do not help us to understand specific social situations of communication where diversity and fluidity are rife.

In the same way that languages are easily essentialised as if they are coherent systems, linguistic classification is used to create social identity categories (mostly presented as social groups) where there is in fact much variety, overlap and contradiction. In general language use, often reflected in the media, social categories such as 'men', 'readers', etc. abound, indicating the need for terms that are useful because of their inherent capacity to permit generalisation. This social categorisation is discussed in the next section with reference to the language debate at the University of Stellenbosch, where terms such as 'Afrikaners' and '*taalstryders*' (language warriors) are often used as if they connote bounded homogeneous social groups. Sociologically speaking, a 'group' is a term that one should rather reserve for use when referring to people who interact and have a common experience, for example a seminar group, a family or an association. All other social aggregates are categories rather than groups, including so-called speech communities. Presenting social categories as social units has, of course, a social function. It is clear that social classifications and essentialist concepts such as 'nation', *volk* (a people) and 'ethnic group' are very useful for political mobilisation in situations of polarisation such as ethnic competition for access to resources, and even more so in extreme situations such as war and genocide. Unreflective language use can contribute to serious social consequences if the assumed social differences implied by social categories of exclusion and domination are unquestioningly perpetuated and reinforced. News reports in the media often contribute to this trend as they feed on and reflect common understandings based on stereotypes and generalisations. The reporting of the Rwandan genocide as 'ethnic' is a case in point. News reports and their captions have to be very economical in the use of time or space and therefore do not leave much room for more complex interpretations. Similar processes of cognitive simplification apply to the other notion referred to in the title of this chapter, namely 'culture', and we now turn to its relation to the analysis of essentialism.

Culture

In the media the use of the term 'culture' mostly reflects its essentialist connotations current in society. The media use this notion to report on what is commonly understood to be cultural and in the process unwittingly also shape its understanding. In South African newspapers many reports and letters on culture and cultural identity can be found on a daily basis. These essentialist understandings are understandable in a country emerging from a long past of cultural exclusion and the abuse of culture for political and racist ends. The problem of culture as a bounded notion is, however, wider than is evident in the South African situation. It concerns the use and abuse of a term, originally deriving from the social sciences, in societies across the world. The anthropological contribution of the term 'culture' to our vocabulary has had unintended consequences. On the one hand it contributed to the move away from the racist and evolutionist concepts that were dominant at the start of the previous century, but on the other hand it replaced these notions with an understanding of culture that was equally essentialist. Cultural relativism and the emphasis on participant observation during fieldwork tended to contribute to the view that cultures (notice the plural) were discrete blocks in a large mosaic. This understanding of culture emphasised the boundaries of separate entities that were seen as being homogeneous, static cultures with a set of essential qualities and lists of characteristics. Underlying systems of shared meanings created identical individuals in these assumed self-reproducing entities (Wright 1998: 8). Such a view articulated very well with the idea of the nation state as well as with the colonial systems of the time, where traditionalist entities were useful mechanisms for indirect rule. A good local example of this older approach in the social sciences was the *volkekunde* (a variant of cultural anthropology popular among white Afrikaans speakers) that was developed at Stellenbosch and other Afrikaans-teaching universities and that became a strong form of support for the policy of separate development. Primary, secondary and higher education, the mainstream Afrikaans churches and the associated media were collectively supportive of the promotion of white Afrikaans identity as an essentialist unitary ideal. The effect of this 'cultural engineering' is still felt today in the wranglings about the place of Afrikaans in the new South Africa, which will be discussed in more detail below. It would be interesting to know how many of the current *taal* (language) panic letters to *Die Burger* (an Afrikaans newspaper in the Western Cape) and other publications are written by people who received their training in *volkekunde* or similarly essentialist social sciences.

New developments in the world, including the postcolonial situation, critical social science and the postmodern understanding of the human condition, have led to a new understanding of culture that is much richer and more useful than the older essentialist notion. Culture is now seen as something diverse, differentiated, fluid and in process, even contaminated. Meanings are understood as contingent rather than fixed. Culture is understood as an active process of meaning creation through contestation between differentially positioned people. Cultures are not seen as bounded, but as parts of a network of linkages that encompass the local and the global. There is an interest in the specific historical process of culture formation; in fact, the emphasis is on culture as a verb ('culturing') rather than as a noun. Also, there is a stronger emphasis on the need to see individual agency and instrumentalism on the one hand, together with structure (including hegemonic cultural systems) on the other, as complementary elements of dialectical relations in complex socio-cultural processes (Wright 1998: 10). Given that the notion of culture in popular understanding, outside of the new view of culture among social scientists, is still overwhelmingly essentialist, some argue for the need to get rid of the concept as being too all-encompassing, simplistic and rigid. At the minimum we need a model of culture that takes into consideration variety, process and contestation. A distributive model of culture (Keesing & Strathern 1998: 19) provides these dimensions, looking at culture as so many flows in which the cultural give and take of differentially situated people takes place continuously.

Neo-Afrikaner nationalism, an ethnicisation process

How do cultural and linguistic processes manifest themselves in South Africa's neo-Afrikaner nationalism and ethnicisation, and how is this related to the way that the media deal with identity issues? Sue Wright convincingly points out that '[e]thnic nationalists are...essentialists, believing that nations are a natural phenomenon whose linguistic and cultural cohesion derive from a common past and whose destiny is to be a single political unit' (2004: 33). Nationalists believe in the fiction of a primordial unity of an ethnic nation for their political process of nation building or ethnic claims. As Anderson (1983) has pointed out, a nation, and we can add an ethnic group, is an 'imagined community', a social category. The supposed members are never all in contact with each other or ever able to know each other, and therefore do not form a real community or a social group. Newspapers, radio and television help to create the idea of a virtual community and reinforce the assumed definite boundaries in a community of communication (Wright 2004: 39–41). This identification process has its particular paradigmatic origin in western Europe in the nineteenth century, but similar nationalistic projects emerged in colonial settings, including in South Africa, where ethnonationalist ideas deriving from Europe permeated the thinking of many in the white population.

In this regard the idea of an Afrikaner community that has existed since the seventeenth century has often been promoted in the service of several cycles of renewed Afrikaans ethnicisation in South Africa. But it is striking that the initial social categories used at the Cape in the seventeenth century were based on religion and on slavery-based contractual relations, rather than on cultural or linguistic ethnicity. Only later, in the nineteenth century, did race emerge as a marker of identity, to be superseded again by culture and language in the twentieth century. It looks as if religion (for example Islam) and contractual relations (reflecting the impact of neo-liberal individuation), in addition to class, are again very salient in our present condition, without replacing older categorisations completely. South African history is littered with labels used to claim or to ascribe identity (religious, linguistic, class, ethnic, national, political, etc.) with regard to various sectors of the population. These essentialising categories were each formed in specific historical situations within the context of the political economy, including colonialism, apartheid and nation building (Kuper 2002). They continue to serve needs as varied as local identity politics and international tourism.

Afrikaner nationalism emerged as an ethnic process amidst the broader conditions of interacting and competing forces during the period of British imperialism. Ethnicity is always a process of identity formation that occurs between two or more social identities that oppose each other. Afrikaner ethnic nationalism emerged in the competition between whites in the nineteenth-century Cape, and was promoted by the experience of alienation of white Afrikaans speakers by English imperialist and exclusivist social, economic and political hegemony. Language difference played an important part in the formation of an ethnic consciousness among white Afrikaans speakers in this context, further reinforced by the trauma of the South African War. Nationalist discourses and Romantic ideas around the formation of a *volk* (a people), a language and a culture were available in the European literature and media accessed by South Africans at that time. These discourses strengthened the ethnicisation process among the Afrikaans-speaking elite, whose ethnic entrepreneurs led the mobilisation of white Afrikaans speakers in the late nineteenth and early twentieth centuries. The National Party, the Afrikaans churches, the Christian Nationalist schools and the Dutch (later Afrikaans) newspapers were very important tools in the formation of an Afrikaner ethnic consciousness. Ideas about a nation state and a national linguistic and cultural identity such as were pursued in European countries, were part of a travelling ethnonationalist model that had a strong influence on the South African political process.

In the Afrikaner ethnicisation process during the last half of the nineteenth century, the Afrikaans language, as supposedly the language of white people, was appropriated from other Afrikaans speakers, whose language perforce became the non-standard variant (Webb 2002: 29). Afrikaans was idealised and romanticised as an essentialist abstract entity, and as such it could also symbolically be personified. The poem by Neef Jan (Jan Lion Cachet 1838–1912), *Di Afrikaanse Taal* (The Afrikaans Language), depicting the Afrikaans language as a girl (Brink 2000: 15), is typical of this tendency:

> *Ek is 'n arme boerenoi,*
> *By fele min geag:*
> *Mar tog is ek fan edel bloed,*
> *En fan 'n hoog geslag.*
> *Uit Holland het myn pa gekom,*
> *Na sonnig Afrika;*
> *Uit Frankryk, waar di druiftros swel,*
> *Myn liwe mooie ma.*
> (I am a poor farmer's girl,
> Detested by many:
> But still I am of noble blood
> And of high family origin.
> My father came from Holland,
> To sunny Africa;
> From France, where the grape bunch swells,
> My pretty, lovely mother.)

Evidently, the statue for the Dutch language in Burgersdorp, in the form of a woman, also expresses the nineteenth-century female objectification of the Afrikaner/Dutch language in a context of having a minority status. More recently, the Afrikaans poet Breyten Breytenbach identified the Afrikaans language monument at Paarl as expressing male symbolism. Male symbolism, granite rocks and concrete structures at the monument in Paarl do perhaps indeed evoke the hegemonic position of the Afrikaans language at that historical moment. The inauguration of this monument took place a year before the 1976 youth revolt against the enforced use of Afrikaans in black schools erupted in Soweto – an event that was ultimately the beginning of the end for apartheid.

Today the annual arts festivals in Afrikaans that have emerged since the South African democratic transition of 1994 still retain some of this veneration of the language as the essence of an ethnic white Afrikaans-speaking identity. These festivals draw strong support from middle-class white Afrikaans speakers, and seem to be socially important for ethnic identification in a context of adjustment to the new political situation. The Klein Karoo Nasionale Kunstefees (Little Karoo National Arts Festival) and Aardklop (Earthbeat) are the two most strongly developed of a still growing series of rural town-based cultural festivals. They are experienced as powerful ethnic spaces and instruments to keep the Afrikaans culture and language alive. Clearly, for many white Afrikaans speakers the link between the standard version of the Afrikaans language and the ideals of a white Afrikaans-speaking ethnic nationalism are very attractive, although they are also being questioned by a growing minority. Since political transformation in South Africa, there has been lively debate in the print and electronic media on what the place of Afrikaans in education, and in the public sphere in general, should be, and how white Afrikaans speakers who identify themselves as Afrikaners should relate to the new South Africa. The Afrikaans media take a leading role in the development of the arts festivals by celebrating them and by supporting them financially. Coloured Afrikaans speakers were marginalised by the racial politics of the past and therefore do not have the same ethnic affinity with the Afrikaans language, although it is still widely used amongst coloured people. For them English is mostly a language of emancipation, and thus no sharp boundaries between Afrikaans and English exist in their consciousness.

The emphasis on using 'pure Afrikaans' as a marker of white neo-Afrikaner ethnicity appears very often in the resistance to an English term or phrase during public Afrikaans discourse. One then needs to apologise when using an English term, to put it in brackets, so to speak, for example as expressed in the often heard phrase '*verskoon die Engelse woord*' (excuse the English word). While purism in language is usually strongest in the context of successful nationalism (Wright 2004: 57), young Afrikaans speakers now often make use of English words and code mixing, as many of them seem to have an emotional need to detach themselves from the Afrikaner nationalism that is associated with a morally tarnished past (Webb 2002: 30). An intergenerational tension emerges in the experiential disjuncture between older and younger Afrikaans speakers. The work of the young author Jackie Nagtegaal, for example her novel *Daar's Vis in die Punch* (There is fish in the punch) (2002), has caused quite a negative reaction amongst the defenders of language purity in Afrikaans. These defenders of the language tend to be older authors and language purists who object to her extended use of English terms. In her work one can read, for instance: '*Edith Piaf het my soulmate geword en ek het gedroom dat ek eendag êrens in 'n rokerige kamer sou staan en perform*' (Edith Piaf became my soul-mate and I dreamt that one day I would stand performing somewhere in a smoky room) (2002: 29). The use of two English words in one Afrikaans sentence is experienced as irreconcilable with 'good' Afrikaans practice by Afrikaans language purists.

When one tries to answer the question 'Why is Afrikaans so important to white Afrikaners and what is its role in the new ethnicisation process?' the answer does not lie in the language itself or in Afrikaners, but in their relationship with significant others in this country and in the nature of identity politics more generally. Afrikaner ethnic nationalism has to be understood in relation to other nationalisms and perceived othernesses as they are played out in the public sphere, often strongly reflected in cultural politics as reported and promoted by the media. I have already referred to the importance of English hegemony in the initial emergence of this ethnic consciousness. I argue that the continued strength of English as a lingua franca, its dominant economic and political role (on top of its role in black liberation and transformation) and its international dominance have kept the ethnic boundary in place. Add to this the experience of suffering in the name of Afrikaner identity, the dominant role of Afrikaans speakers in the previous political system and their experience of relative deprivation presently, and we have a potent combination of historical and current factors that reinforce the essentialising of an identity and the re-emergence of an ethnic consciousness. In the Afrikaans media these issues emerge continually, indicating the need to patrol the boundaries of the ethnic category and to come to grips with a changing context.

Another boundary that is crucial for the essentialist notion of the Afrikaner is the 'racial' divide, especially where there is no link through language, as with African South Africans. Currently there is a wish to include coloured Afrikaans speakers in the Afrikaans-speaking fold in an attempt to strengthen the position of the Afrikaans language. This attempt can be regarded as an example of strategic essentialism around the newly emerged identity of so-called *Afrikaans-sprekers* (Afrikaans speakers) in order to strengthen the claims for a larger public space for Afrikaans, aptly called a '*volkstaat* [nation state] of the mind' by Chris Brink (2006, when he was the vice-chancellor of the University of Stellenbosch). He also indicates that the idea of an Afrikaans-speaking community assumes that such a community exists among white and coloured Afrikaans speakers – a reification of a desire (Brink 2006: 153). In African nationalism the need for unity and the emphasis on political liberation have produced another essentialism that is, however, more inclusive than Afrikaans essentialism and that is connected to other identities. The 'I am an African' speech by then Deputy President Thabo Mbeki in 1996 was a good example of the inclusiveness implied in Africanist thinking. The notion of ubuntu (humanness) as an essentialised positive quality of African people is another good example of this African identification process that seems to be very different from the Afrikaans ethnic identity. As with the idea of an essential Afrikaans culture and language, the idea of an African culture and its expression in the ubuntu morality is built on essentialism. This was politically very useful for finding a common philosophical foundation in the challenging time of transformation, as specifically expressed by Archbishop Desmond Tutu, and since perpetuated by the media and by political leaders.

Talk about multiculturalism, multilingualism, cultural rights and minority rights in the international discourse on diversity has been grist to the mill of a renewed post-1994 ethnic Afrikanerdom, where these terms are interpreted on the basis of an exclusivist and essentialist understanding of the human world as primarily and primordially composed of separate peoples and cultures. It is therefore not surprising that sceptics have questions about the present Afrikaans language movement that is interpreted by many as an attempt to guarantee cultural power for Afrikaans-speaking whites (Webb 2002: 246). Much attention has been given in the media to the developments and debates around the use of Afrikaans as a language of education. The situation at the University of Stellenbosch has become a paradigmatic case of current language politics in higher education, which confronts us with questions about the tension between the need for transformation and the need for protecting minority languages.

The moral panic around *die taal* (the language) at Stellenbosch

What has become known as *die taaldebat* (the language debate) at the University of Stellenbosch, raging on since 2002, is basically a series of strong statements, background articles and letters to the editor in the press and speeches on public platforms. These are reactions by concerned (mainly white) Afrikaans speakers about the increasing use of English in the classroom, within a wider political context in which Afrikaans has lost the dominant position it used to have in the previous political dispensation. The other side of the debate consists of statements, speeches and occasional letters, also widely reported in the media, from those (including the university management) who try to 'promote Afrikaans in a multilingual context'. As South Africans are still grappling with their newly found unity in a new democratic state, and since the inequalities of the past are largely perpetuated in the present, linked as they are to 'race', ethnicity and class, it is understandable that these issues are reflected in the media. More than that, the media have an intense interest in matters of 'racial', cultural and linguistic identities, since the ideal of multiculturalism is not easily achieved and historical differences tend to influence present relationships to a large extent. The Afrikaans media have a further interest in the *taaldebat*, namely to preserve their readership (market sector) and to promote the language medium through which they exist.

In the process of re-ethnicisation among white Afrikaans speakers, the *taaldebat* at Stellenbosch might be understood as a 'moral panic' serving to underscore conservative ideas and interests. A moral panic is a reaction to a perceived threat to 'normal' values and interests, depicted in a stereotypical form by the media. A moral panic prevents considered thinking and debate, it creates its own structure of ideas that are accepted as given, and it becomes a form of essentialism in which justification and explanation are not needed. The language debate at Stellenbosch is part of the wider debate on Afrikaans and the Afrikaner that is going through continuous cycles of navel-gazing. The issues concerning identity come up repeatedly in various rounds of encapsulated contestation within the middle-class white Afrikaans-speaking population. The level of debate is low, with lots of emotion and speculative, one-sided opinions (Webb 2002: 246). What are the implications of the discussion around essentialism for understanding the *taaldebat* at Stellenbosch? Two paradigms, in the Kuhnian sense, about the nature of the social world are in competition with each other. I admit that I generalise about the two positions to some extent, but I need to indicate common elements in each and then contextualise them in relation to the larger complexities in which they are embedded.

The essentialist position claims that the standard form of Afrikaans and the so-called 'Afrikaans character' of the institution need to be preserved at all costs at the University of Stellenbosch. Brink (2006) calls this the 'protectionist' model.

The other side of the debate argues for a more pragmatic, multilingual and multicultural approach in which the challenges of the political and economic context are given a higher priority than purist language preservation. Brink (2006) calls this the 'multiculturalist' model. Maybe the term 'relationalist' suits the situation better, since multiculturalism could also include a strategy for emphasising differences between cultural entities. Terms like 'the A-optionists' and 'T-optionists' are situational labels in the teaching context of the University of Stellenbosch that obscure the deeper political differences between those involved in the debate. These terms refer to the 2003 language policy of the university, which made provision for teaching in either A (Afrikaans), T (*tweetalig* – bilingual) or E (English) modes. The debate erupts in cycles, especially when a decision has to be made by the university on issues that might change its formerly more exclusivist character in relation to student and staff recruitment. Since my appointment at the University of Stellenbosch in April 2002, I have experienced several of these cycles that were predominantly played out in the media. One focused on diversity and the democratisation of *koshuiskultuur* (residence culture) in 2002, another on the regulation of a language policy in 2003, another on the honorary degree bestowed on an Afrikaans communist in 2004, and the latest was a focus on the T-option in the Faculty of Arts and Social Sciences in 2005.

The transfer of power by Afrikaans-speaking whites to a mainly African elite that prioritises the use of English to access the world of work and knowledge, the use of English as the de facto lingua franca in the country and in the globalised world, and the experience of affirmative action all contribute to a sense of loss and alienation amongst conservative Afrikaans speakers. The University of Stellenbosch, as the prime symbol of Afrikaans elitism, is a natural site for putting up a last stand, even if this provides merely symbolic satisfaction. As usual in a process of ethnicisation, the main impetus is given by intellectuals with a social science background. The Afrikaans media are a prime site for the debate.

Hermann Giliomee, a retired professor of history and one of the senior intellectual leaders in the neo-Afrikaner movement, wrote a history, tellingly entitled *The Afrikaners: Biography of a People*, in which the process of Afrikaner ethnic identity formation is described (Giliomee 2003). As the process of ethnicisation is not problematised or theoretically engaged with in this book, the reader is left with a sense of a primordial essence in the conceptualisation of Afrikaners and 'a people'. Giliomee presents his work as 'a biography of the Afrikaner people of South Africa, whose roots in the continent of Africa go back to the seventeenth century' (Giliomee 2003: xiii). The title personifies and essentialises the idea of Afrikaners three times: in presenting these people as 'the Afrikaners', assuming a strong sense on their part of forming a group; by using the word 'biography', whereby the idea of an organic personal entity is evoked; and by using the word 'people', another problematic concept that has to be unpacked theoretically. By using the term 'Afrikaners' uncritically, Giliomee opts for an ethnic interpretation, avoiding a critical theory of ethnicity. In this regard his historical narrative is based on a similar premise to that of the people he discusses, one that is also found widely in media reporting. A theoretical history that does not question and interpret these notions can easily strengthen mistaken common-sense understandings of complex social processes. In his writings on language in the Afrikaans press, one also picks up the notion of 'language community' as a term that is not contextualised or critically analysed.

Another intellectual driving the renewed ethnicisation process is Johann Rossouw, a philosopher who works for the FAK (Federasie van Afrikaanse Kultuurverenigings – Federation of Afrikaans Cultural Associations) and who is the editor of the monthly *Vrye Afrikaan* (Free African) in which he promotes the view that local identities, amongst them Afrikaner identity, are sidelined by globalising neo-liberal forces. In this argument, the complex history of Afrikaner ethnicity and the contextual challenges of South African development are minimised. Many Afrikaans speakers react positively to these sentiments, as they have been brought up to believe that Afrikaner identity is an essentialist entity to be protected at all costs, for example during the *totale aanslag* (total onslaught) of the last decades of apartheid. Now that it is more difficult for white graduates to get jobs in South Africa, the networks of Afrikaans-speaking alumni are of prime importance. An example of their influence is found in the resistance to opening up the university residences, as they represent sites where the old boys' clubs were formed.

In the polarisation around the *taaldebat*, it is interesting to see both sides using forms of essentialism for their arguments. The reference by both to the standardised Afrikaans language as an entity is a way of making a diversified language into one stable, invariant version of itself. The reference to the ideas of the 'other' also rests on an essentialising perspective, typical of a process of polarisation. Yet, despite the essentialisms involved, it is clear that there are many variations on both sides of the debate. The 'coloured' voice is less audible (despite representing most of the Afrikaans speakers demographically), is not so involved in the debate, and tends to take context more into account than the white *taalstryders* (language warriors) do. Women are mostly heard only when they argue against essentialism and for greater flexibility in the language policy. Likewise with the younger generation, although here again these categories are not homogeneous (Van der Waal 2003).

The viewpoints in the debate are related to larger issues with material and ideological dimensions. When large numbers of authors writing in Afrikaans join an action that demands that the University of Stellenbosch remain Afrikaans-teaching, they do so at least partly because of the economics of the Afrikaans book market. Likewise, the old boys' club that I referred to above has a stake in the economic and social capital that is generated at the university. So do the newspapers and the university management, each taking a position that is based on interests in a transforming flux of relationships. These underlying interests are seldom expressed or revealed, due to the common assumption and mystification that the debate is solely about language. Essentialism isolates the phenomena under discussion in a debate without relating them to the broader issues that are at stake. The language issue in higher education is often isolated from the overall dynamics of the educational context, due to the focus on the status of the language in isolation from its functionality. For example, in the teaching of the social sciences, it is my experience that it is preferable to have students from various backgrounds and languages together in one class for the benefit of enriched class discussions that bring in a variety of perspectives and experiences.

Those analysts who do place the language issue in a broader set of relations, such as Chris Brink (2006), argue that Afrikaans speakers need to be understood in the context of the post-apartheid period. They see a need for Afrikaners to reconcile with those in South Africa who have become alienated from them due to the policies and practices undertaken in the name of Afrikaans in the past. Brink argues for a view that includes complexity, and that overcomes the restrictions of the stereotypes of the 'mode 1 world' which functions in terms of either/or logic and is dependent on essential categories. He promotes the idea of a 'mode 2' approach, a world of and/and, with emphasis on complexity and dynamics (Brink 2006: 97, 101). This leads him to argue for an Afrikaans-oriented university that promotes Afrikaans, but not in the context of group identity and group rights which could lead to an Afrikaans enclave. In other words, his is an anti-essentialism approach and, for those who prefer a more democratic and inclusive view of society, therefore a more convincing argument. The anti-essentialism position is much more difficult to promote and achieve in practice, given the strong conservative forces that work for an essentialist interpretation and policy. The Afrikaans media still operate mainly on the basis of an essentialist understanding of identity.

Conclusion

This discussion of language and culture leads to the conclusion that these notions have no essential characteristics; they exhibit more variety than homogeneity. The similarities that are observed have to do with the communicative aspects of culture and language: a critical mass of standardised forms within which huge variation is possible. These cultural and linguistic phenomena are constructed for specific purposes by people who live lives that are characterised by high levels of diversity and unique features. The challenge to social science is to investigate the changing forms of culture and language, to probe for the assumptions underlying the discourses that form part of the encounters in this field, to chart and interpret the interactions that form the micro-contexts for human communication and to contextualise these events. All forms of essentialism need to be questioned and seen as political attempts to frame constructions in a specific way, based on a set of interests and relationships.

As for Afrikaans, its promotion, to the extent that it is desirable and practical, has to be done in full consciousness of the larger political and economic context. Webb (2002: 247) poses the important question of how Afrikaans speakers can contribute to equity, democratisation and development in South Africa. What rights can Afrikaans speakers expect in the context of 10 other language categories? These are useful questions with which one is able to move away from the crippling grip that essentialism has on the minds of many participants in the *taaldebat*.

The political economy of language, the fact that our notions about social and linguistic entities and policies are driven by inequalities, needs to be understood. Given that Afrikaans is not the language of the most marginalised sector of the population, the drive for protection may indicate that vested interests are at stake. This is an indication of how far the European model of ethnonationalism and its associated essentialisms have travelled. In order to get rid of the myths of purity and essentialism that are crippling successful

dialogue, it is necessary to embrace variety and process in their place. The media have an important role to play in this regard as they can be an excellent instrument for liberating the mind. In order to achieve this, they need to:
- reflect the shifting situation of social identities, language and culture on the ground;
- stimulate debate on multilingualism generally, and on the role of language in education specifically;
- reflect on the tendency to essentialise identities as given categories, for example in situations of war, genocide and extremely polarised political competition;
- report and interpret incidents of instigating injustice towards any social category; and
- provide counter-arguments to ethnic exclusivism, especially since this may be harmful to the process of achieving the values enshrined in the South African Constitution.

References

Anderson B (1983) *Imagined communities: Reflections on the origins and spread of nationalism*. London: Verso

Brink A (2000) *Groot verseboek 2000*. Cape Town: Tafelberg

Brink C (2006) *No lesser place: The* taaldebat *at Stellenbosch*. Stellenbosch: Sunmedia

Duranti A (1997) *Linguistic anthropology*. Cambridge: Cambridge University Press

Foley WA (1997) *Anthropological linguistics: An introduction*. Malden, MA: Blackwell

Fuchs S (2001) *Against essentialism: A theory of culture and society*. Cambridge, MA: Harvard University Press

Giliomee H (2003) *The Afrikaners: Biography of a people*. Cape Town: Tafelberg

Grillo R (ed.) (1989) *Social anthropology and the politics of language*. London: Routledge

Huntington SP (1997) *The clash of civilizations and the remaking of the world order*. New York: Touchstone

Keesing RM & Strathern AJ (1998) *Cultural anthropology: A contemporary perspective*. Fort Worth, TX: Harcourt Brace

Kuper A (2002) Today we have the naming of parts: The work of the anthropologists in southern Africa. *Anthropology Southern Africa* 25(1–2): 7–16

Mbeki T (1999) I am an African. In G Maharaj (ed.) *Between unity and diversity: Essays on nation-building in post-apartheid South Africa*, pp. 11–15. Cape Town: IDASA

Morton S (2003) *Gayatri Chakravorty Spivak*. London: Routledge

Nagtegaal J (2002) *Daar's vis in die punch*. Cape Town: Tafelberg

Said EW (1991) *Orientalism*. London: Penguin

Spivak GC (1996) *The Spivak reader: Selected works of Gayatri Chakravorty Spivak*. New York: Routledge

Van der Waal CS (2003) Diverse approaches in a South African debate on language and diversity in higher education. *Anthropology Southern Africa* 25(3–4): 86–95

Webb V (2002) *Language in South Africa: The role of language in national transformation, reconstruction and development*. Amsterdam: John Benjamins

Wright S (1998) The politicisation of 'culture'. *Anthropology Today* 14(1): 7–15

Wright S (2004) *Language policy and language planning: From nationalism to globalisation*. New York: Palgrave

4 'National' public service broadcasting: Contradictions and dilemmas

Ruth Teer-Tomaselli

South Africa moved from formal apartheid to an inclusive multi-party democracy in the early 1990s, culminating in the April 1994 elections. This social and political shift offered a unique testing ground for theories of media and democracy. Political struggles and discourses at every level of the state and civil society were dominated by the demands of pressure groups representing a wide range of constituencies. Little agreement existed on what constituted democracy; on how such a practice could be attained; and whether or not a single nation could be forged out of the linguistic, cultural, ethnic, racial, class and geographical patchwork into which South Africa has been fragmented by apartheid.

The South African Broadcasting Corporation (SABC) was a test case in negotiating disparate ideological conflicts. Established in 1936 as a public service broadcaster under a charter authored by Sir John Reith of the British Broadcasting Corporation (BBC) during the apartheid years, the corporation was used by the National Party (NP) government for apartheid propaganda (Teer-Tomaselli & Tomaselli 2001, Tomaselli et al. 1989). In the early 1990s the SABC became the locus for national struggles – over questions of control, racial composition, news content, language policy, ideology and the whole gamut of what could constitute a 'new South Africa'. What happened in the 'transformation' of the SABC became a litmus test of what occurred in the 'transformation' of the wider society.

In this chapter I focus on two key elements of public service broadcasting in South Africa that have ramifications across most – if not all – of the above categories: economic sustainability on the one hand, and the confused intersection of public and national goods on the other.

Apartheid located South Africa within contradictory relations. The underdeveloped segments in both the rural areas and the cities stood in stark contrast to those sectors (entertainment, banking, media, telecommunications, information) which were inextricably integrated into the global information economy. Subsequent debates on the country's economic modelling emphasised the restructuring of obsolete institutions, based on equally obsolete productive forces, including migrant labour and the maintenance of a large force of cheap labour. The emphasis was on redistribution and the development of a consumer-based mass market, conforming to an emerging commercially driven economy.

In broadcasting, the result was policy decisions which attempted to reform institutions within modernist conditions, as is evident in many of the provisions of the early Independent Broadcasting Authority (IBA) Act. Almost no attention was given to the late capitalist economy into which broadcasting was moving internationally within the dynamics of a postmodern information economy.

The genesis of public service broadcasting in South Africa

Public service broadcasting in southern Africa owes its genesis to the colonial heritage of the Commonwealth model. In these countries, public broadcasting typically preceded the commercial networks and, at least initially, was given precedence over them. The tradition of public service broadcasting is strongest in Britain, embodied in the BBC under its first director-general, John Reith. For a short time, he was the British minister of information (Briggs & Burke 2002: 220).

Reith also wrote the founding documents for the SABC in 1933, as well as the charters for the Canadian, Australian and Kenyan broadcasters, among others. Thus there is a notable formalist similarity among these broadcasters, and public broadcasting principles are still referred to as 'Reithian principles'. A Scottish engineer and the son of a Calvinist minister, Reith had a strong sense of mission. He argued that the radio wave spectrum, or Hertzian radio waves, was a scarce resource, being limited by the availability of sound waves within the electromagnetic spectrum. At the same time, public broadcasting was ubiquitous within the area of transmission. No matter how many people tuned into the airwaves within a particular reception area, there was always plenty of space for others to listen at no extra cost. This strangely paradoxical situation of a scarce resource in terms of the limited spectrum frequency, and a ubiquitous, unlimited ability of the audience to receive a commonly transmitted signal within a specific area, provided much of the early impetus to the usage of free-to-air transmission, first in radio and then in television. Unlike the American experience, where broadcasting was a commercial enterprise from the outset, Reith argued that broadcasting should be developed and regulated in the interests of the nation, assigned through state intervention. Thus, from the outset the state was at the heart of public service broadcasting. The state's stewardship of the airwaves was not only a matter of technological determinacy; it was based on strong normative values as well, since, in Reith's view, to have used broadcasting simply as a medium of entertainment would have been to 'prostitute' it (Briggs & Burke 2002: 221). Broadcasting thus belonged squired in the public domain. Public broadcasting was to be similar in nature to public institutions such as libraries and universities: institutions whose existence can be guaranteed only by the state but which remain resolutely independent of the state in determining what cultural activities they will undertake and how.

This implied a public monopoly of a public good, which would be acceptable only if it were publicly owned and stood equally free from political forces – the government in particular – on the one hand, and various private economic interests on the other. Consequently, in an ideal situation public broadcasting should be financed by a licence fee, and not by advertising, since this would imply that broadcasters would have to pander to commercial interests, something that was anathema to Reith. Public broadcasting was to be 'universal' insofar as it was to serve the interests of the whole public, not just those who could afford to buy it or who had the political clout to receive scarce information.

What is public service broadcasting?

There is no single definition of what constitutes a public service broadcaster; however, it is possible to identify a number of key characteristics which are accepted as common to most institutions that consider themselves to be public broadcasters. All public broadcasters privilege the 'public interest' and the 'public good' by aiming to provide relevant information, balance or fairness on controversial and political issues, and diversity of programmes and services (Mpofu et al. 2000; Raboy 1990, 2003; Scannell 1991, 2000; Teer-Tomaselli 2005). Considered in ideal terms, the classic model of public service broadcasting was underpinned by the following principles summarised by the European Broadcasting Union:

1. Universal geographic accessibility
2. Universal appeal across tastes and interests
3. Particular attention to minorities
4. Contribution to a sense of national identity and community
5. Distance from vested interests
6. Direct funding and universality of payment
7. Competition in good programming rather than for numbers
8. Guidelines that liberate rather than restrict programme makers
(European Broadcasting Union 1985: 18; quoted in Morrison 1986: 13)

These principles have become the accepted basis of all public service broadcasting internationally, although they have been interpreted and applied in different ways.

Public service broadcasting all over the world has faced serious problems in the past two decades. In fact, no 'pure' form of public service broadcasting in its original incarnation exists anywhere in the world today. In South Africa, the worldwide problems which face public broadcasters have been exacerbated by three primary challenges:

- overcoming the historical heritage of a broadcasting milieu which was set up to service the needs of a minority of the population, and which had strong political relationships to the previous apartheid government;
- the financial burden of maintaining an increasingly expensive system in the face of market liberalisation and technological developments; and
- the ongoing temptation to fall back into the old habit of being a 'state broadcaster' rather than a 'national public broadcaster' and, in so doing, replacing the beneficiaries of the old system with beneficiaries of the new, so neglecting the interests of the public.

How 'public' is public service broadcasting in South Africa? One way of addressing the question is to begin to unpack the key distinctions between the 'public interest' and the 'national interest', two concepts that frequently are conflated.

Public interest and the 'public sphere'

A vigorously independent media is intrinsic to the infrastructure required for knowledgeable debate, informed choices and general transparency needed in a mature democracy. This is part of the well-discussed 'public sphere', that space wherein all citizens can freely discuss politics independent of the influence of the state or capital. The 'public sphere' is a concept that has endured long after other theoretical ideas have gone out of fashion. Since the work of Jürgen Habermas was translated into English in 1989 and 'discovered' by academics in the English-speaking world, the concept has been applied to the media with an almost canonical reverence: it has been developed, modified, critiqued, discarded and re-embraced with an enthusiasm verging on faith.

For Habermas, the period of early capitalism in the late eighteenth and early nineteenth centuries seemed to approach the 'ideal speech situation'. During these formative years of capitalism, discussion among the educated elite was intensely political, focusing on contemporary affairs and state policy. Gentlemen's clubs, salons and coffee houses provided the spaces for these informed conversations. The bourgeoisie created networks of information sharing, including newspapers, debating societies, publishing houses, libraries, universities, museums and the like, in order to express public opinion and, more importantly, develop it as a new political force. The outcome is a synthesis of ideas, strongly contested but nevertheless raised to a level of acceptance within the broader society. Habermas held that it is these conditions of argument that lend public opinion its legitimising force; public opinion is thus distinguished from mere 'private' opinion.

The public sphere can be conceptualised as a virtual space in which citizens can have conversations with the guarantee of freedom of assembly and of association and freedom to express and publish their opinions. These ideals are in line with the ideas of the Enlightenment, characterised by four fundamental principles. First, the ideas and their development are independent of church and state power. They represent the thinking of citizens in a 'public' space, and are not prescribed by prior dictates or constraints. Second, in theory at least, discussion is open to all. In practice this was not so; eighteenth-century debating circles were the preserve of the wealthy, or at least of the financially comfortable, and they were mainly the preserve of men. Third, the public sphere was, by definition, distinct from private interests; it served the ideals of the 'public' rather than the individual, and of the 'citizen' rather than commercial interests. Fourth, the public sphere was driven by a quest for general, universal norms supported by scientific and objective legitimation. Thus, discussion and debate within the public sphere axiomatically needs to be governed by the rules of critical reason (Habermas 1989/1995).

Since the publication of Habermas's work, numerous scholars have seen a direct correlation between this idealised schema and public service broadcasting (Bruun-Andersen 1996; Dahlgren 1995, 1998, 2000; Keane 1990;

Murdock 2004, 2005). Indeed, the similarities are beguiling. In the words of Graham Murdock, public service broadcasting seems to offer:

> the chance to universalize the political public sphere by providing open access to three essential cultural resources of full citizenship: comprehensive and accurate information about contemporary events and the actions of power holders; access to the contextual frameworks that convert raw information into usable knowledge by suggesting interpretations and explanations; and access to arenas of debate where contending accounts, aspirations, and positions can be subjected to sustained scrutiny. (Murdock 2005: 178)

The schemas of both the 'ideal' public sphere and the 'ideal' public service broadcaster hide a paternalistic stance in terms of both class and gender, and imply quite undemocratic, top-down practices. In his analysis of the 'structural transformation' of the public sphere, Habermas observed that its erosion was in part due to the growth of the advertising and marketing industries. In other words, while it was the development of widespread capitalism that engendered the public sphere, it was precisely the growth of capitalism that proved to be its greatest nemesis. Habermas contended that media commercialisation excluded political questions from large areas of the public sphere. In particular, he pointed to the tendency towards the consolidation of media ownership and the move towards monopolies, or quasi-monopolies, resulting in the uneven distribution of wealth; the rising cost of entry into the media and other forums facilitating the public sphere; and the resultant unequal access to/control over the public sphere. Whereas in the idealised concept of late-Victorian 'public life', 'publicity' connoted openness, in which the affairs of state were exposed to public scrutiny, the modern conception of 'publicity' has come to mean that which attracts attention for the purposes of journalism, advertising and politics. In such situations, the commercial control of the media stems the flow of 'public' information, just as the persisting dominance of the state over many forms of African media continues to do.

The Reithian inheritance: asymmetrical access and power

Public service broadcasting in South Africa was never premised on a single, rational public sphere, but rather on a fragmentation of peoples, interests, publics and, as a consequence, audiences. This is in direct contradiction to one of the foundations of the model – that is, the idea of a single broadcast to a whole nation.

Reith assumed an audience which in identity terms was relatively homogeneous, capable of making relatively uniform interpretations of programme content and flow (Briggs & Burke 2002: 221). The introduction of public radio in South Africa reflects this position: initially, programming was only in English (the dominant language of the colonial empire). The first quota of Afrikaans programming on the embryonic SABC was a mere 45 minutes per day (Rosenthal 1975: 135), and language equivalency was achieved only years later as a result of considerable agitation on the part of Afrikaans-language pressure groups. In the early years, the media were seen as the preserve of a narrow band of South Africans, who despite their different languages (English and Afrikaans) did constitute a relatively homogeneous group. Ironically, during the 1950s the earlier translocation of the BBC ethos to South Africa continued to suit the NP policy of apartheid, as neither Reith nor the NP recognised black South Africans as part of the listening/viewing audience except on white terms. The first programming in African languages took the form of short inserts in the morning schedules of the English and Afrikaans services.

The media, and especially broadcasting, thus contributed to social and economic disparities. They legitimised apartheid in empowering a small sector of the population working on behalf of the global functions of capital, at the expense of the black-driven motor of the apartheid economy. Herein lay the essential flaw of apartheid. In serving the narrow interests of the South African white capital and the middle classes and oppressing and impoverishing the large majority of people of colour, apartheid could not, in the end, adapt to the needs of late capitalism. This era required an urban, computer-literate, time-conscious and competitively educated workforce.

Capitalism as distorted into a racial form in apartheid South Africa thus reduced the country's ability to interact with the global economy except in a rather asymmetrical kind of way. The suppression of a sufficiently large indigenous market was one result; acquiring the uneven hallmarks of a modern capitalist society was another. South Africa's path to modernity could not be easily derived from too closely linking this country's historical experience to those of the older capitalist societies. Theories of modernity have a different purchase in this partly similar and partly different society. The consequence was a scrambled periodisation of modern, pre-modern and postmodern economic and social forms, which in turn led to the adoption of oppositional ideologies to address these inequities and create the conditions for economic and social growth.

In the apartheid period, ideological positions that were mainstream elsewhere in the world were seen as resistance in South Africa. Liberalism, for example, has always been oppositional. In South Africa it initially opposed apartheid and the tyranny of the minority, and in the 1990s it took issue with an all-embracing African nationalism which threatened to result in the tyranny of the majority. Broadcasting in the 1990s, then, became a site of significant contestation over the image of the 'nation-in-waiting'. This image and struggles over it resulted from a complex accretion of often antagonistic forces: the globalisation of the market versus local content imperatives; plural access versus centralised control; market-driven forces versus a public service ethos; modernity versus postmodernity; centralisation versus regional autonomy; minority pluralism versus majoritarian imposition; and a reverse discrimination uneasily disguised under the discourse of 'affirmative action'.

The 'cultural public sphere'

In a critical repositioning of his own thinking, Habermas reconceptualised his ideas on the public sphere, as evidenced in his writings from 1996 onwards. He points to a second 'cultural' arena, which he dubs as the 'literary cultural sphere'. In this sense, he postulates that great works of fiction allow people to explore what it means to be human in a space parallel to that of the political public sphere. 'But if we if accept that a culture of democracy requires citizens to grasp the links between the good life and good society and see their own life chances as inextricably tied to the general quality of communal life, then the habits of sympathy and projection required by fiction, and the capacity of comedy and art to decentre established ways of looking, are essential resources' (Murdock 2005: 179). These 'affective, aesthetic and emotional modes of communication' (McGuigan 2004) can be seen as a 'cultural public sphere' alongside the political public sphere.

Partly as a response to the growing concern around the issue of social movements (Keane 1990), this second 'cultural public sphere' was seen as a space where the myriad of social interests and grass-roots movements were able to mobilise people as 'communards' (i.e., members of communities) in order to secure a hearing (Habermas 1996). This 'communal' political public sphere could act as an early 'warning system' picking up the early signs of 'social eruptions' and thematising and dramatising them 'in such a way that they are taken up and dealt with by parliamentary complexes' (Habermas 1996: 359).

Applying this to broadcasting, Murdock (2005: 178) has argued that public service broadcasting acts in the same way by mounting pressures from below through developing new forms of representation, including fiction, narrative and entertainment. However, he points to the conclusion that this way of looking at things does little to address another underlying problem with Habermas's formulation: that is, Habermas's model of the political public sphere, with its sole emphasis on information and argument, is set alongside, but not integrated into, his newer idea of the 'cultural public sphere'. Thus, to turn once more to public service broadcasting, this political emphasis translates into an obsession with news and information programming; indeed, news is seen as the test case of the public broadcaster's mandate, a point to which we will return later in the chapter.

Globalisation: reopening the cultural imperialism debate?

In the South African situation, local content programming increasingly attracts greater attention from the majority of viewers and listeners than do imported productions. This observation underscores the point that if public service broadcasting is to continue to play a part in national reconstruction, it must do so largely in the context of its contribution to the local, regional and specific language requirements of the country.

At the same time as technical developments have worked towards globalisation, a parallel development in the ownership and control of broadcast institutions has become apparent. News-flow studies have long indicated that a few major organisations control the distribution of international news. The claim has been that this results in the setting of international news agendas. At the same time, international monopolisation of news programming as well as of entertainment programming brings the very real threat of cultural domination and the erosion of existing communities and cultures.

Given this mixed and ambiguous heritage, the question that we now explore is how public service broadcasting responded to the above-mentioned processes. Public service broadcasting remained an important genre in the light of the need to redress the disparities caused by capital and apartheid in the first place, and legitimated during the apartheid years via broadcasting in the second place. Broadcasting strategies since the early 1990s have attempted to cater for all elements within the South African polity, with mixed success. While programming in African languages, programming for children, as well as news and information programming have increased, the trajectory has been uneven. During periods of financial constraint, particularly in the years following the 'restructuring' of the SABC under the advice of McKinsey & Company, local content programmes were cut drastically, with drama and children's programming being the chief victims (Teer-Tomaselli 2005; Tleane & Duncan 2002).

Despite certain advances, some sectors of the South African public have expressed a perception of exclusion. This is particularly true of the communities that were relatively well catered for under the previous dispensation. Afrikaans-language programming was cut drastically after the channel 'relaunch' in 1996, and only recovered slowly, never reaching the levels previously provided for. English-language programming remains significant, in that the whole schedule of SABC3 is programmed in English, and significant portions of SABC1 and SABC2 are also in English.

Challenges facing public broadcasting

The regimen of advanced capitalism in the twenty-first century has brought massive challenges to broadcasters' ability to adapt to rapid change across a wide front. These challenges, which have been particularly difficult for public broadcasters, include technological change; the problems of soaring cost structures; globalisation and monopolies; the role of broadcasters within a public domain and their susceptibility to government pressure; and the need to redefine the notion of nationalism (see Collins 1992; Keane 1990; Thompson 1990).

Liberalisation and technological innovation

Deregulation, privatisation and liberalisation have been foundational to the multimedia digital era (Herman & Chomsky 1988; McChesney 1997; Mosco 1996; Noordenstreng & Schiller 1993). It is now common cause that the processes of globalisation have resulted in a shift from a world order in which national states exercise significant (though never total) control over their domestic economies to one in which domestic affairs increasingly are open to market forces and economic interdependence. In communications generally this has heralded important historical changes, including the significant break of telecommunications and broadcasting from state control, and concomitant marketisation and commercialisation of communications infrastructures, which were previously considered core public goods.

Commercialisation, by which is meant the funding of media through the sale of advertisements, preceded liberalisation by decades. From the outset, the dominant form of media funding in America was commercial; however, in Europe commercialisation was an anathema. Post-war prosperity and the rise of the consumer society produced significant pressure on governments to accommodate a more commercial regimen of broadcasting. Ironically, Britain, home of the European and Commonwealth model of public broadcasting, was the first to capitulate, with the introduction of Independent Television, ITV, in 1954. This was a dual system of broadcasting provision – the famed 'duopology'. However, ITV was not entirely 'independent'; it was closer to a regulated competition, with the new licensee having significant public service obligations in the way of informational, children's and educational programming, aside from the more openly commercial programming (Murdock 2005). Italy followed the liberalisation process in the early 1980s, when Silivo Berlusconi launched a series of interlocked regional channels, thus getting around the ban on the establishment of alternative national commercial channels.

South Africa provided a variant that was unique at the time: a public service broadcaster with commercial funding in the form of Springbok Radio in 1950. At the same time, the flagship English and Afrikaans services remained advertisement free, so as not to compromise the status of their quality, high-culture programming (Hayman & Tomaselli 2001: 50). It was only in the 1980s that these two stations began to accept advertising. The FM radio stations introduced in the l960s – both the 'Radio Bantu' stations in African languages as well as the English–Afrikaans bilingual regional music radio stations (Radio Highveld, Radio Port Natal, etc.) – were commercial-free from the outset (Hayman & Tomaselli 2001: 61). Until 1972, the SABC's funding from licences outperformed funding from commercials (Hayman & Tomaselli 2001: 61); since 1972, there has been a steady decline in the proportion of licence income. Commercial funding through the sale of advertising space on television was introduced in 1979, within three years of the first screen broadcasts, adding to the commercially derived revenue stream. Thus, commercialisation as such is not a new phenomenon in South African broadcasting; what changed was the liberalisation, or selling off, of previous state-owned assets in the broadcasting portfolio.

The real sea change in global mediascapes was driven by liberalisation, by which is meant 'the legal framework that changes the law and entails removing monopoly of broadcasting exercised by governments' (Carver 1995: 4). In

1980, only two of the broadcasting systems in western European countries had a dual system in which public broadcasters competed with commercial broadcasters. Most public broadcasters relied on a mixture of public and commercial funding models (Siune & Hulten 1998: 27). By the turn of the millennium, fully funded monopolies had disappeared altogether, all countries had commercial competition, and the public service obligations on commercial broadcasters had been severely curtailed (Murdock & Golding 2001). In the decade straddling the millennium, the processes of liberalisation and commercialisation extended beyond western Europe. The collapse of the Soviet Union brought countries in the former Eastern Bloc into the ambit of the European Union economy, and an end to the client relationships that bolstered the bureaucracies of many African countries. In both spheres, market-driven impetuses coursed alongside simultaneous attempts to recast former 'state' broadcasters into 'public' broadcasters.

Globally, the state (in all its manifestations across the world) has been the leading proponent of liberalisation and the concomitant process of deregulation. In the advanced industrial world these policies have been implemented voluntarily, while in the so-called third world, World Bank-led structural adjustment programmes have had similar effects. Middle-ground economies, such as South Africa, find themselves in a situation in which they wish to improve their competitive standing within the global economy, and therefore are drawn to policies of liberalisation; at the same time, they face resistance to the wholesale transformation to a market-driven economy. The long-standing tensions within the political alliance over the transition from the Redistribution and Development Programme to the Growth, Employment and Redistribution programme, and more recently to the Accelerated and Shared Growth Initiative,[1] is testament to these ideological and policy stresses. It is against these broad brush strokes that changes in the broadcasting sector should be seen – and with them, the changing nature of public service broadcasting.

Not only has the number of licensed broadcasters increased hugely but, more importantly, the past quarter century has seen a veritable explosion in the number of channels on both radio and television. The change has been fuelled by two drivers: technological advances and market liberalisation, both of which have allowed multiple terrestrial channels to proliferate. From having a single channel in 1976, the SABC now broadcasts three terrestrial channels. Two further regional channels, sharing the same frequency but beamed across different footprints, are due to come on-stream within two years. In June 2005, the broadcasting regulator ICASA (Independent Communication Authority of South Africa) granted permission for the SABC to apply for licences for SABCTV4 and SABCTV5. The channels, which will broadcast only in African languages, will be funded through a grant from Parliament as well as from advertising or licence fees. The purpose behind the establishment of these two new services is to augment the amount of programming in African languages.

The liberalisation of the broadcasting regimen was effected through the establishment of the regulator (the IBA in 1993, later absorbed into ICASA in 2000). The regulator oversaw the licensing of the first independent, commercial free-to-air channel, e.tv, in 1998. e.tv is owned by a black empowerment group, Hosken Consolidated Investments, and Venfin, a local investment company that until recently held a substantial sector of the mobile telephone giant Vodacom. e.tv's broadcast footprint covers 78 per cent of South Africa's population, and the most recent audience figures indicate a viewership of more than 10.5 million viewers (SAARF 2006).

Equally significant in the process of deregulation (or rather, re-regulation) was the introduction of satellite television. It is sobering to recall that the first licensing legislation undertaken by the IBA in 1993 did not include any mention of satellite broadcasting, since these developments were regarded as so futuristic as not to warrant legislation at that point. Satellite television abolishes the traditional relationship between cost and distance of transmission, and potentially offers new market stratifications. South Africa introduced a KU-band satellite in 1985, which radically altered the pattern of television transmission, creating the conditions for the emergence a decade later of digital satellite TV (DSTV), which broadcasts across Africa. Further, the harnessing of 'super high frequencies', previously useless for broadcasting, made the traditional parameters of spectrum scarcity anachronistic; almost limitless spectrum availability resulted in a plethora of new private stations and community radio across the country (Collins 1990; Teer-Tomaselli 2005). The imminent introduction of digital television, and the increasing use of online (computer-generated) and streamed broadcasting, will exacerbate this situation.

In many countries, multichannel broadcasting has eliminated the public service broadcasting ideal of balance, with commercial imperatives coming to the forefront as public broadcasters battle to retain a competitive edge in order to attract viewers and listeners away from private, profit-driven competitors. In doing so, public broadcasters are at risk of losing their 'distinctiveness' and becoming clones of the commercial broadcasters. The greater number of channels has resulted in more hours of broadcasting, and this increased programming has resulted in more entertainment programmes and, concomitantly, less educational, public affairs, children's and regional fare.

Geographic coverage also suffered. Outlying and rural regions not sufficiently lucrative to warrant expansive capital outlay lagged behind in the provision of communication services, an observation as true of telecommunication as it is of broadcasting. Ironically, satellite transmission has changed this – with a satellite dish and a decoder, it is possible to receive any number of signals. Cost becomes an important issue here, leading to greater inequalities between those who are able to afford unlimited access, and those who for economic reasons are forced to rely on terrestrial transmission. In an effort to even out the effects of the rural–urban divide, at least at a technical level, the SABC invested in the Irdeto satellite distribution system to provide blanket coverage. However, even here the consumer is required to pay for the installation of the equipment, although there is no subscription cost involved.

Ideologically, the emergence of the multichannel society has changed audience profiles and viewing habits and encouraged the rise of market values. No longer is it possible to assume that the entire 'nation' is listening to, or watching, similar programming. Reith's idea of the 'nation speaking to itself' seems an illusion. Having said that, the programming on the SABC should be seen holistically, rather than in isolation. The South African 'public' can as easily be conceptualised as 'publics', with differences of language, age, educational levels and tastes. The argument for the additional two regional channels rests precisely on the need for extra broadcasting time – and space – with which to be able to fulfil the multiplicity of needs that constitute servicing a national audience in 11 different languages. 'Flagship' programming, most notably news, is produced across all SABC channels in different languages.

The reprisal to the fear of audience fragmentation comes from the realisation that the majority of people within Africa, and even in South Africa, remain dependent on terrestrial channels. Audience research indicates that during any given week, approximately 19 million people in South Africa tune into the SABC, whereas the terrestrial commercial channel, e.tv, attracts 10.5 million viewers. The multichannel subscription bouquet, DSTV, has reached a ceiling of approximately 1 million. Seen in this light, fears of the dangers of a multichannel environment seem overstated.

The expansion of the technical possibilities of satellite, digitalisation and other technological advances has produced contradictory effects. On the one hand, through the use of the Irdeto system, satellite transmission has extended the potential of the broadcasting sector to fulfil its mandate as a truly national broadcaster, widening the broadcast footprint to reach the most outlying rural areas regardless of the topographical obstacles. On the other hand, the increase in channels has fractured the national consensus, facilitating a multiplicity of viewing experiences, often dictated by class and access to expensive subscription programming.

Economic constraints

Traditionally, a hallmark of public broadcasting is that it is not reliant on commercial sources of income. To this day the BBC has no advertising, while in South Africa broadcasting was advertising-free until the advent of Springbok Radio in 1956. Nevertheless, fiscal constraints are a body blow to public broadcasters. Internationally, it is no longer possible to depend financially on licence income. Revenue needs to be supplemented by advertising and state allocations, both of which potentially impinge on the independence of broadcasters. In South Africa the position is particularly acute: for close to 20 years now, the SABC has been predominantly dependent on commercial revenue, with approximately three-quarters of the corporation's income coming from advertising and sponsorship, while only a quarter (and in some fiscal years less) comes from licences. Less than 5 per cent is sourced directly from the government, and all of that money is earmarked for specific educational programming.

The perilous financial state of public broadcasters worldwide has resulted from both greater expenditures and diminished income opportunities. On the expenditure side, operating costs are higher in South Africa than in most Western economies, since the country imports its equipment and much of its technical back-up. The aging terrestrial signal distribution infrastructure for the analogue frequency modulation (FM) transmission network, built in the 1960s and 1970s, is now more than a quarter of a century old, and much of it needs to be repaired or replaced. Satellite technology, while cost-effective in the long run, requires enormous initial capital outlay, and needs to be paid for at crippling rates of foreign exchange. As the migration from terrestrial to digital terrestrial broadcasting proceeds, these capital expenses mount. Plans to substitute it with digital terrestrial broadcasting entail a recapitalisation of the broadcasting production capacity at around 1.2 billion rand over a period of six years.[2] The signal distribution arm of the broadcasting infrastructure, Sentech, has estimated that it will require in the order of 1 billion rand to finance the digital infrastructure necessary to transmit the 2010 World Cup soccer.[3]

Programming accounts for the largest expenditure in broadcasting. It is cheaper to import than to produce, a factor which has important consequences for the dearth of national programming and the spectre of cultural imperialism, with wall-to-wall soap operas and German serials dubbed into Afrikaans. In response to the lack of adequate and consistent funding, public service broadcasting genres are being increasingly homogenised. Culturally valuable forms, such as the single play and the innovative documentary, are allotted fewer and fewer resources, and the impulse to co-produce becomes relentless. South Africa has the economic power to appropriate Western technologies and imperatives and reconstitute them into an African context without necessarily sliding into backwardness and an inability to compete in international markets. Concomitantly, there is the increasing potential for economic and programming dependency on the part of third world countries which find themselves locked into a client relationship with the first world giants.

The strategy of breaking the SABC into autonomous business units, which attracted the ire of 'leftist' commentators who saw it purely as a precursor to privatisation (Tleane & Duncan 2002), had a contradictory effect on the possibilities of public broadcasting services. While greater autonomy provided a valuable opportunity for editorial and programming independence, leading to a greater variety of 'voices', the downside was that in circumstances in which individual units are entirely responsible for their financial health, the temptation to ignore culturally valuable but economically less rewarding programming becomes almost insurmountable.[4] Particularly on radio, programme formats became sacrosanct, and any suggested deviation aroused fears of alienating the established audience. Furthermore, the 'trapping' of surpluses in the regions led to even less cross-subsidisation of non-profit national projects.

Market failure

Given that even public broadcasters rely heavily on advertising – the hallmark of commercial broadcasting – why is it necessary to have a public broadcaster, and why don't we simply rely on market forces? There are a number of reasons why the market-led philosophy is inadequate to provide for a service as important as broadcasting, particularly so in a developing country. In a milieu where the value of broadcasting is predicated solely on its marketable popularity, the danger exists that the 'commercial communication promotes the idea that there are no truths, only strategies and claims' (Wintour 2004: 15). Public service broadcasting can, and does, redress market failure. Typically, markets don't produce sufficient quantity and quality of programming in education, research, children's programming (other than cartoons), dramas in minority languages or other specialised programming.

A contrary point of view has been offered by commentators such as Liz Jacka, who have pointed out that commercial private broadcasters often provide quality programming as good as – or better than – public broadcasters (Jacka 2003: 180). Certainly, there are benefits for commercial companies in producing this kind of material, but they are not immediately profitable. An examination of the schedules of any 'commercial' broadcaster will reveal a serious neglect of these kinds of programmes. In short, markets don't work fairly – they don't provide for the poor, the old, the undereducated or those who live in remote areas, away from the urban conurbations.

Social and cultural adjustment

We now return to the central concern of this chapter: the relationship between the broadcaster and the public, the nation and the state.

Public broadcasters frequently see themselves as 'national' broadcasters, and indeed in common parlance the two terms become interchangeable. Furthermore, in debates around public broadcasting, distinctions are made between 'public broadcasters' and 'state broadcasters'. The slide from 'public' to 'nation' to 'state' is insidious, in the discourse as well as in the practice, and is the central issue in discussion of public service broadcasting, citizenship and democracy.

The re-emergence of nationalism, particularly among previously marginalised countries and ethnic groups, became a global factor after the end of the Cold War. The development of nationalist impulses happened simultaneously with the breakdown of transnational barriers among the world's major powers, leading to the rise of 'globalisation' as the most significant epistemological phenomenon of the past decade. Significantly, large, dominant countries read 'globalisation' as an economic discourse, while those who have most to lose see it in cultural terms, frequently reminiscent of the older 'cultural imperialism' thesis.

Modern nationalism 'defined territory as the foundation of the sovereignty and the imaginary community' (Mattelart 2003: 548). In the present context, 'nationalism' is used to cover an ideological position that defines the primary unit of community as 'the nation', predicated on the belief that the interests of national citizens are best served by strong, relatively autonomous states and a resistance to transnationalism. The nation in this sense is famously conceptualised as an 'imagined community' (Anderson 1991).[5] Thus, individual agents constitute themselves as citizens, who are called on to join the national venture and 'encouraged to picture themselves as social agents capable both of remaking themselves and contributing to the public good' (Murdock 2005: 175). The call to nationalism was a call to put aside the particularities of individual identity, and to think of oneself as 'citizen'.

However, in complex modern societies, people are less likely to think of themselves in the first instance as 'national citizens', and are more likely to position themselves within a matrix of multiple and often conflicting identities and loyalties based on such disparate considerations as locality, belief or religion, occupation or class, ethnicity and language, and even gender. These identifications coalesce around networks of support and cohesion, and they have well-developed and sustained narratives and mythologies played out against a rhythm of regular and repeated rituals.

Building an ideological construct of a 'nation' requires, in part, that key institutions of cultural production, including public broadcasters, set out to transcend these particularistic loyalties. The history of the twentieth century, with its turbulent contestations between nations, ensured that national public broadcasters in Europe contributed greatly to the creation of the national imaginary. The role of public broadcasters in cementing a national social solidarity over regional and factional loyalties has already been alluded to. The BBC, for instance, has aired on both radio and television a parade of jingoistic events, from the opening of Parliament; through royal coronations, weddings and funerals; to a myriad of quintessential 'British' events and occasions. In South Africa's recent history, iconic moments of the first democratic elections, the famous fly-past of planes over the Union Buildings in Pretoria to mark the inauguration of the president, and the picture-postcard occasion when then president Mandela donned the green and gold shirt of the victorious Springbok rugby team to celebrate the 1995 World Cup victory have become part of the collective memories of all South Africans. These 'rites of nationhood', to use Paddy Scannell's apt terminology, all contributed to '[m]aking the nation one man' (Reith 1924, quoted in Scannell 2000: 48).

The role of sports in the national psyche poses a particular challenge to public broadcasters. As the rights to international events became more and more expensive, so key tournaments found broadcast homes on pay channels. 'It is an unfortunate reality that the majority of South Africans have for years been denied this right as a result of the introduction of subscription television in this country. Free-to-air television had virtually been starved of coverage of sports events of a national interest as a result of commercial considerations,' opined the then minister of sports and recreation Ngconde Balfour.[6] In a country where 'national pride' is reflected in the performance of national teams, and where the finals of a rugby, soccer or cricket match in an international series are a matter of 'national concern', feelings of exclusion at not being able to take part, even vicariously, are taken to heart. Popular commentator Toni Erling has noted:

> If we cannot watch such events because we cannot afford the subscription service or because the event is only broadcast in a small part of South Africa, we will naturally feel somewhat aggrieved. However, there are also some sports events, such as netball and athletics, which are not as popular and thus need protection by our government to ensure that they are in fact broadcast at all, even if only the highlights are shown.[7]

The Broadcasting Act of 1999 includes a provision that 'subscription services' may not acquire exclusive rights for the broadcast of 'national sporting events as identified in the public interest' (RSA 1999). What constituted a 'national sporting event' was to be determined by ICASA 'in consultation with the Ministers of Communications and Sport…through a public process' (RSA 1999). Such consultations were undertaken in 2002 with the publication of a discussion paper titled 'Inquiry into Sports Broadcasting Rights', followed by hearings and public comment.[8] Arising out of this process, ICASA developed a position paper and a set of regulations, including a list of what were deemed 'national sporting events'.[9] Since that time, the SABC has managed to 'claw back' many of the primary sporting events for live broadcast, while some of the less popular sports have been shown as delayed broadcasts, giving the subscription channels on DSTV the advantage of 'first view'.

The example of sports broadcasting is significant because it points to the great importance of 'national events' to 'national broadcasters', and because it indicates that such events may not always be political, educational or civic in nature, leading to the necessary revision of the rather narrow field inscribed by the Habermasian 'political public sphere'. Nevertheless, most of what is referred to under the rubric of 'public interest' is political in nature, and 'democratic governments could rarely resist pressuring broadcasters to toe the prevailing political line and speak for the "national interest" as they (governments) defined it' (Murdock 2005: 181).

In constructing this 'collective identity', South Africans had to work against the history of the old quasi-'nationalisms' of apartheid. Taken together with the gross disparities in wealth, education and living standards, and the denial of access to social resources caused by an active process of underdevelopment through apartheid, the possibilities of a single post-apartheid consciousness seemed slim. A diversity of culture and language, and the vigorous ethnic consciousness based on language and territorial division, gave grist to the mill of apartheid, which more than any other factor prevented the development of an even minimally homogeneous audience in terms of media consumption.

The first radio services in African languages were based entirely on this logic, with the nine services (named Radio Zulu, Radio Sotho and so on) beamed at those parts of the country that were decreed into being a jigsaw of 'homelands', 'self-governing national states' and the pinnacle of constitutional development, the 'independent TBVC states' of Transkei, Bophuthatswana, Venda and Ciskei. Each of these four 'independent nations' had their own media networks, which in the case of Bophuthatswana and Ciskei were fairly sophisticated. With the devolution of the TBVC states back into a unitary South Africa, these networks were incorporated into the SABC. The debacle left behind by the protracted and litigious reintegration of the Bophuthatswana Broadcasting Corporation is still being played out, with claims and counter-claims being made by the SABC and the Department of Communication as to who should pay the outstanding monies owed on the property, infrastructure and services left behind by this apartheid white elephant.

Even in Europe, where more sophisticated patterns of media consumption developed, the concept of nationalism(s) bedevils the project of an electronic unity. While the potential for an undifferentiated TV market undoubtedly exists, other factors mitigate against it. Localised differences in language and culture have impeded the establishment of a transnational audience in Europe. Attempts to establish a transnational audience-funding programming by delivering international advertising media have not been successful. The preferred model in the world of global satellite distribution is pre-packaged programming, replete with temporal spaces into which local advertising is slotted.

Challenges facing the SABC

Over the past decade and a bit, at least three broad areas of transition have challenged the SABC as a public broadcaster: to change the face and structure of the SABC to reflect the 'new South Africa'; to cater for the developmental and educational needs of the country in a period of rapid change; and to acknowledge in the programming and scheduling the fact that the SABC is part of the African continent.

The first of these imperatives included a reappraisal of the staffing and appointment policies of the corporation. By the end of 1993, the great majority of employees remained white and, among senior employees, Afrikaans-speaking men. A policy of 'employment equity', which translates roughly into 'affirmative action', had been in place since mid-1993, and three men of colour were appointed to senior posts. Two of the three were high-profile members of the African National Congress (ANC), a situation which provoked a considerable outcry both from the black newspapers, particularly the Black-Consciousness *Sowetan*, and the Afrikaans- and English-language newspapers. The appointment of three ANC members was seen as a capitulation on the part of the new SABC board to the new political orthodoxy, and a replacement of one set of political masters by another.

Are we African?

The SABC's official self-description is 'The pulse of Africa's creative spirit', while the news division brands itself as 'Africa's news leader'. The SABC has always had strong ties with the African continent, most notably through its external service. For the past 40 years, the corporation has produced a 24-hour external radio service, Channel Africa, which is funded by the Department of Foreign Affairs. This transnational service broadcasts in the three historically colonial languages (English, French and Portuguese), as well as in three widely spread African languages: Chinyanja (southern and central West Africa, including Angola and Congo); Silozi (south-eastern Africa, including Mozambique, Malawi, Zimbabwe and Zambia); and Swahili (most of East Africa, including Kenya, parts of Ethiopia, Rwanda and the Great Lakes region). Using the media of shortwave, satellite and Internet transmission, Channel Africa covers most of the African continent south of the Sahara.

The SABC's only subscription channel is SABC Africa, an external service beamed at the rest of the African continent. SABC Africa was created by an amalgamation of two previously separate channels. Its namesake, SABC Africa, was a news, current affairs and documentary channel beamed at the rest of the continent, while Africa-2-Africa, an all-entertainment channel, was launched in September 2000, in order to provide a satellite channel broadcasting entertainment made in Africa, for Africa. On 1 April 2003 a hybrid channel was launched, drawing programming from both sources. The channel is housed on the DSTV platform operated by MultiChoice, reaching 49 countries. The channel also serves as an overnight feed on SABC2, one of the three domestic SABC terrestrial channels. In terms of content, the channel has a dual content strategy – to provide news and current affairs as well as entertainment programming. Most of the weekly programming is based on the news/current affairs format, while weekends are predominantly entertainment. The stated philosophy is to 'celebrate the positive side of Africa and being African'. Some programming – approximately a quarter of the airtime, particularly lifestyle, news and current affairs programmes – is specially commissioned for the channel, while a special effort is made to source African movies. Two African-produced dramas are broadcast every week, representing countries such as Tunisia, Egypt, Burkina Faso, Zimbabwe, Guinea Bissau, Cameroon and Ethiopia. For the most part, however, the programmes are rebroadcasts of material shown on the terrestrial channels in South Africa. The majority of programming is broadcast in English, with considerable subtitling in African languages, French and Portuguese.

In 2006, the SABC announced that plans for a 24-hour news channel covering the whole of the African continent were 'at an advanced stage'.[10]

As illustrated by these examples, the SABC has made a conscious attempt to position itself as both a 'national' broadcaster and a leading 'African' broadcaster. What has changed in the past decade has been the corporation's conscious attempt to Africanise its internal services – that is, radio and television programming aimed at domestic South African audiences. This was expressed recently by the chairperson of the SABC board, Eddie Funde, when he reported to Parliament in August 2006 that the SABC planned to increase domestic news coverage of Africa in order to promote the African Renaissance and the New Economic Partnership for Aid and Development, and effectively tell the African story.[11]

In order to do so, the corporation needed to establish its credentials as an independent authority, with the responsibility of developing programming and scheduling discourses, particularly in the areas of news and actuality, which addressed the needs and aspirations of the global, regional (continental) and local constituencies. At the same time, there was a strong sentiment endorsing the idea that in the special circumstances that marked South Africa's move from apartheid, the national broadcaster needed to contribute to the establishment of a national sentiment, to build a 'collective identity'. Thus 'nationalism' in these circumstances took on a more complex character: at once it was both defensive of its cultural territoriality and offensive in its efforts to force, in Antonio Gramsci's terms, a 'national-popular collective will' that incorporated the mythological history of Africa into the concerns and ambit of 'South Africanism'. The double dynamic can be seen as both keeping out 'the other' and strengthening links with those outside the national cordon.

The SABC and the crisis of legitimacy

Viewing the news broadcasts of the SABC more than a decade after the appointment of the first democratically elected board of directors, the one-time mouthpiece of the apartheid government looks very different. Contemporary open-plan newsrooms and younger, mostly black presenters have enlivened the staid, rigid formats of the past. Many of the new stories are critical of the ruling elite; nevertheless, the spectre of the broadcaster as the propaganda arm of the now ANC-led government remains. Media commentators have expressed concerns about the broadcaster's lack of independence from the ruling party: 'I think there's definitely a worrying tendency to move closer to the ANC,' said Anton Harber, professor of journalism at the University of the Witwatersrand.[12] Pointers to the perceived lack of independence come from a variety of sources, four of which are alluded to here: alleged attempts by the ANC-led government to change the 'rules of the game' through the Broadcasting Amendment Act of 2002; the questionable independence of the board of directors; the appointment of ANC stalwart Snuki Zikalala as head of SABC News; and specific news stories that caused popular disgruntlement.

STRUCTURAL ISSUES

At a structural level, the most damaging episode in terms of the SABC's independence from the state has been the promotion of the Broadcast Amendment Act (2002). Tensions between the corporation (then under the chairmanship of Vincent Maphai) and the Department of Communication, under the leadership of Minister Ivy Matsepe-Casaburri, came to a head in 2002 when the minister told the Parliamentary Portfolio Committee on

Communications that an amendment to the Broadcasting Act was necessary because the SABC was not doing its job properly and needed to be made accountable to the public. 'What she meant, of course, was that it needed to be accountable to the government'.[13] Subsequently, the Department of Communications released a Bill to amend the Broadcasting Act, which in due course was promulgated into law. The Bill was highly controversial, especially regarding those aspects that diluted the independence of the public broadcaster by insisting on greater 'accountability' directly to the minister, replacing the onus of reporting to the public via the Portfolio Parliamentary Committee.[14] Following considerable public debate and opposition, the changes to the Broadcasting Act were deemed to be contrary to the Constitution, and ultimately were rejected by an ANC-dominated Parliament. Nevertheless, critics point to the fact that 'the new SABC board that the ANC-controlled portfolio committee on communications proceeded to choose last year has given the government precisely the "accountability" it wanted' (*Sunday Times* 25 July 2004), making the need for the blunt instrument of coercive legislation unnecessary.

INDEPENDENT BOARD?

Unlike elsewhere in Africa – notably neighbouring Zimbabwe, where the government has a tight grip on state-owned media – the SABC has an independent board with a mandate to serve the public and not its sole owner. While the first two boards of the corporation (1993–1996, 1997–2000) were carefully balanced in terms of race, gender and political affiliation, recent incumbents are almost all avowed ANC members, appointed by an ANC-dominated parliamentary committee.[15]

THE APPOINTMENT OF SNUKI ZIKALALA

From the viewpoint of the general public, probably the most damaging aspect of the purported lack of independence of the SABC's news division from the government was the appointment of ANC cadre and struggle stalwart Snuki Zikalala in 2004. 'Fear and discontent stalk the newsroom at Auckland Park as former ANC political commissar Snuki Zikalala forces his underlings to toe the government line' (*Sunday Times* 25 July 2004). Zikalala was educated in Bulgaria during the Soviet bloc's patronage of the ANC in exile. His colourful and chequered career included a stint at the SABC, which he left under acrimonious circumstances in 2001 as a result of the 'bimedia' debacle, when the newsrooms for radio and television were amalgamated.[16] A period of employment as the spokesperson for the minister of labour followed, adding to fears of close government involvement. Zikalala's appointment is credited with leading, directly or indirectly, to the resignation or redeployment of the then chief executive officer, Peter Matlare; the head of television news, Jimmy Mathews; and the head of radio news, Pippa Green. Zikalala's tenure has been marked by a number of highly controversial news stories.

SPECIFIC NEWS STORIES

In April 2005, Zikalala interviewed Zimbabwean president Robert Mugabe. The print media castigated the interview as 'obsequious', avoiding any difficult questions and glossing over the issues of human rights, irregularities in the land-reform programme and possible inconsistencies in the electoral process.[17] Deputy President Phumzile Mlambo-Ngcuka was booed offstage by members of the ANC Youth League, supporters of her predecessor Jacob Zuma, at a rally in August 2005, forcing her to abandon her prepared address to the rally. The SABC reported on the speech but did not mention the booing, leading to claims by e.tv of biased reporting in an attempt to shield the humiliated deputy president. Claims and counter-claims of culpability on the part of the cameraman, the SABC's head of public relations, SABC board members, chief executive officer (CEO) Dali Mpofu, chairperson Eddie Funde and Zikalala himself kept the controversy in the media for weeks, and serious damage was done to the SABC's reputation. After an inquiry, a report was compiled by Tlharesang Mkhwanazi, a Pretoria advocate, and Guy Berger, a journalism professor from Rhodes University. The report has exposed several management weaknesses and instances of interference by board members in the running of the SABC.[18] The SABC was accused of self-censorship in May 2006, when a documentary on President Thabo Mbeki was removed from the schedule. This incident prompted an extended exchange in the print and broadcast media, once again damaging the public credibility of the corporation.

Most recently, in June 2006, radio talk-show host John Perlman accused the SABC management on air of creating a blacklist of commentators not available to SABC journalists. A commission of inquiry, headed by Zwelhakhe Sisulu, the first black CEO of the SABC, and advocate Gilbert Marcus, was appointed by the SABC to investigate the claims. The choice of Sisulu, with his close ANC connections, caused considerable negative comment in the print media. It is therefore somewhat ironic that the commission was highly critical of the SABC and of its news department in particular. Prima facie evidence of a blacklist was affirmed, and a number of political and social commentators, most of whom were black, were identified as *personae non gratae* to the management of SABC News. The process took something of a Byzantine turn when, following the SABC's refusal to make public the results of the commission of inquiry, the *Mail & Guardian* published the entire report on its website.[19] The SABC responded by seeking an injunction against the newspaper, which was refused by the courts. The entire episode took on a carnivalesque façade, reinforcing once more the perception that the news, reporting and documentary outputs of the SABC are partisan and untrustworthy. This in turn has led to an unprecedented billboard war between the public broadcaster and its free-to-air competitor e.tv. The latter erected advertising hoardings in prominent places, proclaiming '0 percent propaganda' and 'Warning: No Government Approval. No fear. No favour'. Both were seen as references to perceived government meddling at the SABC. After losing an injunction to have e.tv's adverts removed, the SABC retaliated with 'We Don't Write the Script: The World Does'.

Just how convincing these slogans are remains for the South African public to decide.

Notes

1 See Mbeki T, State of the nation address, Parliament, 3 February 2006. http://www.southafrica.info/ess_info/sa_glance/government/stateofnation2006-asgisa.htm.

2 www.mybroadband.co.za, 13 February 2006.

3 www.mybroadband.co.za, 12 September 2006.

4 By way of comparison, research done by the Association of America's Public Service Television Stations indicates that the USA's 340 public broadcasting service (PBS) channels are valuable community resources which have found ways of adapting to some of the financial problems identified. PBS serves 89 million viewers during an average week. More people in the USA watch PBS than any of the cable networks, including CNN and HBO.

5 For Anderson, the nation was 'imagined', 'inherently limited and sovereign'. 'It is *imagined* because the members of even the smallest nation will never know most of their fellow-members, meet them, or even hear of them, yet in the minds of each lives the image of their communion.' In this sense he used 'imagined' not as a marker of false pretence, but rather as the 'creation' of bonds of unification, 'indefinitely stretchable nets of (virtual) kinship and clientship…The nation is imagined as *limited* because even the largest of them, encompassing perhaps a billion living human beings, has

finite, if elastic boundaries, beyond which lie other nations. It is imagined as *sovereign* because the concept was born in an age in which Enlightenment and Revolution were destroying the legitimacy of the divinely-ordained, hierarchical dynastic realm... Finally, it is imagined as a *community*, because, regardless of the actual inequality and exploitation that may prevail in each, the nation is always conceived as a deep, horizontal comradeship. Ultimately it is this fraternity that makes it possible, over the past two centuries, for so many millions of people, not so much to kill, as willingly to die for such limited imaginings' (Anderson 1991: 5–7).

6   Comments by the minister of sports and recreation, Ngconde Balfour, on the public release of a position paper and regulations on sports broadcasting rights by ICASA.

7   The Media Online, 25 May 2003. http://www.themedia.co.za/article.aspx?articleid=30937&area=/media_insightlegal_spi/.

8   *Government Gazette* 23713, 8 August 2002. http://www.info.gov.za/gazette/notices/2002/23713.pdf.

9   South African position paper and regulations on sports broadcasting rights by ICASA, Friday 25 July 2003. http://www.info.gov.za/speeches/2003/03072809461008.htm.

10 Da Silva IS, SABC annual results dazzle, 30 August 2006. BizCommunity.comhttp://www.biz-ommunity.com/Article/196/15/12076.html.

11 Da Silva IS, SABC annual results dazzle, 30 August 2006. BizCommunity.comhttp://www.biz-ommunity.com/Article/196/15/12076.html.

12 *Business Day*, 19 November 2003.

13 *Sunday Times*, 25 July 2004. Accessed 29 November 2006, http://www.sundaytimes.co.za/2004/07/25/insight/in02.asp.

14 See Freedom of Information Campaign, e-Archive on Transformation of Broadcasting. http://www.fxi.org.za/archive/Linked/Public%20Broadcasting%20e-archive/Public%20Broadcasting.html.

15 Notable ANC members on the present board include the chairperson, Eddie Funde. A well-known cadre from the struggle days in exile, he is very close to ANC power structures, particularly the minister in the Office of the State President, Essop Pahad. Thami Mazwai, a journalist, was in charge of the previous board's news subcommittee when he told Parliament in 2003 that 'we cannot afford to be driven by old clichés such as objectivity, the right of the editor and so on. These are old clichés and no longer address the challenges of the day'. He has also argued that the Bill of Rights, which enshrines free speech and independence of the public broadcaster, must be interpreted 'in African terms', opposing this to 'Western values and stereotypes'. Christine Qunta was a leading member of the Black Lawyers' Association, which drove the Human Rights Commission's inquiry against the media on the grounds that it

was guilty of racism. The inquiry, which was inconclusive, caused much discussion in both the popular and academic literature. Qunta is famous for her view, published in the *Financial Mail* in 1999, that 'there is no such thing as an independent media. This remains one of the great myths of the Western world' (*Sunday Times* 2 July 2005).

16   Independent Online, 11 October 2001. http://www.iol.co.za/index.php?set_id=1&click_id=13&art_id=ct2001101105414348S1261674.

17   'As usual the SA Broadcasting Corporation followed ANC policy, including an obsequious interview conducted by head of news Dr Snuki Zikalala with President Robert Mugabe on Sunday night. Not a single difficult question was asked.

'Jacob Dlamini, political editor of *Business Day*, suggested that Zikalala poach well-known Zimbabwean journalist and government apologist Reuben Barwe, who sometimes uses the term "we" to describe the regime – and who was awarded a grabbed farm for his loyalty.

'"Zikalala has reportedly told his staff at the SABC that he wants only 'cadres who can work with government' – not free thinkers and independent-minded folks who might (again) cost him his job and pension," wrote a scathing Dlamini, adding that a possible alternative would be to send his current SABC news team to a political re-education camp.' Accessed 8 April 2005, http://www.thezimbabwean.co.uk/8-april-2005/sa-media.html.

18   *Sunday Independent*, 11 September 2005.

19   The authors of the commission's report were quoted as saying 'it would be abhorrent, and at gross variance with the SABC's mandate and policies, if practices of the old order were being repeated in the new, with the effect of again disqualifying South Africans from democratic discourse and debate' (Mail & Guardian Online, 14 October 2006).

References

Anderson B (1991) *Imagined communities: Reflections on the origin and spread of nationalism* (2nd edition). London and New York: Verso

Briggs A & Burke P (2002) *A social history of the media*. Cambridge: Polity Press; Malden, MA: Blackwell

Bruun-Andersen M (1996) *Media and democracy*. IMK Report Number 17. Oslo: Department of Media and Communication, University of Oslo

Carver R (1995) Themes and trends in African broadcasting. In R Carver and T Naughton (eds) *Who rules the airwaves? Broadcasting in Africa*. London: ARTICLE 19 and Index on Censorship

Collins R (1990) *Satellite television in Western Europe*. London and Paris: John Libbey

Collins R (issue editor) (1992) Broadcasting and telecommunications policy in post-apartheid South Africa. *Critical Arts* 6(1): 26–51

Dahlgren P (1995) *Television and the public sphere*. London: Sage Publications

Dahlgren P (1998) Public service media, old and new: Vitalizing a civic culture? The 1998 Spry Memorial Lecture, Montreal, 15 October; Vancouver, 19 October

Dahlgren P (2000) Beyond ratings or quality: Surpassing the dilemmas of entertainment. In P Dahlgren and G Murdock (eds) *Television across Europe: A comparative introduction*. London and Thousand Oaks, CA: Sage Publications

Habermas J (1989; reprinted 1995) *The structural transformation of the public sphere: An inquiry into a category of bourgeois society*. Cambridge, MA: MIT Press; Cambridge: Polity Press

Habermas J (1996) *Between facts and norms: Contributions to a discourse theory of law and democracy*. Cambridge, MA: MIT Press; Cambridge: Polity Press

Hayman G & Tomaselli RE (2001) Ideology and technology in the growth of South African broadcasting, 1924–1971. In RE Tomaselli, K Tomaselli and J Muller (eds) *Broadcasting in South Africa*. Colorado Springs: International Academic Publishers

Herman ES & Chomsky N (1988) *Manufacturing consent: The political economy of the mass media*. London and New York: Pantheon Books

Jacka E (2003) The future of public service broadcasting. In S Cunningham and G Turner (eds) *The media in Australia* (3rd edition). St Leonards: Allen and Unwin

Keane J (1990) *The media and democracy*. Cambridge: Polity Press

Mattelart A (2003) *The information society: An introduction*. London; Thousand Oaks, CA; and New Delhi: Sage Publications

McChesney R (1997) *The global media*. London: Cassell

McGuigan J (2004) *The cultural public sphere*. http://www.lboro.ac.uk/departments/ss/The%20Cultural%20Public%20Sphere

Morrison D (1986) *Invisible citizens: British public opinion and the future of broadcasting*. London: John Libbey

Mosco V (1996) *The political economy of communication*. London and Thousand Oaks, CA: Sage Publications

Mpofu A, Manhando S & Tomaselli KG (2000) *Public service broadcasting in South Africa: Policy directions towards 2000*. Colorado Springs: International Academic Publishers

Murdock G (2004) Dismantling the digital divide: Rethinking the dynamics of participation and exclusion. In A Calabrese and C Sparks (eds) *Towards a political economy of culture: Capitalism and commerce in the twenty-first century*. Lanham: Rowman and Littlefield

Murdock G (2005) Public broadcasting and democratic culture: Consumers, citizens and communards. In J Wasko (ed.) *A companion to television*, pp. 174–198. London: Blackwell

Murdock P & Golding P (2001) Digital possibilities, market realities: The contradictions of communications convergence. In L Panitch and C Leys (eds) *A world of contradiction*, pp. 111–129. London: Merlin Press

Noordenstreng K & Schiller H (1993) *Beyond national sovereignty: International communications in the 1990s*. New York: Praeger Greenwood

Raboy M (1990) *Missed opportunities: The story of Canada's broadcasting policy*. Montreal: McGill University Press

Raboy M (2003) *Public broadcasting for the twenty-first century*. Indianapolis: Indiana University Press

Reith J (1924) *Broadcast over Britain*. London: Hodder and Stoughton

Rosenthal E (1975) *You have been listening: A history of the early days of radio in South Africa*. Cape Town: Purnell

RSA (Republic of South Africa) (1999) Broadcasting Act (No. 4 of 1999). Pretoria: Government Printer

SAARF (South African Advertising Research Foundation) (2006) All media and products survey (AMPS). Johannesburg: SAARF

Scannell P (1991) *A social history of British broadcasting*. London: Basil Blackwell

Scannell P (2000) Public service broadcasting: The history of the concept. In E Buscombe (ed.) *British television: A reader*, pp. 45–62. Oxford: Oxford University Press

Siune K & Hulten O (1998) Does public broadcasting have a future? In D McQuail and K Siune (eds) *Media policy: Convergence, concentration and commerce*. London: Sage Publications

Teer-Tomaselli RE (2005) Change and transformation in South African television. In J Wasko (ed.) *Blackwell companion for television*. London and New York: Blackwell

Teer-Tomaselli RE & Tomaselli K (2001) Transformation, nation-building and the South African media, 1939–1999. In KG Tomaselli and H Dunn (eds) *Media, democracy and renewal in southern Africa*. Colorado Springs: International Academic Publishers

Thompson JB (1990) *Ideology and modern culture*. London: Polity Press

Tleane C & Duncan D (2002) *Public broadcasting in the era of cost recovery: A critique of the South African Broadcasting Corporation's crisis of accountability*. Johannesburg: Freedom of Expression Institute

Tomaselli RE, Tomaselli KG & Muller J (1989) *Broadcasting in South Africa*. Colorado Springs: International Academic Publishers

Wintour P (2004) Media blamed for loss of trust in government. *Guardian*, 8 May

5 Field theory and tabloids
Ian Glenn and Angie Knaggs

The rise of South African tabloids has generated more academic heat than light and has revealed the poverty of existing media theorising in South Africa. The danger is that, as commentators like Rian Malan join the fray and the old broadsheet press and academics become the butt of amused ridicule, the only academic response will be either more heated moralising or belated jumping onto an increasingly powerful bandwagon. (The invitation to Deon du Plessis, the force behind the *Daily Sun*, to speak at the 2005 South African Communication Association conference of media academics shows that some media academics are already suing for peace, so to speak.) And, as advertisers increasingly switch allocation of their resources to tabloids, the theoretical and practical antagonism of media academics and educators to tabloids risks having very real consequences, in that the skills and attitudes they impart to students may not equip them to deal with the new demands of the print marketplace.

Lizette Rabe, a columnist for news24.com and a professor at the University of Stellenbosch, and Professor Guy Berger, the head of the Rhodes University School of Journalism, have been particularly outspoken about their negative views of the role that tabloids play in South Africa. In this chapter we will quote their most extreme views at some length, in order to set them against other approaches, as they are probably highly typical of media academics' views in general. (In the full body of their comments on tabloids, both have a far more complex and nuanced reaction to tabloids than the quotes in this piece may suggest. See, for example, Rabe 2005a and 2005b.)

We suggest two major theoretical approaches – which we can summarise as a) new institutionalism and b) a field theory of social and symbolic capital – to understanding what has been and is happening in the tabloids, and try to show the relevance of these approaches by considering the case of the *Daily Voice* in Cape Town. The editor of the paper is Karl Brophy, a former spin doctor for the Irish government. He subsequently worked for the *Daily Mirror* in London and then for a newspaper called the *Irish Examiner,* before joining the *Irish Independent*. He was then sent to Cape Town to set up the *Daily Voice*. In an interview in 2005, Brophy spoke at length about his sense of tabloids and attacks on them.[1] Through liberal quotation from this interview throughout this chapter, we hope to show that the combination of approaches suggested above comes closer to making sense of the values underlying the paper, and of its success and readers' responses to it, than other accounts have done.

News institutions and the sociology of the newsroom

A major trend in recent American and European media research has been a return to the sociology of news production, with work being done on the conditions in the newsroom and broadcast studio, pressures on reporters, and the economic pressures as felt in practice rather than as theorised (Benson 2004; Benson & Neveu 2004; Born 2004; Schudson 2003). Even if one were not to insist on a title of 'American new institutionalism', as Benson (2004) does, it seems that academics are again spending time examining the real conditions of media labour rather than generalising and essentialising about media ownership and political economy on a grand scale.

One of the surprising features of some of the heated academic strictures on tabloids was precisely the essentialising and othering of tabloids into one category, as though there were not key differences between British and American and South African tabloids, between the *National Inquirer* (USA) and *The Sun* (UK), between the *Daily Sun* (SA) and *Son* and the *Daily Voice* (see, for example, Esser [1999] on some key differences between German and Anglo-American tabloid conventions). Academics, in fact, became guilty of a kind of media racism against which they presumably warn their students:

> They look a lot like newspapers. They feel like newspapers; they even leave ink on your fingertips. Some are owned by newspaper companies. Most are celebrating soar-away circulations.
>
> They're called, of course, the tabloids. But an indication that they are not really newspapers, and that they play in the entertainment market rather than prosecute the business of information, is that they are conspicuously absent from the entrants to the Mondi Shanduka Newspaper Journalism Awards.
>
> Their circulation success dazzles some, and there may even be those admirers who believe this competition should develop special categories to attract them. We'd probably then be

announcing winners for stories such as 'Most creative invention', 'Excellence in hyping', or 'Best adherence to simplistic archetypes like innocent hubby cuckolded by treacherous wife'. (Berger 2005a)

Now what is surprising is precisely that these comments, a kind of media ink on the fingers if not pencil in the hair test, emerged not in an academic piece or an op-ed article, but at the Mondi Awards 2005, in Guy Berger's opening address as convener judge of the awards.[2]

In reality, the division between tabloids such as the *Daily Voice* and other papers may never have been that big and, over time, as other papers have tried to play catch-up, has diminished. In an average week in Cape Town, it is often difficult to distinguish between newspapers by simply going on the banner poster headlines. When comparing stories that are carried by tabloids and other papers, the tabloids often out-report and out-write the supposedly sober and accurate broadsheets. A case in point that a senior media class studied at some length was the reporting and photographing of the bus tragedy on 25 August 2005 on Kloof Nek Road in Cape Town, after a school outing to Table Mountain, in which the *Cape Argus* resorted to sensationalist reporting while the *Daily Voice* reported in far more depth and with greater accuracy. (As far as media ethics go, the tabloids in some respects have adhered to a superior code of conduct – in Cape Town we have had the media scandal of the *Cape Argus* cannibalising material from the *Cape Times* without proper acknowledgement,[3] and in many cases the broadsheets pick up stories broken by the tabloids without acknowledgement.)

What critics have not noticed, or have chosen to ignore, is that the tabloids do far more real reporting – at least in Cape Town – than the other English newspapers, whose reporting staff were gutted by savage budget cuts during the 1990s and early 2000s. Because the *Daily Voice* chooses not to subscribe to news wire services, but rather to invest in local reporters, it has to create its own local stories rather than rely on a heavy proportion of national and international news that is not original, not produced for their particular audience, and does not need any legwork by local reporters. (One of the pernicious features of globalisation may be that major media players have significant financial stakes in big wire services, and thus have every interest in maximising the amount of news drawn from these services rather than investing in local reporters or writers.)

The corollary of this is that the *Daily Voice* has to hire good local writers, including some of the best graduates from the University of Cape Town. One of them, Gavin Haynes, played the part of a modern 'Mr Drum',[4] going into places like morgues and bad hospitals and travelling with garbage trucks to produce reports. In discussion about why he managed to find a job on the *Daily Voice*, but not on other local papers, he made the point that a huge amount of media coverage in South Africa is trivial international celebrity news which can easily bypass local reporting, whereas finding out about the scandal or problems of a local community demands local reporters.

Another corollary to this is that the *Daily Voice* works largely on local news and relies heavily on the local community for tips and leads. They have dedicated phone lines which are staffed constantly to receive such tips. Because the paper follows up on these, it gets more community response and a greater following. The virtuous cycle of reporting and action in making ideas public has made it possible for the *Daily Voice* to be an agenda-setter in regard to several key local issues with major implications for local politics, issues such as the pressure on the African National Congress (ANC) mayor to fire her media advisor, Blackman Ngoro, for racist attacks on coloured people, and on the mayor to cut down a bush where attacks on women and children were taking place.

Brophy reacted fairly vehemently to Berger's criteria for judging the newsworthiness of pieces at the Mondi Awards:

> If Guy Berger wants to talk about us doing good for the community, we have run a number of social issues, particularly the one around the bush in Blue Downs where all the women and children are being raped and murdered. We have consistently, I think from the fourth day of publication, campaigned on that bush, we got the mayor to promise to chop it down. And we have hammered the mayor for months about that bush and now finally, last week it started getting chopped down. It's good, our readers wanted it. We were accused of just doing it for sales. But what people don't recognize is that there is no dichotomy between doing something for sales and doing something that is good. Because if your readers want it and they agree with you and identify with you, they will buy your newspaper. And we are reflecting what they want.[5]

The *Daily Voice* broke more significant stories than all other Cape Town newspapers combined in 2005, yet did not get awards in the newspaper categories at the Mondis, presumably because it is a tabloid. According to Brophy, Lizette Rabe had praised an award-winning story about golf courses entered for the Mondis in 2005 and said it showed a phenomenon 'dividing the nation like never before'. He responded:

> Now, forgive me for thinking that golf courses are not as bad as the Group Areas Act. Or Vlakplaas or Eugene de Kock. And she accuses us of sensationalizing. You know, all of a sudden golf courses are worse than apartheid.[6]

The first key argument of news sociology, then, concerns news values and news production. The middle-class academic view of what constitutes important news finds a robust counter in Brophy's defence of tabloid concerns:

> The thing about this town [Cape Town] is that it has great news. I don't mean it's all good news. The stuff that happens here, it's incredible. One of the criticisms of tabloids is that we sensationalize things; there is absolutely no necessity to sensationalize any news in Cape Town because it's sensational anyway. Like in the last number of months, we have a woman on trial for the youngest contract killing in the world. With a contract killing of a baby, you can't sensationalize that. You know I think South African newspapers are guilty of de-sensationalizing news. Like when the *Cape Times* or *Die Burger* or any other newspaper carries two to four paragraphs on page 8 or page 10 saying that there were 12 murders in Khayelitsha on the weekend, that's de-sensationalizing things.[7]

If one takes local reporting seriously and wants to come to terms with the daily reality of rape and murder, then tabloids are, arguably, far more socially responsible than the broadsheets that, as Brophy suggests, neglect violence and lawlessness in the wider community, but react with horror when whites are the targets of random gang violence.

The second major set of charges levelled against tabloids is that they simply break all the ethical rules of good journalism. Rabe has argued that tabloid journalists in South Africa won't let a lack of factual evidence get in the way of a good story (Rabe 2005c). In her column entitled 'Tabloid journalists watch out!' Rabe attacks South African tabloid journalistic integrity, saying that:

> The sad fact is, it seems, that some tabloids still don't follow the rule or let the facts, indeed, stand in the way of a good story.

A typical example – and it happened a week or so ago: the newspaper – oh, pardon, they are not (yet) worthy of the name newspaper? Okay, then, let's be specific, stick to tabloid, but carry on with the story.

So, the tabloid picks up a rumour. It manufactures its copy based on the rumour. In the process, someone vaguely remembers, hey, they've got to at least verify it against some sort of credible source. Get the other side of the story. Go and check the facts.

And then the rumour turns out to be a non-story. The facts are watertight and above-board. But, heck, let's ignore those facts, and run with the malicious, juicy *skinner* [gossip] instead. With the result, a single-source story. Anonymous, of course. Most probably an individual grinding his or her axe through an unprofessional (or is it naïve?) journalist. (Rabe 2005c)

Joe Thloloe (the chairman of the South African National Editors Forum [SANEF]) has expressed concern that '[t]he challenge for SANEF now lies ahead: whether a point will come when tabloid members should be censured for fabrications, unwarranted invasions of privacy, or other ethical lapses' (Berger 2005b). Thloloe implied that tabloids will inevitably have ethical lapses; it is just a matter of time.

These are huge assumptions to be making about a set of newspapers that have yet to see any significant defamation cases lodged against them; though, given what we have observed above about news production, the tabloids are actually far more at risk, in that they are reporting far more substantially on a daily basis about local events and reputations. Brophy's comments on the quality of his journalists make the obvious points:

> Our rules, the rules that we have on verification and on how we verify and check stories are exactly the same as those followed by the *Cape Argus* and *Cape Times*. Actually, if you talk to our lawyer, he will tell you that we are actually far better at it because we do slightly more aggressive stories we have to be a lot more careful, we have to be absolutely sure of a story because when we take a line on a story we take it very hard, and therefore have to be absolutely sure of our facts.

If you look at our newsroom, it's a senior newsroom; we have more people on higher grades that are young. If you went to speak to Chris Whitfield downstairs in the *Cape Times*, who is a friend of mine, he would kill for any of these journalists. The way that we structured our staff was that we wanted very senior journalists because we have to be very sure of the facts and we expect high productivity out of them.[8]

While the question of audience reactions is properly the subject of further study, the circulation success of the *Daily Voice* suggests that readers find the local reports dealing with their concerns a more palatable repast than the bland international fare of the news wires.

Brophy suggests that their stories, and the fact that the *Daily Voice* is seen as having the interests of the community at heart, give them a community status that no broadsheet enjoys:

I've been out in the West End, at the Galaxy there [a local night club], a couple of months ago, with all our journalists, and they are treated like heroes coming home. The DJ got up into the box and announced that the *Daily Voice* was in the house. And the place went crazy. And it's madness, it's crazy; I have never seen a reaction like that to a publication before.[9]

The frustration felt by those working in the tabloid industry is evident in Brophy's comments. His journalists are actually practising journalism – they are leaving their comfortable offices (and wires), braving the Cape Town weather and gang violence to print socially relevant stories, only to be told that they are not worthy of journalistic recognition. Brophy has some harsh words for the academic critics, suggesting that there are academic blind spots preventing a really constructive engagement with local media:

These people don't know a good story if it hits them in the face, they are sitting up in Stellenbosch, or down in bloody Grahamstown, pontificating on the state of the media. They constantly bemoan the state of the nation's media and completely disregard the fact that their bloody departments produce half the bloody people who work in it. You know a little introspection might be required Mister Berger. You know, if the media is shite, it's probably your fault.[10]

In the next section of this chapter, we look at whether a different understanding of the journalistic field in South Africa might enable a more constructive and comfortable engagement of academics with the tabloids.

Social and symbolic capital and field theory

In criticisms of the *Daily Voice*, as in arguments about media and identity politics more generally, we can discern two major theoretical positions: a Habermasian notion of media as the spaces for a rational social dialogue and dialectic (Habermas 1989, 1992, 2006), and a notion of the media as the proper space for the development of an 'imagined community', as Anderson (1983) defines it. We suggest that the work of Putnam (1995, 2000) and, more particularly, Bourdieu (1979, 1993, 1996, 1998, 2004) provides a better way of understanding the issues of media and identity in general and the tabloids in particular. In the conclusion of this section, we suggest ways in which Bourdieu's work would allow a better understanding of media and identity in South Africa.

The Habermasian ideal reveals itself in idealistic notions of the role that the media should play in constructing a new, better national identity, in line with constitutional values, proper ethical standards and, usually, progressive values. Berger has spelled out this position uncompromisingly. Returning to the issue of tabloids after the SANEF debate on tabloids, he moderated his Mondi tone considerably, but still disputed whether selling 400 000 copies of the *Daily Sun* (whose circulation has since risen to 500 000) could be seen as being as significant for South Africa as the 38 000 sales of the politically and socially influential *Mail & Guardian* (Berger 2005b). He further defended his earlier harsh criticism by arguing that the popularity of tabloid newspapers should not be at the expense of credible journalism, or the promotion of values that are not in line with the South African Constitution:

> My call was to integrate the 'progressive' with the 'popular', else an opportunity for meaningful print journalism catering to the masses would continue to be missed. (Berger 2005b: 2)

This strand of media critique is linked to the view that the tabloids espouse negative values as social intermediaries; in the critics' eyes they are racist, sexist and parochial (accusations to which we will return). The tabloids, critics argue, do not present a progressive world-view, or the broad coverage of the political sphere and the major world events of the time that media critics and journalism professors hope the enlightened media will offer. Nonetheless, as tabloids are demonstrably the print media least affected by business and commercial pressures, they would paradoxically seem to be in the best position to fulfil Habermas's ideal of being uncontaminated by sectional commercial interests.

Another major underpinning of local analysis of identity politics in much South African cultural studies work is Benedict Anderson's *Imagined Communities* (1983), though Anderson's work on how national language and media combine to create a national identity precisely plays down the class, sociolinguistic, regional, racial and ethnic divisions that make the South African media so complex. Very simply put, South Africa never had and still does not have one language of nationalism. It had a (long) moment of Afrikaner nationalism which met many of Anderson's criteria, but that linguistic, political and cultural construction was, precisely, not a national but a group construction – one whose legacies complicate, if not invalidate, any prospect of applying his analysis to South Africa.

In short, while many contemporary South African media appeal across racial lines, South Africa has very few if any media which appeal to the nation as a whole and construct all South Africans as one nation. The closest we have to this is SABC news in African languages, whether on radio or television. But any attempt to create an SABC news service, for example, that sends the same message to the nation as a whole seems, on closer inspection, to have been abandoned in favour of services targeting particular demographic sectors constructed on racial–linguistic lines (Glenn 2006). In the terms of Elihu Katz's gloomy examination of the change in Israeli television, we have been delivered from apartheid into segmentation without, perhaps, ever really sharing a media commonality (Katz 1996).

Several powerful speeches by President Thabo Mbeki have suggested that he and the ANC wish to invoke a new inclusive national identity, an African identity that overcomes old sectarian differences.[11] Nonetheless, the appeal to construct an African Renaissance becomes, in many of its media manifestations, less an attempt to construct a commonality of and for citizens than one that aims to provide an ideological justification for a modernising black elite, which will enable them to delegitimise white and European claims and complaints and also to distance themselves from traditional African sources of authority. (In this respect it is very close to the discourse on negritude by Senghor and others in that it is a modern African elite's recasting of traditional values which they now claim to embody.)

In considering media and identity in modern South Africa in general, and what the tabloids have done and are doing for and to their communities in particular, we would argue that the most useful theoretical approaches lie in considering, fairly dispassionately, the social and symbolic capitals involved in how the tabloids operate in the field of journalism. Recent work by Beaudoin and Thorson (2004, 2006), Benson (1999, 2004), Benson and Neveu (2004), Couldry (2003) and others, drawing on the sociological work of Pierre Bourdieu (1979, 1993, 1996, 1998, 2004), Bourdieu and Wacquant (1992) and Robert Putnam (1995, 2000) in particular, offers interesting comparative and cross-cultural analyses of news values and media production. (Charmaine McEachern's *Narratives of Nation: Media, Memory and Representation in the Making of the New South Africa* [2002], while invoking Bourdieu at points, considers rather different questions.)

In short, Putnam, in well-known articles like 'Bowling alone: The collapse and renewal of American community' (1995), argues that modern American life has lost many of the social bonds that marked earlier communities, and attributes much of this loss to modern media consumption. To live in the television world is to suffer a loss of community, of neighbourhood interaction and social engagement. Very simply, his analysis of social capital suggests that tabloids, rather than contributing to this anomie through coverage of the distant and the abstract, build on and solidify kinds of social solidarity and social capital that traditional broadsheets ignore and snub by omission. A newspaper full of wire stories that say very little about the lived conditions of people on the Cape Flats may appeal to middle-class academic notions of newsworthiness or public discourse, but it in fact does very little to empower or give dignity to local residents facing corrupt police, ongoing white racism, gang violence or government neglect.

Bourdieu's notions of social and symbolic capital and the field as the locus for struggles for value are more complex and more satisfying, we contend, than Putnam's. Let us simply insist on a key feature of Bourdieu's symbolic value and social capital: it is relational, caught in tension and struggle with others. Most of the recent work on Bourdieu and journalism focuses on his work on the professional field of journalism and its relationship to politics (see particularly Benson 2004; Bourdieu 2004; Bourdieu & Wacquant 1992). Nonetheless, as Benson and Neveu themselves point out, 'While field studies in recent years have primarily emphasized processes of cultural *production*, Bourdieu's theory clearly makes room for *reception* as well (see especially

Distinction)' (Benson & Neveu 2004: 7). By attending to the ways in which *La Distinction* links cultural and media consumption with economic and symbolic capital, and looking at the rapid changes and tensions and fault lines of the past decade, we have access to a more complex and complete way of assessing identity than through the use of self-narratives or an examination of media representations alone (see Glenn 2006).

While it seems obvious that media scholars trying to account for identity in a rapidly modernising society should look at who is consuming what media, and how this relates to their background and lifestyles, surprisingly little academic scholarship has shown any interest in the mass media as a, if not the, driving force in identity formation. Media scholars in South Africa need a critical way to look at consumption of mass media and its relation to identity, because they have the use of highly sophisticated commercial databases like the South African Advertising Research Foundation's All Media and Products Survey (AMPS) and various television and radio audience monitoring figures. If media scholars cannot rival the accounts of marketers and commercial commentators on class, race and cultural consumption (see, for example, Steve Burgess 2002), they risk abandoning mass media for counter-culture or cultural studies ghettoes. (See Neveu [2004] for a compelling account of where Bourdieu parts ways with cultural studies, and why.) Our argument is that drawing on Bourdieu's conceptual framework would permit a critical use of important databases for longitudinal and comparative studies. By invoking notions such as habitus and homologies, we should be able to consider how South Africans are constructing their identities as members of churches or unions, graduates, sports supporters, car owners, ratepayers, soap-opera and talk-show fans, and provide a more compelling account than cultural studies or marketing could.

What is the tabloid field?

Bourdieu's account of the interests at work in any professional field certainly suggests why middle-class academics with high social capital attack many of the features of the tabloids. Bourdieu's (1979) dictum that 'taste classifies, and classifies the classifier' should be a caveat inscribed in every journalism classroom.

In this section we will attempt to clarify what the relational notion of symbolic capital means in terms of the everyday practices of the *Daily Voice*. A fuller treatment of this topic would need a far more detailed market analysis of the readership of tabloids, through AMPS figures and local interviews, to flesh out the kind of media and cultural mapping of South Africa that would correspond to Bourdieu's attempt in *La Distinction* to chart the homologies between cultural consumption and capital and symbolic capital (Bourdieu 1979: 140–41). Our task here is to suggest how the concepts of social and symbolic capital explain how and why the *Daily Voice* differs from the *Daily Sun*, what the entertainment and sports focus of the tabloids is, and why.

Some preliminary figures from the *Daily Sun* make it clear that the *Daily Voice* is, in relation, still very much a minority report. Of the *Daily Sun*'s 500 000 daily buyers, the paper's own analysts suggest that over 90 per cent are homeowners. (It is not clear, however, how many of the 2.5 million daily readers are homeowners.) In other words, the readers of this tabloid are, overwhelmingly, in the first stages of petit-bourgeois and bourgeois socialisation, with a need for instruction in the complexities of modern citizenship. The strategic planning of the content of this newspaper to meet this need precisely, underpinned by research undertaken with the input of Jos Kuper and her analysis of tabloids in India in particular, has simply been neglected by most media critics (Bloom 2005).

That its readers still stoutly maintain many traditional African beliefs is something the paper respects, as Rian Malan recounts in his story of decisions taken on how to explain a man moving his bed onto the roof during the night (Malan 2005). The paper decides to take the beliefs of its readers seriously, rather than disregarding or mocking them. Here, then, we have a tabloid coming to terms, as its readers must, with living simultaneously in a world of traditional belief and globalised systems.

In the case of the *Daily Voice*, which has a daily print run of 60 000, the audience consists very largely of multilingual, working- and middle-class coloured readers living on the Cape Flats. While we do not yet have AMPS data or Audit Bureau of Circulation figures for the paper, its own research suggests that 60 per cent of its readers fall within living standards measures (LSMs) 4–7, with home language split fifty-fifty between English and Afrikaans. The research suggests that there are equal numbers of male and female readers. Importantly, 40 per cent of these readers fall within LSMs 8–10, suggesting both that the paper is reaching a more affluent group than critics contend and that it is likely to attract more advertising in future.

The *Daily Voice* appeals, it is true, in many ways to an overwhelmingly coloured Cape Flats working-class community, and takes for granted a coloured identity that the South African political system seems designed to minimise (Piombo 2005). The group designated as coloured is the majority in Cape Town and the Western Cape, and while the political, social and existential dilemmas of this group have been the subject of considerable academic discussion, our argument here is simply that the *Daily Voice* articulates the concerns of a strong, neglected regional group by addressing their social concerns.

Complaints about the social capital of the *Daily Voice* often focus on the most traditional shibboleth of middle-class respectability: being well spoken and using 'proper' English. The paper, notoriously, switches codes, as much of its audience does, using Afrikaans words for emphasis or because the words resonate in ways that the English equivalents do not. If it thinks it will make its point more clearly, a report will say, in the words of one famous banner headline, '*Moffie* hooker shot in *gat*' instead of 'Gay prostitute shot in buttocks'.

Brophy's comments on this issue are revealing in pointing out that all newspapers carry a kind of social capital in the speech codes they use:

> I don't know what language construction you're supposed to use in newspapers. I come from Ireland, and a large amount of words in Irish use have entered the English lexicon around the world. Words like 'Shebeen' have even made it all the way down here. And in terms of numbers, we are predominantly an English newspaper, but, initial statistics suggest that 48% of our readers speak Afrikaans as their home language but they prefer to read English. You know, I hesitate to give you the banal attitude that it's the language that people speak on the street because it's not, no journalism is. Like nobody ever says, 'he slammed the majors' in normal speech. There is a certain lexicon, newsspeak, which has been slightly adapted for our newspaper. But nobody speaks like they write in the *Cape Times*, or the *Cape Argus* either.[12]

To push this analysis further – when the *Daily Voice* switches codes, it validates its readers' peculiar regional ability to move between two language groups and sets of influences. Instead of regarding a bastardised language as a sign of an uncertain racial identity, the *Daily Voice* offers an unapologetic hybridity as a source of moral critique and group knowledge. Where Anderson saw new languages as signs of new identities and political movements, this embrace of the complex ambivalences of the linguistic, cultural and political past allows coloured people to accept themselves unapologetically and claim a moral space on the grounds of this very complexity. In Bourdieu's terms, the paper finds a form of expression homologous to the position of the coloured population caught between languages, social identities and political affiliations, and turns this into a source of strength.

Let us extend this analysis, by way of elaboration, to three other issues: the page three girls, the treatment of sport, and the coverage of television. Many hostile critics have argued that the semi-nude page three girls in the *Daily Voice* reduce women to the status of sex objects. While the *Daily Sun* argues that its readers are too conservative to have bare-breasted page three girls in the tradition of its British namesake, the *Daily Voice* has insisted on this tradition. How are we to account for this decision, which has probably cost them in terms of the tone of the paper and perhaps in making it difficult for them to gain access to certain households, advertisers, and possibly even a greater number of female readers? Here we would argue that middle-class sensibility and hypocrisy combine to stop a lucid consideration of this insistence on what Brian McNair has perceptively analysed as 'the democratization of desire' (McNair 2002). While upper-middle-class magazines such as *FHM* and *GQ* aimed at the white male market have become steadily more sexually explicit over the past decade, we have also seen a huge rise in the amount of sexual material available free-to-air on e.tv and, via satellite, on DSTV. There is a flourishing industry in Internet pornography and other new digital forms of sexually explicit material, such as cellphone aural and visual material. It might be stretching the point to say that access to pornography is part of middle-class amenities in South Africa now, but not by much.

The pictures of the page three girls thus act as a critique of middle-class hypocrisy whereby what must be kept secret, inside wrapped covers, or viewed in the secrecy of the private computer or cellphone, is simply made explicit, normal, not to be apologised for. These pages serve as a kind of *reductio ad absurdum* of the cult of the naked female body and the artistic pretensions surrounding it in most upper- or middle-class erotica, pornography and art. In Bourdieu's terms, the 'distinctions' of middle-class erotica (poses, expensive underwear, make-up) get paid lip service to show that this audience understands the conventions; but the treatment of the images, through techniques like a well-placed deflating Afrikaans expression, also suggests that, after all, a body is only a body, those are only nipples or buttocks. It's only sex. Whereas the *Daily Sun* readers live in a mode of petit-bourgeois respectability, the *Daily Voice* readers, the paper suggests, want their right to partake in postmodern erotic-mediated identity but also to keep a sardonic working-class distance from it.

The second obvious manifestation of this mediated identity lies in the amount of the paper devoted to sport (both local and international) and entertainment. This, it might be argued, runs counter to the argument about local social capital in the previous section, but as Julia Stuart (2005) and others have shown, the Cape Flats has had a long and strong association with British football in particular as a powerful local tradition, in part because of a tradition of British professionals coming here to train local clubs. The success of Cape Flats stars like Benni McCarthy, Shaun Bartlett and Quentin Fortune in European football has also been a source of local pride. English Premier League soccer offers an identity that is new, constructed, multinational. It thus escapes the limits and classifications of the old (or new) South Africa.

To live on the Cape Flats but be a Liverpool or a Manchester United or an Arsenal fan is to inhabit, by extension, a realm of high social capital and achievement. While the *Daily Voice* pays considerable attention to local soccer, rugby and other sports, it shows once again that in terms of social capital, its readers occupy a quite different place to that of *Daily Sun* readers, whose passion is primarily for local clubs like Bucs (Orlando Pirates) or Kaizer Chiefs. The *Daily Voice* accepts the logical corollary of this, which is that many of its readers, however modest their income, will follow sport on the subscription channels of DSTV, and certainly on e.tv and the SABC. (The high proportion of readers in LSMs 8–10 shows that this assessment is quite justified.) And, to insist on the importance of this allegiance for the identity of readers, we can point to ways in which football allegiances reach into other forms of self-expression and identity: wearing club clothing, placing banners on car windshields or bumpers, and Internet usage.

What holds for sport holds also for entertainment. For the Cape Flats, this overwhelmingly means the most democratic broadcast medium, television. While the *Daily Voice* probably favours e.tv over other stations (this channel's programmes are the first listed in the paper's TV guide), it also accepts that some of its readers will have M-Net and that many will watch the SABC. While academic media critics might all wish the readers of the *Daily Voice* to read improving books, or do other worthier things than watch the box, the reality for most of us is that affordable pleasure consists primarily of televised entertainment. Once again, the *Daily Voice* insists that its readers have a full right to views on the range of television options, whereas the *Daily Sun* is concerned primarily with vernacular television.

Part of the failure of previous progressive left-wing Cape Flats newspapers such as *Grassroots* stemmed, according to Lukas Opatrny,[13] from an ideological ambivalence. Editors simultaneously wanted community participation but were also committed to Black Consciousness ideals which had the effect, at some point, of insisting that coloureds should see their identity as one with the majority African population. One of the effects of this, we suggest, might precisely have been to prevent these newspapers from drawing on the particular social capital and cultural experience of their intended audience.

If we accept that social capital is relational, then any paper will necessarily have a stance towards those perceived to be in more or less powerful places on the social and media field. To insist that coloured readers should behave as though they were not holders of specific forms of symbolic and social capital was the cultural equivalent of asking them to subscribe to a radical economic socialism in which they would see themselves as losers.

The advantage of using social and symbolic capital is that it allows us to move away from the highly charged and pejorative charges of racism into broader considerations of class and culture. As Brophy points out:

> Unfortunately in this country there is a correlation between race and class which is always going to be a problem because apartheid was a self-fulfilling and self-perpetuating political system. And unfortunately, at the moment, you can still talk about your readers in terms of race when you really should be talking about readers in terms of class. Elsewhere in the world, everybody deals with newspapers' readers in terms of class. In Britain, in the UK, newspapers are aimed at people in certain classes. Now our newspaper is quite clearly aimed at a working-class population; now unfortunately it so happens because of apartheid, the vast majority of that population happens to be of a certain pigmentation.[14]

The related question is whether tabloids should be required to play the role of social do-gooder because they are aimed at the working class, as Berger (2005b) suggested in his wish for a progressive popular press. Brophy argues that Berger's position is condescendingly classist, because he thinks that the lower classes need to be educated by a progressive press:

We're not social workers, we're not sociologists, we produce newspapers that people want to read. This is a democracy (belatedly). If people have the power and franchise to vote and they are trusted with the vote and they are trusted to select who they want to rule, I'm absolutely confident that they are mature enough to select what newspapers they should be reading and not reading.[15]

That, of course, leaves us with the tantalising question raised by Anton Harber about the *Daily Sun* (Harber 2005). Could the tabloids be the new force on the political scene in South Africa? What influence did the *Daily Voice* have on recent local government elections in Cape Town? What will its coverage of local politics (a recent headline had all the local contenders for political office in Cape Town portrayed as Smurfs) mean for civic participation down the road?

We suggest that the applause heard in the Galaxy club came from the sense that the *Daily Voice* represented coloured Cape Town in a way that no politicians could or would. Media scholars need to watch closely to see if it keeps that close relationship with its readers, and how it uses that power in the months and years ahead.

Notes

1   Karl Brophy interview.
2   The Mondi Shanduka Newspaper Journalism Awards, along with the Mondi Awards for magazine journalism, are widely regarded as the leading industry awards for media in South Africa.
3   See '*Cape Times* news editor canned': http://www.mg.co.za/articlePage.aspx?area=/breaking_news/breaking_news__national/&articleid=142945.
4   Henry Nxumalo, known as Mr Drum, was the investigative journalist for *Drum*, famous for going undercover to reveal dramatic stories.
5   Karl Brophy interview.
6   Karl Brophy interview.
7   Karl Brophy interview.
8   Karl Brophy interview.
9   Karl Brophy interview.
10 Karl Brophy interview.

11 See, for example, Thabo Mbeki's famous 'I am an African' speech, given in Parliament on the adoption of the new Constitution in 1996: http://www.anc.org.za/ancdocs/history/mbeki/1996/sp960508.html.
12 Karl Brophy interview.
13 Lukas Opatrny (2007) The post-1990 demise of the alternative press. Unpublished Master's thesis, University of Cape Town
14 Karl Brophy interview.
15 Karl Brophy interview.

References

Anderson B (1983) *Imagined communities: Reflections on the origins and spread of nationalism.* London: Verso

Beaudoin CE & Thorson E (2004) Social capital in rural and urban communities: Testing differences in media effects and models. *Journalism and Mass Communication Quarterly* 81: 378–399

Beaudoin CE & Thorson E (2006) The social capital of blacks and whites. *Human Communication Research* 32(2): 157–177

Benson R (1999) Field theory in comparative context: A new paradigm for media studies. *Theory and Society* 29: 463–498

Benson R (2004) Bringing the sociology of media back in. *Political Communication* 21: 275–292

Benson R & Neveu E (eds) (2004) *Bourdieu and the journalistic field.* Cambridge: Polity

Berger G (2005a) Remarks at Mondi Shanduka Newspaper Journalism Awards. Accessed 6 June 2006, http://www.journ.ru.ac.za/staff/guy/fulltext/mondi05.doc

Berger G (2005b) SA's tabloids rise in the ranks of journalism. Accessed 6 June 2006, http://www.mg.co.za/articlePage.aspx?articleid=245896&area=/insight/insight__converse/

Bloom K (2005) War talk. Accessed 6 June 2006, http://www.themedia.co.za/article.aspx?articleid=246620&area=/media_insightcover_stories/

Born G (2004) *Birt, Dyke and the reinvention of the BBC.* London: Secker and Warburg

Bourdieu P (1979) *La distinction.* Paris: Minuit

Bourdieu P (1993) *The field of cultural production.* New York: Columbia University Press

Bourdieu P (1996) *The rules of art.* Stanford, CA: Stanford University Press

Bourdieu P (1998) *On television.* New York: New Press

Bourdieu P (2004) The political field, the social scientific field, and the journalistic field. In R Benson and E Neveu (eds) *Bourdieu and the journalistic field.* Cambridge: Polity

Bourdieu P & Wacquant L (1992) *An invitation to reflexive sociology.* Chicago: University of Chicago Press

Burgess SM (2002) *SA tribes: Who we are, how we live and what we want from life.* Cape Town: David Philip

Couldry N (2003) Media meta-capital: Extending the range of Bourdieu's field theory. *Theory and Society* 32: 653–677

Esser F (1999) 'Tabloidization' of news: A comparative analysis of Anglo-American and German press journalism. *European Journal of Communication* 14(3): 291–324

Glenn I (2006) Racial news? How did SABC1 Nguni news and SABC3 English news cover Zimbabwe in 2004? In DP Conradie et al. (eds) *Communication science in South Africa: Contemporary issues. Proceedings of the 2005 Annual Conference of the South African Communication Association,* pp. 136–149. Juta: Cape Town

Habermas J (1989) *The structural transformation of the public sphere: An inquiry into a category of bourgeois society.* Cambridge, MA: MIT Press

Habermas J (1992) Further reflections on the public sphere. In C Calhoun (ed.) *Habermas and the public sphere.* Cambridge, MA: MIT Press

Habermas J (2006) Political communication in media society. Does democracy still enjoy an epistemic dimension? The impact of normative theory on empirical research. Paper presented at the International Communication Conference, Dresden, June

Harber A (2005) Rich diet at bottom of trough. *Business Day,* 12 April. Accessed 6 June 2006,http://www.journalism.co.za/modules.php?op=modload&name=News&file=article&sid=2293

Katz E (1996) And deliver us from segmentation. *Annals of the American Academy for Political and Social Science* vol. 546, The Media and Politics: 22–33

Malan R (2005) The great white hyena. *Spectator,* December 17

McEachern C (2002) *Narratives of nation: Media, memory and representation in the making of the new South Africa.* New York: Nova Science

McNair B (2002) *Striptease culture: Sex, media and the democratization of desire.* London: Routledge

Neveu E (2004) Bourdieu, the Frankfurt School and cultural studies: On some misunderstandings. In R Benson and E Neveu (eds) *Bourdieu and the journalistic field,* pp. 195–213. Cambridge: Polity

Piombo J (2005) Political parties, social demographics and the decline of ethnic mobilization in South Africa, 1994–99. *Party Politics* 11(4): 447–470

Putnam R (1995) Bowling alone: America's declining social capital. *Journal of Democracy* 6: 65–78

Putnam R (2000) *Bowling alone: The collapse and renewal of American community.* New York: Simon and Schuster

Rabe L (2005a) Galactic tabloid wars. Accessed 6 June 2006, http://www.news24.com/News24/Columnists/Lizette_Rabe/0,,2-1630-1714_1680379,00.html

Rabe L (2005b) License to kill. Accessed 6 June 2006, http://www.news24.com/News24/Columnists/Lizette_Rabe/0,,2-1630-1714_1685951,00.html

Rabe L (2005c) Tabloid journalists watch out! Accessed 6 June 2006, http://www.news24.com/News24/Columnists/Lizette_Rabe/0,,2-1630-1714_1767193,00.html

Schudson M (2003) *The sociology of news.* New York: Norton

Stuart J (2005) The cult of soccer on the Cape Flats. Paper presented at the Youth and Media Conference, Centre for Film and Media Studies, University of Cape Town

Interview

Karl Brophy (2005) Editor, *Daily Voice.* Interviewed by Angie Knaggs for an honours project, Cape Town, September 2005

6 Identity in post-apartheid South Africa: 'Learning to belong' through the (commercial) media

Sonja Narunsky-Laden

Beyond the fault lines of political economy and race

This chapter considers some of the principal ways in which post-apartheid South Africa has begun to redefine itself as a newly emergent social entity. In what follows, I describe, and attempt to theorise, the kinds of engagement with collective and individual identity options currently being enacted by growing numbers of people inhabiting South Africa's urbanising environments. I also outline a number of the procedures through which these identity options are regularly being concretised in people's everyday lives.

I refer specifically to two primary thematic threads which appear to be firmly interwoven into, and central in steering the dynamics of, South Africa's reconstituting social fabric. The first relates to the rise of a prevailing consumer culture in South Africa and the way this comes to bear on identity making – collective and individual, social and personal – during apartheid, after its demise, and post-apartheid. The second concerns the extent to which the racialised discourse of identity that underpinned the apartheid state continues to inform, shape and constrain how new identity options, spanning individual and social senses of 'selfhood', are currently being mediated and enacted in post-apartheid South Africa. For the purposes of this chapter, these themes comprise two interrelated arguments, each of which, however, also asks to be examined separately. Further, this line of thought is advanced here as a set of *working hypotheses* which necessarily calls for further corroboration, closer scrutiny, and a comparative perspective with other thematic aspects of identity formation mediated in post-apartheid South Africa's public debate(s).

The themes mentioned above are alluded to in a recent article by Comaroff and Comaroff (2005: 33–56) in which they reflect on the nature of democratic citizenship in post-apartheid South Africa. The authors discerningly point out that in South Africa, as in other postcolonies 'which are endemically heterogeneous' and where neo-liberal capitalism prevails, a predominant *politics of difference* inevitably *runs up against the limits of liberal citizenship*, ostensibly seeking to undermine the very terms of shared collectivity or 'citizenship' in which it is ethically anchored (Comaroff & Comaroff 2005: 35; my emphases). My concern here lies less with the limits of liberal citizenship than with the matrix of identity suggested in the discussion, in which the authors further observe that in social entities such as these, a new sense of citizenship seems to have crystallised which is marked by the way:

> identity has become, *simultaneously*, a matter of volition and self-production through consumption *and* a matter of ineluctable essence, of genetics and biology. (Comaroff & Comaroff 2005: 43)

They further suggest that this is a mode of citizenship which aspires to be global even as it registers a vague sense of national belonging that is also compatible with other modes of being in the world (Comaroff & Comaroff 2005: 35). This conceptual, yet at the same time accurately formulated, grasp of identity is aptly captured in a recent series of Hansa advertisements disseminated in the print media by South African Breweries. An analysis of the (extremely aesthetically styled) images in these ads is not included as this would extend the chapter beyond its limits. However, I will indicate the gender of the models used in each image. The copy reads as follows:

1) *I HATE BEING BLACK. If it means some people think they know my criminal record. My rhythm. My level of education. Or the role affirmative action has played in my career. I'm not someone else's black. I'm my own. I LOVE BEING BLACK. (Male model)*

2) *I HATE BEING WHITE. If it means some people think that I'm not a real South African. That I'm a racist. Privileged. Paranoid. Or Baas. I'm not someone else's white. I'm my own and I LOVE BEING WHITE. (Male model)*

3) *I HATE BEING BEAUTIFUL. If it means some people see that I'm just a pretty face. Superficial...An airhead...vain or immature. I'm not the world's sex idol. I'm my own. I LOVE BEING BEAUTIFUL. (Female model)*

4) *I HATE BEING INTELLIGENT. If it means some people think that I'm boring. Humourless and unapproachable. That I can't be sexy or spontaneous.*

I didn't choose my IQ. I did choose who I am. I LOVE BEING INTELLIGENT. (Female model)

5) *I HATE BEING FAMOUS. If it means some people think that I'm rude, shallow, that I only do things to get attention, that I think I'm better than everyone. I'm not me because I'm famous. I'm famous because I'm me. AND I LOVE BEING FAMOUS.* (Female model)

6) *I HATE HANSA. If it means some people think it's the same as any other beer. Looks the same. Tastes the same. Refreshes the same. It's not. It's a Pilsner. Brewed with the kiss of the SAAZ hop to refresh like no other. It's my beer and I LOVE HANSA.* (Bottle of Hansa)

Despite having been accused of manifesting a bias toward white perceptions and verbal competencies,[1] these articulations are strikingly symptomatic of how advertised identities in general are typically presented as 'authentic' productions of the idealised self which are at once culturally encoded and predetermined. In these advertisements the formal patterns of language used foreground, by way of exemplification, the breaking and remaking of socio-cultural meaning (Jakobson 1960). This is noted in their structures of parallelism, which deviate from the norm in advertising copy, their structures of repetition (I Hate Being Black/White/Beautiful/Intelligent/Famous/Hansa) and inversion (I Love Being Black/White/Beautiful/Intelligent/Famous/Hansa), and the way the consumer's persona (the Hansa drinker) is evoked as though the consumer her/himself subscribes to the identity conveyed.

We note a deviation in the meaning and repeated use of 'I Hate' at the beginning of each advert – the norm would be to begin with a positive declaration. Moreover, these formulations all disparagingly foreground racial or social stereotypes (black, white, beautiful, intelligent, famous) by articulating the shortcomings currently considered to be socially representative of each stereotype. However, the speakers here all knowingly anticipate and undermine the main ways in which they might be disparaged, by themselves articulating the shortcomings others might ascribe to them. Finally, the speakers themselves ultimately invert their maligning opening statements, ending on a note of celebration whereby the stereotypical label is now positively evaluated: 'I love being Black/White/Beautiful/Intelligent/Famous.'

We further note an ironic play here on South Africanness, generated by presenting inverted stereotypical representations of the 'racialised other' alongside a range of non-specific, globally relevant clichés, which indicate the select yet commonplace middle-class aspirations (beauty, brains, fame) presumably meaningful to Hansa's potential consumers. Michael Pickering's formulation, in which stereotypes are seen to 'operate as a means of evaluatively placing, and attempting to fix in place, other people or cultures from a particular and privileged perspective' (Pickering 2001: 47) is apposite here. Interestingly, too, Pickering has sought to reassess the analytical correspondence between the stereotype and the 'other' at more or less the same time as an interesting convergence of stereotypical 'othering' seems to be prevalent in South African promotional culture. The extent to which this kind of advertising discourse indeed constitutes a mode of social redress is a moot point and falls beyond the scope of this chapter, but I believe these adverts, and others like them, do also serve a social-semiotic function. Whether or not their creators intended them to, they articulate a minimal range of identity markers that young, middle-class South Africans presumably hold to be most desirable. They denote the 'ideal' middle-class identity currently regarded as most socially viable for young beer drinkers in South Africa: ideally, whether one is black or white, one should aspire to be beautiful, intelligent, famous and able to afford Hansa.

As everyday artefacts through which 'the work of the imagination is transformed' (Appadurai 1997: 9), the Hansa advertisements exemplify one of the ways in which commercial media discourses in South Africa today provide 'a staging ground' (Appadurai 1997: 7) from which 'strategies of action' (Swidler 1986) may be constructed. They represent sources of data which generate new understandings, images and concrete instructions for recommended social and individual conduct. Frequently representing aspired to, not necessarily given, states of affairs, it is their evocative power (see McCracken 1990: 104–117), and that of the cultural commodities and beliefs they recommend, that concerns us here; these are the means by which they provide valid ways for people to imagine as plausible alternative realities which may be structurally opposed to their existing reality. In so doing, they provide 'a series of elements…out of which scripts can be formed of imagined lives' (Appadurai 1997: 35); or, more specifically, following Swidler, they comprise part of the 'tool kit or repertoire from which actors select differing pieces for constructing lines of action' (Swidler 1986: 273). As such they are conducive both to sustaining existing strategies of action for identity formation and constructing new ones.

Media discourses on consumption in South Africa are not perceived reductively as a straightforward insistence by Africans on 'going West' (see Nyamnjoh 2000: 9–10), but rather in terms of the ways they enable people to devise new ways of doing things in life (see Even-Zohar 1997), and access new resources and sets of strategies directed at the social and individual production of selfhood (Laden 2001a, 2001b, 2001c). In this regard we should be attentive to the transformative power and local reworkings, not merely the culturally homogenising effects, of commercial media discourses, consumer culture and patterns of consumption, and their impact(s) on people's senses of social membership and individual selfhood. For as Appadurai points out, in the second half of the twentieth century consumption appears to have:

> ...become the civilizing work of postindustrial societies...not the horizon of learning but its engine for vast numbers of consumers in contemporary industrial societies...*a serious form of work*, if by work we mean the disciplined (skilled and semiskilled) production of the means of consumer subsistence. (Appadurai 1997: 41–42)

Appadurai's view of practices of consumption as a 'force of habituation', as a central means of regulating, among other things, 'the rhythms of accumulation and divestiture that generate particular states of material wealth' (Appadurai 1997: 26), converges with my own view of consumer culture as a means of regulating procedures of change, thereby increasing the stabilising effect of the emerging social order, and standardising global stuctures of common difference(s) in the age of globalisation (Wilk 1995).

In the context of current socio-cultural approaches to identity, which Jenkins (2004) distinguishes broadly as 'interactionist' (i.e. concerned with a 'general theory of identification') vis-à-vis 'cultural' (i.e. concerned with local and historical specificities under shared 'postmodernist' concerns, whatever these might be), I take a socio-semiotic approach to identity and identification, which takes into account the socio-cultural determinants entailed in the mediatory mechanisms of consumer culture and the commercial media in South Africa. My interest lies in how these have been brought to bear on options for the (re)production of individual selfhood and collective identity among all South Africans, but especially among black South Africans in urbanising environments.

Here I advance, without demonstrating, two methodological assumptions regarding the broader interplay of factors I believe are pertinent to the overall study of identity formation and social change: (1) new identities are frequently fostered in climates of complex heterogeneity, yet are determined in more or less the stable terms of how possible, impossible or feasible they are for

members of specific social coteries at given moments in time; and (2) change
and the dynamics thereof are frequently far less radical or revolutionary than
we might assume, especially when the survival of a social group or entity,
and its individual members, is at stake. In other words, although new identity
formulations are often appropriated and processed more or less unconsciously,
I believe they are best regarded as voluntarily, cognitively chosen mechanisms
of actively negotiated consent.

Imagining South Africa

My own approach to identity is significantly informed by Anderson's concept
of the nation as an 'imagined community' (Anderson 1983) whose members
will never really come to know one another, but are nonetheless bound(ed) and
bonded by 'the image of their communion' (Anderson 1983: 15), and whose
communities are set apart from one another through '*the style in which they are
imagined*' (Anderson 1983: 15; my emphasis). Anderson further points out the
centrality of the newspaper and the novel, as concrete forms of print-capitalism,
in instilling in their readers a sense of themselves as characters moving
simultaneously through 'homogenous, empty time' (Anderson 1983: 37)
within the limits of a single social entity. South Africa's anticipated emergence
into a 'collectivity of communities' or a 'national entity' is most profitably
accounted for through what Foster has dubbed *commercial* rather than
strictly political or ideological 'technologies of nation making' (Foster 1999:
265–267; Foster 1997). As Foster points out, social historians have long
since understood the reciprocal links between mass consumption and the
constitution of national entities (see Boorstein 1973; Bronner & Kellner 1989;
Ewen & Ewen 1982; Fox & Lears 1983; Marchand 1985). In the context of post-
apartheid South Africa, the 'commercial' technology of nation making alludes
to ways in which advertising, for instance, and other forms of mass media
such as soap operas, talk shows, magazines, chat rooms and blogs, enable the
heterogeneity of South Africans to activate processes of objectification (Foster
1999, 2002; Miller 1995) through which they come to constitute a sense of
themselves as sharing a proliferation of discursive patterns, images and objects
(see also LiPuma 1997). In so doing, South Africans (will) come to believe
that collectively they constitute 'a nation' which exists, as it were, 'outside
themselves'.

In this respect, one might say that processes of colonial conquest and the
'civilising' missionary enterprise in southern Africa were more or less directly

responsible for transforming the printing press into a mechanism that prefigured shared mass media consumption on a large scale. The printing press facilitated knowledge production and dissemination and social mobility, and provided a leading channel for conducting intercultural contacts in South Africa. As facilitators of 'cultural interference', print commodities are also primary means through which black (i.e. African, coloured and Indian) South Africans have long been able to access new resources and repertoric options, and motivate socio-cultural change. As De Kock points out, the printing press:

> ...made it possible to realign an entire cultural order...[serving] as the basis for a strong literary role in the cultural conversion of people. Meanwhile, cultural codes for the inculcation of new forms of identity would touch on almost every aspect of living. Housing, clothing, forms of labour and agriculture, modes of belief and worship – in short, almost every daily cultural practice – would be affected by the representation of the missionaries. (De Kock 1996: 40)

In other words, even as De Kock acknowledges that 'literacy was at the core of colonisation in South Africa' (De Kock 1996: 64), he is also well aware that literacy was at the same time 'the basis of what became an informing, knowledge-creating representational order' (De Kock 1996: 65). Once the literacy imparted by 'the colonisers' was mastered and could actively be reproduced by 'the colonised', as both producers and reading subjects, black South Africans began to transform the print medium into an enabling apparatus for the production of various kinds of knowledge and social practices that served many of their own interests. Similar functions might be ascribed to other forms of media, a whole range of visual and media literacies, and the workings of consumer culture and patterns of consumption in South Africa, for contemporary understandings of consumer culture clearly both rely on and can be seen to extend the 'development of print-as-commodity' or 'print-capitalism' as crucial to the conceptualisation, emergence and shaping of new social and cultural entities and the identities of their fellow members (Anderson 1983: 37, 40).

It would appear that at least from the 1930s on, there were additional factors at play which contributed significantly to the reorganisation of the lives, experiences and sense of identity of black South Africans. These hitherto unacknowledged factors pertain to the introduction of routinised, regulated options for everyday living among ordinary black South Africans, and new modes of subsistence, in particular consumption practices and consumer patterns. Seminal in this regard was the black commercial press in South Africa, which was a crucial mechanism for the dissemination of perceptions of regulated activities of consumption as viable ways of successfully reorganising the social, political, economic and cultural lives of its black readers. The black commercial press, exemplified by such publications as *Bantu World* and *Zonk!*, paved the way to new, alternative methods of imagining collectivity in South Africa (see Laden 2003). In this respect, the black commercial press provided a vehicle for 'imagining' the future 'post-apartheid nation'.

Elsewhere I have addressed some of the ways consumer magazines for black South Africans function seminally as 'cultural tools' that perform the task of cultural (re)ordering by codifying, disseminating and legitimising specifically urban, middle-class repertoires for black South Africans living in urban(ising) environments (see Even-Zohar 1994, 1997; Laden 2001a, 2001b, 2001c, 2003, 2004; Swidler 1986). Among other things, I show that as particularly styled print commodities geared to the changing relations between persons, objects and ways of mediating the world in modern-day South Africa, consumer magazines shape social action by ascribing significance to, without always putting into action, a newly imagined, shared 'tool kit' (Swidler 1986: 273) of middle-class, everyday habits, experiences, lifestyle options and social practices. Consumer magazines, then, are documents or sources of data which generate new understandings, images and concrete instructions for recommended social and individual conduct. In so doing, they provide 'a series of elements... out of which scripts can be formed of imagined lives' (Appadurai 1997: 35) or, more specifically, following Swidler, they comprise part of the 'tool kit or repertoire from which actors select differing pieces for constructing lines of action' (1986: 273). As such they are conducive both to sustaining existing strategies of action and constructing new ones (Swidler 1986: 273). As an operative set of 'cultural tools', the magazines function on several different yet interrelated levels: they are instrumental in establishing new praxes of everyday social, cultural and behavioural norms for their target readerships, organised largely through a new range of middle-class goods, lifestyles and cultural activities; this includes the magazines themselves. By analogy, all mass media in South Africa can be seen to operate in similar ways, and are both commercial cultural products in their own right, and vehicles through which consumer culture and new identity options are regularly disseminated.

In South Africa the emergence of print commodities, coupled with the rise of consumer practices and patterns of consumption, has contributed significantly to the construction and implementation of repertoires of 'middle-classness' in general, and to introducing new, and reshaping existing, senses of collective and individual identity among black South Africans in urbanising environments. This mode of collective identity has been concerned not only with maintaining a sense of survival and stabilisation within the context of apartheid, and facilitating social change, but is currently also interested in *overtly proclaiming the social membership of black South Africans in South Africa's changing economy in modern, urbanised environments, even as community-based and rural modes of economy still prevail* (see Lamont and Molnar 2001 for an account of how consumption ostensibly shapes the collective identity of black Americans). The import, borrowing and translation of identity options, alongside the desire to render more visible the involvement of black South Africans in driving the transition of South Africa's economy into a more liberal-democratic one, is not simply imposed from above, but is also more or less consciously undertaken by black South Africans themselves.[2] Through a range of 'tale types', human-interest stories, anecdotes and parables, alongside more directly informative, instructive and educative accounts, the mass media in South Africa suggest options for desirable social conduct and promote notions of 'social correctness', while marketing a full range of Western commodities, values and beliefs, including literacy and education, entertainment and popular culture, and notions of liberal democracy. Subscribing to and promoting the relevance of consumer consciousness among black South Africans, the commercial mass media are committed, on the one hand, to imparting information on career guidance, financial services, vocational training, changing legal rights, graduate education, tertiary studies, and instances in which customary law and constitutional law are not readily reconciled. The commercial mass media further recommend the consumption of 'cultural', recreational or leisure-oriented practices, many of which are perceived as 'entertainment', such as music, sport, television viewing, and dance and drama performances. They also provide black South Africans with efficient means for integrating and transforming indigenous oral traditions such as public debate, oral poetry and song, storytelling and historical narrative, all received sources of African 'cultural capital', into literate modes of print culture and 'urban ways of knowing'. In so doing, the media reinstate their own participatory nature as public forums and modes of urban 'performance' culture enhanced by technologies of print and broadcast (see Laden 2001a, 2004). Many of the discursive and thematic options authorised in the South African commercial media have contributed to (re)forging a strong sense of interconnectedness and interdependence among black South Africans. In some ways, this interconnectedness underlies aspects of South Africa's contemporary corporate climate, promoting a new 'middle-class' discursive and popular cultural idiom that is in many ways typically 'South African'.

The mass media in South Africa can therefore be said to function centrally as didactic and aspirational tools, geared toward helping audiences/readers/viewers acquire new skills and devise new ways of doing things in life, enabling them to access new knowledge, social options and cultural resources. Didactically, the mass media engage their audiences/readers/viewers on at least two different levels: the first is oriented toward formulating a technology of verbal and visual literacy, while the second outlines a repertoire of cultural references and practices that invoke, and may be invoked by, the social processing of media technologies. Significantly, then, the mass media seek to provide audiences/readers/viewers with the very skills and methods of comprehension required to access and retain the knowledge they wish to impart. And seminally, too, the mechanism of regularised repetition inherent in many media forms, in which a given repertoire is constantly reiterated, thereby reconfirming its validity, is also a technological device which enables audiences/readers/viewers to actively participate in the daily recreation of their culture by repeatedly renegotiating it among themselves (see Davis 1994).

Toward a cultural economy in South Africa: historical and theoretical underpinnings

The salience of consumer culture in South Africa is almost self-evident: we note the overwhelming and virtually undisputed predominance of commercial media discourse(s) in the South African public sphere, and a virtually unconditional endorsement of market forces among the country's political and corporate institutions and leaders. These discourses of consumption, consumer culture and promotional culture constitute the dominant register of public debate in post-apartheid South Africa today, and precisely because they are so integral to mainstream media (especially print and broadcast media), and their consumer-oriented tenor is so obvious, they indeed appear to be constituting the underpinnings of South Africa's new 'civil society'. My concern here is not to call for policy and other prescriptive forms of change in this regard, but rather to pursue a fuller understanding of how this state of affairs came about and why it appears to be enduring and/or sustainable.

In other words, I am interested in understanding why the predominantly commercial orientation of South African media appears to have successfully taken hold, and what about it promises to be viable and/or beneficial to vast numbers of South Africans. A partial answer, I suspect, lies in the way the commercial orientation of the media today enables the mass media in South Africa to function most effectively in the service of identity formation at both national and individual levels that are also social, political, cultural and economic. I will return to this point later.

Much of South Africa's commercial media discourse today plays a central role in propagating processes of identity formation among black South Africans. Indeed, I maintain that alongside the South African state's regulated modes of exploitation consolidated through the apartheid regime, at the level of their unofficial social practices black South Africans have long since been actively engaged in forging new forms of more or less organised sociability, generating new *cultural and social identity options.* Moreover, I view this apparent proneness to formulating new forms of 'civil' sociability and new repertoires of cultural identity options as an enterprising response to the oppressive circumstances induced by various modes of British and Afrikaans colonialism and racialism. For it would appear that social groups often manufacture a sense of social cohesion precisely in the face of economic, political and ideological pressures that seek to tear them apart, especially, I suspect, when there is little or no agreement about the modes of social cohesion and solidarity through which a broad sense of collective identity can be manifested and regulated over time. The predominance of a racialised identity discourse, structures of power, and the ostensible linkages between apartheid, capitalism and processes of modernisation in the recent history of South Africa, have necessarily led to ongoing public and scholarly engagements with the political–economic constraints imposed on South Africa, and countless assessments of their role in shaping the country's socio-political history. Although it is clearly the case that for decades disenfranchised black South Africans were formally excluded from official decision-making processes in most socio-political and economic spheres, the point I wish to make here is that despite the shackles of race and the apartheid regime's official attempts to determine identity in South Africa along a racial fault line, *black South Africans have long been actively pursuing identity options of their own.* They have long been more than passive subscribers to, and casualties of, colonialist legacies and the apartheid regime. The transition from a recognised number of rural lifestyles to a far broader range of newly acquired urban lifestyle options has inevitably resulted in considerable changes in the social structurations and cultural patterns of South Africa's black population in urban settings.

More specifically, these nodes of collective social action strongly suggest that in Africa, received 'colonial dichotomies of ruler and ruled, white and black, colonizer and colonized only reflect...part of the reality in which people lived', for the 'meanings of institutions, bureaucratic habits, and cultural styles set up in the colonial era were continually being reshaped' (Cooper & Stoler 1997: 34, 33; for an extension of this argument see also Cooper 1997: 406–435). On another level entirely, I contend that most earlier debates on the construction of social identity and selfhood in South Africa were too frequently, and all too restrictedly, grounded in reductive articulations of the colonial situation and the subsequent modernisation of Africa. These discussions seem to have promoted a unilateral view of power and domination in (South) Africa and a wrongful disregard for historical manifestations of human agency in specifically African contexts. Perhaps this is because, as Cooper has suggested, 'the colonial state...created a system vulnerable to challenges in precisely those areas they did not want to think about' (Cooper 1997: 411).

Following both Cooper (1997) and Bayart (1993), then, I believe many scholars and intellectuals, both Western and non-Western, have failed to identify as legitimate and adequately historicise a whole range of practices and idioms that do not always meet declared Western ideals of 'acceptable' social practice. As manifestations of African social experience, many of these practices fall outside 'universalistic' principles of egalitarian social organisation and received understandings of the procedures entailed in processes of democratisation. The apparent disregard, largely on the part of non-Africans, for manifestations of human agency in African societies may even be an extension of the anxiety manifested by colonial officials who failed to discern, let alone consider, 'social categories that fell outside their boundaries' (Cooper 1997: 410). For most intellectual engagements with colonial power tend to focus almost exclusively on categories derived more or less directly from the repertoire of colonial politics; hence they often ignore, or choose to denigrate, how indigenous social autonomy and stratification may be articulated among African elites and individuals through establishing, and maintaining over time, new and/or alternative socio-cultural figurations and options. These may include deliberate constructions of dependency and social stratification, and the valid institutionalisation of African urban elites, often formulated in terms of a 'politics of the belly' (Bayart 1993). This can be manifested in the accumulation of wealth; conspicuous access to possibilities of social mobility, and the exercise of power through alternatively regulated social relations; frequently evidenced indigenous, locally regulated practices and discourses relating, say, to relations of intimacy (such as concubines, mistresses and/or unofficial wives); nepotism (perceived in the West as a sign of 'corruption'); witchcraft and sorcery; traditional medicine; forms of indigenous knowledge; and customary positions of authority, such as village and/or tribal headmen and inherited or appointed chieftainships (Bayart 1993; Durham 2002; Geshiere 1997; Geshiere & Nyamnjoh 1998; Niehaus 2001).

Received views of the South African media in terms of political economy correspond with, and often confirm as self-evident, conventional understandings of South African history. In so doing they frequently echo the 'official' story of South African history in general, and represent an 'official' history of the South African media in particular. Attempting to expose the tensions between the political economy of the South African media and the socio-semiotic complexities of a cultural economy of consumption, consumption patterns and consumer practices, promises to denaturalise this 'official' story and give voice to 'unofficial' versions of South Africa's modern-day socio-cultural history that may well be no less valid and/or relevant. However, it is important to note that 'official' and 'unofficial' versions of South African history are by no means mutually exclusive; quite the contrary – they are discerned here as frequently overlapping sites of investigation which promise to cross-fertilise one another. Thus, unravelling the similarities and tensions between political, economic and cultural factors and agencies, and examining how these are brought to bear on the everyday lives of media consumers, readerships and audiences, promises to facilitate new understandings and cross-analyses of a distinctively South African cultural idiom and its diverse manifestations in the media.

Reciprocal relations between the spheres of 'culture' and 'economy', traditionally rendered analytically distinct, were recognised by Sahlins (1976) and Appadurai (1986), and have latterly begun to be acknowledged, to various critical ends, by a range of writers (see, for instance, Barry & Slater 2005; Gough-Yates 2003; Granovetter 1985, 1992; Hunter 1988; Miller 1997, 2002; Ray & Sayer 1999; Turner 1992; Wernick 1991; for an informative outline of many these arguments see McFall 2004: 61–88). Two noteworthy volumes in which the concept of cultural economy has recently been crystallised are Du Gay and Pryke (2002) and McFall (2004). However, my own conceptualisation and endorsement of a *cultural*-economy approach to the South African print media occurred well before any of these studies came to my attention, and is methodologically grounded in the work of French sociologist Pierre Bourdieu and American anthropologist James Carrier. I begin my discussion of this approach by clarifying my own grasp of a cultural economy in the context of South Africa's print media, and later comment on its fit with the work represented in Du Gay and Pryke (2002) and McFall (2004). Telling correspondences between the metaphorical notions of a *political* economy and a *cultural* economy may be drawn from (1) Bourdieu's grasp of the convergences obtaining between the economic and symbolic orders, whereby the logic that orders each is the logic of 'capital', and (2) Carrier's problematisation of the market model as an adequate representation of Western economy (Carrier 1997). Bourdieu's argument goes roughly like this: fields of cultural production where economic capital is produced are always oriented toward, even as they seem antithetical to, symbolic capital; at the same time, fields where intellectual and/or artistic capital are produced always strive to conceal their underlying market motivations (Bourdieu 1984, 1995). That is to say, although all enterprises of production seek to keep market values and symbolic values relatively separate and independent of one another, it cannot be denied that these two seemingly inverse 'economic logics' are strongly linked. Both are based on an accumulation, by people and/or objects, of the 'capital of consecration' (Bourdieu 1995: 148), which bestows value upon them and enables them to make profits. What distinguishes them is the 'objective and subjective distance of enterprises of cultural production with respect to the market and to expressed or tacit demand' (Bourdieu 1995: 141–146) or, in other words, the changing ways in which their agents, semiotic markers and practices are apprehended and distinguished by various cultural agencies. Economic capital necessarily includes both material objects, many of which have symbolic value, and intangible attributes and properties such as prestige, status and authority (i.e. symbolic capital), and cultural capital (culturally valued taste and consumption patterns) (see Bourdieu 1984). As pointed out in Harker et al. (1990: 13), 'for Bourdieu, capital acts as a social relation within a system of exchange', so that the term relates to all material and symbolic goods which are perceived as worth aspiring to or are indeed sought after in particular social situations. Crucial here is the way Bourdieu extends 'the use of the term "economic" and its correlate "capital" to include the exchange of anything of value' (Harker et al. 1990: 207), so that the power dimensions of cultural, symbolic and economic capital are relatively interchangeable, although not always equally so in all directions (that is, cultural resources and social networks might be forms of capital, but they are not always equivalent to money and/or property). Nonetheless, the notions of culture and access to cultural production as capital pave the way for establishing structural homologies or analogies between cultural and economic forms of capital and cultural production, while perceiving symbolic capital as a particular instance or exemplification of economic capital. No less significant is Bourdieu's reconceptualisation of fields of cultural production to include the notion of a 'habitus', a matrix of preferred cultural dispositions which enables us to reassess how human agency impacts on the ways social reality is constructed, both practically and intellectually. (On the concept of 'habitus' see Bourdieu 1984; Harker et al. 1990: 10–12, 137–141; Sela-Sheffy 1997; Swartz 1997: 290–291.)

On another level, Carrier (1997) postulates that it is important to distinguish between understandings of Western economy produced by formal economists (frequently replicated, I might add, by politicians), and those commonly held by non-specialist members of the entities this economy purports to organise and describe (Carrier 1997: 1–67; 129–157). Carrier points out the complex relationship between what he calls the 'market model' and the ways in which people actually think about and go about conducting their economic lives. Further, he usefully argues that the model of the market is 'as much concerned with defining the difference between self and other as it is with its putative purpose of describing a form of socio-economic activity' (Carrier 1997: 32). Carrier goes on to interrogate essentialised associations of the market model with constructions of the modern West (most notably with the USA), advocating an unpacking of the socio-cultural underpinnings of the socio-economic patterns and practices entailed in and affiliated with a capitalist market-driven economy. In these constructions, the market is reductively construed as analogous with 'impersonality, self-regard and calculation', and market actors are typically perceived as autonomous individuals looking out primarily for their own best interests, at all times seeking 'to avoid pain and seek pleasure' (Carrier 1997: 34). Carrier stresses the need to investigate instances in which the market model may be manifested as a collective social enterprise in which choice and autonomy culminate in forms of social constraint, and which is often grounded in the very socio-cultural interdependencies and values that market model adherents would seek to deny. Finally, then, following both Bourdieu and Carrier, we would be well advised to critically and reflexively question, or objectify, our own prior knowledge of South Africa's economic and political past, and it is to this task that I now turn, in the hope of providing a more nuanced analysis of cultural change in contemporary South Africa.

My own approach to 'cultural economy' is aligned with recent attempts by Du Gay and Pryke (2002) and McFall (2004) to assess how practitioners' actual behaviour in concrete instances of material practice might best be 'done'. This approach lends itself to extending analyses of the South African media beyond the frameworks of political economy into the realm of a strategically managed, and concretely manifested, cultural economy. The contributions in Du Gay and Pryke (2002) view cultural economy as a means of trying to discern how economic life is constructed from a range of disparate but at all times culturally conditioned elements, or as a series of assertions suggesting that economic and organisational life are at present more culturally determined than they appeared to be in the past. Both aspects of this view tie in with my own, and reinforce my sense that it is vital to extend the analyses of the South African media beyond the frameworks of political economy into the realm of a strategically managed cultural economy.

Consumer magazines for black South Africans comprise a particularly telling case study for 'doing' cultural economy, since their ongoing, systemic publication (from 1951 on) cannot readily be accounted for, nor fully explained, in purely economic terms of supply and demand, or political economy terms relating to the ownership and control of their producers and/or publishers. Nor is the cultural 'work' performed by these magazines adequately described by neoclassical economic perceptions of human agency as motivated solely by self-interest, utility and actual material gain. For not only do consumer magazines for black South Africans nicely illustrate that 'not all economic action arises out of what are traditionally thought of as economic motives' (Fukuyama 1995: 18), they further urge us to perceive their ongoing viability as commercial goods as the result of 'an intricate interplay of economic and cultural norms across the institutional field of given markets, industries and organizations' (McFall 2004: 69).

It is in this sense that I believe that analyses of the South African media stand to benefit from broadening their scope from standard *politico-economic* factors (i.e. the South African state and its institutions, state corporations and their convergences with private capital, and how these have shaped the black press and other media) to the *socio-cultural* determinants entailed, among other things, in the ways the consolidation of the commercial black press in South Africa came to bear on the (re)production of individual selfhood and collective identity among black South Africans in urbanising environments. This *cultural* economy would focus, say, on procedures of social stratification, and the various and shifting ways in which demographic change (migrant labour and urbanisation) has impacted on existing and new socio-cultural networks, practices and representations within black urban culture. It would also consider the various and changing uses to which material and cultural goods are put, the agency of individual consumers and consumer groups, and the dynamic workings of the cultural institutions and practices, frequently unofficial, entailed in the culture of consumption.

Revisiting racialised identity

Questions of identity in South Africa have long been both prejudiced and coloured by essentialism. That is to say, the discourse of identity has typically been predicated on racialised understandings of identity, manifesting a complicity with imposed racial and/or ethnic categorisations, and has accordingly been conducted in terms of (more or less) fixed racial, ethnic, linguistic, religious and other *differences* formalised by apartheid and its oppressive structures of discrimination and domination. Given the ways in which the machinery of apartheid insisted on foregrounding racial difference, it is not surprising that racial difference has set the tone, and provided the dominant discursive framework, for discussions about identity in South African public media discourse.

However, while the collusion between proponents of apartheid and racialised understandings of identity is self-evident, less obvious perhaps is the unintended contribution by apartheid's opponents and critics to perpetuating a racialised discourse of identity in South Africa. It seems that ideologues and institutions of apartheid, and advocates of the struggle against apartheid as well as academic communities in South Africa that sought to promote a discourse of non-racialism, all came to adopt, at different points in time, similarly normative, prescriptive stances toward a predominantly racial identity politics. Both group and individual identities in South Africa have long been constituted, to one extent or another, through racial distinctions.

More specifically, the discourse of identity in South Africa has been all too narrowly focused on more or less fixed racial/ethnic categorisations, and has underplayed, if not totally disregarded, perceptions of the non-racial aspects of human identity and lived experiences, and the ways in which the human imagination may be brought to bear on revising the 'interactional constitution of identity' (McFall 2004: 7) of the personal and social 'self', especially in people's everyday lives. South African leaders, intellectuals and scholars alike have tended to overlook the social construction of identity as *process*, as the dynamic outcome of human interaction, expressed by means of 'agreement and disagreement, convention and innovation, communication and negotiation' (Jenkins 2004: 4). I therefore recommend pursuing a framework that would probe beyond apartheid, and register the perceived nuances of many people's lived experiences and sense(s) of self and personhood, as represented in the South African media. In this regard I propose a 'cultural economic' approach to South African identity options as mediated through a variety of media discourses, popular culture (whatever this might mean), consumption patterns and everyday-life routines, both local and global. This should enable us to better understand and analytically describe some of the recurrent signs of personal and collective change, social mobility, stratification, group affiliation and personal and collective identity options currently discernible in the South African media.

There have been, to date, relatively few descriptions of how people's non-racial options for identity in South Africa actually 'work' or 'are worked' (McFall 2004: 5) in real social contexts. It is therefore understandable that questions of identity as a meta-concept denoting *shared* and *divergent* types of distinctiveness, both individual and collective, and equally operative in human interaction (see Jenkins 2004: 3–6, passim), have yet to be studied in depth in South Africa. This scholarly bias may be on the verge of shifting, as there is today a sizeable body of scholarly literature, in a variety of fields, which overtly seeks to transcend questions of racial identity in order to probe questions of 'new' identity in South Africa *beyond the limits of apartheid*. Not surprisingly, though, many of these studies also reactivate racial difference as an analytical category, thereby repositioning it at the forefront of the 'new South Africa', whatever this might mean. This corpus includes, among others, Alexander 2006; Alexander et al 2006; Bratton et al 2005; Burgess 2002; Ceruti and Mudau 2006; Chidester et al. 2003; Distiller and Steyn 2004; Dlamini 2005; Dolby 2000, 2001; Grossberg et al. 2005; Laden 2003; Mangcu 2001; Masenyama 2005; Morrell 2001; Morrell and Ouzgane 2005; Nuttall 2004, 2006; Nuttall and Michaels 2000; Pieterse and Meintjies 2003; Posel 2001; Simpson and Dore 2004; Ratele 2006; Ribane 2006; Wasserman and Jacobs 2003; Zegeye 2001; Zegeye and Harris 2003; and Zegeye and Krieger 2001.

Race appears to linger, and raises issues of re-racialisation in post-apartheid South Africa, especially in the widely mediated debates regarding official policies of black empowerment, affirmative action and black economic empowerment, and the Native Club, which strongly suggests that race is being re-essentialised. Such allegations have recently been denied, less emphatically than one would hope, by Mangcu (2001), Posel (2001) and Nuttall (2006), but as yet there has been no really convincing attempt to shed light on the relevance of race in post-apartheid South Africa. I would like to position my comments here alongside my analysis of identity markers in the Hansa advertisements addressed earlier in this chapter.

On the matter of re-racialisation, I would like to point out that although inherited identity markers such as race and ethnicity have far from disappeared or been rendered discursively and functionally obsolete in South Africa, newly relevant constructions of racialised identity are becoming increasingly perceptible, acquiring their own social and symbolic capital, and promising to motivate new forms of social change. An intriguing instance which may be symptomatic in its own right is the ostensibly unorchestrated initiative undertaken at more or less the same time (between November 2004 and February 2005) by three independent publishers, to launch three new magazine publications targeting black South Africans, namely *BL!NK*, *Real* and *Move!* While the simultaneous targeting of 'black' readerships is clearly a market-driven initiative undertaken by both black and white magazine producers, it may also attest, however implicitly, to recognition of a proneness among black South Africans to identify with a renegotiated, affirmative view of what choosing to be 'black' might mean. This implies a *newly normative use of black identity mediated by popular global notions of what 'being black' might mean in the global arena today*, and presents another form in which black South Africans might proclaim social membership in South Africa's middle class(es), while distinguishing their own collective identity therein. In this sense then, the appellation 'black' is optimised not as a racial category in a discriminatory or sectarian sense, but rather as a viable cultural option, one that is increasingly aspired to, and proudly so. It seems to me that a decision by black South Africans to choose to identify themselves as 'black', by producing cultural artefacts and commercial media products intended also, but not exclusively, for black readerships, resonates with the Hansa advertisements, and echoes the inclusion there of being 'black' and being 'white' as equally viable middle-class options.

Although the hypothetical suppositions voiced above clearly require extensive ethnographic verification, further inquiry in this regard should provide us with an empirical basis for more generalised theoretical conclusions regarding the motivations underlying people's choices of specific identity options, while mediating modes of what Jenkins calls 'internal self-identification' and its external categorisation (Jenkins 2004). I hope this chapter has gone some way toward suggesting that commercial media discourses and manifestations of consumer culture (be they discursive patterns, images or material goods) may provide valuable insight into what Lofgren calls 'the microphysics of learning to belong' (Lofgren 1996) and into the ways in which black South Africans in urban environments might imagine themselves as individuals, and collectively. In some sense then, I trust that I have shed light on how the mass media in post-apartheid South Africa grant black South Africans access to a vast 'marketplace' of global and local commodities, routines, linguistic practices, identities and aspirations, both trivial and esteemed, and motivate them to be actively participant in manufacturing the new fabric of their everyday lives.

Notes

1   Personal communication with Simpiwe Mpye, former editor of *BL!NK* magazine, May 2005.

2   Given present constraints, the empirical evidence in this regard cannot be presented here, but is readily available elsewhere (see Laden 2001a, 2001b, 2001c, 2003, 2004).

References

Alexander N (2006) Racial identity, citizenship and nation building in post-apartheid South Africa. Lecture delivered at the East London Campus, University of Fort Hare, 25 March

Alexander P, Dawson MC & Ichharam M (eds) (2006) *Globalization and new identities: A view from the middle*. Johannesburg: Jacana

Anderson B (1983) *Imagined communities: Reflections on the origins and spread of nationalism*. London: Verso

Appadurai A (1986) Introduction: Commodities and the politics of value. In A Appadurai (ed.) *The social life of things*, pp. 3–63. Cambridge and New York: Cambridge University Press

Appadurai A (1997) Consumption, duration, and history. In D Palumbo-Liu and HU Gumbrecht (eds) *Streams of cultural capital*, pp. 23–46. Stanford, CA: Stanford University Press

Barry A & Slater D (eds) (2005) *The technological economy*. New York and London: Routledge

Bayart J-F (1993) *The state in Africa: The politics of the belly.* London and New York: Longman

Boorstein DJ (1973) *The Americans: The democratic experience.* New York: Random House

Bourdieu P (1984/1979) *Distinction: A social critique of the judgement of taste.* Trans. R Nice. London, Melbourne and Henley: Routledge and Keagan Paul

Bourdieu P (1995) The market for symbolic goods. In *The rules of art: Genesis and structure of the literary field*, pp. 141–173. Trans. S Emanuel. Stanford, CA: Stanford University Press

Bratton M, Mattes R & Gyimah-Boadi E (2005) *Public opinion, democracy and market reform in Africa.* Cambridge: Cambridge University Press

Bronner S & Kellner D (eds) (1989) *Critical theory and society.* New York: Routledge

Burgess S (2002) *SA tribes: Who we are, how we live, what we want from life.* Cape Town: David Philip

Carrier J (ed.) (1997) *Meanings of the market: The free market in Western culture.* Oxford and New York: Berg

Ceruti C & Mudau R (2006) Perceptions about class in Soweto: Preliminary results. Paper presented at the Sociology Seminar, University of Johannesburg Soweto Campus, 10 March

Chidester D, Dexter P & James W (eds) (2003) *What holds us together: Social cohesion in South Africa.* Pretoria: HSRC Press

Comaroff J & Comaroff J (2005) Reflections on liberalism, policulturalism and ID-ology: Citizenship and difference in South Africa. In S Robins (ed.) *Limits to liberation after apartheid: Citizenship, governance and culture*, pp. 33–56. Oxford: James Currey; Athens, OH: University of Ohio Press; Cape Town: David Philip

Cooper F (1997) The dialectics of colonization: Nationalism and labor movements in postwar French Africa. In F Cooper and AL Stoler (eds) *Tensions of empire: Colonial cultures in a bourgeois world*, pp. 406–435. Berkeley and Los Angeles: University of California Press

Cooper F & Stoler AL (1997) Between metropole and colony: Rethinking a research agenda. In F Cooper and AL Stoler (eds) *Tensions of empire: Colonial cultures in a bourgeois world*, pp. 1–56. Berkeley and Los Angeles: University of California Press

Davis J (1994) Social creativity. In CM Hann (ed.) *When history accelerates: Essays on rapid social change, complexity and creativity*, pp. 95–110. London: Athlone Press

De Kock L (1996) *Civilizing barbarians: Missionary narrative and the African textual response in nineteenth-century South Africa.* Johannesburg: Wits University Press and Lovedale Press

Distiller N & Steyn M (eds) (2004) *Under construction: 'Race' and identity in South Africa today*. Sandton: Heinemann

Dlamini SN (2005) *Youth and identity politics in South Africa, 1990–1994*. Toronto: University of Toronto Press

Dolby N (2000) The shifting ground of race: The role of taste in youth's production of identities. *Race, Ethnicity and Education* 3(1): 7–23

Dolby N (2001) *Constructing race: Youth, identity, and popular culture in South Africa*. Albany: State University of New York Press

Du Gay P & Pryke M (eds) (2002) *Cultural economy: Cultural analysis and commercial life*. London and New Delhi: Sage Publications

Durham D (2002) Uncertain citizens: Herero and the new intercalary subject in postcolonial Botswana. In R Werbner (ed.) *Postcolonial subjectivities in Africa*, pp. 139–170. London and New York: Zed Books

Even-Zohar I (1994) Culture planning and the market: Making and maintaining socio-semiotic entities. Paper presented at Dartmouth Colloquium, Dartmouth College, 22–27 July

Even-Zohar I (1997) *Culture repertoire and the wealth of collective entities: Parameters for contrastive culture analysis*. Accessed 3 February 2000, http://www.tau.ac.il~itamarez

Ewen S & Ewen E (1982) *Channels of desire: Mass images and the shaping of American consciousness*. New York: McGraw Hill

Foster RJ (ed.) (1997) *Nation making: Emergent identities in postcolonial Melanesia*. Ann Arbor: University of Michigan Press

Foster RJ (1999) The commercial construction of 'new nations'. *Journal of Material Culture* 4(3): 263–282

Foster RJ (2002) *Materializing the nation: Commodities, consumption and media in Papua New Guinea*. Bloomington and Indianapolis: Indiana University Press

Fox RW & Lears TJ (eds) (1983) *The culture of consumption: Critical essays in American history, 1880–1980*. New York: Pantheon Books

Fukuyama F (1995) *Trust: The social virtues and the creation of prosperity*. New York and London: Free Press

Geshiere P (1997) *The modernity of witchcraft: Politics and the occult in postcolonial Africa*. Charlottesville and London: University of Virgina Press

Geshiere P & Nyamnjoh F (1998) Witchcraft as an issue in the 'politics of belonging': Democratisation and urban migrants' involvement with the home village. *African Studies Review* 4(3): 69–91

Gough-Yates A (2003) *Understanding women's magazines: Publishing, markets and readerships*. London and New York: Routledge

Granovetter M (1985) Economic action and economic structure: The problem of embeddedness. *American Journal of Sociology* 91: 481–510

Granovetter M (1992) Problems of explanation in economic sociology. In N Nohria and R Eccles (eds) *Networks and organizations: Structure, form and action*. Boston: Harvard Business School Press

Grossberg A, Struwig J & Pillay U (2005) Multicultural national identity and pride. In U Pillay, B Roberts and S Rule (eds) *South African social attitudes: Changing times, diverse voices*, pp. 54–76. Pretoria: HSRC Press

Harker R, Mahar C & Wilkes C (eds) (1990) Bourdieu's class. In R Harker, C Mahar and C Wilkes (eds) *An introduction to the work of Pierre Bourdieu: The practice of theory*, pp. 109–131. London: Macmillan

Hunter I (1988) *Culture and government: The emergence of literary education*. Basingstoke: Macmillan

Jakobson R (1960) Closing statement: Linguistics and poetics. In TA Sebeok (ed.) *Style and language*, pp. 350–377. Cambridge, MA: Harvard University Press

Jenkins R (2004) *Social identity*. London and New York: Routledge

Laden S (2001a) Making the paper speak well, or, the pace of change in consumer magazines for black South Africans. In 'South Africa in the global imaginary', ed. L De Kock, L Bethlehem and S Laden, special issue, *Poetics Today* 22(2): 515–548

Laden S (2001b) Consumer magazines for black South Africans: Toward a cultural economy of the South African (print) media. *Scrutiny2* 6(1): 3–16

Laden S (2001c) Magazine matters: Toward a cultural economy of South Africa's (print) media. In K Tomaselli and H Dunn (eds) *Media, democracy and renewal in southern Africa*. Denver: International Academic Publishers

Laden S (2003) Who's afraid of the black bourgeoisie? Consumer magazines for black South Africans as an apparatus of social change. *Journal of Consumer Culture* 3(2): 191–216

Laden S (2004) Making the paper speak well, or, the pace of change in consumer magazines for black South Africans. In L De Kock, L Bethlehem and S Laden (eds) *South Africa in the global imaginary*. Pretoria: University of South Africa Press; Leiden: Koninklijke Brill NV

Lamont M & Molnar V (2001) How blacks use consumption to shape their collective identity: Evidence from marketing specialists. *Journal of Consumer Culture* 1: 31–45

LiPuma E (1997) The formation of nation-states in national cultures in Oceania. In RJ Foster (ed.) *Nation making: Emergent identities in postcolonial Melanesia*, pp. 33–68. Ann Arbor: University of Michigan Press

Lofgren O (1996) The nation as home or motel? On the ethnography of belonging. *Anthropologica Newsletter* (October): 33–34

Mangcu X (2001) Liberating race from apartheid. *Transformation* 47: 18–27

Marchand R (1985) *Advertising the American dream: Making way for modernity, 1920–1940.* London and Berkeley: University of California Press

Masenyama KP (2005) National identity in post-apartheid South Africa: SABC TV's contribution. MA thesis, University of Johannesburg

McCracken G (1990) *Culture and consumption: New approaches to the symbolic character of consumer goods and activities.* Bloomington and Indianapolis: Indiana University Press

McFall L (2004) *Advertising: A cultural economy.* London and New Delhi: Sage Publications

Miller D (1995) *Acknowledging consumption: A review of new studies.* London and New York: Routledge

Miller D (1997) *Capitalism: An ethnographic approach.* Oxford: Berg

Miller D (2002) The unintended political economy. In P du Gay and M Pryke (eds) *Cultural economy: Cultural analysis and commercial life*, pp. 166–184. London and New Delhi: Sage Publications

Morrell R (2001) *Changing men in southern Africa.* London and New York: Zed Books

Morrell R & Ouzgane L (eds) (2005) *African masculinities: Men in Africa from the late nineteenth century to the present.* New York: Palgrave; Pietermaritzburg: University of KwaZulu-Natal Press

Niehaus I (with E Mohlala and K Shokane) (2001) *Witchcraft, power and politics: Exploring the occult in the South African Lowveld.* Claremont, Cape Town: David Philip

Nuttall S (2004) Stylizing the self: The Y generation in Rosebank, Johannesburg. In 'Johannesburg: The Elusive Metropolis', ed. A Mbembe and S Nuttall, special issue, *Public Culture* 16(3): 430–452

Nuttall S (2006) A politics of the emergent: Cultural studies in South Africa. *Theory, Culture and Society* 23(7–8): 263–278

Nuttall S & Michaels C-A (eds) (2000) *Senses of culture: South African cultural studies.* Cape Town: Oxford University Press

Nyamnjoh F (2000) 'For many are called but few are chosen': Globalisation and popular disenchantment in Africa. *African Sociological Review* 4(2): 1–45

Pickering M (2001) *Stereotyping: The politics of representation.* Basingstoke: Palgrave

Pieterse E & Meintjies F (eds) (2003) *Voices of the transition: The politics, poetics and practices of social change in South Africa.* Sandton: Heinemann

Posel D (2001) What's in a name? Racial categorisations under apartheid and their afterlife. *Transformation* 47: 50–74

Ratele K (ed.) (2006) *Inter-group relations: A South African perspective.* Cape Town: Juta

Ray L & Sayer A (eds) (1999) Introduction. In L Ray and A Sayer (eds) *Culture and economy after the cultural turn.* London: Sage Publications

Ribane N (2006) *Beauty: A black perspective.* Pietermaritzburg: University of KwaZulu-Natal Press

Sahlins M (1976) *Culture and practical reason.* Chicago and London: Chicago University Press

Sela-Sheffy R (1997) Models and habituses: Problems in the idea of cultural repertoires. *Canadian Review of Comparative Literature* 24(1): 35–47

Simpson J & Dore B (2004) *Marketing in South Africa: Cases and concepts.* Pretoria: Van Schaik

Swartz D (1997) Culture and power: The sociology of Pierre Bourdieu. Chicago and London: University of Chicago Press

Swidler A (1986) Culture in action: Symbols and strategies. *American Sociological Review* 51: 273–286

Turner C (1992) *Modernity and politics in the work of Max Weber.* London: Routledge

Wasserman H & Jacobs S (eds) (2003) *Shifting selves: Post-apartheid essays on mass media, culture and identity.* Cape Town: Kwela Books

Wernick A (1991) *Promotional culture: Advertising, ideology and symbolic expression.* London and New Delhi: Sage Publications

Wilk R (1995) Learning to be local in Belize: Global systems of common difference. In D Miller (ed.) *Worlds apart: Modernity through the prism of the local,* pp. 110–133. New York and London: Routledge

Zegeye A (ed.) (2001) *Social identities in the new South Africa.* Vol. 1 of *After apartheid.* Cape Town: Kwela Books and SA History Online

Zegeye A & Harris RL (2003) *Media, identity and the public sphere in post-apartheid South Africa.* Leiden and Boston: Brill

Zegeye A & Krieger R (eds) (2001) *Culture in the new South Africa.* Vol. 2 of *After apartheid.* Cape Town: Kwela Books and SA History Online

Media restructuring and identity formation after apartheid

7 Finding a home in Afrikaans radio

Johannes Froneman

The performance of a communication system can be measured by determining if it is 'a public cultural space that is open, diverse and accessible' (Golding & Murdock 1996: 18). As has been argued numerous times, South Africa did not meet these criteria prior to 1990 (see Tomaselli et al. 1987). Although it is also widely accepted that huge changes have taken place since that time, no definitive, comprehensive history of these changes has been written. Although some attempts have been made to describe these changes, they tend to be somewhat impressionistic (Berger 2001; Froneman 1997, 2006; Teer-Tomaselli & Tomaselli 2001; Van Kessel 1998). I will not attempt (another) 'overview' of the total industry here, but instead focus on a facet of this unfolding story within the broadcast sector, while recognising that these developments were not unrelated to changes happening in the rest of the media industry.

This chapter will therefore give a brief overview of the broadcast media inasmuch as it forms the backdrop to the micro-histories or case studies offered here, namely those of two Afrikaans radio stations: the present radiosondergrense (radio without borders), more commonly known by its acronym RSG (formerly Radio Suid-Afrika/Afrikaans Stereo of the South African Broadcasting Corporation [SABC]), and Radio Pretoria, a community radio station. The focus is on how these Afrikaans radio stations contribute to a variety of voices befitting a plural democracy, thereby providing homes to a diversified ethnic group and those who merely regard themselves as 'Afrikaans'.

How Afrikaans radio stations have developed since 1990

RSG and Radio Pretoria are products of the interplay between the political, economic, cultural and social changes which characterised the 1990s. In this period the Afrikaner establishment ceded control of the SABC to the new ruling class, that is the black majority, mostly represented by the alliance of the African National Congress (ANC), the South African Communist Party (SACP) and the Congress of South African Trade Unions. A new, more representative board with a black (ANC-supporting) chairperson was appointed and old-guard executives were replaced, mostly by black people, that is, Africans, coloureds and Indians (in the parlance of old apartheid South Africa, subsequently perpetuated by the new government). While the SABC had always been owned by the people of South Africa, there were obviously huge implications for policy and content when the black majority gained control (i.e. ownership) of the national broadcaster.

Since television broadcasts commenced in 1976 it had never been financially feasible to have separate television channels for all languages. Channels were thus divided between an Afrikaans/English channel and one for African indigenous languages. This reflected more than mere cultural and language realities; it was apartheid thinking in action, and inevitably had to change when the country was put on the road to a multiracial, multi-ethnic, multilingual democracy. A policy of deliberately mixing the ethnic, racial and language diversity of programming was applied to television with ideological fervour. It was a concerted attempt at forging a new 'rainbow nation'. All SABC viewers were effectively forced to watch the same channels, but the policy was flawed as many viewers were confronted with programmes in languages they did not understand. After a time some common sense prevailed, but the essence of the changes was retained, that is, Afrikaans was relegated to a less prominent position (Froneman 1994). This trend has continued. News continues to be presented in all 11 official languages, but although the Constitution makes no such provision, English is, consistent with government practice, given pre-eminence.

Although the SABC has a clear public service obligation, commercial imperatives have become more prominent. Ideological power struggles have also left their mark. Key positions (chairperson, chief executive and head of news) have changed hands regularly. Not surprisingly, commentators have questioned the concentration of 'absolute powers' within the organisation, and suggested that the 'new ruling elite' has the potential to be just as bad as the apartheid authorities they have replaced (Pamphele, quoted in Nyamnjoh 2005: 65). The news service in particular has been a target of critics, who claim that it is biased towards the ANC/SACP government. While much more balanced than in pre-1990 days, the serial power struggles and suppression of critical voices do not help to allay fears of an authoritarian undercurrent at the national broadcaster.

The typical nation-building rhetoric of the development media model was espoused by the ANC and its allies even before the 1994 elections (Froneman

& De Beer 1993) and subsequently introduced in the SABC's slogans (for example, 'We are one'), news coverage (as in its treatment of developmental issues, particularly regarding the poor rural population), and programming, even in popular TV soap operas (such as the Afrikaans series *Sewende Laan* [Seventh Avenue]).

Concurrently with the changes at the SABC, satellite television, controlled by Multichoice, a South African company with reach into many African countries, has become a dominant player. This illustrates the commercial (or market) character of modern television, with its emphasis on never-ending choice: live sport, 24-hour news, movies, reality shows, music video channels, and a dedicated Afrikaans channel, kykNet, a small reminder that the SABC cannot adequately cater for this language group in terms of its ideological preferences and commercial imperative.

The same commercial imperative motivates e.tv, the only free-to-air non-SABC channel. The e.tv news programmes have a stronger Cape Town flavour, a notable departure from the usual Johannesburg-centred SABC broadcasts. The station insisted for some time on using Cape Town as a starting point for its weather forecasts (but has since relented and adopted the SABC norm of a Gauteng starting point), and gives reporters and presenters from the coloured (mixed-race) and Indian communities significant airtime. This may be motivated purely by commercial interests, aiming to capture a larger audience amongst certain viewers, particularly from the two minority groups which are arguably under-represented on the SABC's television channels. But e.tv also gives these groups (and the geographic areas where they predominantly live, the Western Cape and KwaZulu-Natal) a greater visibility on the news programmes.

Most of the SABC's regional radio stations were sold to private, black empowerment companies, creating powerful new media players focused overwhelmingly on the goal of financial success. The bilingual (Afrikaans/English) format was discarded in some instances (Radio Port Natal, Radio Algoa and Highveld Stereo), presumably to attract bigger, more profitable audiences who accept English as a radio lingua franca.

The English radio service, with its somewhat elitist style, was rebranded SAFM, rid of many of its white, BBC-sounding announcers, and recreated as a vehicle for all South Africans who spoke and/or understood English. This was not unlike the changes made at RSG, as discussed below.

A development of huge importance was the creation of the totally new community radio sector. Some 90 community radio stations were licensed by the newly created Independent Broadcast Authority (now called the Independent Communication Authority of South Africa [ICASA]). This created new zones of public discourse never before experienced in South Africa. Minority religious groups (such as Islam) and smaller ethnic groups (for example, Greeks and Chinese) have been afforded the opportunity to start radio stations. This development was particularly important to all minority groups, including Afrikaans communities stripped of their former status and power (Froneman 1995).

Adding to the ever-expanding mix of radio stations, an even smaller group, the San, received help from the SABC to start a community radio service. !Xu-Kwe, or X-K FM, has been set up for this small, near-extinct group of people, the original inhabitants of large parts of southern Africa who mostly speak Afrikaans (*Mail & Guardian* 2000; SABC 2006).

While the broadcast media have thus become significantly more commercially driven and prone to domination by large companies, ethnic groups have gained access to and representation in some areas of the media. But these developments have not significantly empowered people with little or no media access, particularly those in poor rural areas and townships. The government has reacted to this situation by launching the Media Development and Diversity Agency (see Froneman & Pretorius 2000; MDDA 2006).

Notwithstanding perceived and real problems, the South African broadcast media system has democratised significantly. It has become a more open, diverse and accessible sector, based on a core public service broadcast system encircled by private music stations and a variety of community radio stations (see Curran 2000: 148).

Underlying these changes is, on the one hand, a strong drive to create an idealised 'South African nation' free from the boundaries set up and maintained by the apartheid system; but, on the other hand, the reality of 11 official languages, ethnic and cultural differences and significant internal differences within ethnic groups has to be faced (see Blom 1998: 74–85).

Against this background the reconstruction of the SABC's Afrikaans radio service and the creation of a reactionary Afrikaans community radio station, Radio Pretoria, have taken place. These developments go to the heart of the

reality of being a minority ethnic group, and the former oppressor; they touch on the question of whether the Afrikaner group should:
- accept incorporation into a wider South African 'nation', inevitably losing its distinct language; or
- accept incorporation into a wider South African 'nation', but only as part of an inclusive Afrikaans-language community; or
- emphasise its ethnic identity and maintain boundaries aggressively, if need be (see Barth 1998: 33).

As Gandy (2000: 50) notes, complex factors 'push and pull individuals towards diffusion and assimilation or the maintenance of social–cultural distinctiveness within the dominant society'. How have these and other political, cultural and commercial factor shaped RSG and Radio Pretoria? And how have these radio stations become sites of struggle in the creation of meaning for an ethnic and language group stripped of former securities as well as political and economic power? How has RSG become a new zone of interracial unity built on shared language and religious interests?

The reconstruction of the Afrikaans radio service

As the flagship of the old SABC, Radio Suid-Afrika/Afrikaans Stereo had a distinct character. It was a conservative cultural station with a formal style, strong Afrikaner establishment links and far better resources than the radio stations for indigenous languages. To survive in a new democratic, non-racial, market-driven environment, the station had to shed its staid apartheid image and reinvent itself step by step with a much smaller budget (see *Beeld* 1996; Raubenheimer 2004a). Afrikaans Stereo (as the station was then called) was rebranded as RSG in 1996. This signalled its break with its conservative past, particularly regarding the maintenance of a narrowly defined Afrikaner identity (see Retief 2004). (Omitting 'Afrikaans' from the name was part of a corporate decision by the new SABC; all 11 public service radio stations were rebranded as part of the transformation process.)

A large number of white staff was retrenched or put on early retirement, cutting staff numbers from 105 to 29 (*Beeld* 1998; Breytenbach 1995). These steps by the new SABC management, perceived to be attacks on Afrikaans, initially caused an outcry. Meanwhile a station manager (Mohamed Shaikh), announcers and journalists from a coloured background were appointed, stressing the non-racial character of this Afrikaans station (see Nieuwoudt 2003a, 2003b; Steyn 2003). This perhaps contributed to the acceptance of the concept of a non-racial Afrikaans-language community within the broader South African nation (see Du Plessis 2006). The present station manager, Magdaleen Kruger, the first woman to be appointed to the position, notes that certain white announcers now have a huge personal following amongst coloured listeners; likewise, coloured announcers enjoy enthusiastic support from white listeners.[1]

Programme formats were adapted, for example by introducing more live programmes and interactive phone-ins, and having less music during the day which could be described as 'elitist' (i.e. classical music). For the first time white and coloured Afrikaans speakers shared a zone of public discourse cheek by jowl. More importantly, controversial topics are now addressed freely. Programmes such as *Praat saam* (Join the conversation) and particularly *Sê wie?* (Says who?) have become institutions, allowing ordinary people to air their diverse views via the telephone – thus offering interactive radio in the democratic-participatory mould (see McQuail 1989: 121–123).

This move towards freedom of expression has been informed by the new political paradigm. Not surprisingly, RSG sees its task as breaking down old barriers by encouraging reconciliation and tolerance.[2]

To give momentum to the non-racial, inclusive policies of the new SABC, even programme names which could somehow be connected with old-style apartheid were scrapped or adapted to fit the new, inclusive approach (Froneman 1997). The programme *Alle volke loof die Here* (All peoples praise the Lord) was changed to *Loof die Here*, thus omitting the word '*volk*', a central word in the vocabulary of *volksnasionalisme* (people's nationalism). Thus, while being adapted, programmes important to the station's predominantly Christian listeners have been retained, albeit now produced by an independent Christian media group. A recent straw poll conducted on RSG's website indicated that the vast majority (70 per cent) of those taking part in the poll regarded the religious programmes as the most important (RSG 2006). While this does not provide a definitive snapshot of all its listeners' preferences, it underscores why RSG's managers have been careful not to offend the religious sensibilities of listeners. It also supports the contention that owners, advertisers and managers 'cannot always do as they wish' (Golding & Murdock 1996: 15).

Another subtle change was made to the language programme *Die taal wat ons praat* (The language we speak). The singular *taal* (language) was replaced with the plural *tale* (languages), thus shedding any suggestion of exclusion. But in practice, the programme still focuses on Afrikaans, the common denominator of the listenership. A noteworthy broadcast was a Christmas play in colloquial Afrikaans in 2004 (*Beeld* 2004). This underscored RSG's acceptance of different forms of Afrikaans.

The use of correct Afrikaans was, in line with the prevailing nationalism of the time, an important characteristic of the old Afrikaans radio service. A full-time language adviser helped to implement a policy of strict adherence to standards. This was discontinued as deep personnel cuts were implemented. The emphasis shifted to a more relaxed attitude towards Afrikaans and broadcasting in general; Sarel Myburgh, a former programme manager who did much to transform RSG, acknowledged this (Nieuwoudt 2000a). This has resulted in sporadic media debates and a steady stream of letters bemoaning the perceived neglect of Afrikaans by the SABC in general and RSG in particular (for example Nieuwoudt 2003c; Olivier 2003; Raubenheimer 2004b). Now the pendulum has shifted back somewhat; a part-time language adviser has been appointed and a significant amount has been invested in a computer programme which gives announcers instant access to correct language usage and pronunciation.[3]

Although some white listeners migrated to newly founded community radio stations which preserved the more conservative ethos of the old Afrikaans radio service, RSG's listenership numbers shot up as coloured Afrikaans-speaking listeners previously excluded were attracted in large numbers (Nieuwoudt 2000b). Some 35 per cent of RSG's listeners are now drawn from the coloured community and this figure is set to rise as the station plans to offer even more programmes, presenters, topics and guests aimed at attracting listeners from this group.[4]

RSG's public service mandate requires it to offer a broad spectrum of programmes, including programmes sensitive to the developmental needs of its listeners. Educational or service programmes form a popular part of the station's mix, supplemented by the station's growing support of 'community service investment', that is, social responsibility towards all needy Afrikaans speakers.[5]

RSG has broadened its focus even further, now aiming to inform, educate and entertain all who can understand Afrikaans. This even includes black Sotho speakers.[6] The station's inclusive approach has resulted in a marked increase in listeners: in the past 7 years listenership has grown from just above 500 000 to nearly 1.9 million.

This could not have happened without retention of the bulk of white Afrikaans-speaking listeners. While they may not all support the station manager's views on ethnicity ('I don't regard myself as an Afrikaner, but I am proudly Afrikaans...' [Retief 2004]), they have, at least to some extent, embraced being Afrikaans in a non-racial context. This is remarkable, considering the fact that 50 per cent of all RSG listeners are over 50 years old.

However, more conservative-minded (white) listeners express their views clearly enough, for example on talk shows and in letters to the press. But while management is careful when considering changes, station manager Magdaleen Kruger denies pandering to these listeners.[7]

While there is no indication that RSG wants to maintain any boundaries other than those set by its language, the station still offers a home to more conservative Afrikaners. Could it be that in some instances this is merely because RSG has a countrywide footprint, and respects the cultural and religious views of its more conservative listeners? For other Afrikaners unimpressed by the more progressive attitude permeating RSG, Afrikaans community radio stations (often with a strong Christian character) already provide an alternative sphere where meaning is constructed in a manner compatible with their sensibilities.

To some extent RSG's management finds itself squeezed between conflicting philosophies and commercial and political demands (see Nieuwoudt 2003a; Prins 2003).[8] It has to tread a fine line when targeting the 'modern, progressive' under-50-year-old Afrikaans-speaking community, as the SABC's website claims (SABC 2007).

Fortunately, RSG's station manager embraces this objective without writing off the 50-plus age group. In any case, it cannot be assumed that the 50-plus group is all-white and reactionary. Likewise, there is no solid research to indicate which socio-economic class dominates RSG's listenership, which negates any attempt at relating RSG's changes to purely or even predominantly economic forces (see Golding & Murdock 1996: 15 [AU: Again, this item not in the References list; please supply details.]). The same applies to Radio Pretoria.

The construction of Radio Pretoria

The founding of Radio Pretoria, a station for 'Boer Afrikaners', in 1993 was a direct result of the collapse of Afrikaner hegemony in the early 1990s. The loss of political power, the general fear of lawlessness as experienced in many African countries when colonial powers withdrew, and the transformation of the SABC and its Afrikaans radio station, created a vacuum which Radio Pretoria and a number of other Afrikaans community radio stations could potentially fill.

Radio Pretoria was textbook radio for the people, by the people and gave a voice to those with an exclusive definition of Afrikaner identity which they did not want to sacrifice in the name of a multiracial democracy or 'rainbow nation'. Initially the station was at the heart of reactionary resistance to the new democratic dispensation (see for example Stofberg 1994). Later, spokesperson Jaap Diederichs was more accepting of the new dispensation, but with an important requirement. He stated, 'We don't want to go back to apartheid, we want more say in a real, new South Africa that accommodates all our differences' (Carrol 2002). He even mentioned a positive contribution that the station could make to the new South Africa, but once again with an important caveat:

> We aim at maintaining and strengthening Afrikaner identity, we are a '*volk*' [people's] radio station...a station of interest for Boere Afrikaners...We are making a good contribution to the new South Africa in our own way, in our own style. (Media24 2003b)

The station, which is owned by a not-for-profit company, encountered strong opposition from other Afrikaners from the outset (see for example Fourie 1993) and the former (white) Nationalist government (Grobler 1993; Lötter 1993). After the ANC came to power, the station was granted a licence by the then Independent Broadcasting Authority (Bezuidenhout 1995), but its battle to stay on the air continued. It broadcast 'legally', but without a licence, for some time, pending a ruling by the court of appeals (De Bruin 2005; Kruger 2006; Media24 2003a; *Volksblad* 1999, 2000). The court ruled in Radio Pretoria's favour in 2007 (De Bruin 2007).

Earlier, it had taken ICASA a year to release its reasons for refusing Radio Pretoria a licence in 2003. The reasons were, inter alia, that the station did not employ any people of colour and that there was no need for Radio Pretoria as it did not add anything to what was already offered by RSG, the Afrikaans-language service of the SABC (Media24 2004). This claim is rejected by Radio Pretoria as ludicrous.[9]

What, then, does Radio Pretoria offer its listeners? Unlike the SABC's RSG, Radio Pretoria does not embrace the new political dispensation, although it (now) accepts that it has to abide by the laws of the land. It is unashamedly conservative and refuses to accept the symbols of the new South Africa; for example it still plays the old apartheid-era national anthem, *Die Stem*. The station still refers to places in South Africa and further afield by obsolete geographic names such as the Transvaal, South West Africa (Namibia) and even Rhodesia (Zimbabwe).

On a cultural level, Radio Pretoria to some extent echoes the content and style of the old SABC Afrikaans service (see Radio Pretoria 2006; Roscher 1999). It is, however, not elitist (as the old Afrikaans service was). But to make its position unequivocal, Radio Pretoria adopted the slogan '*Radio met grense*' (Radio *with* borders), in direct opposition to RSG's earlier slogan and present name (*radiosondergrense*, i.e. radio *without* borders).

Ex-announcers and presenters on the SABC's old Afrikaans service continued through the years to crop up amongst the small band of committed Radio Pretoria staff, adding to the feeling that this station is, to some extent, the spiritual successor to the former Afrikaans service.

In content terms, Radio Pretoria offers a mixture of music, news, sport, service and educational programmes. It plays a mixture of Afrikaans and other popular music, notably also nostalgic German music, but avoids music with 'too much beat' (Media24 2003b).

News bulletins focus regularly on crime and issues of direct importance to Afrikaners. According to management, the station struggles to find enough positive news to fill news bulletins, resulting in much publicity for the opposition Democratic Alliance (DA).[10] However, Radio Pretoria is not pro-DA; it supports *volksgerigte* (i.e. Afrikaner-centred) parties. The station's news commentary (which is a throwback to the old apartheid-supporting news commentary broadcast by the SABC prior to 1990) takes strong conservative views on issues relevant to its listeners' safety and survival as a people (Radio Pretoria 2006).

The station's Christian ethos is reflected in its broadcast of, inter alia, church services, *huisgodsdiens* (family worship) and other religious programmes. But critics will certainly question the whites-only policy of Radio Pretoria and ask if this is consistent with Christian love and charity.

Given Radio Pretoria's *raison d'être*, it is not surprising that its social responsibility programme is titled *Volkshulp 2000* (Helping our people 2000). Other programmes also reflect the nationalist inclinations of the station: *Volksmikrofoon* (People's microphone) and *Vandag uit ons volksverlede* (Today in the history of our people).

Notwithstanding its roots in *volksnasionalisme*, as confirmed by the Boer flags and portraits of victories over the Zulus in the studio, Diederichs insists that Radio Pretoria is about the politics of the future, not nostalgia (Carrol 2002). It is about self-sufficiency and claiming the right of not wanting to form part of the Mandela-inspired 'rainbow nation' (Robinson 2004). According to Diederichs, the station is forward-looking and aims at giving Boer Afrikaners courage to face the future.[11] It claims the right to produce meaning in a manner consistent with its world-view. It contradicts the SABC's political correctness as well as the homogenising hegemony of commercial music radio stations.

While it serves a relatively small section of the white Afrikaans community, it receives enough support from small donors and non-mainstream advertising to claim to be in good financial health.[12] As such it survives on the non-corporate economic power of small-time Afrikanerdom – a far cry from the much more corporately reliant RSG, which can also count on the support of traditional Afrikaans institutions such as the ATKV (Afrikaanse Taal- en Kultuurvereniging).

Conclusion

While the SABC's Afrikaans radio service has been reconstructed as a non-racial station in step with the new political dispensation, Radio Pretoria could be regarded as ideologically reactionary by clinging to Afrikaner *volksnasionalisme*. In a sense it takes the listener back to a bygone era, but it insists on being focused on a self-sufficient future.

While RSG accepts incorporation into a wider South African 'nation', it actively supports the construction of an inclusive Afrikaans-language community, but within the ideological and economic framework prescribed by the ruling class. Radio Pretoria, on the other hand, emphasises its *Boere Afrikaner* ethnic identity and tries to maintain its boundaries without compromise. The stations thus represent fundamentally different philosophies and economic bases. While RSG pays its way handsomely by treading a careful ideological path in an environment less accommodating towards the former 'language of the oppressor', Radio Pretoria chooses the opposite.

Both are entrenched in ideological positions vis-à-vis the new political dispensation: RSG provides a home for those who accept a non-racial country, with some recognition of language and cultural diversity; Radio Pretoria insists on the right to reject the dominant political paradigm, while pragmatically seeking to find some minimum accommodation and ensure cultural and economic survival.

But both (RSG by implication and Radio Pretoria explicitly) reject incorporation if this would put Afrikaans terminally at risk. Those Afrikaans speakers who are becoming anglicised have probably already migrated to the wide range of English-language radio stations on offer locally (or overseas). The reality is that those who regard themselves as Afrikaners, or merely Afrikaans-speaking, are a highly diversified 'group' which ideally needs diverse stations, particularly if one accepts that Afrikaans speakers are part of different socio-economic groups. This is, of course, equally true for all other ethnic and language groups.

Should ethnic boundary maintenance become impossible within a public service SABC which only pays lip service to diversity and access, or restricts its meaning to superficial language differences, more ethnic Afrikaners comfortable within a multicultural plural democracy could decide to seek a cultural and spiritual home with stations which do not shy away from giving substance to their ethnicity.

If this argument is correct, economic considerations are clearly insufficient to explain the depth of emotional commitment towards Afrikaans as a language of discourse and carrier of certain cultural and religious values.

Notes

1   M Kruger interview (2006a).
2   M Kruger interview (2006a).
3   M Kruger interview (2006a).
4   M Kruger interview (2006a).
5   M Kruger interview (2006a).
6   M Kruger interview (2006a).

7   M Kruger interview (2006b).
8   See also M Kruger interview (2006a).
9   J Diederichs interview.
10 J Diederichs interview.
11 J Diederichs interview.
12 J Diederichs interview.

References

Barth F (ed.) (1998) *Ethnic groups and boundaries*. Long Grove, IL: Waveland

Beeld (1996) Afrikaans Stereo se begroting verklein. 11 June. Accessed 10 March 2006, http://152.111.1.251/argief/berigte/beeld/1996/06/11/4/1.html

Beeld (1998) RSG groei sterk ondanks kwaai mededinging. 3 September. Accessed 10 March 2006, http://152.111.1.251/argief/berigte/beeld/1998/09/3/4/6.html

Beeld (2004) RSG bied propvol Kersprogram. 24 December. Accessed 9 March 2006, http://152.111.1.251/argief/berigte/beeld/2004/12/24/B1/18/02.html

Berger G (2001) Deracialisation, democracy and development: Transformation of the South African media. In K Tomaselli and R Dunn (eds) *Media, democracy and renewal in southern Africa*. Denver, CO: International Academic Publishers

Bezuidenhout N (1995) Radio Pretoria wettig terug met uitsaailisensie. *Beeld*, 28 April. Accessed 10 March 2006, http://152.111.1.251/argief/berigte/beeld/1995/04/28/6/7.html

Blom J-P (1998) Ethnic and cultural differentiation. In F Barth (ed.) *Ethnic groups and boundaries*. Long Grove, IL: Waveland

Breytenbach P (1995) Baie woelinge by Afrikaans Stereo. *Beeld*, 17 August. Accessed 10 March 2006, http://152.111.1.251/argief/berigte/beeld/1995/08/17/5/1.html

Carrol R (2002) Radio Pretoria rallies supremacists. *Guardian*, 26 November. Accessed 11 March 2006, http://www.guardian.co.uk/international/story/0,,847626,00.html

Curran J (2000) Rethinking media and democracy. In J Curran and M Guscvitch (eds) *Mass media and society* (3rd edition). London: Arnold

De Bruin P (2005) Radiostasie saai uit sonder lisensie. Accessed 8 March 2006, http://152.111.1.251/argief/berigte/volksblad/2005/11/08/VB/6/04.html

De Bruin P (2007) Pretoriase radiostasie wen regstryd oor lisensie. Accessed 24 October 2007, http://152.111.1.251/argief/berigte/beeld/2007/06/11/B1/3/aabatars_08-06-07 (13-31-51)pdbruin-347.html

Du Plessis T (2006) Hoekom Maties so woes baklei. *Rapport*, 12 March. Accessed March 2006, http://www.news24.com/Rapport/Standpunte/0,,752-823_1896325,00.html

Fourie C (1993) Radio Pretoria wil nou 12 uur per dag uitsaai. *Beeld*, 2 October. Accessed 10 March 2006, http://152.111.1.251/argief/berigte/beeld/1993/10/2/10/13.html

Froneman JD (1994) Elke keer ander redes om Afrikaans kant toe te klap. *Die Burger*, 22 November

Froneman JD (1995) Mediatransformasie: ons almal se kans. *Woord en Daad* Somer: 14–15

Froneman JD (1997) Mediatransformasie dek tafel vir nuwe joernalistiek. *Literator* 18(3): 199–220

Froneman JD (2006) Expanding the zones of free public discourse in post-apartheid South Africa, 1990–2005. Paper presented at conference on Modern Mass Media and Public Sphere: New Challenges and Opportunities for Democracy, Moscow, Russia, 13–16 June

Froneman JD & De Beer AS (1993) The Afrikaans press: Heading for demise or a constructive role in a plural democracy? *Communicatio* 19(2): 52–64

Froneman JD & Pretorius K (2000) Towards a common-sense typology and democratic philosophy for South Africa's community media. *Communicatio* 26(2): 60–64

Gandy OH (2000) Race, ethnicity and segmentation of media markets. In J Curran and M Guscvitch (eds) *Mass media and society* (3rd edition). London: Arnold

Golding P & Murdock G (1996) Culture, communication and political economy. In J Curran and M Guscvitch (eds) *Mass media and society* (2nd edition). London: Arnold

Grobler L (1993) Regse radiostasie voldoen nie aan Kabinet se riglyne nie. *Beeld*, 19 November. Accessed 10 March 2006, http://152.111.1.251/argief/berigte/beeld/1993/11/19/15/8.html

Kruger E (2006) Gemeenskapstasies kry lisensieskok. Accessed 7 March 2006, http://152.111.1.251/argief/berigte/volksblad/2003/10/13/VB/3k/06.html

Lötter F (1993) Stem van AKB se Radio Pretoria is stilgemaak. *Beeld*, 21 September. Accessed 10 March 2006, http://152.111.1.251/argief/berigte/beeld/1993/09/21/2/16.html

Mail & Guardian (2000) A voice in the wilderness. 20 December. Accessed 15 March 2006, http://www.mg.co.za/articledirect.aspx?area=mg_flat&articleid=162596

McQuail D (1989) *Mass communication theory*. London: Sage Publications

MDDA (Media Development and Diversity Agency) (2006) *Home page of the Media Development and Diversity Agency*. Accessed 10 March 2006, http://www.mdda.org.za

Media24 (2003a) Radio Pretoria may fight on. 27 March. Accessed 8 March 2006, http://www.news24.com/News24/South_Africa/Politics/0,,2-7-12_1339413,00.html

Media24 (2003b) 'Volk' radio station bugged. 12 November. Accessed 8 March 2006, http://www.news24.com/News24/South_Africa/News/0,,2-7-1442_1444426,00.html

Media24 (2004) Radio Pretoria airs its views. 14 May. Accessed 8 March 2006, http://www.news24.com/News24/South_Africa/News/0,,2-7-1442_1527304,00.html

Nieuwoudt S (2000a) Radio sonder grense op TV en internet. *Beeld*, 13 October. Accessed 9 March 2006, http://152.111.1.251/argief/berigte/beeld/2000/10/13/17/1.html

Nieuwoudt S (2000b) Maphai is beïndruk deur Afrikaans se programgehalte. *Beeld*, 20 October. Accessed 9 March 2006, http://152.111.1.251/argief/berigte/beeld/2000/10/20/17/1.html

Nieuwoudt S (2003a) Jong Afrikaanse kultuur in SAUK nodig. *Beeld*, 16 May. Accessed 9 March 2006, http://152.111.1.251/argief/berigte/beeld/2003/05/16/15/2.html

Nieuwoudt S (2003b) Oor teen die grond SAUK-hoof kan nie vir 'n oomblik stilsit nie. *Beeld*, 24 May. Accessed 9 March 2006, http://152.111.1.251/argief/berigte/beeld/2003/05/24/11/5.html

Nieuwoudt S (2003c) Boetman met die een gesig. *Beeld*, 31 May. Accessed 9 March 2006, http://152.111.1.251/argief/berigte/beeld/2003/05/31/15/4.html

Nyamnjoh FB (2005) *Africa's media, democracy and the politics of belonging*. London: Zed Books

Olivier C (2003) Afrikaans is SAUK se Aspoestertjie. *Beeld*, 27 October. Accessed 9 March 2006, http://152.111.1.251/argief/berigte/beeld/2003/10/27/B1/12/09.html

Prins J (2003) RSG-skuiwe laat gaping. *Beeld*, 2 July. Accessed 9 March 2006, http://152.111.1.251/argief/berigte/beeld/2003/07/02/B1/10/05.html

Radio Pretoria (2006) *Home page of Radio Pretoria*. Accessed 15 March 2006, http://www.radiopretoria.co.za

Raubenheimer L (2004a) Niekie is g'n geskors nie. *Noord-Son*, 27 August. Accessed 9 March 2006, http://152.111.1.251/argief/berigte/beeld/2004/08/27/SN/04/01.html

Raubenheimer L (2004b) Keurig. Keurig. Kleurvol. *Noord-Son*, 24 September. Accessed 9 March 2006, http://152.111.1.251/argief/berigte/beeld/2004/09/24/SN/05/01.html

Retief H (2004) G'n Afrikaner nie, maar trots Afrikaans. *Rapport*, 13 June. Accessed 14 March 2006, http://152.111.1.251/argief/berigte/rapport/2004/06/13/R1/16/01.html

Robinson S (2004) Learning to let go. *Time*, 11 April. Accessed 11 March 2006, http://www.time.com/time/europe/html/040419/afrikaner.html

Roscher AFC (1999) Die koei en die bus. *Volksblad*, 16 September. Accessed 8 March 2006, http://152.111.1.251/argief/berigte/volksblad/1999/09/16/6/26.html

RSG (2006) *Listeners poll on the question: Which programmes do you regard as most important?* Accessed 9 March 2006, www.rsg.co.za

SABC (South African Broadcasting Corporation) (2006) *Home page of the SABC.* Accessed 15 March 2006, http://www.sabc.co.za/portal/site/corporate/menuitem.01b93ed679dcd7e48891f2e75401aeb9/

SABC (2007) *Home page of the SABC.* Accessed 24 October 2007, http://www.sabc.co.za/portal/site/corporate/menuitem.01b93ed679dcd7e48891f2e75401aeb9/

Steyn J (2003) Afrikaans betaal vir transformasie. *Beeld,* 27 May. Accessed 9 March 2006, http://152.111.1.251/argief/berigte/beeld/2003/05/27/12/11.html

Stofberg A (1994) Regses brand nuwe vlag omdat hulle bose 666 daarin sien. *Beeld,* 19 November. Accessed 10 March 2006, http://152.111.1.251/argief/berigte/beeld/1994/03/28/7/4.html

Teer-Tomaselli R & Tomaselli K (2001) Transformation, nation-building and the South African media. In K Tomaselli and R Dunn (eds) *Media, democracy and renewal in southern Africa.* Denver, CO: International Academic Publishers

Tomaselli R, Tomaselli K & Muller J (eds) (1987) *Narrating the crisis.* Bellville: Anthropos

Van Kessel I (1998) Mass media in South Africa: From liberation to black empowerment. Paper presented at the African Studies Centre seminar 'The role of media in Africa', Leiden, The Netherlands, 8 October. Accessed 14 March 2006, http://www.ascleiden.nl/GetPage.aspx?url=publications/wmjvankessel

Volksblad (1999) Hofsaak noop OUO om uitreiking op te skort. 18 October. Accessed 8 March 2006, http://152.111.1.251/argief/berigte/volksblad/1999/10/18/3/11.html

Volksblad (2000) Openbare verhore van media aanbeveel. 23 January. Accessed 8 March 2006, http://152.111.1.251/argief/berigte/volksblad/2000/01/23/2/25.html

Interviews

Diederichs J (2006) Spokesperson for Radio Pretoria. Interview by email. Reply received 21 April 2006

Kruger M (2006a) RSG station manager. Interview by email. Reply received 1 March 2006

Kruger M (2006b) RSG station manager. Interview by email. Reply received 1 April 2006

8 The rise of the *Daily Sun* and its contribution to the creation of post-apartheid identity

Nicola Jones, Yves Vanderhaeghen and Dee Viney

An alternative to the boring, serious, expensive, elitist, formal, difficult-to-read newspapers in South Africa, one that would reach its target readership – township dwellers, workers with low English proficiency – in a way that is entertaining, informative and relevant – that is the goal stated by the publisher of the *Daily Sun* when it was launched in Gauteng in June 2002 (Du Plessis 2005, interview). This goal was explicitly set within the framework of a developing democracy in which people needed to be empowered to become part of the new citizenry.

Interestingly, such a goal and the subsequent delivery of South Africa's first 'tabloid' editions brought with it immense criticism from many quarters, ranging from the academic to the mainstream press. Criticisms have included the views that tabloids pander to the lowest common denominator of public taste; simplify and/or twist complex issues; display emotionalism, sensationalism and oversimplification; and generally fail to provide information that citizens need in order to make informed political judgements – a task largely assumed to be performed by the mainstream press, which is commonly viewed as rational–intellectual and able to contextualise issues. Consequently, tabloids are generally seen to 'lower the standards of public discourse' (Örnebring & Jönsson 2004: 283).

However, this chapter claims that changing notions of popular culture shape both the commercial and the textual forms of popular media. Building on Örnebring and Jönsson (2004), it argues that emotionalism, sensationalism and simplification are not necessarily opposed to serving the public good. It explores the rise of the *Daily Sun*, and the relationship between cultural consumption and questions of cultural identity. Following Sen (1999), it contends that people will become free only if they are given 'social opportunities' to engage with social issues in a new democracy. It explores the concept of a public sphere, and whether the *Daily Sun* is operating in only one of a multiplicity of public spheres, as articulated by Fraser (1997).

The chapter discusses how the *Daily Sun* has taken the step from representing its readership in the abstract, in the realm of debate, into that of direct representation, thereby creating its own public space. Where readers of the *Daily Sun* are concerned, the chapter explores how this newspaper contributes to changing identity through offering 'tools of identity making' – providing information that contributes to social skills of readers, thus giving them a sense of self. Issues dealt with in the *Daily Sun*, such as violence, corruption, gender power struggles and so on, provide opportunities for 'conversations' which lead towards specific discourses that help empower readers. To the extent that this newspaper creates an avenue of hope, of validation for people as human and social beings, the chapter argues that the *Daily Sun* serves democracy by contributing to a sense of empowerment. Mob justice, for example, may not be pretty, but it is a sign of empowerment. Reporting on mob justice is also a clear sign of the existence of a free press, a key indicator of a functioning democracy.

The rise of tabloids in the South African context

Under the apartheid regime, the white minority controlled the print media, both English and Afrikaans, serving only a small, select group of regular newspaper readers. The so-called quality newspapers served to 'inform, educate and comment', and did so under the ever-watchful eye of the government. The Nationalist government fined or banned newspapers (usually from the independent English press) that criticised its policies. Most Afrikaans newspapers were funded by government and used for government propaganda. A very small number of black-owned, independent newspapers were started up, but few survived. It is not surprising, then, that by 1989 English newspapers were in trouble, plagued by stagnant readership and circulation. Ken Owen, then editor of the *Sunday Times*, said newspaper readers wanted 'to see their own views and emotions reflected in newspapers. They want a voice to speak for them much more than they want to be informed.' They wanted a 'user-friendly product' that was quite different from the existing 'serious broadsheet newspapers' (Diederichs 2005: 1). However, media groups continued to produce traditional newspapers aimed at a select few and circulation continued to stagnate.

The emergence of the *Daily Sun* in 2002 – with its human-interest stories about ordinary people for ordinary people – undoubtedly changed the face of newspapers in South Africa. Under apartheid, most black people were not interested in reading about a society they were not part of. The end of apartheid saw 'a surge of newspaper reading', since black people were no longer alienated from mainstream culture and politics (Harrison 2005: 2).

Ironically, the previously English-owned Independent Group (now with substantial black ownership shares) turned down the offer to start the *Daily Sun*. Instead, the previously Afrikaans group, Naspers, took control of it and now owns 'the leading papers in the country today', which are 'independent, party-politically unshackled papers to serve the buying public' (Vosloo 2004: 152–153). The *Daily Sun*'s target market of Living Standards Measures 4 and 5 has quadrupled its income since the demise of apartheid, and the launch of the *Daily Sun* has coincided with the realisation that the political power of this target market is potentially explosive (Bloom 2005: 3). It is important for this discussion to consider the specific socio-political and economic system within which the tabloid, as a cultural product, is produced, distributed and consumed. As Strelitz and Steenveld (2005: 3) point out, 'such an investigation does not imply an uncritical celebration of popular preferences, but rather points to a need to understand how they have come about, and what dimension of the social structure they either challenge or hold in place'.

The success of the *Daily Sun* has had a significant effect on journalism in South Africa. It seems to have initiated the process of 'turning South Africa's traditional newspaper model on its head' (Bloom 2005: 2). The country's mainstream newspapers reacted to the paper only when it started to achieve record sales and thus posed a commercial threat. For example, in terms of the latest available figures describing newspaper readership trends from the South African Advertising Research Foundation (their All Media and Products Survey), from March to September 2005, the *Daily Sun* had a daily readership of 3 444 000, as opposed to 535 000 for *The Star*, 96 000 for *Business Day* and 1 640 000 for the *Sowetan* for the same period. Papers like *Business Day* traditionally have a low readership per copy because the paper serves the buyer's individual needs, while the *Daily Sun* has more readers per copy as it tends to be passed around more in households with more inhabitants than in affluent homes – an indication of the different uses a newspaper serves in a community, including direct information needs, literacy exercises and practical household usage. The Audit Bureau of Circulation figures for April to

June 2006, largely believed to be a far more accurate assessment, put the *Daily Sun* circulation figure at 463 691 per day, as opposed to 168 878 for *The Star*, 131 562 for the *Sowetan*, and 42 022 for *Business Day*.

The initial response from the mainstream media to the unprecedented *Daily Sun* sales was to 'resort to tabloid bashing', criticising the 'trashy' tabloid and accusing it of unethical, bad journalism and of pandering 'to the lowest common denominator of public taste' (Strelitz & Steenveld 2005: 1). Now, other newspapers like the *Son, Sunday Sun, Daily Voice, Sowetan* and *Citizen* are copying its format (though the latter two do not classify themselves as typical tabloids), and media analysts are vigorously engaged in discussing 'paradigm repair' of the mainstream press and moving towards accepting tabloids as a 'new kind of journalism' in a South African democracy. More interesting, perhaps, is the fact that *The Star* has also followed a more 'tabloid' line, employing louder headlines and a more activist tone on occasion. It should also be noted that while the mainstream papers are striving for reader involvement through SMS, MMS, blogs and other online strategies, the *Daily Sun* relies on old-technology phone lines.

One could ask whether tabloids in general and the *Daily Sun* in particular are playing a more socially acceptable role in a developing culture than are the mainstream media. Harber (2005: 2) describes the irony of the situation as follows: 'Apartheid and its repression brought us some courageous, outspoken, probing journalism that won international admiration and few readers; democracy and normality have brought us popular sleaze. The price of freedom is that the bottom feeders also enjoy it.' This comment encapsulates the ambivalent attitudes towards the tabloid in the new democracy: on the one hand, the 'snobbish moralists' (Harber 2005: 1) are bemoaning the loss of mores and norms of good journalism; on the other, many are heartened by the idea of democratic freedom and the concomitant notion of millions of new readers, and the possibility of new 'citizens'. The arrival of the *Daily Sun* and other tabloids has seen an increase in literacy in the country, and this will result in millions of people being able to participate in and 'affect the quality of our democracy' (Harber 2005: 1). Whatever the answers, there is widespread agreement that a proper understanding of the tabloid newspaper will contribute to the development of journalism in South Africa (Wasserman 2005).

In explaining the popularity of the tabloids among the British working classes, Sparks (1988: 216–217) postulates that political and economic power in a stable democracy is so far removed from the real lives of the majority of the population that they have no interest in monitoring its disposal. In other words, in a stable democracy the popularity of the tabloids says more about the relationship of ordinary working people to the social and political processes that govern their lives than it says about the press. Strelitz and Steenveld (2005: 2) argue that it is not insignificant that during the 1980s, when popular political activity was at its height in South Africa, the country witnessed the emergence of the 'alternative' press: 'This media had an explicitly political purpose, expressed in their aim to "popularise, educate and organise", and thus focussed on social and political issues – traditionally defined in relation to the anti-apartheid struggle.' Strelitz and Steenveld point out that it is noteworthy that the current tabloid explosion has occurred just 10 years after the first democratic elections in South Africa. They state that it is worth considering whether the growth of the tabloid press is a sign of the alienation felt among the working classes from the formal political processes in this country, or whether it is a sign of 'struggle fatigue'. As Gripsrud notes with regard to the popular press in Norway, it 'remains a pervasive fact that most people prefer pleasure to politics, and this may be understood as a *choice* made on the basis of some sort of recognition of their social conditions' (Gripsrud in Dahlgren & Sparks 1996: 92).

Strelitz and Steenveld (2005) contend that the 10 years of democracy may be significant in another way. The rise of the mass-circulation popular press in both America and Europe coincided with the growth of a new reading public, an outcome of the introduction of mass education and the resulting growth in literacy: 'In similar vein, perhaps we are witnessing the growth of new reading publics with their own "specific socio-cultural traits and contingencies" (Dahlgren 1995: 16). If this is so, we need a sociological understanding of how such publics are constituted, and the role of journalism and other entertainment media in this process' (Strelitz & Steenveld 2005: 3). They argue:

> As Örnebring and Jönsson (2004: 285) observe, while there is arguably a mainstream mediated public sphere dominated by elite sources, the structural elitism (who is quoted, what kinds of stories are covered) of this sphere in turn creates a need for one, or several, alternative public spheres. Tabloid journalism has, according to these authors, the ability to broaden the public, giving news access to groups that have not been previously targeted by the prestige press. Similarly, Sparks (2000: 63) notes that the British press consists of different kinds of print media that are produced

for different social classes and that they have to be understood as part of the differing cultural lives of those classes. The place and content of a newspaper in working-class culture is quite different from that in middle-class or ruling-class culture. The press, he argues, is not, and never has been, a single self-evident and undifferentiated category. (Strelitz & Steenveld 2005: 3)

We would argue that the majority of readers want to see themselves as they are, as they wish to be or as a complex blend of both. Consider the manner in which some mainstream and alternative media dealt with images of political violence during the struggle era, when there was a professional imperative to publish and sometimes be damned, as in the case of the then *Weekly Mail* and *The Witness*. Various newspapers within the mainstream press, such as *The Witness*, struggled under apartheid with various ethical issues surrounding political coverage. One of the most urgent of these was that of coverage of events such as funerals, which in terms of Western journalism ethics are considered private and personal. During the era of extreme internecine violence between the African National Congress (ANC) and the Inkatha Freedom Party, *The Witness* reporters were sent out every weekend to cover funerals, interview grieving family members and take intimate photographs. These newsroom debates flowed over into coverage of the actual violence itself, particularly where photographs were concerned, as from an ethical point of view it ran against tradition to publish images of overt violence or corpses. But during those years, 'people wanted that. They felt it validated their circumstances; they understood it was a way of telling the world what was happening to them. The media was thus extremely welcome' (Vanderhaeghen 2006, interview). Similarly, under apartheid the *Sowetan* styled itself as a paper that articulated the opinions of the black intelligentsia, as it was both psychologically and politically necessary, implicitly or explicitly, to rebut the white supremacist idea of blacks as stupid primitives, and one way of doing this was to engage at the level of ideas.

All of this served to undermine the moral ground of the powers that were, and validated the experience of the oppressed under apartheid. Some quibbled about such issues as privacy and reader sensitivities, but it was generally accepted to be a good thing to get those pictures and stories out. A desperate populace seeking a voice found one. There are distinct similarities with the *Daily Sun* and its community coverage.

This situation reversed during the immediate years after the unbanning of the ANC and the country's first democratic elections, as the media realised they were no longer operating in a conflict situation, and they thus began behaving in a more traditional way. However, the tendency to reveal more than is allowed according to Western ethical criteria has shown itself clearly in the *Daily Sun*, where stories and photographs that are shocking in terms of mainstream coverage are fairly common.

And yet one could argue that this is what the audience – the readers – want. Publisher Deon du Plessis's response to criticisms is that the paper 'makes blue overall values [its] values' (Ismail 2006: 1). A poster on the *Daily Sun* newsroom wall reminds its reporters: 'We believe in witches.' And to Du Plessis, these 'blue overall values' represent the common people on the street and what they want to read. For many academic and mainstream journalist critics, that is not good enough. The academic argument tends to be that matters which the public may have a *desire* to know about are to be distinguished from those which they have a *right* to know about. Du Plessis's response is simple: satisfying the audience and making money in the process is all he is required to do.

And although there have been numerous calls to study what constitutes tabloid news, it is interesting to note that perhaps all the *Daily Sun* is doing is delivering stories which appeal to the social, cultural and traditional beliefs of its readers – more successfully than broadsheets, which often tend to run similar stories, but perhaps in more muted (or more polite, as opposed to impolite) terms. In Pietermaritzburg, for example, *The Witness* annually runs stories about the Delville Wood cross weeping. The *Post* newspaper in Durban, which has a large component of readers from a traditional Indian spiritual environment, regularly runs stories about phenomena such as weeping portraits and ghostly apparitions, which are presented in a deadpan and factual manner. Vanderhaeghen, deputy editor of *The Witness*, points out that when a natural disaster such as a hurricane occurs, reporters have sometimes been faced with a situation in rural areas where people have described the event in folk-mythology terms, such as a huge snake coming down from the sky: 'If this is what people are saying, who are journalists to judge? If we were going to be judgemental, the place to do this would be on the opinion pages, where one has the choice to apply gullible or cynical criteria. Such descriptions may be alien to a sophisticated urban audience, but if it is what people are saying, we can't laugh at them and ignore them. They also have a right to be heard' (Vanderhaeghen 2006, interview).

It is also vital to note that even the legal system in South Africa is starting to take into account traditional and spiritual beliefs. In KwaZulu-Natal a recent court case involving a man who murdered relatives because he believed in bewitchment is a case in point. The judge stated that the man should have known right from wrong, but also acknowledged in his judgment that the man's belief system had to be taken into consideration. Such is the necessity in a pluralistic democracy.

Engaging the public sphere

These kinds of developments have led to much recent debate over journalism in the public sphere. Following Jürgen Habermas, a number of media scholars have used the concept of the public sphere both to describe and evaluate the role of the mass media – particularly news – in public life. Scholars such as Dahlgren (1995), for example, have argued for the increasing centrality of the media as a public arena where the public can access societal dialogues: 'As such, the media play an important part by providing this access, and it is relevant to talk about a mediated public sphere' (Dahlgren 1995: 9).

An egalitarian multicultural society requires a plurality of public arenas in which groups with diverse values and rhetorics may participate. These alternative public spheres may then in turn allow for talk and debates across these 'different publics' to form a 'new post-bourgeois conception of a public sphere' where issues that concern them all can be addressed, allowing for differences in culture (Fraser in Calhoun 1997: 124). This raises the question, 'Can everyone be accommodated within one and the same public sphere?' (Dahlgren 1995: 17) and suggests that through the creation of a multiplicity of public arenas, the exclusionary nature of the bourgeois public sphere may be overcome.

Örnebring and Jönsson argue that whereas the central struggle in the bourgeois public sphere was the struggle of one particular class to find a new place in society (by criticising traditional authorities and power elites), the central struggle in the mediated public sphere is the struggle for visibility – that is, the struggle to be seen and heard in the first place: 'This struggle for visibility seems to indicate that there might not be just one mediated public sphere, but instead the media landscape could be described as consisting of a mainstream and a number of alternative spheres – spheres from which marginalised groups strive to gain access to, and representation in, the mainstream' (Örnebring & Jönsson 2004: 285).

Fraser (in Calhoun 1997) discusses the notion of a mainstream-mediated public sphere, and argues that the type of structural elitism at play within this sphere in turn creates a need for one or several alternative public spheres, in which different people create different issues in different ways. She suggests that creating possibilities for alternative public spheres to exist and thrive is a way of promoting democratic participation and open public debate:

> This historiography records that members of subordinated social groups – women, workers, peoples of colour, and gays and lesbians – have repeatedly found it advantageous to constitute alternative publics. I propose to call these subaltern counterpublics in order to signal that they are parallel discursive arenas where members of subordinated social groups invent and circulate counterdiscourses to formulate oppositional interpretations of their identities, interests and needs. (Fraser in Calhoun 1997: 123)

Pointing out that Fraser is discussing the role of the public sphere as an arbiter of cultural recognition, Örnebring and Jönsson use her argument as a basis for conceptualising alternative-mediated public spheres as being 'alternative' in four different but related ways:

- Alternative might be taken to mean that the discourse itself takes place somewhere else other than in the mainstream-mediated public sphere.
- It might be alternative in the sense that other participants than those normally dominating media discourse have access to and a place in the debates and discussions taking place.
- It might be alternative in the sense that other issues than those commonly debated in the mainstream are discussed.
- 'Alternativeness' may derive from the usage of other ways or forms of debating or discussing common issues than those commonly used in the mainstream, for example forms which encourage citizen participation and non-parliamentary direct action. (Örnebring & Jönsson 2004: 286)

They use 'alternative' to indicate criticism and questioning of the political, economic and cultural elites and the societal status quo – the possession of some kind of emancipatory potential: 'Tabloid journalism can help affect social change in addressing issues not previously open to debate, including new publics and using new forms – thus introducing new areas of discourse into the mainstream mediated public sphere' (Örnebring & Jönsson 2004: 287).

Sen (1999) proposes that what is needed for development is removing the sources of 'unfreedom', such as social deprivation, and giving 'social opportunities', as in freedom to exchange words, goods, gifts and so on – all part of how humans interact with one another. He argues that development can take place only by removing the sources of unfreedom, including poverty, famine and tyranny. And he believes that individual agency is central to addressing these deprivations, as in this way people become 'active agents of change' (Sen 1999: iii, 6).

We believe that the *Daily Sun*, by giving access to information, does provide for 'societal dialogues' and a 'marketplace of ideas' on common concerns essential for a working democracy. This helps to create a public sphere that could prepare readers for more 'political involvement' (McQuail 2000). The crucial point is that, instead of trying to compare and contrast this new public sphere with that of the traditional notion of the public sphere, one should view this as a unique public sphere that comes about as a result of participation by a unique group of people in a particular socio-political and economic context. This kind of public sphere could then interact with other 'public arenas'.

What the *Daily Sun* has managed to do, albeit for primarily commercial reasons, is attract a new public by speaking to them about issues previously ignored, in new, clearly understandable ways. Readers get so absorbed in the stories and issues raised by the newspaper, such as violence, crime and the police's inability to deal with these, that dedicated phone lines are staffed continuously to receive public tip-offs and journalists are invited to investigate crimes or events, often at the moment they are happening. The *Daily Sun* receives around 10 000 letters to the editor each month. In addition, in an average edition of 36 pages, at the most only 6 of these contain 'sensational' or ordinary news, and the bulk of the rest contains what the publishers call 'social-skilling' initiatives and community news: photographs sent in by readers, self-help articles ranging from how to negotiate a bank loan to how to fix a broken toilet, an agony column, a free home-repair service, a free service to find missing people, general knowledge material, educational articles and a variety of other 'non-news' items. Viney puts it this way: 'The pages of the *Daily Sun* engage the readers in a way that could contribute to self-development in terms of literacy, knowledge acquisition and "social skilling"' (Viney 2004: 17). This points to the mobilisation of a group of people who were previously powerless, voiceless and passive towards taking action to improve their lives, albeit at a very unsophisticated and basic level. In this sense, the *Daily Sun* is fulfilling an important task by 'contributing to the development of an identity of citizenship not too formal and not too substantive' within the 'hetero-cultural context' of South African capitalist democracy, and thereby contributing to the functioning of the public sphere (Andersen 1997: 43).

Some ideas on identity through tabloids

As we have seen, Sen argues that development can take place only by removing the sources of 'unfreedom' and that 'individual agency is central to addressing these deprivations' (Sen 1999: i). We would like to explore the extent to which the *Daily Sun* is providing its readers with the 'instrumental freedom to exchange words, goods and gifts' and, in so doing, empowering them to become 'active agents of change' (Sen 1999: iii, 6). Following on from work by theorists such as Williams, Hall and Barker (Barker 2002: 71), in this context we rely on descriptions of culture as democracy, and of the capacity of ordinary people to construct a shared, meaningful 'popular' culture that is valuable to them even 'in the face of high cultural disdain'. Given the freedom to explore media relevant to them (including the *Daily Sun*), members of this sector of South African society now have access to making choices that could impact on their identities as active citizens.

The concept of 'writing for the person waiting for the bus' is a fairly normative approach in many newsrooms. Mainstream newspapers – assuming they have a role in providing authority and leadership in society – tend to believe they are writing for the 'ordinary' individual, although this is obviously very simplistic, as each newspaper has a specific market and audience for whom it provides stories. The *Daily Sun* has an extremely well-identified idea of its target market. Gripsrud (1999) argues that well-known features of the tabloid press, such as sensationalism, personalisation and the focus on private concerns, parallel the main components of melodrama which developed in the last century and has attained a prominent position in tabloids. He argues that these elements of the tabloid press are popular precisely because they provide ways of understanding the world which are different from the idealised notion of how the mainstream press works. Although his research was not on South African tabloids, it is useful here to note some examples of the sorts of news headlines found in the *Daily Sun*: 'Save us from VIP toilets'; '27 corpses moved due to power cut'; 'Our bus journey is hell'; 'DIY taps, pipes give brown water'; 'School of mud'; 'Death of a thug'; 'Boy drowns in open hole'; 'Fired after disclosing HIV status' (Harber 2006: 1). All these stories deal with the hardships of everyday life and would seldom make a mainstream newspaper. For the *Daily Sun* readers, such stories are articulating their daily lives and struggles, and it is unlikely they would see themselves similarly featured in most of the rest of the media.

Nightingale and Ross point out that 'critics have been pontificating about the salacious excesses of newspapers for generations; even mainstream news has always been torn between what practitioners see as a duty to inform, and their need to entertain and engage their audience' (2003: 67). While critics are baffled by the fact that readers do prefer 'human-interest' stories that seem trivial, it is useful to look at 'the difference in the way that journalists/critics and audiences define news and how it is used' (Nightingale & Ross 2003: 68). Carey (1988: 73) refers to the 'transmission' view, whereby audiences consume news to be informed about the world, 'but everyday definitions of news focus more on how these stories are inserted into people's daily lives, growing and becoming the subjects of speculation and discussion'. Most of what the audience reads in the newspaper is either ignored or forgotten almost immediately; from the audience perspective, relevant news consists of stories that take on a life of their own outside the immediate context of the newspaper.

Woodward describes the concept of identity as follows:

> Identity can be seen as the interface between subjective positions and social and cultural situations...Identity gives us an idea of who we are and of how we relate to others and to the world in which we live. Identity marks the ways in which we are the same as others who share that position, and the ways in which we are different from those who do not. (Woodward in O'Shaunessy & Stadler 2002: 209)

She emphasises the role of symbolic systems – the media, images and language – in contributing to our identities: 'Representation as a cultural process establishes individual and collective identities, and symbolic systems provide possible answers to the questions: Who am I? What could I be? Who do I want to be?' (Woodward in O'Shaunessy & Stadler 2002: 209). We believe that part of the *Daily Sun*'s immense success is based on the fact that readers enjoy the representation of themselves that they discover in its pages.

It should be noted that many of the broadsheet newspaper companies in South Africa have started their own small tabloid newspapers, and that there is increasingly substantial overlap in the South African newspaper industry between what were previously known as 'community newspapers' and conventional tabloids. Historically, community newspapers dealt with the small, everyday stories that the broadsheets deemed not to be of national or provincial interest, often focusing on local community gossip, school news, municipal problems and so on. They make full use of graphics such as photographs and illustrations, and use far less erudite language than one would find, say, in a *Business Day* editorial. These strategies display yet another similarity with the *Daily Sun*, which tends to use a personal tone and far more colloquial language than the 'Queen's English' generally espoused by the broadsheets. In focusing on the textual strategies of American tabloids, Fiske (1982: 46) argues that they produce subjectivities that are different from those produced by the address of the mainstream press. The latter presents information as objective facts selected from empiricist reality, acting on the assumption that good, 'objective' investigation produces the truth. The tone is serious, official and impersonal, aimed at producing understanding and belief. In other words, the mainstream press addresses the reader from the position of one who knows and is providing information for those who don't. In contrast, the tone of tabloids is more conversational, using the language of its readers. In this way, they set up a more 'egalitarian' relationship between themselves and their readers. They don't pontificate.

According to Fiske (1982: 48), the last thing the tabloids want to produce is a believing subject. Indeed, they appear not to take themselves too seriously: 'One of [their] most characteristic tones of voice is that of a sceptical laughter which offers the pleasure of disbelief, the pleasures of not being taken in. This popular pleasure of "seeing through" them (whoever constitutes the powerful them of the moment) is the historical result of centuries of subordination which the people have not allowed to develop into subjection.' It follows that people who read these different publications often tend to create part of their identity around what they read, and in the South African context this is interwoven with varying literacy levels and the widespread perception of status associated with the reading of English-language papers.

Although there is no clear definition of the term 'tabloidisation', some themes are consistent, including the 'storytelling' style and a focus on personal narratives about individuals. There is also 'the increasing predominance of the visual image over analysis and rational description' (Sparks 1988: 39). Sparks maintains that through tabloidisation, 'the popular conception of the personal becomes the explanatory framework within which the social order is presented as transparent' (Sparks 1988: 39).

In deliberately giving the readers what they want, and allowing them to contribute substantially to the content of the news section of the paper, the *Daily Sun* is giving the audience content that they can relate to and which they are able to interpret in terms of their own lives. Readers are looking at themselves as the subjects of what is happening in their environment and, through interpretation of these texts, are placing themselves in a position where they can make choices. One could argue that readers' responses to this content will help give them tools for personal empowerment – even if it is in as simple a way as knowing how to open a bank account. This creation of identity around the reader – the action and interaction – could be seen as an embryonic level of citizen journalism.

Conclusion

We have argued that much of the criticism levelled against the *Daily Sun* has been based on a set of values that to a large extent coincides with the values of cultural and political elite groups in South African society, some of whom have obviously not taken too kindly to the competition for resources and attention that the *Daily Sun* has offered. However, by no means are we arguing that all criticism is class-based, as the newspaper can be legitimately criticised in many ways. Kruger (2006) has pointed out that one of the ethical criteria necessary for journalism is that stories can't be invented ('Gorilla raped me' was one particular headline which invoked much criticism). He argues that journalists have to take some responsibility for what they put into the public domain, and he questions whether a newspaper should uncritically buy into the worst prejudices and superstitions of its audience. Also, sensationalism, emotional appeals and new forms of presentation, while not necessarily bad in themselves, may well mean that news – in particular, facts and fairness – may suffer.

However, we would argue for greater openness when making normative judgements about the phenomenon of tabloid journalism. In whatever sphere of journalism one investigates, there is good journalism and bad journalism. The point is this: while tabloid journalism may have many faults, it can also be seen as an alternative arena for public discourse, wherein criticism of both the privileged political elites and traditional types of public discourse plays a central role. Tabloid journalism has the ability to broaden the public knowledge base as well as widen the reader demographic, giving news access to groups that previously were not targeted, and to effect societal change by redefining previously undebatable issues in need of debate, as the *Daily Sun* has done with regard to many areas, such as health, education and housing. The newspaper has given rise to a new form of journalistic discourse which is unquestionably more accessible to its audience and less deferential to traditional authority. Moreover, the much criticised appeal to emotion could actually stimulate political participation, by speaking to people's feelings rather than simply to the rational mind.

It is also interesting to note that in spite of all the criticisms levelled at the *Daily Sun*, including that it trades in 'stereotypes, xenophobia and fear' (Harber 2004: 156), the Press Ombudsman's Report for 2005 showed that surprisingly few complaints were being made at this level. Out of a total of 185 complaints made in 2005, only 21 were laid against the tabloids *Daily Sun, Daily Voice* and *Son*, and only one complaint against the *Daily Sun* was upheld.

What the *Daily Sun* has managed to do is position itself, in different ways, as an alternative to the issues, forms and audiences of the mainstream press in South Africa – as an alternative public sphere. A superficial glance leaves one with the impression that the *Daily Sun* carries no politics, and it is true that there are few in-depth looks at the workings of Parliament, the politicians and the parties. But it is filled with the issues and trivia of the hardships of daily life – whether the drains are blocked and the rubbish is being collected, whether jobs have managed to be found and the hospital system is working – and of the occasional victory over these issues when housing has been gained or the police solve a case. We believe politics over the next few years will be framed around lower- and middle-class satisfaction with the areas of practical governance that facilitate and improve the lives of these citizens, in which case the *Daily Sun* should be seen as an important potential political force. In Harber's words: 'The politicians are not taking much notice now, but at some point in the next few years they will notice that the staff and readers of the *Daily Sun* have become more important to the next election than *Business Day* or the *Sunday Times*. And things will never be the same again' (Harber 2004: 158).

References

Andersen MB (1997) Television, political culture and the identity of citizenship. *Critical Arts* 11(1–2): 28–45

Barker C (2002) *Making sense of cultural studies: Problems and critical debates*. London: Sage Publications

Bloom K (2005) War talk. *Mail & Guardian*, 4 August

Calhoun C (ed.) (1997) *Habermas and the public sphere*. London: MIT Press

Carey J (ed.) (1998) *Media, myths and narratives: Television and the press*. London: Sage Publications

Dahlgren P (1995) *Television and the public sphere: Citizenship, democracy and the media.* London: Sage Publications

Dahlgren P & Sparks C (eds) (1996) *Journalism and popular culture.* London: Sage Publications

Diederichs P (2005) The tabloids: There are two sides to every story. Paper presented at the South African Communication Association (SACOMM) Annual Conference, Pretoria, 19–21 September

Fiske J (1982) *Understanding popular culture.* London: Routledge

Fraser N (1997) Rethinking the public sphere: A contribution to the critique of actually existing democracy. In C Calhoun (ed.) *Habermas and the public sphere.* London: MIT Press

Gripsrud J (ed.) (1999) *Television and common knowledge.* London: Routledge

Harber A (2004) The *Daily Sun* shines in gore and glory over a changing land. *Ecquid Novi* 25(1): 156–159

Harber A (2005) Rich diet at bottom of trough. *Business Day*, 17 August

Harber A (2006) Of rags and riches. Accessed 30 March 2006, http://www.big.co.za/wordpress/2006/03/11/of-rags-and-riches/

Harrison R (2005) No holding back as SA tabloids take off. *Pretoria News*, 28 July

Ismail S (2006) What makes news in the *Sun*? Accessed 9 June 2006, www.journalism.co.za

Kruger F (2006) Sex, soccer and superstition: But is it news? Accessed 30 March 2006, http://www.mg.co.za/printPage.aspx?area=/insight/insight_columnists/&articleID=26.html

McQuail D (2000) *McQuail's reader in mass communication theory.* London: Sage Publications

Nightingale V & Ross K (eds) (2003) *Critical readings: Media and audiences.* Maidenhead: Open University Press

Örnebring H & Jönsson AM (2004) Tabloid journalism and the public sphere: A historical perspective on tabloid journalism. *Journalism Studies* 5(3): 283–295

O'Shaunessy M & Stadler J (2002) *Media and society: An introduction.* Oxford: Oxford University Press

Sen A (1999) *Development as freedom.* New York: Alfred A. Knopf

Sparks C (1988) The popular press and political democracy. *Media, Culture and Society* 10: 209–223

Strelitz L & Steenveld L (2005) Thinking about South African tabloid newspapers. Paper presented at the South African Communication Association (SACOMM) Annual Conference, Pretoria, 19–21 September

Viney D (2004) Investigating the role of the tabloid newspaper in the new South Africa. Unpublished paper, University of KwaZulu-Natal

Vosloo T (2004) On accepting African power and adapting in the media world. *Ecquid Novi* 25(1): 152–158

Wasserman H (2005) Tackles and sidesteps: Normative maintenance and paradigm repair in mainstream reactions to tabloid journalism. Paper presented at the South African Communication Association (SACOMM) Annual Conference, Pretoria, 19–21 September

Interviews

Du Plessis D (2005) Publisher, *Daily Sun*. Johannesburg, 21 March

Vanderhaeghen Y (2006) Deputy Editor, *The Witness*. Pietermaritzburg, 20 May

9 Online coloured identities: A virtual ethnography

Tanja Bosch

In post-apartheid South Africa, racial identity has come under the spotlight more than ever before. As some artificially created but now established racial identities have given way to more fluid ones, centred on class, religion or culture versus ethnicity or race, others have exhibited increased assertiveness in the face of perceived marginalisation. The so-called coloured[1] identity is one such example. The coloured people of South Africa, constituting around 9 per cent of the total population (Statistics South Africa 2005), are usually described as being of mixed race, including descendants of the indigenous Khoisan, Dutch and English settlers, indigenous Africans, and the Javanese, Malay and Indian slaves.

This chapter presents the findings of a virtual ethnography of the Internet portal Bruin-ou.com – The Brand, The People, The Lifestyle, in order to explore some of the meanings of coloured identity, and the ways in which this identity is constructed and contested via the site. While the physical characteristics of race are absent in online interactions, online discussion groups created specifically to discuss racial and cultural issues are often appropriate settings for exploring the organisation of online racial identity (Smith & Kollock 1999). This study was conducted over a five-month period, and forums, discussions and transcripts of email interviews with users were analysed. The presentation and self-expression of coloured users was of particular interest.

Background

The site

Bruin-ou.com – The Brand, The People, The Lifestyle is described on its website as being 'the only portal about South Africa's mixed-race people'. No similar sites were located using a variety of Internet search engines. The site is located at http://www.bruin-ou.com and offers a range of services including news, entertainment, sports, job listings, local music downloads, as well as creative writing, chat rooms and numerous forums on a range of topics. The website posts the following description:

> We are NOT trying to create a racial divide between ourselves and other groups within South Africa. Instead, we are endeavouring to educate the South African and world population at large on what exactly it means to be coloured. In much the same manner that programmes like Eastern Mosaic and the like exist to educate people about their cultures, Bruin-ou.com exists to forge and promote Coloured culture in all its facets. With the many varied questions surrounding the topic of 'Coloured identity', Bruin-ou.com exists as a business vehicle through which the many stereotypes and question marks surrounding Coloured identity can be dispelled, thus enabling the Coloured community at large to be included in this country's great cultural resurgence. Bruin-ou.com has absolutely no political or religious affiliation whatsoever. Bruin-ou.com is ABOUT coloured people but for EVERYBODY who has an interest in learning more about our urban culture and our people. Register now and experience Coloured culture (whatever that may be), first hand. (www.bruin-ou.com; accessed 20 May 2007)

Site founders Charles Ash and Lester Ash say that the portal name was originally an acronym for 'Bring Real life, Understanding, Individual Need to Operate in Unity'. The site celebrated its one-year anniversary in April 2006, at which time it listed a membership of 4 168, with some 6 000 members on the email mailing list. On 9 January 2006, the cellphone version of Bruin-ou.com was launched, allowing those with WAP-enabled phones and a GPRS connection to access limited features. According to webmaster Charles Ash, limited connectivity necessitated this decision:

> With this in mind, we realised that the best way for us to reach the masses with Bruin-ou.com would be to make the site accessible on a cellphone. So we began work on a feature-limited, scaled-down version of Bruin-ou.com that would allow the public easy access to our content. (www.bruin-ou.com)

He also reports that future projects include a television magazine show, a radio station for coloured youth, a compilation CD, and hip-hop tours across the country by unsigned groups. Bruin-ou.com has also formed a soccer team which competes in Randburg. This chapter focuses only on the online content of the site.

Website manager Lester Ash describes how Bruin-ou.com was developed by his then 21-year-old brother Charles, at which time the page attracted 75 000 page views per day. Charles says that he found coloured people in the country to have a romanticised notion of Cape Town, and that his own such views were shattered when he first visited the city and saw the conditions on the ground, particularly the socio-economic impoverishment on the Cape Flats. He believed that the Internet would be the best place to start to 'educate people about enduring questions about coloured identity, to connect the community divided by race and language', and felt that 'if I could reach the influential members of the community, then I could make a difference. The coloured community has serious problems and no-one can solve it but us'.[2] Today, his posting on the site says that it is 'unapologetically coloured…to me, coloured is nothing more than a noun, a naming word used to describe people of mixed race, finished en kla!'

The site is funded exclusively by the Ash brothers, and was created to serve as a discussion forum, to reach opinion leaders and to promote the idea that problems in the coloured community need to be tackled by the community itself. Charles explained how the idea for the website was born around a braai stand:

> I saw an opportunity to initiate a social exercise that could be feasibly tested. What if there was a website targeted at coloured people of South African origin? What if there was a meeting place for those people to meet and connect no matter where in the world they were? For me, the question of my social identity is something I can neither outgrow, nor is it something I can leave in the hands of people who couldn't care less. What about my two kids? Will they be equally encumbered with questions surrounding their social identity? No doubt my kids will be better off asking 'what happens to a particle accelerated to near the speed of light?' rather than 'what is a coloured and where do I fit in?' So for me there is no question, the buck stops here! (www.bruin-ou.com)

Bruin-ou.com is understood as a virtual community, which is a 'self-defined electronic network of interactive communication organised around a shared interest or purpose, although sometimes communication becomes the goal in itself' (Castells 2000: 386). A virtual community is also understood as 'a social aggregation that emerges from the Net when enough people carry on those public discussions long enough, with sufficient human feeling, to form webs of personal relationships in cyberspace' (Rheingold 2000: 277). While virtual communities are not necessarily different from 'real' communities, they operate according to their own rules and dynamics. Furthermore, groups that consider themselves marginalised may be more likely to use the Internet for communication, because of the protection this medium affords them (Wasserman 2002).

Coloured identity

The apartheid South African state officially created four classifications of South Africans – black, coloured, Indian and white – with legislation maintaining physical segregation and impacting on the socialisation and identity formation of the members of each group.

Coloured is a complex identity, arising out of slavery, genocide, rape and perceived miscegenation (Hendricks 2005). Slavery was an important form of labour for the Dutch East India Company, with slaves imported from East Africa, Madagascar, the Indonesian archipelago, Bengal, South India and Sri Lanka (Keegan 1996). Hendricks (2005) argues that coloureds are descendants of sexual liaisons between colonialists, slaves and the indigenous Khoisan, and that while this 'mixing' took place centuries ago, state-enforced self-reproduction was largely the means through which the group multiplied. An ongoing process of absorption and miscegenation between European colonists, the indigenous Khoikhoi people of the Cape, slaves and the so-called Bantu-speaking people gradually created a heterogeneous group of mixed people who were later called coloured (Pickel 1997).[3]

On the other hand, Erasmus stresses the ambiguity and ceaseless fluidity of coloured identity formations, and argues that these identities are based not so much on 'race mixture' as on 'cultural creativity, creolized formations shaped by South Africa's history of colonialism, slavery, segregation and apartheid' (Erasmus 2001: 14). They are cultural formations born from appropriation, dispossession and translation in the colonial encounter, 'with various elements of the different cultures appropriated, translated and articulated in complex and subtle ways' (Erasmus 2001: 21).

Moreover, Adhikari argues that coloured identity is primarily a product of its bearers, and that a separate coloured identity was asserted in the late nineteenth century, after the introduction of large-scale mining resulted in 'a wide range of people being thrust into the highly competitive and more diverse environment of the newly established mining towns' (Adhikari 2005: 3).

More often, however, 'coloured' has been conceptualised as a residual identity, and constructed as a category midway between white and black. In an often-quoted speech given at a white nursing home in the former Transvaal, Mrs Marika de Klerk (the wife of the former state president) put it as follows:

> You know, *they* [coloured people] are a negative group. The definition of a coloured person in the population register is someone that is not white and not black, and is also not an Indian, in other words *a non-person*...They are left overs. They are the people that were left after the nations were sorted out. They are the rest...The coloureds were always under the wing of the whites. They have never been on their own. They have no history of governing themselves...They must be supervised. (quoted in Scheper-Hughes 1994; italics in original)

Others have argued that through identification with an African American hip-hop culture, coloured youth look to a blackness based on urban marginalisation and a US-based struggle against racism, and articulate a blackness that links up with global understandings of blackness based on oppression and discrimination (Yarwood 2006). Yet, ironically, in South Africa these youth are particularly far removed from the category of 'black', largely through their inability to speak any African languages, and for the predominance of Afrikaans (perceived by black South Africans during apartheid as the language of the oppressor) as a mother tongue.

More than a decade after the demise of apartheid, coloured identity remains problematic. The identity is experiencing rapid change 'as old sensitivities die down and as new concerns and agendas impinge on people's consciousness' (Adhikari 2005: xv). Many coloured intellectuals and activists discard the term as being an artificial one imposed on them by the apartheid state as part of its divide-and-rule policy and prefer to self-identify as black. Neville Alexander, for example, has denied the reality of coloured identity, arguing that it is white-imposed, reactionary and indicative of new forms of racism – an apartheid relic best left behind (quoted in Erasmus 2001: 15). However, many others proudly self-identify as coloured, and with the first democratic elections came a reassertion of the identity, together with the emergence of coloured nationalist political organisations such as the *Kleurling Weerstandsbeweging* (Coloured Resistance Movement) and Brown Nationalist Front.

During both the 1994 and 1999 elections an overwhelming number of coloured individuals voted for the National Party, which had created and enforced the apartheid system (Yarwood 2006). This political conservatism of predominantly coloured working-class communities in the Western Cape has further intensified debates around their identity, and has reinforced the inability of many South Africans to include coloureds under the umbrella term 'black'. As Erasmus reflects, at the roots of coloured identity formation was the notion of being '*not only* not white, but *less than white; not only* not black, but *better than black*' (Erasmus 2001: 13).

The term 'coloured' has thus been rehabilitated into public discourse since the recession of the rejectionist tide after 1990 (Adhikari 2005). According to Adhikari, the assertion of coloured identity has been the result of a desire to project a positive self-image in the face of negative racial stereotyping, a fear of African majority rule and the perception of being marginalised. For the Ash brothers, they perceive their identity as marginal. According to Lester:

> If I am neither black nor white, then why can't I reject both identities? If black people don't accept me as black, then why should I identify as black? I don't speak Zulu or any other indigenous language. I'm coloured.[4]

Methodology

The methodology for this study consisted of a virtual ethnography, in which the researcher aims 'to gain an in-depth understanding of the issue at hand; although not generalisable, the rich data obtained is useful to understand the intricacies and binding characteristics prevalent in a community' (Dowling 2001). The Internet represents a place where culture is formed and re-formed, with computer-mediated communication providing a rich form of interaction and a space for community formation (Hine 2000; Rheingold 1993). Indeed, racial identity is achieved, maintained, questioned and re-established in Internet discussion groups (Smith & Kollock 1999).

The Internet is thus understood to be a product of culture (Woolgar 1996), and as such is both discursively performed culture and cultural artefact (Hine 2000). Electronic networks renew community 'by strengthening the bonds that connect us to the wider social world while simultaneously increasing our power in that world' (Smith & Kollock 1999: 4).

Morley and Geertz assert that the value in ethnographic methods 'lies precisely in their ability to help us "make things out" in the context of their occurrence – in helping to understand…media consumption practices as they are embedded in the context of everyday life' (quoted in Murphy 1999: 208). Ethnography sets aside the notion that behaviour is rule-governed or motivated by shared values and expectations, and maintains that social structures are locally produced, sustained and experienced (Holstein & Gubrium 1999).

The first phase of my research was observation only, where I 'lurked' and explored all the pages of Bruin-ou.com, reading postings and news, following newsgroup discussions, and so on. A lurker is a non-participating member of a discussion group (Dowling 2001). At this stage I did, however, partially enter the role of participant through site registration with a user name and password. This observation-only phase of the ethnography and experience in negotiating my way around the site gave me the confidence to risk a more active entry into the field (Lindlof & Shatzer 1998).

During the next phase of the research I contacted the webmaster and the project manager of the site via email. Charles and Lester Ash, based in Durban, agreed to be interviewed on the telephone. I also contacted Bruin-ou members directly, through a posting on the site requesting participation in my study. The initial forum posting which was sent was modelled on a previous study conducted by Hine (2000) and read as follows:

> Dear Bruin-ou.com members,
>
> I am a researcher in communications at Stellenbosch University and am very interested in issues of coloured identity. Being a Bruin-ou myself, it was with great interest that I stumbled across this website. I would very much like to interview members, and hope that you will take the time to share some thoughts with me on coloured identity and your participation on Bruin-ou.com. As a frequently misunderstood and under-researched community, I'm sure you'll agree with me that more research and writing is needed – in particular, we need to write about ourselves! I would be very

grateful if you could spare a little of your time by answering a few questions. If you agree to help, I'll mail you some questions. You could really help me by spending as little as 10 minutes and your answers can be as long or short as you like. If I use anything you say in my writing, you will remain anonymous. Please email me on drbosch@sun.ac.za for a list of questions. Thanks in advance. If you want to check out my credentials go to http://academic.sun. ac.za/journalism/bosch.htm

tebza

I signed using my user name, but referred members to a website to confirm my authenticity as a researcher. I posted the message in the 'Seriously Speaking' forum, which falls under Discussion Central. This forum is accompanied by the description, 'If it's important to you, this is where you discuss it'. The first positive response came into my inbox only seconds after I had made the posting. My data thus consisted largely of printouts and files of webpages and newsgroup postings, as well as emails to and from participants. I also collected field notes, recording thoughts and observations which arose during the course of the ethnography. I read and reread the data several times in order to identify recurrent themes.

With regard to ethical issues, while this study acknowledges that the Internet is a public sphere, the route of informed consent versus covert research was followed. My intentions were clearly stated to the website manager and to members. Furthermore, as any reader can log onto the website and read the postings, members' and interviewees' anonymity was partially maintained by using only their online screen names and not their real names (which I had access to when they responded to my request for participation in the study).

One main criticism of Internet research in the United States has been that as computers are only available to a sample of the population, Internet-user populations represent a dramatically skewed sample. However, several studies have shown that Internet and non-Internet samples generally do not differ dramatically in terms of sexual orientation, marital status, ethnicity and education, but tend to differ only in terms of age and sex. Furthermore, my research questions did not require representative samples, as the ethnography is concerned not with making broad generalisations, but with exploring and elucidating individual perspectives (Hewson et al. 2003) – in this case, how coloured identity is understood and performed in one particular online community.

According to the Goldstuck Report (2005), 3.6 million South Africans were to have Internet access by the end of 2005. However, there are no data to indicate how this distribution breaks down in racial terms, and one might conclude that only a tiny percentage of coloured South Africans have regular access to a broadband Internet connection to allow participation in forums like Bruin-ou, whose membership numbers only 4 168 out of a population of 4.1 million (Statistics South Africa 2005). It is thus only the class of 'digiterati' who are included in this study. As Wasserman (2002) points out, virtual South Africa largely reflects the polarisations of the 'real-world' South Africa, with the average South African Internet user being white and earning more than R11 000 per month, while less than 1 per cent of the country's black population have access to the Internet (Smith & Kollock 1999).

Thus this chapter cannot provide a holistic account of coloured identity, but instead uses Bruin-ou.com as a site for exploring some of the meanings and performances of this identity at this specific historical juncture. Of course, a certain degree of reflexivity was necessary, as I was classified as coloured by the apartheid state, though I prefer to self-identify as black, and it is acknowledged that this political positioning may have tempered my interaction with the site and with participants.

The ethnography was conducted over a five-month period from 28 March 2006 to end August 2006. During this period I visited the site every day, sometimes several times a day. In total, I spent approximately 130 hours online.

Discussion

Explicit discussions of identity

While many of the postings on the site do not specifically deal with identity, several ongoing conversations do. User mondlimsomi started a post labelled 'The term coloured and Coloured people as a race', in which he describes his meeting with a professor on a plane while travelling to New York as an exchange student. This professor told him that being coloured is not a race, but a subcategory of being black, and that the category was created in South Africa to serve the government's purpose of divide and rule. Mondlimsomi writes:

> Me, not knowing the sensitivity of the word 'Coloured', I just used it as I grew up in a country being identified as 'Coloured'. But in the US and in many other major countries in Europe I am seen as

Black and not as 'Coloured'...which was a culture shock for me. I guess my culture shock was becuz here in SA we as Coloured people are not classified as part of Black people although we fall within the sub-category of Black people and that is obviously due to apartheid legislation of divide and rule. (19 April 2006)

User Cjoe responds:

More classification. Is there any reason we should accept classifications handed to us by Europeans and Americans? Whatever WE decide we are, I'm happy with, but that decision must come from us. (20 April 2006)

User Critikill points out that the NAACP[5] gains more power in terms of numbers as more mixed people claim the black identity as their own:

That is why the NAACP is vehemently opposed to the emergence of many multiracial/ mixed groups advocating improved representation for mixed race people...As a mixed race person I think it is incredibly unfair that my racially mixed genetic data is tabulated according to the whims of people who seek to retain accrued political power... There are many multicultural societies like ours which are grappling with mixed identity issues. Take Brazil for example, they have a very large mixed-race population, and hell yes they have a name which they use to identify themselves with. That's just my 2 bob. For me, I'll be a Coloured... until further notice. (20 April 2006)

Another user, bhekza, clearly identifies himself as black in the following exchange:

For the older people being coloured was the in thing, which meant a better life and better benefits, so I don't blame them. My problem is with young people these days that still think you are better because you are so-called coloured. Let's break the chains of the people that enslaved us and start to realise that we are one. We were separated to be destroyed. We need to understand that there is no such thing as a grey zone, it's either black or white. (20 April 2006)

User titoM then responds, pointing out the problematic nature of the notion of 'mixed' race and starting a rather heated exchange.

...from a point of view of the dominant group, racial distinctions are a necessary tool for dominance. Who better to know than the

> Coloured people of South Africa. Brainwashing Tutorial 101, if you want to break down any subject mentally successfully, first strip him or her of his identity. It is worth remembering though, we all have genetic material from a variety of populations, and we all exhibit physical characteristics that testify to mixed ancestry. Biologically speaking, there have never been any pure races – all populations are mixed. (21 April 2006)

Bheka angrily rejoins the conversation with the following:

> Now you want to say everybody is mixed. It is clear you don't know where you come from or what you are. Instead you believe what people that came from across the oceans tell you. I don't want this to sound like I'm insulting you, but my brother please with the respect, go figure out where you come from and who you are before you will decide on calling yourself coloured. (21 April 2006)

The argument ends there, except for a couple more postings on the thread. There is one powerful line from user Cjoe, which demonstrates the deep attachment to the identity and the need for a descriptive marker:

> Before I was coloured I wasn't born. (22 April 2006)

This particular thread ends with contributions of coloured pride, which show clearly how the identity has been claimed and reinvented by many individuals. User Likwidzoe's use of language and interspersion of Afrikaans phrases and words also indicates his membership of the community:

> You check when I see myself in the mirror, when I look at my friends, my families, we bruin mense in general…I honestly don't believe there is a race more diverse and varied ekse. Ag no, my roots aren't 100% African (too many over-friendly Hottentots, Xhosa, Khoisan maidens and horny slave masters running around back in the day) and what not. That is why I don't claim any other ethnicity. I'm proud to walk this earth as a kleurling. (19 April 2006)

Language and identity

The Afrikaans vernacular distinctive to the coloured community has been 'customarily stigmatized as a mark of social inferiority' (Adhikari 2005: 16). Language is an important marker of individual and group identity as an identification badge both for self and outside perception (Saville-Troike

1982). 'The fixed reference of the body is online transformed into the largely immutable text of the message' (Smith & Kollock 1999). It is thus the perspectives of and language in the messages on the site that reveal the writers' racial identities as coloured, in the absence of any physical cues.

During the discussion of identity, Tiger1 posted the following:

> Being a bruin-ou is the best thing ever. We have invented a way of life that every other race wants to follow. Everyone wants to be just like us!!! Our tongue (slang) here in Durbs, there isn't one person that knows not a word of it. Our dress is unique and undoubtedly the freshest and hottest on the market. Life clothing for coloureds made for coloureds. Playa clothing for coloureds made by coloureds. Everybody wears these clothes, mostly because they've seen us wearing these items. All stars, Pointer t-shirts, Dickies pants, Chuck Taylors, Jack Purcell. Name one person you know who hasn't owned one of these in their lifetime. Peeps, we are special, no doubt!! I'm bruin-ou up to my eyeballs and daaaammmnnn proud of it. (20 April 2006)

Here it can be seen how online discussions that remain within racially defined systems can make use of 'fine-grained racial distinctions that are a meaningful framework for members within the group' (Smith & Kollock 1999: 11). In other words, the way language is used on the site in conversations between users reflects membership of the community. For members of the coloured community in particular, their usage of English is associated with the grammar of non-native language speakers, with more working-class members often displaying second-language proficiency and grammatical interference from Afrikaans. This is very similar to African American vernacular language and the use of Ebonics; and in the same way, language becomes a form of self-differentiation that fosters group membership and group pride. In fact, UNESCO recognises Coloured English as a specific variant of South African English.

A posting on the Bruin-ou site that deals explicitly with language is Ou-cabulary, which features group slang. Slang is constantly changing, and the need to post coloured slang on a site targeted at coloured people indicates the fluidity of language use. It is also assumed that use or knowledge of this slang indicates group membership.

Fashion as a currency of identity

In another posting Tiger1 highlights another common point of identification: fashion. He demonstrates how clothes communicate as though the wearer were an actor on stage. Clothes have become a currency of identity, and here we see how fashion allows us to assume another identity and join a subculture that insulates us from other styles (Finkelstein 1997).

As Hebdige (1988) notes, fashion goods can be weapons of exclusion. The coloured community is generally perceived as being fashion conscious. Youth especially are often seen sporting clothing and sports shoes with the latest fashion labels, and even working-class members own high-status technology items like DVD players, flat-screen televisions, MP3 players and fancy cellphones. Like African Americans in the United States, coloureds tend to be brand conscious, with certain brands (for example, sports items) linked to race consciousness.

This is similar to the trend in the Congo in the 1970s and 1980s, when young, unemployed, lower-class Congolese men known as *sapeurs* dressed in the labels of Parisian *haute couture*, perceived as symbols of refinement. For the *sapeur*, clothing became the essence of his identity: although he was black, unemployed and a discarded colonial relic, he was existentially equal to his European master if he dressed in the same style, pursued the same desires and shared the same sensibilities (Friedman 1992). Often, obtaining these branded items means living beyond ones means, and in a country where race is still often equivalent to class, this aspiration to a middle-class lifestyle can be interpreted as a desire to 'be white' or take on some kind of 'European' identity: a fetishisation of white culture (Klein 2000). In South Africa, under the Group Areas Act even coloured communities were separated by class. With certain sections of the population able to purchase property, for example, the acquisition of material goods was often seen as a way to achieve a higher social status – status seeking via conspicuous consumption. This is also manifested in the travelogues, as discussed below.

Travelogues

Another forum, entitled 'Social', contains the postings of members who share their experiences of travel abroad. Interestingly, all are about trips to Europe or North America, with the exception of one short description of a trip to Nairobi (found in another section of the site). The other descriptions are fairly standard travelogue-like descriptions of places and landmarks visited, first impressions and so on. The very first posting on the forum states that its purpose is to share stories of 'achievement' in order to inspire others. In other words, one marker of achievement is making your way to Europe.

In a posting entitled 'Living La Vida in London', an anonymous member writes about his strategy for adjusting to life abroad:

> At first, I was really homesick and made hundreds (no exaggeration) of phone calls to lost friends in London and family back home. It wasn't long before I moved into the friendly South African circles of the 'coloured community' in London. Life was great; every weekend there was a party and there was always a group of friendly South African guys and gals looking for a good time. (13 July 2005)

This user also describes how the time spent with other coloureds eased his culture shock:

> On the weekends, the coloured South Africans normally get together and banter over a 'few' drinks, which sometimes turns into all-weekend binge benders. This is either at someone's place, a bar, pub or club. Now that it is summer, we have been getting together and playing football in the various beautiful parks that London has to offer (my favourite being Clapham Common in South London), then having braais afterwards. It makes for a lovely social outing and allows one to unwind after a long week at the office and find out from other bruin-ous what their week was like and what they've been up to. We have all become quite a close-knit family. (13 July 2005)

Similarly, another user, also sharing reflections about a trip to London, writes:

> Another enjoyable event was a SA club onboard a boat on the Thames. I think it would be fair to say that I had consumed more than just a fair amount of alcohol, so the recollection of events from that evening is not too clear. I do remember though that it was really great and there were many South Africans, many of whom I knew and hadn't seen in a really long time. The boat had 3 levels each playing their own type of music. It's amazing that we travel so far to stick to our own. The kwaito was happening on the one level and there were 99% Blacks on that floor. On the lower

level there was Hip-hop and RNB and that's where all the Bruin-ous were. (16 February 2005)

In this way, these postings reveal the writers as tourists. And tourists desire experiences they can legitimise as authentic in order to underpin their own sense of self as culturally authentic (Nakamura 2002: 55). Another user writes about his trip to France and Spain and his acute awareness of his racial identity there:

> I thought everyone liked Bruin-ou's in Paris; apparently they do in Madrid too. Most Spanish people consider themselves mixed-race, which is either 'mullatto' or 'mestizo', the former being a mix of black and white. It is not surprising, as Spain has had a history of frequent invasions by other cultures, most notably the Arabs who ruled for centuries. So with all that mixing, racism is virtually non-existent, and inter-racial marriages the norm. Can you see how the world is eventually going to be full of Bruin-ou's! (27 April 2005)

Interestingly, the description of the trip to Uganda via Nairobi does not conform to the format of the other travelogues, which primarily mention highlights and tourist attractions. Instead it emerges that this was a business trip, and in expressing his dismay at the fact that the roads were very bad and that the lifts in his hotel did not work, the writer advises 'please erase all images of South African standards – this was hard-core Africa!'

The predominance of descriptions of trips to Europe and North America indicates that these locations are valued much more highly than trips to other parts of Africa. For the *sapeur*, a pilgrimage to Paris, the source of all things civilised and luxurious, was a necessity, with the final achievement being status of *parisien* or elder – that is, one who had been there and lived the life (Friedman 1992). Throughout the lengthy apprenticeship, a *sapeur* would return to Brazzaville to show his progress in the accumulation of *la gamme* (social status) (Finkelstein 1997). We see this in many of the descriptions above.

One user writes of how he moved his family to New Zealand because of crime in South Africa, and how they return 'home' annually because they miss it so much, but also as a reminder of why they left in the first place. In the 'Expat' forum, another user, Sassy, further reflects on this perceived marginalisation:

> I am proudly South African but look forward to getting British citizenship soon. Dual citizenship to my advantage and the people

I will empower through the pounds and experience I am able to earn here [sic]. I don't miss home as much as I used to and would rather settle here than return some day...let's face it...people are dying like flies from Aids, crime is getting worse, food is so expensive, less opportunities for bruin-ou's now than ever before... IT'S OFF-PUTTING! (30 March 2006)

These links to North America and Europe are also seen in the site's design. There are many links to mixed-race websites originating in the USA, and Bruin-ou.com advertises its partnership with www.multiracial.com.

Music and identity

Several users in the travelogues refer to hip-hop and R & B (rhythm and blues), with the unspoken assumption that these genres of music are most popular within the coloured culture and in a sense define that culture. Battersby (2003) argues that coloured youth in the 1980s used hip-hop to work through the tensions of being racially marginalised and to identify with black people around the globe based on a common oppression and struggle against racism. Similarly, Yarwood argues that a new generation of young coloured South Africans uses black popular culture as a means of actively engaging with, reworking and creating identities that do not necessarily conform to South African notions of race:

> Additionally, a new generation of musical artists are using hip-hop to speak specifically to issues affecting working class coloured communities, the perceived marginal experience of coloureds in post-apartheid South Africa, and as a way to work through issues of coloured identity in contemporary South Africa. (Yarwood 2006: 52)

What is interesting is that through music, coloureds reverse the return to Africa, by looking to black American popular culture (rather than black South African culture) to help them define their identity. Young coloureds attempt to link up with global notions of blackness based on common understandings of dislocation, displacement, rootlessness, marginalisation and racial oppression, as contemporary coloured identity becomes a continued interaction between local experiences of identity construction and global black popular culture (Yarwood 2006).

Conclusion

Like other media, the Internet is a reflection of the cultural imagination, a collectively authored, synchronous, interactive hybrid medium. In addition, through borrowing from other media, it is particularly sensitive to shifting figurations of race and thus a good place to see how race is enacted and performed (Nakamura 2002: 55). Coloured identity continues to be vigorously contested in post-apartheid South Africa, and this chapter suggests that Bruin-ou.com has emerged as one vehicle to critically engage with and reinvent a coloured identity and as one key site for identity formation. As Adhikari (2005: xiv) puts it, a 'great advantage of text written by coloured people for coloured readers is that it addresses a specific constituency, communicates in a language broadly accessible to them, through ideas that resonate with them'.

Moreover, the Internet is a theatre of performed identities (Nakamura 2002). Through an analysis of the site it becomes clear that coloured identity does not belong to one place or location, but is instead influenced by a plurality of languages and cultures. It is a community struggling to define itself conclusively, and often looks to Europe and North America for self-definition. In particular, we see that coloured identity is more linked to global notions of blackness than to a South African black identity. In this sense, one might argue that it is an obsolete identity, forged out of a shared history, but disintegrating together with old apartheid geographic boundaries as people become more linked by class than race.

However, from the analysis it is clear that for now, coloured identity is still more than a dated apartheid label; it has been invented and reinvented by coloured people themselves in their attempts to make meaning of their everyday lives (Erasmus 2001). As such, Bruin-ou.com has become a vehicle for the exploration of that identity. While academic and activist arguments about the datedness of the term are valid, and while many so-called coloureds self-identify as black, in reality, coloured identity remains a problematic historical milestone which requires further research.

This chapter also argues that the creation of virtual communities in cyberspace facilitates cultural empowerment, as minority groups are able to consolidate their cultural identities despite geographic borders or other constraints (Wasserman 2002). In this way Bruin-ou.com creates the opportunity for the affirmation and reiteration of the existing cultural identity known as coloured, and also sets the platform for the re-imagining of this identity.

Cyberspace and everyday space are enmeshed and interpenetrating, continuous with and embedded in other social spaces (Lister et al. 2003; Miller & Slater 2000). While users of Bruin-ou.com leave their bodies behind, presumably to gain a more fluid identity, the site reflects new ways of making private practices of identity construction public, and highlights the Internet as an arena for negotiating issues crucial to the conduct of social life. Moreover, this study has highlighted that Internet usage by racial minorities is a necessary, but not sufficient, condition for a meaningfully democratic Internet (Nakamura 2002: 27), while acknowledging that new media are only a part (albeit a significant part) of the impact of broader historical, economic and cultural change on identity (Lister et al. 2003).

Notes

1. As the author self-identifies as black, the term 'coloured' is prefixed by the words 'so-called'. For convenience, from this point onwards the term will be used without any prefixes or quotation marks, though the problematic nature of the identity/term is fully acknowledged.
2. Telephonic interview with Lester Ash, 28 May 2006.
3. This is not to say that any other racial classification is 'pure' if coloured implies mixed.
4. Telephonic interview with Lester Ash, 28 May 2006.
5. National Association for the Advancement of Colored People, a US organisation.

References

Adhikari M (2005) *Not white enough, not black enough: Racial identity in the South African coloured community*. Research in International Studies. Africa Series. Athens, OH: Ohio University Press

Battersby J (2003) Sometimes it feels like I'm not black enough: Recast(e)ing coloured through South African hip-hop as a postcolonial text. In S Jacobs and H Wasserman (eds) *Shifting selves: Post-apartheid essays on mass media, culture and identity*, pp. 109–129. Cape Town: Kwela Books

Castells M (2000) *The rise of the network society*. Oxford: Blackwell

Dowling Z (2001) Research methodology and the Internet: A study of the Internet as a data-capturing tool. MPhil thesis, Stellenbosch University

Erasmus Z (2001) *Coloured by history, shaped by place*. Cape Town: Kwela Books

Finkelstein J (1997) Chic theory. *Australian Humanities Review*. Accessed 20 April 2006, http://www.lib.latrobe.edu.au/AHR/archive/Issue-March-1997/finkelstein.html

Friedman J (1992) Narcissism, roots and postmodernity: The constitution of selfhood in the global crisis. In S Lash and J Friedman (eds) *Modernity and identity*. Oxford: Blackwell

Goldstuck Report (2005) *Internet access in South Africa 2005*. Accessed 25 May 2006, http://www.theworx.biz/access05.htm

Hebdige D (1988) *Hiding in the light*. London: Routledge

Hendricks C (2005) Debating coloured identity in the Western Cape. *African Security Review* 14(4). Accessed 10 June 2006, http://www.iss.co.za/pubs/ASR/14No4/CHendricks.htm

Hewson C, Yule P, Laurent D & Vogel C (2003) *Internet research methods: A practical guide for the social and behavioural sciences*. London: Sage Publications

Hine C (2000) *Virtual ethnography*. London: Sage Publications

Holstein J & Gubrium J (1999) Phenomenology, ethnomethodology and interpretive practice: Strategies of inquiry. In N Denzin and Y Lincoln (eds) *Handbook of qualitative research* (3rd edition), pp. 483–505. Thousand Oaks, CA: Sage Publications

Keegan T (1996) *Colonial South Africa and the origins of the racial order*. Cape Town: David Philip

Klein N (2000) *No logo*. New York: Picador

Lindlof T & Shatzer M (1998) Media ethnography in a virtual space. *Journal of Broadcasting and Electronic Media* 42(2): 170–189

Lister M, Dovey J, Giddings S, Grant I & Kelly K (2003) *New media: A critical introduction*. London and New York: Routledge

Miller D & Slater D (2000) *The Internet: An ethnographic approach*. Oxford: Berg

Murphy P (1999) Media cultural studies' uncomfortable embrace of ethnography. *Journal of Communication Inquiry* 23(3): 205–221

Nakamura L (2002) *Cybertypes: Race, ethnicity, and identity on the Internet*. London and New York: Routledge

Pickel B (1997) *Coloured identity and ethnicity: A case study in the former coloured areas of the Western Cape, South Africa*. Demokratie und Entwicklung Series No. 28, Hamburg

Rheingold H (1993) *The virtual community: Homesteading on the electronic frontier*. Reading, MA: Addison-Wesley

Rheingold H (2000) The virtual community: Finding connection in a computerized world. In H Mackay and T O'Sullivan (eds) *The media reader: Continuity and transformation*. London: Sage Publications

Saville-Troike M (1982) *The ethnography of communication*. Oxford: Basil Blackwell

Scheper-Hughes N (1994) *Mixed feelings: The recovery of spoiled identities in the new South Africa*. Accessed 20 April 2006, http://nationalhumanitiescenter.org/publications/hongkong/scheper.htm

Smith M & Kollock P (eds) (1999) *Communities in cyberspace*. London: Routledge

Statistics South Africa (2005) *Mid-year population estimates 2005*. Accessed 25 May 2006, http://www.statssa.gov.za/publications/P0302/P03022005.pdf

Wasserman H (2002) Between the local and the global: South African languages and the Internet. *African and Asian Studies* 1(4): 303–321

Woolgar S (1996) Technologies as cultural artefacts. In W Dutton (ed.) *Information and communication technologies: Visions and realities*. Oxford: Oxford University Press

Yarwood J (2006) Deterritorialised blackness: (Re)making coloured identities in South Africa. *Postamble* 2(1): 46–58

10 The mass subject in Antjie Krog's Country of My Skull

Anthea Garman

> Trying to understand the new South Africa without the Truth and Reconciliation Commission would be futile; trying to understand the Commission without this book would be irresponsible.
>
> André Brink, on the back cover of *Country of My Skull*

Transition, the TRC and Krog

The Truth and Reconciliation Commission (TRC) is arguably the most significant of the new South African state's attempts after 1994 to deal with all the fraught and complex events of the past which stood in the way of forging a single new nation with a sense of oneness and wholeness. The commission leaned heavily on the news media as its means of information dissemination, believing that the participation of all South Africans via radio and TV especially (but also through print) would have the effect of drawing everyone in the country into a vicarious participation in this process of discovery, forgiveness and healing.[1] The medium that did the most to track the entire process of the TRC was the SABC radio service, involving a team that was dedicated to this task alone for more than two years. This team was headed by poet Antjie Krog.[2]

Soon after the TRC's hearings got under way Krog was approached by Anton Harber, editor of the *Mail & Guardian*, to write a piece as part of a focus called 'Two years of transition: A series by leading South African authors, celebrating the second birthday of our democracy and exploring the nuances of a changing society'. Starting on 24 May 1996 with 'Pockets of humanity', Krog wrote a series of articles about her experiences of reporting on the TRC.[3] The printing of these five articles (from May 1996 to June 1997) had two results: Krog was to win a prestigious journalism award,[4] and to come to the attention of book publisher Stephen Johnson of Random House. This resulted in the publication of *Country of My Skull* (Krog 1998, 2000), one of the first accounts of the TRC, in April 1998.[5]

Beyond journalism

But the book is much more than journalism. It is also a brave and honest confrontation with the commission process from a highly personal point of view and occasionally in searingly poetic language (Olivier 1998: 221).

Despite the attention given to the highly charged emotion, poetic language and affect written into *Country of My Skull*, it is a fast-paced narrative which spans the life of the TRC and owes a great deal of its value to the fact that its roots – both the actual materials used and the techniques employed – are in the actual journalism activities, the interviewing, and the direct observations and experiences of the author of the processes and the people. Hours and hours of actual voices caught on tape by the SABC radio reporters are the raw material that forms the backbone of this book. Access to the actual words of those who experienced and those who perpetrated some of the most notorious events of the past, insight into the side discussions and the behind-the-scenes decisions and manipulations not normally open to the public are here to be read, and thus known. In the book the author reveals what the journalist could not say at the time, and often in present-tense language which carries the same urgency and immediacy that news journalism as a form imparts. It is difficult to pigeonhole *Country of My Skull* in a genre, not because journalism hasn't been successfully worked into book form before (New Journalism was pioneered out of exactly this kind of genre mutation), but because of the context of atrocity and because of Krog's taking up the particular position of *witness* to the testimony of atrocity. This stance of witness is evident in her radio journalism, her essays for the *Mail & Guardian* and ultimately – and most effectively – in her book.

Reviewer Gerrit Olivier said of the radio reports:

> In her characteristic Free State Afrikaans accent Samuel[6] combined factual reportage with strong involvement in the process…despite her many doubts Samuel has been an advocate of the process… not surprisingly some listeners objected to what they perceived to be the moral and ethical pressures emanating from Samuel's journalism. (Olivier 1998: 221)

Turning to the book, he notes that Krog provides here the rationale for the advocacy of her journalism – the forcing of 'headlines...into the national consciousness' – and says that she brings to the book the same 'moral, philosophical and linguistic issues that have come to characterise her *oeuvre* as a poet' (Olivier 1998: 222).

While not denying that the TRC journalism[7] generally played a significant informational role in alerting South Africans to the events and debates around the commission process, I want to focus on Krog's particular performance as the witness in the pages of *Country of My Skull* and highlight this for the purpose of making an argument about a particular writer experimenting with identity formation through the creative use of the materials and knowledge generated by the TRC. Through the use of arresting metaphors and highly embodied language – which is very often activated to indicate states of distress or extremis – and constant injection of the 'I', the writer makes herself the listener, observer and witness to all she relates. The book is her vehicle for doing what could not be done through news journalism. Journalism's procedural adherence to 'objectivity' as a norm and prohibition of the injection of the 'I' of the journalist into the reporting mean that reporters must find another means to declare, express or enact their reactions to the TRC process, which involved them as South Africans, citizens or fellow humans.

Krog's journalism was considered controversial in that she did not always adhere to these procedural norms. In *Country of My Skull* she not only explicitly performs the responses of an 'I', but also engages in the debates surrounding the seeking and telling of truth and the connections between language and extremities of experience and their implications for a sense of national home and belonging. While noting that the book has other uses beyond our borders (for example, its use as a window text into the post-apartheid situation and its use as a seed text for a film about the TRC), I am postulating that *Country of My Skull* is taken up with such effect within South Africa because it is a text that enables readers to participate in a 'mass subjectivity' that allows for an imaginary yet unified 'we', as South Africans. In building the argument that *Country* enables public participation in a particular kind of mass subjectivity, I need to explore certain crucial components that Habermas (1991) outlines as being of importance to the functioning of a public sphere, and which are taken up and inflected by Michael Warner (2002) for today.

The concept of the 'mass subject and the mass public'

In outlining an argument about 'mass subjectivity' and its formation through reading, the first component I want to deal with is the crucial nature of the text–reader relationship. Thomas McCarthy points out in the introduction to *The Structural Transformation of the Public Sphere* that Habermas 'traces the *interdependent* [my italics] development of the literary and political self-consciousness' of the new class that gave rise to the eighteenth-century bourgeois public sphere. McCarthy says Habermas 'weaves together accounts of the rise of the novel and of literary and political journalism and the spread of reading societies, salons, and coffee-houses into a *Bildungsroman* of this child of the eighteenth century' (Habermas 1991: xi–xii). In other words, Habermas shows through his study that the primary vehicle for the functioning of the public sphere was the literary in its multiple forms, and that the realisation of 'public-ness' in its new public-sphere form, and 'public opinion' as mobilised by this new class, was via the literary. But what McCarthy emphasises is that the literary was more than vehicle or means; it was also a site of changing consciousness. Warner takes this further by emphasising the literary as integral to the rise of the sense of 'public' *as a mode of being* when he says 'the imaginary reference point of the public was constructed through an understanding of print' (2002: 162). Thus, for Warner it is in reading printed information that one participates in the awareness that the 'same printed goods are being consumed by an indefinite number of others'. This awareness comes to be built into the meaning of the printed object and the reader is therefore partaking in mass subjectivity (as part of a public) by reading. As José van Dijck puts it, 'material inscriptions mediate between individuality and collectivity as well as between past and present' (2004: 270).

A particular sense of being a public, which has its origins in eighteenth-century Europe, is still with us today. In the introduction to *Publics and Counterpublics* Warner insists that 'much of the texture of modern social life lies in the invisible presence of these publics that flit about us like large, corporate ghosts' (Warner 2002: 7). A great many of our activities in the world are orientated around our 'practical sense of what publics are' (Warner 2002: 8), even if we cannot pin them down as social entities. This 'practical fiction', which permeates our modern world and drives many of its permutations, has its roots in the formation of the public sphere that Habermas seeks to understand as evolving in the mercantilist economies of eighteenth-century Europe. Via the literary (in the broadest sense), says Warner, we apprehend the public, participate in the public, come to have a sense of public personhood and become the 'mass-public subject'.

It is the nexus of these two components (the literary and the subjective and their interpenetration in a particular dimension called 'public') that I am holding on to in my quest to set a theoretical platform on which to examine the a/effect of *Country of My Skull*. Warner says that inherent in the single reader's experience of the book is the knowledge that the publishing industry makes possible a multiplicity of readers and so the single reader is, through printing, placed knowingly in a 'public' context. Texts and publics, says Warner, are 'mutually defining'. Circulation of texts is, therefore, 'more than textual' (Warner 2002: 16); it also facilitates the formation of a particular type of subjectivity operating en masse. Warner outlines the components of this public subjectivity:

> To address a public or to think of oneself as belonging to a public is to be a certain kind of person, to inhabit a certain kind of social world, to have at one's disposal certain media and genres, to be motivated by a certain normative horizon, and to speak within a certain language ideology. (Warner 2002: 10)

He also notes that a public subjectivity is a 'different style of embodiment, a new sociability and solidarity, and a scene for further improvisation' (Warner 2002: 14). It is important to keep in mind that Habermas does not see 'high literature' as the only means of public-ness. All forms of textual production of the time could act as 'carriers'[8] of public-sphere activities, and many of them were deeply intertwined in the emerging capitalist economies of the era.[9] Warner also points out that 'the contexts of commodities and politics share the same media and the same metalanguage for constructing our notion of what a public or a people is' (Warner 2002: 170).

This changing sense of human subjectivity in the eighteenth century into a double public–private individual is implicated in the rising sense of a taking on of 'public' by private people as an outgrowth of the previously private sphere. Although Habermas's concern in his inquiry is not primarily subjectivity, it is evident through his explanation of the development of the bourgeois class and the shifting understandings of private and public[10] that subjectivity is itself being rearranged under these changed circumstances. Warner takes this idea much further by asking what kind of subject a public/mass subject is and suggests that all human beings in the modern world have two conditions of being (here quoting Hannah Arendt and Mary Dietz): a private subjectivity and a public subjectivity (2002: 59). In public, human beings are not just an aggregation of private people and not just private people who create public practices. 'As subjects of publicity – its hearers, speakers, viewers, and doers – we have a different relation to ourselves, a different affect from that which we have in other contexts' (Warner 2002: 160). It is this condition of public subjectivity that is the focus of Chapter 3 of *Publics and Counterpublics*.[11] Warner quotes Habermas: 'In the *Tatler*, the *Spectator*, and the *Guardian* the public held up a mirror to itself... The public that read and debated this sort of thing read and debated about itself' (2002: 165). Warner adds: '...but in reading and debating it as a public, they adopted a very special rhetoric about their own personhood' (2002: 165).

From 'public' to 'nation'

Benedict Anderson, in the text *Imagined Communities* (1991), makes the same point about the discovery through print of a public of other reading individuals, but takes this further, linking it to the shift in consciousness which began to loosen up from older ideas of community and to engage with the incipient idea of 'nation'. Covering the same historical territory as Habermas, he looks at how burgeoning print industries and the shift from the 'sacred language' of Latin to multiple vernaculars facilitated a change in consciousness about community. He says the 'possibility of imagining the nation' arose when three fundamental cultural conceptions shifted in seventeenth- and eighteenth-century Europe (Anderson 1991: 36ff): the status of the 'sacred language' of Latin which primarily bonded people to the Church as their first community began to erode; the concentration of political power in the hierarchical and centripetal 'high centres' (the divinely ordained monarchs in their city states) which began to move outward with growing administrations and seek manageable boundaries; and the growth of an idea of time which allowed for the conception of multiple others existing in the world simultaneously. The two forms of print he sees as most influential in facilitating these changing ideas were the novel and the newspaper. Because the readers of these texts were addressed intimately through these vehicles as a 'we', the knowledge of there being a simultaneous group of others also reading was reinforced. Anderson points out that the writers of these publications assumed that there was a bond connecting all their unknown readers – the bond of reading this very text. This, then, is the experience that allows for a different kind of imagination about a community that exists but cannot possibly be known – the 'imagined community'. The centrality of print's power was that it enabled 'rapidly growing numbers of people to think about themselves, and to relate themselves to others, in profoundly new ways' (Anderson 1991: 36). The shift in the three social factors pointed to above, coupled with the penetration of print across communities and territories in the vernacular languages, enabled a new community to be thought into being – the nation.

Craig Calhoun puts it like this:

> Communications infrastructures have facilitated space-transcending linkages which encouraged people to give up the narrow outlooks of their native villages for an understanding of themselves as (individually) members of the nation. (Calhoun 1997: 117)

This state of mass subjectivity is our inheritance and our disposition as modern people in a media-saturated world. The idea of 'public' as a functioning experience in our world is so much the air we breathe as to be unremarkable, and the bifurcation of our subjectivity is so taken for granted that we cannot conceive of an alternative or a prior condition. Likewise, our sense of belonging to a nation and our sense of the nation as an actual entity seems so real and tangible that the imaginary and mediated aspects of it escape our common-sense understandings. But it is this very construction of public–private subjectivity in relation to texts that allows for participation in an imagined, public and unknowably large community. This idea and practice, perfected over the centuries via the mediated and textual, allows for people to conceive of a different kind of personhood and nationhood.

The return of the body

But the public sphere, its activities and the construction of mass subjectivity have a corollary denial of individuality and bodily particularity. Warner's crucial insight is that the idealised and normative public sphere not only enables 'strangers' to discover a 'we' (a mass subjectivity) through the public-sphere vehicles (such as texts), but it simultaneously abstracts its participants from their individual subjectivities rooted in class, race and gender. This Warner calls the inherent 'bad faith of the *res publica* of letters' and says it requires 'a denial of the bodies that gave access to it' (Warner 2002: 176). The ideal of the public sphere is that anyone, regardless of power, position, riches or education, should be able to engage in public in rational-critical debate, but in effect the 'actually existing' (to use Nancy Fraser's phrase [1992: 109]) public sphere favours middle-class white men, who have been groomed to exercise its practices. The contradiction is that the public sphere both allows for a desirable abstraction into a mass subjectivity and at the same time makes evident that each individual's bodily particularity precludes entire participation in the mass public-ness. Warner comments: 'I'm suggesting...that a fundamental feature of the contemporary public sphere is this double movement of identification and alienation' (2002: 182).

The way the modern public sphere resolves this contradiction, according to Warner, is through the reactivation of the category 'publicity':

> Responding to an immanent contradiction in the bourgeois public sphere, mass publicity promises a reconciliation between embodiment and self-abstraction. This can be a powerful appeal, especially to those minoritised by the public sphere's rhetoric of normative disembodiment. (Warner 2002: 181)

In both Habermas's and Warner's use, the word 'publicity' acts as a package term meaning the dissemination of texts, ideas and discussions (and their forms) as well as the characteristics and a/effects attached to the person operating in the public sphere. In Habermas's study, in the prior public sphere of the autocratic ruler, 'publicity' referred to the status and representativity of the only truly public person who carried this as an 'aura' of power. In the bourgeois public sphere, 'publicity' retains some of these notions (for example, the 'display' aspect) but is no longer confined to the ruler or the members of the state. Habermas takes a dim view of the publicity attached to persons, approves of its decline in the classic public sphere in favour of cerebral activities, and sees the return in modern-day media to the display of public figures as a 'refeudalising' of the public sphere and a diminishing of its ideals and power for rational-critical debate.

Warner warns us about the alienating capacity of the public sphere. He argues that in today's public sphere, we see people mobilising publicity and their individual and bodily particularities in order to engage the terms and limits of what takes place in public. Warner's argument hinges strongly on his activation of the body as a vehicle and he turns to the news media to make this case. Using the example of the 'discourse of disasters' (Warner 2002: 177), he shows how the reporting of injury to other people's bodies (and this works particularly well when masses are affected by major cataclysms) draws a public into witnessing on a mass scale and causes them to understand themselves, in this moment, as having cohered into a 'non-corporeal mass witness'. He goes on to say that the 'mass media are dominated by genres that construct the mass subject's impossible relation to a body' (Warner 2002: 179) and says reports of horrors, assassinations, terrorism and even sports are in this category of journalism which he calls 'mass-imaginary transitivism'. This transitive participation includes the tabloid coverage of celebrities, who are endlessly dissected for their human failings. The same knowledge ingrained in print culture, that by reading one is joining a public, is activated in the consumption of the mass-media publicity of disasters and celebrity reporting, but in these cases the individual is joining a public of witnesses in a vicarious body.

Warner concludes this argument as follows:

> The centrality of this contradiction in the legitimate textuality of the video-capitalist state, I think, is the reason why the discourse of the public sphere is so entirely given over to a violently desirous speculation on bodies. What I have tried to emphasise is that the effect of disturbance in the mass publicity is not a corruption introduced into the public sphere by its colonisation through mass media. It is the legacy of the bourgeois public sphere's founding logic, the contradictions of which become visible whenever the public sphere can no longer turn a blind eye to its privileged bodies. (Warner 2002: 182–183)

The subject matter of Krog's journalism and book is precisely the disastrous, the catastrophic and the impacts on actual bodies both in the telling of the testimonies by those who appeared at the TRC and in the experiences of the author. Warner's insight enables us to see why this resurgence of the bodily and the personally particular is important and why this 'transitive' and vicarious participating in a mass body has relevance for the detection of new South African identity construction in this text.

Autobiographical writing and testimonies of atrocity

Australian literary theorist Gillian Whitlock writes about the spate of commissions, hearings and public engagements around the world which have taken place within the last decade and which mainly focus on atrocities perpetrated against ostracised peoples. She says:

> Testimonial forms of autobiographical expression elicited by Commissions of Inquiry are at the forefront of debates about race and identity, most particularly in thinking about the role of

the State in the politics of race and reconciliation. The meaning
of reconciliation as a strategy, policy, and ethics, is being shaped
as a global politics, albeit one which finds quite different local
formations and expressions. Testimony is at the heart of this
struggle. (Whitlock 2001: 201)

Whitlock's interest is the 'stolen children' issue, which became public in 1997 in Australia,[12] but she makes points that are strongly applicable to the South Africa of and post the TRC, and to the uses of and responses to public testimonies. It is most often the case with such commissions that while some prior evidence usually exists of suffering and abuse on a large scale, the gathering of testimonies and the holding of public hearings brings into the public domain 'a mass of voices'[13] never previously heard. This demands a response from the public at large never previously elicited. Carli Coetzee remarks: 'Reviews of *Country of My Skull* repeatedly stress the fact that the text allows the "voices of the voiceless" to be heard, an image that ignores that Black South Africans have always had a voice, that it was the ear that was lacking' (2001: 693). Meira Cook comments that the 'TRC's attempt to uncover narratives of violence was instrumental in bringing many lost stories back into symbolic currency and social circulation' (2001: 73). It is quite evident in the text of *Country of My Skull* that Krog the author is aware of these arguments and is deliberately, as both a journalist and a poet, doing her part to put these voices into the public domain. In the literature that deals with trauma, theorists stress the act of listening as critical, perhaps not to the healing of the trauma sufferer, but certainly to rooting the perpetration of the atrocity in reality and therefore in history.[14]

Whitlock's most useful insight, which I want to pick up on and apply to *Country of My Skull*, is that the silenced people who spoke at these hearings took on the authority and position of the 'first person' (using a grammatical metaphor and a concept of subjectivity rooted in language) and forced the hearers (and very often the enfranchised, empowered and usually complicit) into the listening position of the 'second person' who is required to respond ethically and relationally to the first person. 'The presence of the first and the second person, the narrator and the witness, is vital to the narrative exchange established through testimonial speaking and writing' (Whitlock 2001: 199).

Whitlock's interest is in the person who is placed 'in this textual economy as the second person', the addressee, the recipient (Whitlock 2001: 199–200). The burden now placed on this second person is to become a witness who 'affirms the experience and trauma of the first person', who 'reflect(s) upon the self, upon his/her own responsibility and implication in the events being narrated by a traumatised subject' (Whitlock 2001: 200). She comments that in this transaction the burden of shame shifts to the listener and by extension to the dominant culture. In response 'the politics of reconciliation comes into play...as a quite specific discursive framework, as a personal and collective strategy which recognises the complex dynamics of this shaming as a catharsis' (Whitlock 2001: 200). Thus:

> The politics of reconciliation as it is currently emerging in Africa, Australia and North America requires in the second person a subjective identification, contrition, introspection, and finally a change of heart. (Whitlock 2001: 210)

It becomes evident why autobiography as a textual vehicle is the most powerful means for such a transaction. Calling Krog's *Country of My Skull* 'a brilliant autobiography of the second person', Whitlock notes that:

> the fragments of traumatic memory spoken by victims to the South African Truth and Reconciliation Commission are braided together with Krog's autobiographical narrative. Krog struggles to get the relationship between these narratives right. Like Carmel Bird,[15] Krog too produces her book as an apology and as a recognition of complicity. (Whitlock 2001: 210)

The textual transaction that Whitlock outlines is not just first person–second person dialogue. It also includes an implicit third person – the readers to whom the text is addressed and who 'must be told and reminded repeatedly to respond from the heart' (Whitlock 2001: 209). Positioning the readers into this appropriate response also becomes the responsibility of the second-person writer, and holding the boundary between complicity, culpability and denial is an ongoing, arduous task. At this point I want to join Whitlock's grammatical categories (first person, second person) to Warner's understanding that the purpose of engaging in a text is to join a 'we', a shared incorporeal subjectivity, which is first-person plural. Krog's TRC-inspired text is not only the second-person performance of ethical listening to the thousands of new and previously silenced voices, but also a means to enable the third-person readers to join Krog and the first-person speakers in an imaginary 'new South African' subjectivity. It is interesting to read the reviews of the book in this light and to note that the reviewers take up the positioning by, firstly, themselves responding as ethical hearers of Krog's story (and of the first-person stories she hosts) and, secondly, urging their readers to do the same.[16]

New South African selfhood

It now remains to root these insights in wider processes of the South African transition after 1994 and to refer back to the ideal of the public person acting/speaking in the normative public sphere. Deborah Posel, in a recent paper presented at 'The Reasons of Faith' colloquium, said 'a particular kind of faith in the production of selfhood is at the heart of the South African Constitution'.[17] And in dealing with the divided, atrocity-littered past, the idea that 'speaking is healing, has become common sense'. Posel's argument is that the TRC became the 'first vector' of the project to reconstitute the South African self through the constitutional provision that every single South African has the right to speak. Via a series of individual performances involving victims and perpetrators held *in public*[18] and engaging an audience both real and virtual (via the media processes which broadcast the hearings), 'the mutuality of damage and the shared need to be healed gives access to a shared community and a shared humanity predicated on the shared experience of pain'.

Posel proposes that 'Foucault's logic of the secular confessional was appropriated by the TRC and extended to the national self, through multiple individual performances' and points out that this logic has had several outcomes, two of which are useful for my argument. Firstly, dealing with its shameful past has allowed South Africa to rejoin an international community, but it has also entered the 'global community of suffering…which leads to mutual humanity' – a certain late twentieth-century understanding of mass and national selves. Secondly, the post-apartheid moment is filled with instances of speaking about this construction of a new national self, particularly evident in popular media such as radio talk shows. Posel commented after delivering the paper that the notion of the person which underlies liberal democracy is the rational, deliberative subject (the classic public-sphere persona as espoused by Habermas's study). But the TRC – as well as the many processes like it around the world – has ushered in a different notion, the 'emotional, affective, damaged' subject.

If Warner's insight that the corollary need for those participating in mass subjectivity is to experience transitive participation in a mass body is joined to Posel's understanding that the new national subject can be one which is damaged and affected, one can then see the evocative power of a text like Krog's which deals precisely with a people newly allowed into the public sphere to declare their damage and affectedness, and asserting their rightfulness in belonging to the democratic South African state.

Conclusion

I am asserting that Krog's radio journalism, print essays and ultimately the book *Country of My Skull* show an ethical performance being played out of a journalist/writer as the witness and listener to the speakers of testimonies of atrocity who had newly entered the South African public domain. By using public-sphere theory and focusing particularly on how people use media hermeneutically to craft subjectivity, I am suggesting that at the moment of the TRC in South Africa, a text such as Krog's was instrumental in showing (in particular white) South Africans how to think and behave differently in relation to who the 'we' of the new nation could be. This 'we' is a departure from the rational–critical subject usually constructed by the nation state and includes an acknowledgement that the national body as a whole is wounded and scarred. A text which models hurt, affectedness and apology provides a hermeneutic vehicle for those seeking a new understanding of – and a place within – a new collective.

But I want to put it more simply. I want this hand of mine to write it. For us all; all voices, all victims:

because of you
this country no longer lies
between us but within
it breathes becalmed
after being wounded
in its wondrous throat

in the cradle of my skull
it sings, it ignites
my tongue, my inner ear, the cavity of my heart
shudders towards the outline
    new in soft intimate clicks and gutturals

of my soul the retina learns to expand
daily because by a thousand stories
I was scorched

a new skin.

I am changed for ever. I want to say
    forgive me
    forgive me
    forgive me

You whom I have wronged, please
take me
with you
(Krog 1998: 278–279)

Notes

1   For an account of the TRC's reliance on and relationship with the news media, see Anthea Garman, 'Pressure on the press' (*Natal Witness* 12 February 1997) and 'Media creation: How the TRC and the media have impacted each other' (*Track Two* 6(3/4); accessed 14 October 2007, http://ccrweb.ccr.uct.ac.za/archive/two/6_34/p36_garman.html).

2   By this point in her life Krog was an established award-winning poet, with seven volumes of poetry in print and the prestigious Hertzog Prize for *Lady Anne* (1989).

3   Krog's other articles for the *Mail & Guardian* series are 'Truth trickle becomes a flood' (1 November 1996); 'Overwhelming trauma of the truth' (24 December 1996); 'The parable of the bicycle' (7 February 1997); and 'Unto the third or fourth generation' (13 June 1997).

4   The Foreign Correspondents Award shared with Justice Malala (at that time senior writer for the *Financial Mail*). The SABC radio team was also honoured for their journalism, receiving the Pringle Award from the South African Union of Journalists.

5   The book had an immediate and powerful impact. It was widely reviewed by English and Afrikaans newspapers and magazines, and it drew substantial attention internationally. In the next two years it garnered the following awards for Krog: the Sunday Times Alan Paton Award (shared with Stephen Clingman for *Bram Fischer: Afrikaner Revolutionary*); the BookData/South African Booksellers' Book of the Year prize; the Hiroshima Foundation Award (shared with John Kani); and the Olive Schreiner Award for the best work of prose published between 1998 and 2000. *Country* received an honourable mention in the 1999 Noma Awards for Publishing in Africa and it also appears as one of 'Africa's 100 Best Books of the Twentieth Century' (an initiative of the Zimbabwe International Book Fair). It has been made into a film (called *In My Country*, directed by John Boorman, with Juliette Binoche and Samuel L Jackson) and has been prescribed in many universities around the world as essential reading for students studying South African history or issues of dealing with the past. Krog became internationally known as an expert on national reconciliation and healing, political transition, trauma and memory, resulting in many invitations to speak around the world on these subjects.

6   Samuel is Krog's married name and the name she chose to use as a TRC journalist.

7   This journalism took many forms: the *TRC Special Report* edited by Max du Preez which aired once a week on national TV; a dedicated radio channel allowing listeners to tune into the live hearings; and of course all the newspaper reports. The commission also drew the attention of foreign media at significant points.

8   A very useful word used by Habermas to capture not only a medium but a dimension of public sphere (see Habermas 1991: 23).

9   See his discussion of the 'unique explosive power' of the press in its many forms (Habermas 1991: 20–26).

10 In Chapter 1 of *Transformation* Habermas outlines a prior situation in which 'public' was only the province – and status – of the absolute ruler. In the bourgeois public sphere, there are two significant changes which grow out of the prior states of public (the ruler) and private (the people): the autocratic ruler has become a multifaceted state which considers its various organs (army, administration, judiciary, courts and their edicts and buildings) to be 'public'; this state addresses a people which it also considers to be the 'public'. The private people via the mercantile class consider themselves to be operating in public as the 'public' and constituting 'public opinion' which judges and calls the state to account for its actions.

11 This chapter was written for a 1989 conference introducing the English translation of Habermas's *Transformation*.

12 In 1997 *Bringing Them Home*, the report of the national inquiry into the Australian aboriginal children who had been separated from their families, was released. It claimed that a tenth to a third of aboriginal children had been removed from their families by the state between 1910 and 1970. The commission travelled the country, heard 535 personal stories and collected another 1 000 in written form.

13 Krog's words, speaking about the thousands of TRC testimonies on 2 November 2005 at the Boekehuis launch of *'n Ander Tongval*. Whitlock calls it an 'unprecedented outpouring' (2001: 210). According to Fiona Ross (1998), the TRC collected 21 000 statements.

14 See, for example, Laub (1992).

15 Author of *The Stolen Children: Their Stories* published by Random House (1998).

16 This, of course, is different from their sometimes quite critical comments of her style or use of material. In my archive search for reviews in South African media, I collected 23 from the period 19 April to 8 December 1998, including responses by reviewers to other reviewers. It is remarkable that only one reviewer rejected Krog's positioning of the reader (Terence Friend in the *Citizen*, 19 May 1998) and positioned Krog herself as the 'Tutu-worshipping Krog'.

17 My notes from the verbal presentation on 18 October 2005 at the Wits Institute for Social and Economic Research, Johannesburg. See Posel (2005).

18 Unlike many other similar commissions, this was a crucial commitment made by the TRC.

References

Anderson B (1991) *Imagined communities: Reflections on the origin and spread of nationalism* (2nd edition). London: Verso

Calhoun C (1997) *Nationalism*. Buckingham: Open University Press

Coetzee C (2001) 'They never wept, the men of my race': Antjie Krog's *Country of my skull* and the white South African signature. *Journal of Southern African Studies* 27(4): 687–696

Cook M (2001) Metaphors for suffering: Antjie Krog's *Country of my skull*. *Mosaic* 34(3): 73–89

Fraser N (1992) Rethinking the public sphere: A contribution to the critique of actually existing democracy. In C Calhoun (ed.) *Habermas and the public sphere*. Cambridge, MA: MIT Press

Habermas J (1991) *The structural transformation of the public sphere: An inquiry into a category of bourgeois society*. Cambridge, MA: MIT Press

Krog A (1998) *Country of my skull*. Johannesburg: Random House

Krog A (2000) *Country of my skull: Guilt, sorrow and the limits of forgiveness in the new South Africa*. New York: Three Rivers Press

Laub D (1992) Bearing witness, or the vicissitudes of listening. In S Felman and D Laub (eds) *Testimony: Crises of witnessing in literature, psychoanalysis and history*. New York: Routledge

Olivier G (1998) The 'fierce belonging' of Antjie Krog: Review of *Country of my skull* by Antjie Krog, Random House, Johannesburg, 1998. *African Studies* 57(2): 221–228

Posel D (2005) The post-apartheid confessional: Faith in the self. Paper delivered at The Reasons of Faith: Religion in Modern Public Life Colloquium at the Wits Institute for Social and Economic Research, Johannesburg, 17–20 October

Ross F (1998) From a 'culture of shame' to a 'circle of guilt'. *Southern African Review of Books* (June). Accessed 27 August 2001, http://www.uni-ulm.de/~rturrell/sarobnewhtml/ross.html

Van Dijck J (2004) Mediated memories: Personal cultural memory as object of cultural analysis. *Continuum* 18(2): 261–277

Warner M (2002) *Publics and counterpublics*. New York: Zone Books

Whitlock G (2001) In the second person: Narrative transactions in stolen generations' testimony. *Biography* 24(1): 197–214

Expressing identities

11 Crime reporting: Meaning and identity making in the South African press

Marguerite J Moritz

'I was the blood-and-guts king of the *Cape Argus*...and I enjoyed it!'

Press photographer

News in the United States is replete with examples of sensational crime stories. The 'Barbie doll' murder of JonBenét Ramsey, the high school shootings at Columbine, the OJ Simpson trial, the Laci Peterson disappearance – these are but a few recent examples of stories that have not only dominated US headlines, but also captured the media spotlight around the world. Despite their enormous appetite for crime narratives, US journalists have set some self-imposed limits, especially around issues of visual representation. As a general practice, for example, mainstream US news workers are reluctant to use close-ups of graphic images or shots of corpses. There is no absolute prohibition, but professional codes and practices make it clear that images of dead bodies, bloody scenes and body parts as well as close-ups of the victims of crimes, terrorist attacks and natural disasters are highly problematic for mainstream news organisations, and typically their use is discouraged (see, for example, Fishman 2003; Moritz 2003).

Similarly, crime reporting in South Africa is a chief component of the news, '"omnipresent" with horrendously graphic descriptions', in the words of Philip Scheiner (2006, interview), a South African communications consultant. But in the South African case, searing headlines and sensational narratives are often accompanied by graphic images. The practice, especially in newspapers, has been routinely valorised, hence the comment from the photographer whose quote opens this chapter. South African journalists acknowledge that the impact of their approach to crime reporting has been largely unexamined by journalists and by the media organisations they work for.

Yet the use and framing of crime stories and images raise many questions: What is the impact of these practices on journalists, on their subjects and on their audiences? What meanings do these stories create as they circulate and recirculate through an increasingly interlocking media system? What meaning does crime reporting have for the national self-image of South Africa and for its international image? These are the questions that I address in this chapter as part of a broader research agenda on the professional codes and practices of journalists who cover traumas. While I can speak with some knowledge in this area from the US side, my experience in South Africa is limited. Rather than making knowledge claims, I am instead offering observations and raising issues for discussion, debate and further inquiry.

My primary data are drawn from transcripts of recorded focus groups and in-depth interviews conducted with dozens of South African journalists in May 2002. In all, 11 different focus-group sessions were held with journalists in Cape Town, Pretoria, Johannesburg and Nelspruit. Each session had at least 5 participants but most had between 10 and 30. Participants included both print and broadcast reporters, editors and photographers working for national, regional and local news organisations. Their testimony and reflections offer important insights into journalistic processes and beliefs, which in turn impact on subjects and audiences at a time when the very identity of South Africa is being reshaped both at home and on the international stage.

News texts and value judgements

Fictional films and entertainment television have long provided audiences and scholars alike with a rich variety of words and images that offer a deeply revealing window into a national psyche. Although not studied in nearly the same detail, news texts are no less meaningful and, like their counterparts in the entertainment industry, no less subject to manipulation. While reporters and editors argue that they don't make the news, they just report it, viewers and critics may see a different reality. There is a long history in the field of communication research, and in feminist film theory as well, that more than adequately demonstrates the constructed nature of news (see, for example, Epstein 1973; Gans 1980; Tuchman 1978). Indeed, news texts do far more than relate the specifics of a particular event; they also offer rich material for analysis into the ways in which societies see themselves and the rest of the world. Particularly in the era of 24/7 coverage via cable, the Internet, podcasting and other instant communication tools, increasingly it is the news text that helps shape and reinforce national norms and values.

In his classic study of mainstream US news organisations, Herbert J Gans notes that journalism aims to be objective but that story selection and story writing are in and of themselves value statements: 'Value exclusion is therefore accompanied by value inclusion both through story selection and as opinions expressed in specific stories' (Gans 1980: 182). Thus, in a very real sense value-free news is an impossibility, not simply in the United States, but in any cultural and political context. Precisely because values are reflected in every story selection, what journalists elect to cover is labelled news and what they choose to ignore is labelled not newsworthy. Beyond that, the way a story is covered – and this would include the selection of images, the choice of words, the juxtaposition of words and images, the location and size of headlines and many other aspects of production – further confounds the notion of objectivity and neutrality.

What journalists actually have instead of objectivity is a set of codes and professional practices that combine to offer a road map or set of guidelines for creating a professionally acceptable story. If there is a formula for this, it often is expressed as getting 'both sides'. Thus news is conceived in terms of conflict, and the reporter's role is often to represent the proponents and the opponents of the latest economic plan or the new highway project. In covering crime and disasters, the reporter's role is often descriptive, at least initially. After the account of what happened, the next question answered may be why it happened. Here, reporters may invoke their normative role as watchdogs of government, business and other powerful entities. Theoretically, there is a clear line between opinion/commentary and news reporting, which is supposedly confined to factual information. But the very choice of what to cover and what to ignore is itself a statement of opinion as to what does and does not matter, whose voice should be heard and whose can be ignored. This is classically called the agenda-setting function of the press.

Crime reporting

Sensational reporting on crimes has been a mainstay of US news since the era of yellow journalism in the late 1800s, when newspapers began to see the profit potential of serving a mass audience rather than an elite one. Stories about 'crimes, disasters, scandals and intrigue' made money for publishers and exciting reading for the public (Campbell 1998: 218). That reporting tradition later became associated with the tabloid press. But the general decline in newspaper readership, the emergence of cable news and the rise of the Internet all helped push mainstream US news organisations towards an increasingly tabloid approach to reporting.

Not only do crime stories sell newspapers and attract audiences, they are relatively simple to report and inexpensive to produce. Typically, they offer little or no context. Instead, they present the world in stark terms of good and evil, victim and villain. In *Covering Violence*, William Cote and Roger Simpson use the idea of a three-act play to describe how news narratives, particularly stories involving traumatic crimes and disasters, unfold in contemporary media:

> Act I includes the reporting right after an event, telling readers, listeners, or viewers the traditional '5Ws' – who, what, when, where, and why. Act II, by contrast, portrays the longer-term effects of trauma, profiling the victims months or years later and describing how they cope in the continuing recovery process. (Cote & Simpson 2000: 113)

Act III involves coverage that puts events 'within broader sociological, historical or even economic contexts' (Cote & Simpson 2000: 120) and by definition requires perspective that emerges only over time.

Journalists, especially those working for broadcast radio, television and daily newspapers, look for what is new and changing. News, certainly in the US context, is driven by the 24/7 imperatives imposed by cable and increasingly by websites, which are already effectively responding to the competitive environment. News reporters and photographers know and accept these parameters. As a result, they typically operate in an 'Act I' environment. This makes a difference in what they look for, think about and record. In other words, it makes a difference in professional practice.

The culture of competition

South African news workers are clearly aware of a culture in which competition is a driving force. 'I came from a radio station that really encouraged you to push yourself all the time – and to get the story, and to get the leads. I think I definitely had an appetite for that. I was very ambitious as a journalist' (Cape Town focus group, 2002). South African journalists frequently noted the importance of being first with a story – beating the competition, getting an exclusive – and of submitting stories with memorable or sensational details. Such stories were important markers of success:

> And a whole family of seven, from a baby – the baby must have been about a couple of months old and the grandfather must have been in his eighties. They'd been slit from the throat down to their abdomen. And I could actually see what they had for supper. And I was excited because I got a scoop. I got the story first. (Cape Town focus group, 2002)

South African news workers who can deliver dramatic crime narratives are applauded by bosses and peers. Managers accept and stress the premise that emotional content is a hallmark of excellent journalism, and reporters agree. As one local journalist described her work: 'It's about writing the story so well, that somebody is going to cry when they read it and say, "I am going to do something." I think that is my goal with all stories' (*The Star* focus group, 2002). A television anchor said she was given high praise for her work as a reporter because of its emotional impact on the audience:

> The year that I gave up reporting, or that I gave it a break, I had been to 14 funerals. And of the 14 funerals, 12 of them were [for] children...I was there as a reporter. By the time I wrapped up, I was crying along with the people. I was becoming an emotional wreck with the story. And, a lot of the commendation I was getting from editors was – they were saying, 'Fantastic. You put a lot of emotion into your pieces. You're empathising with the victims of crime.' (Cape Town focus group, 2002)

In the case of South Africa (and in the US), an aggressive approach to crime reporting has been linked to corporate imperatives. In his book on media ethics in South Africa, Johan Retief notes that:

> ...certain sections of the media deserve the blame for reporting sensitive matters in an insensitive and sensational way. All too often, it is the bleeding victim, crying relatives, dead bodies and insensitive questions that dominate news reports. Events are often dramatised and presented so as to attract attention – in order to sell. (Retief 2002: 171)

Many journalists said the ethical dimensions of crime reporting are the subject of newsroom debates ('We had a windy debate'; 'I stormed out'; 'We had huge fights'). Nonetheless, the news imperative almost always ensures that reporters will cover sensational crimes. An editor at the *Sowetan* recalled his early days as a reporter:

> You know, I started off as a print journalist covering the struggle – so we called it – and people were being killed every day, in every manner possible you could think of. As a journalist, I never featured and none of my colleagues ever featured, about what might be happening to us. What was happening was, well, 'Where is the next issue? Where is the next story?' (*Sowetan* focus group, 2002)

Aggressive techniques are accepted as an unavoidable consequence of the competitive news environment. In her work on trauma reporting, Michelle Pieters describes this phenomenon, noting that 'some journalists may feel bad about pushing a microphone in the face of a crying mother, but they know their professional rivals will do it' (quoted in Retief 2002: 173).

Even when news workers are traumatised by the crimes they witness, they accept their news routines as inevitable: 'I said [to a paramedic on the scene], I hope you don't take offence…but this is what we have to do. It is not nice, but you either do it or you have to find another career' (*The Star* focus group, 2002). Another journalist said: 'You question what you are doing, whether you should be doing what you are doing, because this person is dying. But you are doing it because it is your job' (*The Star* focus group, 2002).

News photography

I have said that a common assertion among journalists is that they don't make the news, they just report it. This sentiment is closely aligned with the so-called mirror theory, which maintains that news simply holds a mirror up to our world and reflects it back to us – the readers and viewers. But positing the photojournalist as innocent bystander does not withstand serious examination. In photography as in news generally, choices are continually made, favouring one set of options over another. The fundamental reality of picture taking is that the photographer has agency.

'No matter what social role an image plays, the creation of an image through a camera lens always involves some degree of subject choice through selection, framing, and personalization' (Sturken & Cartwright 2001: 16). Photographic images, whether beamed to viewers on live television or shot and processed for later publication, are not reality but a construction of reality. The photographic image is, in the words of Bill Nichols, always 'a *representation* of the world we already occupy. It stands for a particular view of the world' (Nichols 2001: 20). Furthermore, that view is not arbitrary; it is the result of the photographer's beliefs, values and background, often influenced by cultural and institutional training and expectation. John Berger puts it succinctly: 'The way we see things is affected by what we know or what we believe' (Berger 1972: 8). This is as true of news images as it is of family snapshots and documentary studies. 'Every image embodies a way of seeing…Every time we look at a photograph, we are aware, however slightly, of the photographer selecting that sight from an infinity of other possible sights' (Berger 1972: 10).

At the same time, professional codes and practices insist on photographic authenticity. Staging a shot is unethical in news settings and simply not part of the documentary tradition of the still photo or the moving film image.

> The emphasis – harking back to Lumiere – was on action caught on the run, from any revealing vantage. Permissions were never asked. Stage action was abhorred. Concealed camera positions were used to catch moments in marketplaces, factories, school, taverns, streets. (Barnouw 1993: 57)

Photoshop notwithstanding, the idea then and now is to capture a moment that shows something that is a representation but a truthful one, not an invented one.

South African news photographers report being socialised into a newsroom culture that underscores the importance of sensational coverage. This description captures the typical process of older workers indoctrinating younger ones: 'And I remember commenting that this is bad and asking, "Are we going to use this picture?" And they would say, "You are still young. You haven't seen nothing yet."' Getting pictures of even the bloodiest events is an accepted part of the job:

> Your job is to get the pictures. What you do with those pictures is a different thing. Whether you offer them for publication, on the one hand – or keep some of those unpublishable pictures for competitions – or sometimes just to have them. You know, it's a unique event, and you've got a unique opportunity. And you're really the messenger of the community. You're the person they

pay for your newspaper. They pay to buy your newspaper. So, they pay your salary. You're there to get the pictures. (Cape Town focus group, 2002)

Because of the equipment they carry, photographers are easily identifiable and often subject to criticism. 'As a photographer, you're targeted all the time. You'd like to be left alone to do your work, but you cannot' (*The Star* focus group, 2002). Photographers frequently reported being confronted with ethical decisions about when to take pictures:

[I was] covering Mozambique and the floods, and there are 15 000 people who are starving who are determined that they are going to get on the chopper before you and they cannot. You have to push and shove kids out of the way. It's rough. (*The Star* focus group, 2002)

The commonly cited rationale of 'just doing my job' can come into conflict with other realities. A case in point was described by a photographer in Cape Town:

It had just started raining. There was a freeway. There was an old car lying on its side and it was burning. And wedged in between the tarmac and this burning car was this body of a man that had fallen through the window. And I had a camera with me. When the first flash went off, the guy's eyes opened, and he said, 'Help me. Help me.' I dropped the camera, it still hung around my neck, but there was nothing I could do. And then, then he died. But there I was, confronted with a decision-making, a split-second decision-making situation. Am I going to lose a good picture or should I help the person? Can I help? And if I can't help, should I carry on taking pictures? What are the people around me thinking? I had to deal with many decisions there – that it just screwed my mind for a long time. (Cape Town focus group, 2002)

Post-traumatic stress

South African photographers and reporters were often aware of the emotional toll that crime reporting takes on them. As Cote and Simpson note, journalists are first-responders to tragedies and disasters just as police, fire and medical workers are. They are also vulnerable to stress reactions, including post-traumatic stress disorder (PTSD), which is a medically recognised diagnosis that increasingly is being made for news workers. Symptoms of PTSD include having flashbacks to the event in question, being emotionally numb to daily events and having a heightened startle response (Cote & Simpson 2000).

Even though news workers in South Africa who cover crime stories are especially vulnerable to stress reactions, many say they have had no counselling or training with respect to the highly emotional content of their work. Some people noted that showing any reaction to difficult stories is often considered unacceptable. Being a journalist is being 'macho'. The phrase repeatedly used in these discussions was 'cowboys do not cry'. Many said it is part of the job to 'put on a brave face'. Some said that they had never discussed their emotional responses to reporting on crime because this was frowned upon: 'To this day, I have never received, whether by self-prompting or by anyone suggesting, some debriefing and de-traumatisation counselling on these things that we were experiencing' (*Sowetan* focus group, 2002).

Others said showing emotions can be acceptable as long as one can keep on working:

> I have cried behind the lens a million times, I don't care. If anybody is going to think less of me because of it, that is their problem. If I hold it in I won't be able to do my job. If it enables you to do your job, you just do it. (*The Star* focus group, 2002)

Some said they had a sense of fearlessness because they managed to survive: 'I had so many people shot and killed all around me. And the fact that I survived, I think has also made me almost immune to fear and to the trauma' (*Sowetan* focus group, 2002).

Photographers are especially vulnerable to stress reactions and South African photojournalists recognised this:

> You have to look at the scene. I mean journalists don't have to look. They can glance at the scene and get an idea of what's happening. You – it's frozen in your memory. You're looking through the lens, close. (*The Star* focus group, 2002)

One photographer said he is haunted by a picture he took that appeared on the front page of his newspaper. He carried it with him to the focus-group meeting. It shows a dead man hanging by a noose next to his dead child who is also hanging from a rope.

I've got a picture that I took in 1999 of a man who killed himself and his child. This will always remain with me and it has changed my attitude towards children. And, to such an extent, that as a grandparent, I dote on my, on my grandchildren because of what I've experienced. And this will always be with me. And it's, it's sort of sobering to find that the industry is that way – [breaking down] sorry. (*Sowetan* focus group, 2002)

News managers

Focus-group members described a range of approaches on the part of management to crime reporting and crime reporters. Many said the macho image of journalists persists and is encouraged by managers. One reporter described the attitude this way: 'No matter what sex you are, you have to be man enough to do the job.' Another reporter said her request for a bulletproof vest was repeatedly turned down when she was covering the crime beat in Cape Town. Eventually, her lawyer wrote to the newspaper, saying the management would be sued for damages if the reporter was wounded or killed on the job. Soon thereafter, an editor threw a vest at her in disgust as she came into the newsroom.

A news manager acknowledged that media executives are not in the field and don't appreciate the demands placed on reporters and photographers who cover crime stories every day: 'I'm conscious of the negligence of the industry, and of the newspaper, and of me – as an executive. You know, of coming to the guys that deal with crime to say, "Hey, how is it? How do you feel?"' (*Sowetan* focus group, 2002).

Reporters at *The Star* said the arrival of a woman in the editor's job had made a positive difference:

> [She] has an office that overlooks the newsroom. And there has been a couple of times when I have been so stressed, and she says, 'Okay fine. Lie on the couch.' And I know that no one can see me. And I just lie there for a while and she just acts like I am not there. And sometimes she will pop her head up and say, 'Is there anything you want to talk about?' And I say, 'No.' (*The Star* focus group, 2002)

Crime-reporting debates

The issue of sensational reporting, particularly of crime and corruption, has been the subject of extensive debate in South Africa. Thabo Mbeki and many government officials have complained that the press is 'undermining the interests of the country by giving prominence to reports on crime' (Retief 2002: 21). The development model of the media suggests that journalism is obligated to help improve the image of South Africa both at home and abroad. Critics say the failure to accentuate the positive and the insistence on splashing negative images on front pages has had damaging results to national identity. 'You ask a person what they know about South Africa and they say, "crime"' (Scheiner 2006, interview). In his analysis of contemporary photography in Africa, *New York Times* critic Holland Cotter makes a similar point:

> War, disease, poverty, heartbreak and nothing else. That's exactly how most of the world sees Africa: filtered through images of calamity. 'Afro-pessimism' is the diagnostic term that Okwui Enwezor, the Nigerian-born art historian and curator, uses for the syndrome. (Cotter 2006: C1)

Arnold S de Beer has noted that this image is especially tied to South Africa, where rates of murder, rape and domestic violence are among the highest in the world. Added to this are 'perceptions, conveyed in the international news media, of Africa being on the brink of total collapse due to unbridled corruption, civil wars, the scourge of HIV/AIDS sweeping over the continent' (De Beer 2003: 98).

Not surprisingly, journalists defend their right to publish. The media's response is that media critics are 'targeting free speech and press freedom' (Jere-Malanda 2002: 146). Journalists argue that news stories are appropriate as long as they are accurate, and precisely *because* they are accurate. The concept of 'sunshine journalism' has been denounced as a thinly veiled effort to hide government failures. Crime reporting may sell newspapers, but it also informs citizens about their communities. Some note that rather than too much crime reporting, there may be too little:

> A lot of people think there is under-reporting of crime in South Africa. The private security industry is bigger than the police force and it is not the police who arrive on the scene of many crimes – and these are not reported. Crimes where the victim knows the aggressor are not reported. And then the conviction rate for crimes

is so low that people often don't bother to go to the police because it will be just another dossier. (Scheiner 2006, interview)

Crime reporting and race

Although journalists rarely mentioned the issue of race when they discussed their reporting on crimes, media scholars and critics have made clear connections. De Beer sees a persistent fear of the black majority as being apparent...especially [in] the conflict-ridden reports on crime...Racial polarization is again the order of the day through news reporting that creates the perception of blacks being the cause for the tide of crime engulfing the country, while it fuels white fears and new racial strife (De Beer 2003: 100). Philip Scheiner (2006, interview) agrees that 'when the victim is white and the attacker is black, the story has much more resonance. It's what people expect to read. It fits their world-view'.

Robert Entman's research looks at the ways in which news coverage stereotypes blacks in the US, but his observations have application to the case in South Africa:

> [T]he specific realities depicted in single stories may accumulate to form a summary message that distorts social reality. Each in a series of news stories may be accurate, yet the combination may yield false cognitions within audiences. (Entman 1994: 509)

News stories about corruption have been criticised for an underlying racism, with more attention put on black mayors taking home big salaries than on white corporate executives doing the same thing. 'In white parlour conversation, the focus is on the black mayors' (Scheiner 2006, interview).

Regina Jere-Malanda notes that 'the issue of race continues to be a major theme in South Africa as both black and white journalists operate in a still white-dominated newspaper industry' (Jere-Malanda 2002: 146). The charge of 'subliminal racism' levelled against the primarily white-owned media 'did not come as a shock' especially in light of South Africa's history of apartheid: '[M]any South Africans agreed that the post-apartheid press has been used to fuel anxieties among whites about their future in a South Africa under black leadership' (Jere-Malanda 2002: 150).

Issues of identity

The chicken-and-the-egg question repeatedly asked is whether media shapes the culture or is shaped by it. Journalists, like other citizens, are products of the culture in which they function. Before they became South African journalists, they were students in South African schools, members of South African churches, children in South African families. They come to the profession already enmeshed in their nation's culture, already shaped by the generation in which they came of age. But unlike most of their fellow citizens, journalists are mediators of culture. The work they produce forms a bridge between politicians and citizens at large, between corporations and consumers, between sports teams and fans, to give just a few examples. Journalists are shaped by their culture, but they also play a collective role in shaping their culture. I say collective role in an effort to acknowledge newsroom culture – that is, the common perspectives, viewpoints and approaches that newsrooms tend to produce.

Journalists are exposed to newsroom culture by virtue of working in a team setting on a creative product. Over months and years, they acquire a similar set of beliefs about the nature and definition of news. These become mutually reinforcing among newsroom personnel. Contrary viewpoints may be raised, but if a person strays too far from the prevailing attitudes about what stories should be covered (agenda setting) and how stories should be presented (framing), that person is likely to become marginalised. Rarely if ever are there formal mechanisms for controlling the perspectives journalists bring to their reporting. Instead, a powerful common culture emerges from the daily experience of working together on a news product.

My interviews with South African journalists reveal some commonly held views about crime stories: they are an important aspect of the news; their graphic details should be conveyed in both words and images; they sell in print and in broadcast contexts; aggressive, dramatic crime reporting is applauded by news managers and recognised within the profession; even though crime reporting creates emotional trauma for reporters and their subjects, it is considered a necessary part of the job. Failing to report on crime or downplaying crime can be seen as capitulating to government pressure, which in turn is viewed as a threat to free speech. Crime reporting often has racial implications that resonate with white readers and viewers.

Does crime reporting contribute to South Africa's national identity? I would argue that the approach to crime reporting in South Africa is shaped by national identity and national history. At the same time, crime reporting itself continues to help shape national identity in the post-apartheid period. It is a dynamic and mutually reinforcing interaction. South African journalists come to their work with a world-view or perspective shaped by their individual and collective experience, which has profound racial underpinnings. Crime reporting in the South African news contributes to a national identity in which race is a key factor. Most South African journalists who I interviewed are white. While they reject apartheid, they are also products of a culture in which racism has a long history.

The same has been said of US journalists, who are predominantly white and who were particularly criticised for racial aspects of the Hurricane Katrina coverage. This was not a conspiracy, but cultural history does help to explain why images taken during Katrina overwhelmingly showed whites in active roles such as being rescuers and blacks in passive roles such as being rescued, according to a study of images in *The New York Times*, *USA Today*, *The Wall Street Journal* and *The Washington Post* (Kahle et al. 2007).

Many South African journalists referred (with pride) to a macho image within the profession. Being macho may set a certain tone that pushes news reporters and editors to capture, show, describe and disperse the most difficult image. The idea of being 'man enough' to do the job captures that same sensibility, that determination not to shrink from showing the worst, not to pull back from describing brutality. As Entman has noted, the accuracy of individual crime stories is not necessarily in question. Stories may be completely accurate in terms of individual reporting, but the collective archive of crime reporting may create, reinforce and reify a world-view in which crime is linked to race.

To the extent that journalism in South Africa relies on Western models (the latest newspaper to emerge in South Africa is the *Daily Sun*, which patterns itself after the UK paper *The Sun*, complete with the page 3 girl), the future does not look good for media reform or improvement. As Cote and Simpson correctly point out: 'One of the hallmarks of tabloid journalism always has been the use of sensational photographs and illustrations, often related to crime and violence.' And as noted at the beginning of this chapter, examples of mainstream journalism 'taking on the trappings of supermarket tabloids' are abundant (Cote & Simpson 2000: 131). At the same time, particularly in television and online, immediacy has reached the point where audiences are seeing the news-gathering process unfold before them. Gone are the days when reporters spent time checking out the accuracy of stories and interviews. As former CNN vice president David Bernknopf has described it, 'The time to check things, find out if they're true, has shrunk to nothing' (quoted in Moritz 2003: 92).

Diversity issues with respect to ownership and employees alike are also problematic. As Clive Barnett points out, even if South Africa can diversify its ownership structure, more stations will be competing for the existing audience, which is 'a relatively narrow segment of society, the affluent minority' (Barnett 1999: 660). News routines are based on models that existed during apartheid and remain to a large extent entrenched. News workers may over time become more diverse, but that diversity must lead to a change in news culture and in the very definition of news in order for change to be brought about.

References

Barnett C (1999) The limits of media democratization in South Africa: Politics, privatization and regulation. *Media, Culture and Society* 21: 649–671

Barnouw E (1993) *Documentary: A history of the non-fiction film*. New York: Oxford University Press

Berger J (1972) *Ways of seeing*. London: Penguin

Campbell R (1998) *Media and culture*. New York: St Martin's Press

Cote W & Simpson R (eds) (2000) *Covering violence: A guide to ethical reporting about victims and trauma*. New York: Columbia University Press

Cotter H (2006) Colorful and clashing: Looking at Africa. *New York Times*, 17 March

De Beer AS (2003) A long walk to freedom, and a steep road to nation building: The role of the media in post-apartheid South Africa. In K Ross and D Derman (eds) *Mapping the margins: Identity politics and the media*. Creskill, NJ: Hampton Press

Entman RM (1994) Representation and reality in the portrayal of blacks on network television news. *Journalism Quarterly* 71(autumn): 509–519

Epstein EJ (1973) *News from nowhere*. New York: Random House

Fishman JM (2003) News norms and emotions: Pictures of pain and metaphors of distress. In L Gross, J Katz and J Ruby (eds) *Image ethics in the digital age*. Minneapolis: University of Minnesota Press

Gans HJ (1980) *Deciding what's news: A study of CBS Evening News, NBC Nightly News, Newsweek and Time*. New York: Random House

Jere-Malanda R (2002) Press freedom and the crisis of ethical journalism in South Africa. In JB Atkins (ed.) *The mission: Journalism, ethics and the world*, pp. 143–152. Ames, IA: Iowa State University Press

Kahle S, Yu N & Whiteside E (2007) Another disaster: An examination of portrayals of race in Hurricane Katrina coverage. *Visual Communication Quarterly* 14(2): 75–89

Moritz M (2003) Instant transmission: Covering Columbine's victims and villains. In L Gross, J Katz and J Ruby (eds) *Image ethics in the digital age*, pp. 71–93. Minneapolis: University of Minnesota Press

Nichols B (2001) *Introduction to documentary*. Bloomington: University of Indiana Press

Retief J (2002) *Media ethics: An introduction to responsible journalism*. Cape Town: Oxford University Press

Sturken M & Cartwright L (eds) (2001) *Practices of looking: An introduction to visual culture*. New York: Oxford University Press

Tuchman G (1978) *Making news: A study in the construction of reality*. New York: Free Press

Interview and focus groups

Cape Town focus group, May 2002

Scheiner P (2006) Lecturer, Communication Program University of Paris IV, and consultant on South African business initiatives. Telephone interview, Paris, 9 October

Sowetan (Johannesburg) focus group, May 2002

The Star (Johannesburg) focus group, May 2002

12 Afrikaner identity in post-apartheid South Africa: The Self in terms of the Other

Wiida Fourie

On 2 February 1990 the social reality of white South Africans was turned upside down when former president FW de Klerk announced the unbanning of the African National Congress (ANC) and the release of Nelson Mandela. Commentators described the socio-political changes as 'bizarre' (Louw 1994: 38), while the changing position of the Afrikaner was described as that of one who was in power, to one who was willing to share power, to one who was finally powerless (Kriel 1997: 75). Some 14 years later, on 17 April 2004, newspapers announced the final demise of the once-mighty National Party (NP).

How did Afrikaans-speaking white South Africans cope with these sudden changes in their social reality? Which terms did they use to explain these changes to themselves and others? How did newspapers articulate these changes? In particular, how did white Afrikaans-speaking South Africans cope with the changes in terms of who they are and what they stand for? In this chapter I attempt to answer these questions by looking at the letters column of one of the major Afrikaans newspapers in South Africa, the Gauteng-based *Beeld*. *Beeld* is one of four Afrikaans daily newspapers owned by Media24, originally known as Nasionale Pers (National Press).[1] *Beeld* is generally regarded as an Afrikaans-establishment newspaper. Its journalists, editors and directors are firmly rooted in that establishment and are very sensitive to their readers' interests (Boshoff 1992, interview; Muller 1990: vii–viii).

In this chapter I argue that, while the letter-writers did adjust their typification of the Self, no fundamental review of their typification of the Other (black South Africans) took place. Looking at themselves, letter-writers managed to free themselves of the baggage of apartheid after De Klerk gave up power in 1990 and declared white South Africa ready for negotiations for a new democratic order. Together with giving up power, letter-writers also freed themselves from the aspect of Christian nationalism, one of the fundamental building blocks of Afrikaner character. The Afrikaners of 2004 seem to be a white minority, proud of their language and culture, and fighting for their right to speak and hear Afrikaans. However, it seems as if no major revision of the perception of the Other has taken place. Rather, letter-writers have adjusted their perception of black people only insofar as it became practically relevant to do so for survival in the new South Africa. Very few, if any, fundamental changes in terms of the perception of racial or cultural superiority have taken place.

My analysis reflects the social phenomenology of Alfred Schutz (1899–1959), an Austrian-born philosopher and sociologist and one of the most important exponents of phenomenology in the United States in the 1960s.[2]

The phenomenological approach

Communication science began taking note of the phenomenological approach as a viable method to understand and analyse human communication only towards the late 1980s. Thanks mainly to the work of Alfred Schutz,[3] phenomenology found a home in the work of ethnomethodologists such as Garfinkel (1967), in Goffman's (1959) framing concept and in Berger and Luckmann's (1967) social-construction-of-reality approach. All these theories emphasise the central role of the individual in actively constructing social meaning.

It is important for the researcher wanting to apply the phenomenological approach first to understand its underlying philosophical perspectives. Thus I begin by addressing the question, what is phenomenology? I then discuss the social phenomenology of Alfred Schutz.

What is phenomenology?

Unlike other disciplines in the social sciences, phenomenology cannot claim to be a clearly defined discipline with its own methodologies. It is better described as a movement with certain fundamental assumptions. The most basic of these assumptions lies in phenomenology's criticism of positivism – namely, that there is a radical difference between man and nature and that one cannot use the same methodologies to study natural and social phenomena. The critical difference between man and nature is man's ability to give meaning to his actions (Jansen 1989: 6): 'Anything that is within us as knowledge…actually exists and is unquestionable evidence' (Moustakas 1994: 44).

Another basic assumption is that man actively and consciously creates his own social reality. The father of phenomenology, Edmund Husserl, asserted that the individual's world is a world that exists apart from and above the objective and external world. Individual reality comes into being the moment the individual becomes aware of an object, interprets it and gives it meaning: 'Human life is not only meaningful; it is also articulate; it expresses its own meaning which we can understand' (Rickman 1961: 41). Husserl called this reality the everyday life-world of the individual. The most important characteristic of the life-world is its taken-for-grantedness. Furthermore, the individual accepts that everyone shares in the same reality – that the life-world is a collective world.

It is the purpose of phenomenology to grasp the essence of this everyday life-world by analysing the individual's thought processes (Jansen 1989: 50). For Husserl, to understand the essence of something is to understand its meaning. Although social phenomena do not have an objective existence, they do have an essence which affirms their objective validity: 'Only essences are knowable at all. We know to the extent that we grasp essences. Beyond that we opine' (Lauer 1965: 62).

Husserl's phenomenology is complex and difficult to understand. His work was made more accessible by Schutz, who was also influenced by Max Weber and GH Mead, the father of symbolic interactionism.

Schutz's social phenomenology

Phenomenology accepts that the world of everyday life is the human being's fundamental and pervasive reality. Most people take 'this world' for granted, assume it is the same for everyone and act accordingly – an approach that Schutz calls the natural attitude: a blind and naive belief in the existence of a shared world (Jansen & Steinberg 1991: 53; Schutz 1970: 320; Schutz & Luckmann 1974: 3).

Schutz focuses on the analysis of this natural attitude because it, more than anything else, exposes the structures of the life-world (Jansen 1989: 52): 'The central and most cunning feature of the taken for granted everyday world is that it *is* taken for granted' (Natanson 1973: xxvi). Explaining the natural attitude, Schutz makes use of concepts such as the social stock of knowledge, typifications and intersubjectivity to explain how people interpret their everyday reality so that it becomes meaningful to themselves and others in communication.

In this regard Schutz's social phenomenology is an ideal framework for the analysis of a newspaper letters column. A letter represents the writer's comprehension of his or her social world, and the mere fact that the letter is published means that other individuals share in the writer's ideas and that it forms part of the larger stock of social knowledge. The letters column thus represents a revealing interaction between the subjective life-world of the individual and the larger social reality 'out there'.

THE EVERYDAY LIFE-WORLD, THE SOCIAL STOCK OF KNOWLEDGE AND INTERSUBJECTIVITY

According to Schutz the everyday life-world of the individual consists of shared general knowledge and taken-for-granted interpretations of everyday life (the so-called natural attitude) (Schutz & Luckmann 1974: 3). This life-world exists above and apart from the real social and physical world. It functions as a type of reference framework according to which the physical world can be ordered and understood by interpreting and then categorising certain aspects of it.

Although individuals find themselves each in their own unique biographical situation, they also exist within a world of shared social meaning – the social stock of knowledge. While the individual may be unique, all individuals share the same knowledge of the social conventions, rules of behaviour, norms and practices prevalent in their community. The social stock of knowledge is made up out of standard recipes or typifications. Typifications are generated from certain social structures long before the individual became a part of that structure. In the present, it acts as a socially determined frame of reference for the individual (Schutz 1962/1973: 208; Schutz & Luckmann 1974: 319). The social stock of knowledge becomes integrated as part of the individual's subjective Self.

It is the social stock of knowledge that makes communication between members of the same group possible. For Schutz, intersubjectivity is key to understanding the social world (Natanson 1973: xxx). We take it for granted that others hold the same stock of knowledge that we do and that we can exchange experiences – 'the general thesis of the reciprocity of perspectives' (Schutz & Luckmann 1974: 60, 85). The interaction between the individual's unique biographical situation and that of the larger objective social stock of knowledge, and thus with other individuals, can be depicted as shown in Figure 12.1.

Figure 12.1 Interaction between individuals and social stock of knowledge

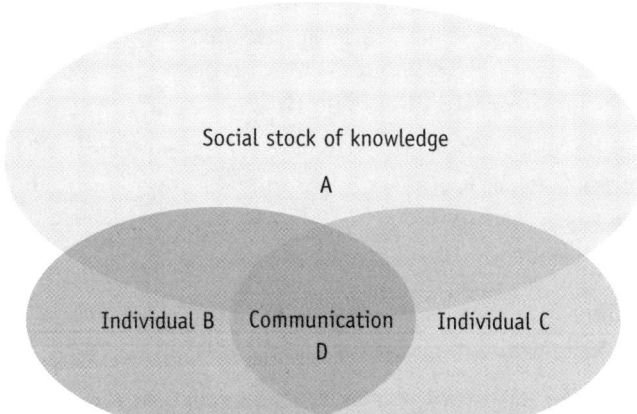

Both Individual B and Individual C have their own unique circumstances. At the same time they share in the same social stock of knowledge (A). Where A, B and C overlap, communication (D) can take place. Schutz describes the interaction between the individual's biographical situation and the social stock of knowledge as a dialectic between individual and society (Schutz & Luckmann 1974: 319). Schutz is concerned with those meaning structures existing at a given time in the life-world of a society (Jansen 1989: 53).

In the South African context, one can argue that the average white Afrikaans-speaking child was born into a readily interpreted and organised South African reality. This ready-made reality would have been presented to the child by parents, family, teachers and other authoritarian figures as taken for granted and logical. In addition, the child could fall back on a whole supply of ready-made interpretations (typifications) to interpret and confront his or her social reality. The task of the phenomenologist would be to question the taken-for-grantedness of this life-world and identify its underlying principles (or essences).

Here typifications become important as the essential building blocks of the social stock of knowledge. According to Schutz (1970: 24–25), typifications help us to make sense of the world. These typifications, or ways of looking at the world, are communicated primarily by means of language.

LANGUAGE AS MEDIUM OF OBJECTIFICATION

Language is the primary means by which a subjective experience is objectified and taken up into the social stock of knowledge (Schutz & Luckmann 1974: 264). The most important criterion for objectification is the relevance thereof for the larger social stock of knowledge:

> What the typical problems are, whose typical problems are involved, who has to transmit the solutions, and to whom the solutions are transmitted are for the most part predetermined in historical societies. The answers to the questions are themselves elements of the social stock of knowledge. By this means the transference of socially relevant knowledge is anchored in the social structure. (Schutz & Luckmann 1974: 291–292)

In communicative acts over the course of time the original language action becomes further and further removed from the original experience, and therefore less likely to be questioned. The relationship between black and white South Africans before 1990 is a good example of how far removed the objectified language element became from the original experience. Many white South Africans' experience of black people was limited to the news on television and in newspapers, and their only direct experience was with 'types', such as cleaners and gardeners. The average white person's perception of black people was mainly in terms of objectified language constructions (with very little chance to correct those stereotyped constructions in reality). In the words of former newspaper editor Ken Owen: '[W]e have steadfastly ignored the single most important truth about South Africa: this is a land so deeply divided that nobody can see across the gulf. We deal not with each other but with illusions of one another' (Owen 1985: 23).

A typification is kept alive only as long as it can find solutions to relevant problems (Schutz 1964/1976: 234–235). The moment a problem becomes irrelevant, or the existence of a group is at stake, typifications are radically questioned and revised. Normally this questioning first takes place on a philosophical, religious or scientific (thus ideological) level before it trickles down to the everyday stock of knowledge (Schutz & Luckmann 1974: 296–297). In the South African situation, it can be argued that average white South Africans had no choice but to start questioning their typification of the Self and the Other (black people) as changes in the socio-political situation became a reality with the unbanning of the ANC in 1990.

Schutz is particularly pragmatic when it comes to the formation of typifications. All individuals have a practical interest in the intersubjective world: to make it work for themselves and their fellow humans (Schutz 1962/1973: 208–209). Members of the in-group actually create their social reality. Therefore they have to act in such a way as to maintain that specific social reality. If, then, white Afrikaans-speaking South Africans defined their reality in such a way that, in order to survive in Africa, black South Africans were to be subordinate, then white Afrikaans-speaking South Africans would have to act in such a way as to maintain this predefined reality.

It is unlikely that the individual would give much thought to such actions, until it becomes necessary for survival. In daily life, most people concentrate mainly on those aspects of the social world relevant to their own survival (such as a salary, security, food on the table, good schools, yearly vacations and so on). For the purposes of this chapter it will be argued that, until the 1980s, white South Africans did not need to question their 'democracy'. The situation was under control, and for the average white South African the problem of survival was solved 'until further notice'. It took a radical questioning of their social reality for white South Africans to wake up and begin searching for alternative solutions (typifications).

TYPIFICATION OF THE SELF AND THE OTHER

In the South African context the notion of the Other has developed to such a level of anonymity that the 'typical black' stands independent of any unique black individual a white South African may meet in real life. Most of the time the manners and lifestyle of the Other remain inexplicable and inferior to the in-group, with far-reaching consequences. The truths held by the in-group are a 'matter of course' and 'self-evident', while the ways of the Other are looked at 'with repugnance, disgust, aversion, antipathy, hatred or fear' (Schutz 1964/1976: 246–247). Fourie (1991: 2, 4, 5) notes that even in the 1990s the South African media were communicating in the binary oppositions of apartheid ('us' versus 'them'), describing the ANC as enemy number one and black people as generally 'barbaric'.

The typification of the Other has a determining influence on individuals' definition of the Self and their behaviour. By defining the Other's role beforehand, the individual takes on a predefined role: 'In typifying the Other's behaviour I am typifying my own, which is interrelated with his, transforming myself into a passenger, consumer, taxpayer, reader, bystander, etc.'

(Schutz 1962/1973: 19). The fragmentation of the Self into certain typical roles explains how Afrikaners could call themselves Christians in one role, but still regard themselves as superior to black people in another role. It also explains why many white South Africans change the tone of their voice and the language they use the moment they speak to a black person (as if they are talking to a child). The same goes for black South Africans who address white people as '*baas*' or '*miesies*' in certain situations.

The subjective meaning of a group implies that the group members consciously share in the same circumstances, with similar typifications and relevancies. Individuals in a group are more or less determined by the same historical situation, thereby sharing the same general world-view (Schutz 1964/1976: 251–252). A group's social stock of knowledge is generally regarded as sufficient. It is carried over from one generation to another without questioning by people in positions of authority (Schutz 1964/1976: 96). However, the group will experience a crisis the moment elements of the shared stock of knowledge are questioned (Schutz 1964/1976: 96).

In this study I argue that the typical white South African's perception of a black South African is based mainly on typifications and very little on direct experience. When direct and relevant contact did take place, typifications were either affirmed or revised. The extent to which a typification was questioned was related to the direct interest of the person involved. In other words, while white South Africans were 'in control' of the country and its governance, they did not have a direct interest in revising their typification of the typical black person. The situation changed radically with the unbanning of the ANC and the first democratic elections in 1994, introducing a black government and a black president. Suddenly it became very important for white South Africans to revise their typification of the Other.

I provide here a short historical overview of the development of Afrikaner nationalism to give insight into the possible typifications existing in the stock of social knowledge of the Afrikaner. I then look at the typifications as manifested in the *Beeld*'s letters column.

The everyday life-world of the Afrikaner

The first signs of a unique Afrikaner nationalism can be traced back to the British annexation of the Transvaal in 1877. Later historical events such as the Anglo–Boer War, British repression and the concentration camps, the 1910

Union and the failed 1914 Rebellion all led to a stronger Afrikaner sentiment (Kenney 1991: 66). It is significant to note how the typification of the Other contributed to the typification of the Self in the formation of a national identity for the Afrikaner.

TYPIFICATION OF THE OTHER

Until the Second World War, the average white South African's perception of black people did not differ much from that of the rest of the Western world. In South Africa, the term 'racism' in the 1940s was restricted to feelings of animosity between Afrikaans- and English-speaking South Africans and had nothing to do with colour (Mervis 1989: 30–31). The old Voortrekkers' perception of black people was generally negative – they were portrayed as 'barbarous, predacious, bloodthirsty and treacherous' (Van Jaarsveld 1985: 17). In addition, God willed that the children of Ham should remain cursed eternally, as hewers of wood and drawers of water (Van Jaarsveld 1985: 21).

By the 1940s this typification had not undergone any significant changes. The Afrikaans poet and theologian, JD du Toit (alias Totius, 1877–1953), describes the 'evil spirit' of this 'darkened part of the world' in his poem 'Die Gees van Donker Afrika' (The Spirit of Dark Africa). The poem is filled with references to this 'sunken race' and 'degenerate creature' (with reference to the San), and to the black giant of Africa who will spear those who dare defy him (Du Toit 1944: 11).

In 1945 and 1947 two books, regarded as the intellectual foundation of apartheid, appeared. Geoff Cronjé, a professor of sociology at the University of Pretoria, published *'n Tuiste vir die Nageslag* (A Home for Future Generations; my translation) in 1945, and in 1947 Cronjé, Nicol and Groenewald published *Regverdige Rasse-Apartheid* (Fair Race-Apartheid; my translation).

Cronjé (1945: 11–20) dedicates an entire section to the biological differences between the races, delivering the scientific 'proof' of the intellectual inferiority of black people. The differences between the two groups are in direct opposition and irreconcilable – for example 'white' in contrast with 'black', 'blond' in contrast with 'dark', 'honest' in contrast with 'thievish' and 'industrious' in contrast with 'lazy'. The basis of this racially based nationalism was the assumption that different races are essentially incompatible because of the inherent inferiority of the black race (Thompson 1985: 104, 41). Cronjé (1945: 168–183) justifies the necessity of complete racial segregation in terms of the ultimate survival of the white race in southern Africa. He lists the following dangers facing the white race: miscegenation; the ruin of their native land by the blacks; undermining of the general health and welfare of the (white) nation; the degradation of moral and cultural standards; the damaging of (white) property (by blacks); the increase in whites' economic responsibilities towards blacks; the formation of a non-white front and last but not least, the threat of communism.

By far the most attention is given to the dangers of the total bastardisation of the white race: a *mengelmoes-samelewing* – literally meaning a mishmash society leading to a mishmash race (Cronjé 1945: 49). Cronjé (1945: 71) provides 'authoritative and convincing proof that the miscegenation between the black and white races in South Africa will be biologically detrimental, producing human material which will be physically and mentally inferior to the quality of the European race'. Therefore, unqualified equality will never work in South Africa, because it will eventually lead to the complete debasement of the European race (Cronjé 1945: 40).

Coetzee (1991) describes Cronjé as one of the most important formulators of apartheid policy. Cronjé's work shows that apartheid in all its early manifestations (including separate residential areas, separate amenities, work reservation and resettlements) was indeed a reaction against desire. Any form of desire between black and white had to be prevented on all levels in order to prevent miscegenation – that terrible mishmash society. Miscegenation was not only contrary to the ideal of an Afrikaner nation, it was also against the will of God (Coetzee 1991: 6–13, 18).

This argument was later used to justify total apartheid, and not just separation in terms of residential areas. Complete racial segregation was justified for the sake of racial purity and the prevention of any further instances of miscegenation. Apartheid was, in contrast with segregation, a systematic and exhaustive policy meant to solve the race problem forever and ensure a home for future generations of white South Africans (Cronjé 1945: 117). Cronjé was well aware of the fact that white people would not be able to maintain control based solely on white superiority or supremacy – aptly called *baasskap* in Afrikaans. The ideal solution was the complete separation of the different races and the opportunity for each to develop on its own (Cronjé et al. 1947: 148–155).

Alternatives to this final solution were voiced, but definitely not heard. The Afrikaner writer and philosopher NP van Wyk Louw pleaded for a more critical disposition among Afrikaner intellectuals. According to Louw, the Afrikaner's struggle for survival should have been fought on a moral high ground: 'I would rather go under than continue to exist through injustice... How can a small nation continue to exist for long when it becomes something abhorrent and evil to the best inside – or outside – itself?' (Louw 1958: 58, 63). Some Afrikaans-speaking journalists did start to question the morality of so-called petty apartheid (such as separate toilets and service counters for black people and white people). Journalists such as Piet Cillié and Schalk Burger argued as early as the 1960s that the future of the Afrikaner could only be worked out with the cooperation and agreement of black South Africans. However, while several Afrikaner intellectuals criticised the derogatory aspects of petty apartheid, few went as far as questioning the morality of apartheid itself (Mouton 2002: 34).

The typification of the Other before 1940 can be summarised as shown in Table 12.1.

Table 12.1 Typification of the Other before 1940

Negative typifications	Positive typifications
Drawers of water and hewers of wood	Loyal resistance against injustice
The children of Ham	Criticism of petty apartheid
Intellectually inferior	Future of Afrikaners depends on black cooperation and agreement
Black, dark, thievish, lazy	
Danger of miscegenation and a bastardised society	
Africa is a black morass; the black giant of Africa	

TYPIFICATION OF THE SELF

What is a real Afrikaner? In 1877, a real Afrikaner was described as someone with an Afrikaner heart, as opposed to a Dutch or English heart (Van Jaarsveld 1985: 18). From the 1940s until the 1960s, a true Afrikaner nationalist was someone who supported the NP and its leaders (Mouton 2002: 35).

Nationalism was built into the Afrikaner's social being as a kind of instinctive mechanism to prevent absorption by the English on the one hand and miscegenation with black people on the other (Van Jaarsveld 1985: 19). An important aspect of this nationalism was the theological justification thereof: it is God's will that nations should live apart and maintain their own identity. To be an Afrikaner was to be a Christian, resulting in the concept of Afrikaner Christian nationalism. Combined with being in Africa, the Afrikaner's Christianity manifested in two ways: (1) being part of a chosen people with a mission, and (2) white guardianship of an inferior black population.

Afrikaners as a chosen people with a mission

In the 1930s a number of young Afrikaner academics doing research at European and especially German universities were impressed by Germany's ability to rise up after the humiliation and economic depression of the First World War (Sparks 1995: 148).[4] These intellectuals were especially impressed by the new ideas prevalent in Europe about the holy right of each nation to a separate existence – especially Abram Kuyper's theology of sovereignty. The argument went as follows: The wonder and richness of God's creation exists in its diversity. Therefore, in order to honour God's creation and maintain its diversity, people should remain separate and diverse as well (Olivier 1985: 17). In Afrikaner nationalism, the people (*die volk*) always came first. The individual could become fully human only through his people. Nationalism was defined as an ideal, a principle, leading the individual (Diederichs 1936):

> [M]an is not only a social being; he is also a national being. Man is not only called upon to be part of a society, he is also and especially called upon to be a member of a nation. And without the uplifting, ennobling and enriching influence of this highest all-embracing unity we call our nation, man can never reach the highest ideal of being human…The nation is the fulfilment of the individual life. (Diederichs 1936: 17–18; my translation)

This idea of nationalism was also given a deeper spiritual and religious dimension:

> Nationalism is necessarily religious because it regards each nation as a creation of the almighty Creator, destined to fulfil a destiny and contribute its share to the realisation of God's plan for the universe…Service to my nation is thus part of my service to God. (Diederichs 1936: 63; my translation)

The white man's arrival at this southernmost point of Africa was willed by God to make an end to the 'dark ages' (Du Toit 1944: 11). The *boer* nation was 'a new type, created out of a wondrous confluence of blood', knocking at 'the dark gateway' to Africa (Du Toit 1944: 11). This new, God-willed creation had a particular calling. In the words of Hendrik Verwoerd on 16 December 1958:

> Perhaps it was meant for us to have been planted here at the southern point within the crisis area so that from this resistance group might emanate the victory whereby all that has been built up since the days of Christ may be maintained for the good of all mankind. (quoted in Pelzer 1966: 211)

The Afrikaner nation became a *volk* with a divine right to exist and with an ordained mission to make sure that all other races (*volkere*) in South Africa develop their own nationhood (Sparks 1995: 153–154). Afrikaners could now be Christians and guard their nationhood (and that of others) with a 'holy zeal' (Coetzee 1991: 14; Nicol 1947: 20–21). In the words of a letter-writer to *Beeld* in 2004:

> I regard the National Party [now the New National Party; NNP] as the vehicle for the conscience and strife of the Afrikanerdom for the past 90 years. That is why the party cannot simply disband… The NP has always been the embodiment of the Afrikaner's character. It has never been just a party, but the representative of the soul of the *volk*. (Du Preez 2004)[5]

The moral legitimacy of apartheid was questioned in 1960 during the Cottesloe conference in Johannesburg, when eight Afrikaans- and English-language churches came together under the banner of the World Council of Churches to discuss the race situation in South Africa. In the resulting Cottesloe declaration the churches declared that no one may be denied entrance to a church on the basis of race, and that no scriptural grounds exist for the prohibition of marriage across the colour line. Prime Minister Verwoerd regarded the declaration as a direct attack on his authority and vilified the South African delegation of the Dutch Reformed Church in the press. One of the delegates, Beyers Naudé, refused to repudiate the declaration and was eventually driven from the church (Mouton 2002: 42–43).

In the same fashion Verwoerd made short work of a group of 13 Pretoria academics in 1955 when they protested against the removal of coloured voters from the common voters' role. Verwoerd managed to unify Afrikaners into a 'rocklike unity…a tight ideological consensus which could not tolerate any deviation or critical enquiry' (Du Toit 1983: 15). Only in the 1980s would the church's justification of apartheid come under fire again with the publication of *Stormkompas* (1981, as quoted in De Klerk 1984: 50–51). This work proclaimed that the Bible is the only legitimate authority and that a church cannot be built on unifying factors such as blood, land, ownership, culture, language or status. In June 1982, 123 officials of the Dutch Reformed Church wrote an open letter stating that the church may not have any criteria for membership other than the profession of belief in Christ (De Klerk 1984: 50–51).

White guardianship

Afrikaners were convinced that they should act as the guardians of the childlike and intellectually immature African. White people had a responsibility to accept this guardianship because they represented a higher civilisation, were intellectually superior, were the carriers of Christianity and possessed economic and political power (Cronjé 1945: 20). White guardianship was justified because it was made out to be in the best interest of Africans:

> The true-born Bantu see their salvation in the just apartheid policy of the *Boer* nation because they realise that they will only be able to survive as a race along that route...The true-born natives are prepared to subject themselves to the guidance and guardianship of the white man because they know that it is in their own best interest. (Cronjé 1945: 102)

White guardianship became a God-given task, requiring 'commitment and guidance' (Cronjé et al. 1947: 143). However, Cronjé did admit that this guardianship could not last forever: no society can justifiably keep another group subservient indefinitely. Nonetheless, he had the perfect solution to that problem: as soon as Africans were on the same level as Europeans, they could be given self-determination (Cronjé et al. 1947: 148, 149).

THE OLD VERSUS THE NEW AFRIKANER

The first cracks in Afrikaner unity began showing after the assassination of Verwoerd on 6 September 1966. Verwoerd was an autocratic leader: in addition to crushing any dissent or criticism of NP policies, he also created a false sense of security among Afrikaners (Du Toit 1983: 15; Mouton 2002: 45).

On 6 October 1966 Professor Willem de Klerk of Potchefstroom University pointed out the differences among the Afrikaner rank and file. De Klerk criticised the so-called enlightened Afrikaners as 'shallow and fashionable radicals', while the narrow-minded Afrikaners were caught up in the past and resistant to any form of change. Ideal Afrikaners were the 'positive' Afrikaners who were prepared to change without renouncing their heritage. The etiquette of the enlightened Afrikaner later became synonymous with that of the positive Afrikaner, but without the negative connotations. The terms 'enlightened' versus 'narrow-minded' (*verligte* versus *verkrampte*) Afrikaner became popular descriptors of the differences within the NP (Kenney 1991: 206). In 1985 Van Jaarsveld described the difference between the two types of Afrikaners as follows:

...an orthodox, traditionalistic, archaic Afrikaner who fears the present and the future and who wants to resurrect a colonial past long gone, and a grown-up Afrikaner who supports reform because he knows that apartheid was an utopia, that the old past is gone forever, and that a future for the Afrikaner can only be built if he is prepared to accept the South African society in its totality, i.e. that group identities are safeguarded by means of self-governance, so that 'South Africa' eventually can speak with one voice to the outside world...The emphasis has thus shifted from race to 'civilised values'. (Van Jaarsveld 1985: 29)

However, while the new, enlightened Afrikaner was economically stronger and more independent, he was not overly concerned with the morality of apartheid. This enlightened Afrikaner was rather someone who sat back, enjoying the fruits of economic growth and political domination. Afrikaners now focused on material growth rather than their ideological well-being (Kenney 1991: 235; Munroe 1995: 10–11).

This is not to say that there were no critical voices – only that they were not listened to. According to Giliomee (2003: 555–556), critical thinkers such as Johan Degenaar, a philosopher from Stellenbosch, and Breyten Breytenbach, a poet and writer, were heard only outside party ranks. In June 1965 Breytenbach wrote a letter to the Afrikaans daily newspaper *Die Burger* in which he stated that he hates apartheid: 'If I could renounce my being an Afrikaner I would do it. I am ashamed of my people' (Giliomee 2003: 556). By the 1980s few white South Africans still believed in the viability of separate development, but instead of becoming critical of apartheid, the new urbanised bourgeoisie had to be united using a different strategy (Sparks 1995: 317).

THE MYTH OF THE TOTAL ONSLAUGHT

By the 1970s two neighbouring African countries, Angola and Mozambique, gained independence from their colonial masters. This development gave new momentum to the struggle inside South Africa, and provided a springboard for the ANC on South Africa's borders (Sparks 1995: 300–301). In order to counter this new political development, the NP government launched a strategy of military domination and destabilisation of the region (Sparks 1995: 307).

The myth of South Africa as the target of the 'total onslaught' orchestrated from the heart of Moscow gradually began to displace the previous ideology until it became an ideology in itself (Sparks 1995: 309). Struggle organisations such as the ANC, the South African Communist Party (SACP) and the United Democratic Front were made out to be instruments in the hands of an international communist conspiracy: 'South Africa has for a long time been subjected to a total and protracted revolutionary onslaught...The onslaught is not just military: it is political, diplomatic, religious, psychological, economic and social' (General Magnus Malan, former minister of defence, quoted in Pauw 1997: 22). A new concept, so-called neo-apartheid, replaced the previous apartheid policy. The NP realised that reform was inevitable and that Afrikaners, being a minority group, needed the co-option of other minority groups (coloureds and Indians) to protect them against the total (black and communist) onslaught – power-sharing without giving up control (Kenney 1991: 300–302, 307).

PW Botha and his government, however, were not prepared for the angry reaction of black South Africans. The tricameral Parliament was seen as a final attempt to exclude black South Africans from the political process and relegate them permanently to second-class citizenship (Kenney 1991: 336, 338–339). Widespread rioting and so-called black-on-black violence led to the declaration of a state of emergency in 1985 and again in 1986 (Kenney 1991: 350, 353, 365).

The Botha-led government managed to create a psychosis of fear among white South Africans to merge them together as a group: their throats would be cut and their land taken away if they should lose control of the country. All white people had to stand together against the threat of the total onslaught (Sparks 1995: 327–328). The ANC was a barbaric and heathen organisation – cold-blooded murderers of innocent people (Pauw 1997: 36). The struggle for survival was no longer about the inferiority and immaturity of Africans, but the struggle of the Western Christian civilisation against the godless powers of Africa and the total onslaught of the *rooi gevaar*, namely communism (Pauw 1997: 256; Sparks 1995: 279, 311). 'It is a struggle between the powers of chaos, Marxism and destruction on the one hand and the powers of order, Christian civilisation and the upliftment of people on the other...we will not surrender' (Botha quoted in Pauw 1997: 22).

Botha's autocratic and militaristic leadership came to a sudden end after he suffered a stroke on 18 January 1989. In March that year FW de Klerk became state president and began the final dismantling of the apartheid monolith (Kenney 1991: 392–395). Table 12.2 lists the typifications of Self prevalent in the social stock of knowledge of white Afrikaans-speaking South Africans by 1990.

Table 12.2 Typification of the Self by 1990

Before 1940	1940–1990	
Chosen people with a God-given task: the self-preservation of the white minority against a black majority; fear of miscegenation and equality	*The narrow-minded Afrikaner*: caught up in the past; resistant to any form of change; 'true' Afrikaners	*The enlightened Afrikaner*: urbanised; economically well off; more liberal and less ideological; not as dependent on government protection; not really concerned with morality of apartheid; albatross of apartheid hampering progress in the world; neo-apartheid (power-sharing without losing control); fashionable radicals; sell-outs
Sovereignty of the people: an Afrikaner *volk* with its own language, philosophy of life, history and traditions		
White guardianship: had to act as guardian of the childlike and intellectually inferior African		
	Myth of the total onslaught melds groups together: fear psychosis among whites; struggle of Western Christian civilisation against the godless powers of dark Africa and communism	

Later in this chapter I examine to what extent these typifications were taken up in the social stock of knowledge of letter-writers to *Beeld* and to what extent they were used to cope with the sudden changes in their social reality.

CHANGE IN (DIS)COURSE: AFRIKANER, *QUO VADIS*?

De Klerk had a major task ahead of him: to convince white South Africans to replace their nationalism with an inclusive South African nationalism based on a shared value system, regardless of race or culture. The NP achieved this by making use of the deep-seated religiosity of white South Africans. Where the political dividing line before 1990 was based on colour, it now became a question of values and principles (Louw 1994: 40–41).

However, white South Africans got much more than they bargained for. The Afrikaner's social reality changed from being in power, to sharing power, to being powerless (Kriel 1997: 75). Ten years after the new dispensation, the NNP received only 2 per cent of the votes in the 2004 national elections. It seems as if white South Africans had lost their trust in the NNP's ability to negotiate a place in the South African sun. This disillusionment with the previous government's policies came to light with the so-called *Boetman* debate in 2000.

This debate began with the reaction of an Afrikaans journalist, Chris Louw, to the book *Afrikaners: Kroes, kras, kordaat* (De Klerk 2000), in which young Afrikaners are accused of 'genocide' because of their aversion to being Afrikaans. Louw's response to the book was one of utter disillusionment. He and other young men like him had fought in the bush wars against the ANC and the communist *gevaar* (danger); they were misled by Afrikaners like De Klerk and his cronies; and they were exploited in political power games. Louw's generation now finds itself picking the bitter fruits of a failed ideology, while the leaders of the previous regime enjoy retirement. Louw expresses his anger in no uncertain terms: 'Damn you! Damn you for your arrogance, your self-justification, your rationalisation, your denials, and all your lies' (Louw 2000: 13).

The debate opened a Pandora's box of anger and disillusionment among Afrikaners. It raged for weeks in the letters columns of Afrikaans newspapers and led to a book, a drama and several discussion programmes. Ten years after the changes, Afrikaners were still struggling to come to self-knowledge about their role in apartheid. At the same time the question was asked whether the Afrikaner has managed to create a new identity and indeed whether it is worthwhile to do so: 'Who would willingly associate with the concept *Afrikaner*?...They used and misused political power to advance their nationhood and racial identity. What are most of them going to do now that they have become politically powerless?' (Slabbert 1999: 55).

In several disciplines debates raged about the creation of a new South African nationalism and the possible future or demise of the Afrikaans language. For example, of all the survival strategies that Van Niekerk suggests (including emigration, settlement in a white *volkstaat* [nation state], renouncement of Afrikaner identity and adoption of a struggle mentality), he prefers the radical renewal of Afrikaner identity, implying the democratisation of Afrikaans (which means embracing coloured Afrikaans speakers) and the empowerment of Afrikaans by taking up contact with the Dutch–Flemish culture (Van Niekerk 2000: 365). Webb and Kriel (2000: 42–43) maintain that Afrikaners are busy with a process of redefining themselves and their role in the new South Africa after 'totally and finally' losing all political power after 1990, while Bosch (2000: 55) describes the tendency among Afrikaans-speaking South Africans to distance themselves from Afrikaans, choosing English as the language of instruction for their children, without giving up their Afrikaner identity.

In Afrikaans newspapers and magazines the debate about the survival of Afrikaans has been described as the 'third language struggle'.[6] However, the debate is marked by a tendency towards language purism with undertones of nationalism and a religious moralism (Kriel 1997: 76). Any attempt to further the boundaries of a 'pure' language can thus easily be interpreted as a threat to the nation itself – its autonomy, unity and identity (Cattell 2000: 144–145; Kriel 1997: 79). In addition, there seems to be some relation between speaking a 'pure' language and a high moral standard of living, in contrast with 'impure' language and moral degeneration (Kriel 1997: 80). However, Nash (2000: 362) warns that Afrikaners will be able to lay claim to language rights only if they can convince themselves and others of the legitimacy of their aspirations.

Eventually the question is raised about the moral right of the Afrikaner to survive after 1994 (Degenaar 2000; Du Toit 1983; Van Niekerk 2000). Degenaar (2000: 311) refers to Louw when he asks whether the concept of Afrikaner can or should survive given that it was founded on injustice. Degenaar (2000: 313) describes the role of the Afrikaner in the new dispensation as one of 'creative continuation to exist';[7] this presupposes not only a moral responsibility, but also continuous vigilance as a minority group in a multicultural democracy (Degenaar 2000: 317). However, there is a certain 'evilness' associated with being an Afrikaner. In that sense, it is valid to ask whether it is worthwhile for the concept of Afrikaner to survive when it carries so much historical–ideological baggage (Van Niekerk 2000: 371).

It is clear that much remains to be said about the continuing existence of the Afrikaner in the twenty-first century. Various organisations and intellectuals are engaged in a process of redefinition and recontextualisation of the identity, norms and values of the Afrikaner. The next sections attempt to trace the recontextualisation of Afrikaner identity from the perspective of Afrikaans letter-writers to the Afrikaans daily newspaper *Beeld*.

Why *Beeld*?

The history of the Afrikaans press in South Africa is interwoven with the history of the Afrikaner. The establishment of Nasionale Pers with the first Afrikaans daily newspaper (*De Burger*) in Cape Town in 1915 was, in the first instance, an attempt to advance the Afrikaans language and culture against English domination as well as to provide a political mouthpiece to propagate Afrikaner nationalism (Muller 1990: 118).

However, the establishment in 1974 of the liberal *Beeld* newspaper in the former Transvaal (now Gauteng) was seen as a direct threat to NP hegemony, representing a more critical stance towards party policy (Kenney 1991: 209). In the first editorial, then editor Schalk Pienaar voiced the idea of an inclusive South African nationalism:

> The Afrikaner nation has no hope for the future if [the Afrikaner] does not accept himself as part of a South African nation. The South African nation cannot hope for a future existence if it does not regard itself as part of a Southern African complex of nations and societies…The Afrikaner nationalism, growing stronger and stronger into a South African nationalism, believes that it knows the road on which it will find answers to co-existence in Southern Africa. (Pienaar 1974/1984: 2)

The newspaper prided itself on speaking to a new generation of Afrikaners, while it accused far-right Afrikaner groupings of obduracy (Scholtz 1992: 312, 315). *Beeld* was especially critical of the right-wing politics of Andries Treurnicht, an up-and-coming young Turk in the NP ranks and later minister and leader of the Transvaal NP:

> He is undeniably the most often repudiated deputy minister. But here, there and everywhere he continues in the same old key…The emphasis with him is on separation, on apartheid, on resistance against developments which could possibly lead to contact between white and black South Africans. It is always negative. No, no, no! Has he ever offered a positive thought, a practical suggestion as to what we can do about the current crisis in South Africa? (Scholtz 1992: 316)

Although *Beeld* never regarded itself as a mouthpiece for the NP, it did support party policies (Scholtz 1992: 318). In practice this meant that while editors such as Pienaar criticised petty apartheid, they still believed in the ideal of great apartheid (*groot apartheid*) (Mouton 2002: 111). Against this backdrop *Beeld* welcomed De Klerk's historical speech on 2 February 1990 and even suggested that the NP open its doors to all race groups (Scholtz 1992: 323).

In the 1990s the political reform process dominated *Beeld*'s pages: 'The country was at knife's edge. *Beeld* strongly supported a political settlement… *Beeld* saw it as its responsibility to guide its readers by propagating political change and a settlement' (Kruger 2002, pers. comm.). During this time *Beeld*'s circulation rose sharply due to intense interest in the reform process, regardless of the fact that the newspaper's political views were more progressive than its readers' views. According to the then editor of *Beeld*, Willie Kühn, the newspaper's role in the 1980s and 1990s was to lead the Afrikaner establishment peacefully into the new dispensation:

> We knew the high circulation and thus potential influence of *Beeld* was seated...in the suburbs with their schools, churches, clubs, etc. If we could convince those structures and societal institutions to accept change, we could prevent a civil war and create a truly democratic dispensation. We succeeded, despite death threats and even an explosion. (Kühn 2003, pers. comm.)

Afrikaans newspapers distanced themselves structurally and philosophically from the NP only after 1990 (Van Deventer 1998: 79). They came to support certain basic values, such as a liberal multi-party democracy, human rights, media freedom, a free-market economy and the protection of minority rights. *Beeld* had to manoeuvre itself very carefully away from its 'NP umbilical cord' to become a truly independent newspaper. At the same time, the paper had to be very careful not to let the 'objectors' take over the letters column:

> When the newspaper takes up a progressive or even daring viewpoint, it is easy to let the objectors take over the letters column and shoot those viewpoints down with burning arrows. That is why one needs the heavyweights to give guidance or to support you. This is an absolutely non-official, unorganised partnership between the newspaper and those intellectuals and/or leaders, but essential for the work to be done. (Kühn 2003, pers. comm.)

Methodology

Although phenomenology can claim no specific methodology, there exists general consensus about how qualitative data should be analysed – namely by description, classification and interpretation. This study employed the following general procedure in the analysis of the *Beeld* letters:
- *Epoché*: The researcher needs to distance himself/herself from personal preconceptions and suppositions and open up to the meaning constructions of the participants.
- *Horizonalisation*: Husserl called the different perceptions of a phenomenon 'horizons'. During horizonalisation all meaningful statements regarding a phenomenon are listed.

- *Cluster forming*: With this step, the different statements, reduced to their essence, are grouped into themes.
- *Textural and structural description*: Based on the previous analysis, the research describes *what* the individuals experienced (textural description) and *how* they have experienced it (structural experience) (Creswell 1998: 54, 144–145, 147, 235–237; Jansen 1991: 36; Moustakas 1994: 33–36, 60).

The study focuses on letters to the editor published in *Beeld* during 1990 to 1992, three very turbulent and historically significant years in modern South African history, and on letters published during 2004, the year of the demise of the NP. During 1990–1992 a total of 3 462 letters were published, of which 2 010 letters with a socio-political theme were selected. A random sample produced 572 letters for analysis. In 2004, 1 756 letters were published. A random sample produced 148 letters with a socio-political theme. Ultimately 720 letters in total were analysed.

Discussion of the results

Typification of the Other

All significant statements referring to the ANC, black people, Nelson Mandela, black political parties, black politicians and leaders were listed and then clustered together as it became evident that they were functioning on the level of typification. A brief summary of the most significant typifications evident in the letters from 1990–1992 and in 2004 is presented in Tables 12.3 and 12.4.

Table 12.3 Typification of the Other (ANC, Mandela, black people, black government)

1990–1992	2004
Antichrist	*Evil, devilish*: cannot be trusted
Dark Africa: fear of the black majority, black hate, chaos, barbarism	*Black government does not care for white people*: will destroy everything that is Afrikaans or white, is encouraging racial hatred
Chaos: the country is burning, third-world tyranny	*Black majority*: numbers!
Black people cannot govern: do not respect democracy, will destroy the economy, cannot be trusted; inability of a black government	*Black government incapable*: disgraceful, ineffective, does not keep promises, 'gravy train', deterioration of the countryside, uses apartheid as excuse for its own incompetence
A home for future generations: no future for white people	*White taxpayer is keeping new South Africa afloat*

1990–1992	2004
White superiority: white taxpayer is keeping the country going/built South Africa; black people will not be able to govern without white help	*Total onslaught*: totalitarian, cannot stand opposition, communists, revolution
	Insuperable differences between Africa and the West
White guardianship: arrogance and thanklessness of black leaders; 'our blacks'	*Black people hate white people*: violent crime, farm murders
Total onslaught: communists	
Different groups	*Corruption, moral decay*
Moral decay	
Black people are also human: understanding reasons for mass action; understanding reasons for violence	Black government isn't that bad
	Black government is sympathetic towards white fears
	Black people are also human

Table 12.4 Typification of the reform process and the new South Africa

1990–1992	2004
NP/FW have sold out the white volk	*Trauma of crime*
Reform is a sin	*Police/judicial system is failing society*
Reform is part of the total onslaught	*Government doesn't act against crime* because most of the victims are white
Politicisation of sport, education	
Lowering of standards: education	*Comparisons with the previous government*
Afrikaners will not give in to the ANC's demands (humiliating)	*Minority feels threatened*: white people will have to look after themselves because the government is not going to do it
Police are the keepers of law and order	
A home for future generations: who has a plan for the future of white South Africans?	*Absurdities of the new South Africa* as evidence that black people cannot govern
Burden/guilt of apartheid: FW de Klerk is a saviour	*Reverse discrimination/affirmative action*: causes white people suffering, brain drain, disillusionment of white middle-aged men, white people are forever paying for the sins of their forefathers, double standards
	The bubble is going to burst: drop in standards; medical profession/education/air force/defence force in general decline; poor Afrikaans symptomatic of low educational standards, sport is going down the drain
	New SA economy: prices are sky-high
	Success of black government thanks to apartheid

POWER, POLITICS AND IDENTITY IN SOUTH AFRICAN MEDIA

1990–1992	2004
	*Where are the so-called values of the Constitution if...*prisons are overflowing; rights of awaiting-trial prisoners
	Police: inept, powerless, incompetent, corrupt
	Comparisons with the rest of Africa
	Opposition parties are powerless: NNP is powerless, insignificant, no longer the saviour of the Afrikaner, in the ANC's claws; ANC is playing cat-and-mouse games with smaller parties
Positive towards reform in terms of new value systems: redress of past injustices, suggestions for a new NP	Jail terms are effective
	New South Africa is on the right track
	Affirmative action is a correction of an unjust past
Third Force's 'dirty tricks'	
Understanding of need for new national symbols	Not everything is worse now (the past wasn't that wonderful either)
White people are part of the new South Africa	
Qualified acceptance of the new South Africa	Changes in the country thanks to FW de Klerk
Unacceptability of the church/party relationship	NNP operates within reality of African politics
NP government is clever/outsmarting the ANC	(In)effectiveness of the media, opposition parties

It becomes clear from the data summarised in these tables that, especially in 1990–1992, letter-writers tended to fall back on existing recipes in their social stock of knowledge in order to understand the new reality facing them. Quite significant were the references to the ANC as the Antichrist and the many references to darkest Africa, white guardianship, a home for future generations and the total onslaught.

It is especially significant to note in what terms Mandela was described in 1990–1992. It is as if he personified everything that has ever been associated with the Other: atheist, Antichrist, heathen, murderous, symbolisation of murder and murderousness, an old man, tirades, standing with a begging hand, impudent, communist, obstinate, tactician, politically immature, inferior to white people, should address the state president with more respect, doesn't deserve to be addressed as mister, doesn't know his place. There are only a few references to Mandela as an acceptable leader.

TYPIFICATION OF THE OTHER AS THE ANTICHRIST

While the average white South African probably came into contact with black South Africans on a daily basis by 1990, it is likely that very few of them ever met an 'ANC member' in real life. With the unbanning of the ANC and the release of Nelson Mandela in 1990, white South Africans were suddenly engulfed with television images of and newspaper discussions about their former arch-enemy. The letter-writers refer to the ANC in very abstract terms – the most abstract typification being that of the ANC as the Antichrist: 'Pres. F.W. de Klerk must know that, when he is sitting around the table with heathens, he does not represent me nor my fellow citizens at CODESA [Congress for a Democratic South Africa]' (Kemp 1992).

In 2004 there were still letter-writers who referred to the ANC in similar terms: 'This small story represents the world of the police officer in this evil country' (Hugo-Tritter 2004) and 'When the president of our country lights a bunch of grass to call the forefather spirits to bless a memorial garden, then it is dark' (Vister 2004).

FROM THE TOTAL ONSLAUGHT TO VIOLENT CRIME TO THE LANGUAGE STRUGGLE

The fear psychosis of the total onslaught was very effectively internalised by many white South Africans. To them, the unbanning of the ANC was an irresponsible and ill-considered act with chaotic consequences: the country is burning, there is absolute anarchy and a third-world tyranny of poverty and deterioration awaits – that which Afrikaners have been fighting against since they arrived in (darkest) Africa: 'South Africa is now only seeing the beginning of the hell that has broken loose in the country since the unbanning of the ANC and the SACP' (Engelbrecht 1992, letter).

More pertinent, however, is that which underlies the fear psychosis: the continuing existence of white people in a totally new dispensation. This fear is kept alive by the wave of violence and crime engulfing the country. Many letter-writers do not foresee a future for themselves. There exists a very real fear that white South Africans are going to be slain or that there exists an orchestrated murder campaign against farmers in order to get their land. There is a perception of violence, crime, murder and mayhem, barbarism and a lowering in quality of life because of crime. Letter-writers are especially concerned about the shocking and senseless murders of the elderly:

> For the umpteenth time this year white elderly people were barbarically murdered by sadists with pangas. They attacked them like animals. (Besorg 1990)

> Bloodthirsty barbarians are busy with the meaningless and cruel killing of people. (Venter 1991)

> Unrest, murder, joblessness, economic and moral decay and the lowering of standards are the order of the day with the NP's policy of reform. (Lotz 1992)

The myth of the total onslaught is also manifested in the perception that the ANC is a communist organisation interested only in the total overthrow of the existing order. There are hardly any references to the ANC as a liberation movement involved in a legitimate struggle: 'The ANC is a fourth-rated, communist-inspired and terrorist organisation' (GJ Steyn 1990). Letter-writers think that the ANC is interested not in negotiation, but in a scorched-earth policy in order to finally 'take over' (Van Tonder 1992). There is, however, some insight into the legitimacy of protests. Black people still cannot vote and protest marches are the only way they can express their opinions: 'History will show who were the guilty ones and who were the martyrs in South Africa' (Brand 11 September 1992).

By 2004 letter-writers do not necessarily refer to the ANC as a communist organisation. They do, however, warn against the ANC's hidden agenda. Typical of communism, according to letter-writers, are the dictatorial and totalitarian tendencies of the ANC, intolerant of any opposition and slowly but surely leading the country to revolution (Van Oostrum 2004). 'The fact that the ANC cannot tolerate opposition stands out like a sore finger' (De Kock 2004) and '[N]ow that the NP is firmly caught in the claws of the ANC it cannot be regarded as an opposition party any more' (Saunders 2004).

Another manifestation of the 'hidden agenda' of the black government is its seeming inability to act against the high levels of crime in the country. Apart from the letters complaining about the inefficiency of the police and the justice system, most letter-writers are concerned with the government's seeming inability to take action:

> Why do we have to bring our side by voting, but the people whom we are voting for feel nothing for us or our property? (Jacobs & Jacobs 2004)

> And apparently the present government approves of it [the murders] because no attempt is being made to improve the situation. (Oosthuizen 2004)

Pres. Thabo Mbeki, when will you listen to the cries of your nation? (Lucas 2004)

There is a strong perception that the government does not act because the victims are white:

Why can the fear of whites from Cullinan not be stated without beating around the bush, namely that they live in fear of black men who do not hesitate to murder during robberies...? (Du Plessis 2004)

Call a spade a spade and forget about your 'white guilt'. It's plain blatant discrimination, or even more, it's plain racism. It is high time that the ANC should be addressed in no uncertain terms about its discrimination, and that black-against-white racism and intolerance are exposed. We all live in fear. (Henson 2004)

In 2004 letter-writers' mistrust and fear manifest in the perception that the ANC government is set to destroy the Afrikaans language and everything associated with it. Letter-writers are extremely emotional about the proposed name changes of cities and towns:

Or is it the aim of the new lords to change ALL Afrikaans names? (De Lange 2004)

That the ANC and its tentacles are busy with a campaign against everything that is Afrikaner or Afrikaans is evident not only because of the changes of solely Afrikaans place names. I understand (with shock) that the total Afrikaans bookery built up over decades in state libraries [is] now also...being slaughtered, as apparently is the case with the farm murders where there is an onslaught against Afrikaans farmers. (Erasmus 25 June 2004)

However, the same letter-writer is very careful to note that the struggle for the survival of Afrikaans should be part of a legitimate struggle for the survival of all 11 official languages. Otherwise it is back to apartheid (Erasmus 25 June 2004).

WHITE SUPERIORITY

In 1990–1992 the concept of white guardianship manifests in terms of white superiority and the perception that black South Africans, especially Mandela, should be more thankful (for what white people have done for them), less arrogant and more respectful towards (especially) De Klerk. One letter-writer states that he will never stoop so low as to address Mandela as '*oom*' (a familiar but respectful way to address elderly people in Afrikaans):

> I enjoyed reading Johan van Wyk's *Potjiekos*...But when I read that Johan van Wyk addresses Nelson Mandela as 'Uncle Nelson', I felt like giving birth to a porcupine. Nelson Mandela may be Van Wyk's uncle. He is really and truly not my uncle...The title 'uncle' may never be granted to Mandela and his kind. (Anti-Mandela 1990)

The feeling of white superiority manifests in letter-writers' tirades against Mandela. He is an old man, impudent, stubborn, full of tricks and politically immature. There is a feeling in 1990–1992 that De Klerk should put Mandela firmly back in his place:

> It is my humble opinion that Mandela should be thrown off his pretended little throne. (JA Venter 1990)

> One day the State President is going to lose his temper with Mr Mandela...The State President definitely needs the wisdom of Moses and the patience of Job to deal with the irresponsible actions of Mr Nelson Mandela. (EV 1992)

Most letter-writers regard the NP's negotiations and concessions to the ANC as a sign of weakness: 'How far yet is FW de Klerk going to bend backwards to accommodate the ANC's wishes and demands?' (De Bruyn 1991). There exists an awareness of the possibility of power-sharing, but not yet black majority rule based on one person, one vote. Letter-writers are unhappy about the fact that the ANC is already acting as if it is in power: 'Many people are acting as if the ANC is already the boss' (Crous 1990).

With reference to black people in general in 1990–1992, letter-writers write about their inherent barbarity, the consequences if a black person should become one's neighbour, the general lowering of standards and even chaos on the beaches:

> Blacks only came into contact with civilization less than two hundred years ago. (Piet Patriot 1990)

> It is repulsive and disgusting that most blacks swam in their clothes and underwear. (Bekommerd 1990)

South Africa with its thousands of millions of rands will show the rest of the world that one cannot raise blacks to First-World standards. (Vaderlander 1991)

There is only slim reference to black people as 'normal' people who should be regarded as fellow citizens: 'The time has come that we as whites should refer to the black man's language and cultural goods without it sounding inferior' (Mocke 1991).

By 2004 one rarely finds any kind of racist remarks in the letters column. There is a general perception that 'blacks' are also people with emotions, people who grieve when a child dies a tragic death in a water pipe. However, there is still a level of anonymity or typification present when letter-writers write about affirmative action, violent crime and murder. There is a strong perception that black South Africans actually hate white people: 'I...am shocked by the brutal way in which people all over our country are murdered...I can think of many reasons for the murders and violence, but poverty? No ways' (Du Toit 2004).

Other examples of white superiority manifest in letter-writers' references to the dangers and consequences of AIDS, the population explosion as well as the inherent unproductivity and laziness of black people:

Sanctions have always been just a pretext for businessmen who [weren't] prepared to state in the open that they are not prepared to invest in a country with so many unproductive workers, unrest and stay-aways. (Joubert 1991)

Maybe blacks...should teach their own to...work more productive[ly]. (Jordaan 1990)

There are inherent differences between black and white people: 'But am I really the same as the black in spirit, body and being?' (AG Strydom 1991). The most significant reference to the Other is when JHC du Toit (1990) writes that 'my fellow white countrymen should seriously consider how it will be if a black man moves in next to him'. With this simple statement a Pandora's box of white fears and presuppositions is opened. This is probably one of the best examples of Schutz's concept of intersubjectivity: how a few words can call up instant understanding from fellow Afrikaners raised on the ideological elements of Afrikaner nationalism. An entire frame of reference, a cognitive field of related associations, instantly rises to the surface of intersubjective understanding. That is what makes the use of the word 'them' in South Africa so significant. In 1990–1992 'they' are responsible for all the chaos in the country, 'they' are on a stay-away again, 'they' will hijack your car. 'They' are the personification of everything that is black, without 'them' ever being given a chance to defend themselves or give evidence to the contrary: '"They" are blamed for everything, whether "they" are Jews, blacks, Catholics or Martians' (Allport 1958: 12).

By 2004 two types of black people appear in letter-writers' social stock of knowledge. The one type is a human being with feelings (Van Rensburg 2004) and a certain value system – and as long as he can play good rugby, '[w]e shout our lungs out for any player – white, black or brown because they are all part of the team' (Bester 2004). There is, however, the feeling that this type of black person is the exception to the rule. The other type is a remnant from the past: the young black man who commits the most horrific murders (Du Plessis 2004, Du Toit 2004).

The typification of the Other in terms of white superiority has certainly lost its crude, racist elements, but it is doubtful whether the typification of the Other has undergone any fundamental changes to its racist essence.

TYPIFICATION OF THE OTHER IN TERMS OF WHITE GUARDIANSHIP

In 1990–1992 and definitely by 2004 there are hardly any references to white guardianship per se. Rather, letter-writers state that they, the white people of South Africa made it into what it is today and black people should be more thankful for all that they have done for them over the years. In other words, it seems that Cronjé's (1945: 179) idea that white people should accept economic responsibility for black people has become widely accepted. Letter-writers point out that white South Africans built up the country and that black people developed only by accepting their guardianship:

> Just think about everything FW de Klerk did for blacks. The only thing he is getting from them now is the accusation that he is responsible for the terror in the black townships. There are signs of unthankfulness and spite from blacks towards everything he has done for them. (Van Eeden 12 May 1992)

More subtle, however, is the inherent paternalism underlying letter-writers' references to 'our blacks'. For example, there is a general perception that the ANC is not representative of the average, honest black citizen: 'The atrocities of the ANC and its adherents…are not really the traditions, insight or social norms of our black citizens' (Van der Merwe 1990). In 1990–1992 white guardianship becomes the white taxpayer keeping the country afloat; black people are now going to have to work very hard in order to govern the country effectively: 'In the new South Africa manna is not going to fall from heaven' (Maré 1990) and 'It is only the presence of the whites in South Africa which makes this country stand out head and shoulders above its neighbouring states...If the whites leave South Africa, the country will fall apart' (Patriot 1990).

There is also a feeling that white taxpayers are no longer prepared to keep the new South Africa going. Previously it was done in their own interest, then out of a feeling of guilt about the past. Now black South Africans have to take responsibility for their own problems and circumstances: 'We whites have paid for the new South Africa for long enough now. Now it is the coloureds' turn to pay' (Van der Merwe 1991). By 2004 this typification sports yet another new jacket: it is still the poor white taxpayer who is keeping the country afloat, but the ANC's bubble is going to burst when medical, educational, justice and other structures finally collapse under mismanagement, incompetence and corruption: 'The reality will hit them like the Black Death of yesteryear' (De Klerk 2004) and 'Corruption on every terrain is feeding like fishmoths at the economic system; low moral standards find devastating embodiment in AIDS; at the general crime front (murder, robbery, rape) South Africa is world champion' (Levinson 2004).

A more sarcastic version of the above (and still indicative of innate white superiority) refers to the 'absurdities' of the new South Africa – as if these kinds of things could only happen under a black government: 'And there stands the South African high commissioner in Malaysia...straight-backed behind the South African flag...and he cannot see his flag is upside-down! Shame! Poor thing, Dr Nkomo!' (Van Zijl 2004) and 'The saying that this "can only happen in the new South Africa" got new meaning' (Jordaan 2004).

In 2004 the black government's seeming incompetence (and the seeming superiority of the letter-writers) is manifested in its poor language usage, especially when trying to use Afrikaans. It becomes the ultimate example of a failing government: 'Shocking advertisement indicates poor education' (Van Dyk & Coetsee 2004).

The most interesting debates centre on affirmative action, with competing typifications struggling for acceptance in the social frame of reference. On the one hand, letter-writers are tired of suffering for the sins of their fathers.

On the other, they admit that they now have to take what they formerly dished out:

> I am a white man of 39. The benefiting started before I was born ...Today people who do not deserve it are being pushed into posts because they were previously disadvantaged. Please note, not because they have the right qualifications or the capability to do the job, but because of their skin colour. That is why we are bitter ...What is happening here is not 'transformation', but reversed discrimination! Now the shoe is on the other foot and, believe you me, I am not planning to endure this for another 40 years. (Kuhn 2004)

Versus:

> For more than 40 years your skin colour determined your progress in life. Why do whites complain like this after only 10 years? How should those who had to live with this system for 40 years have felt? Why was it okay that a certain portion of the people in this country was advantaged and now they cannot swallow their own medicine? (Transformaat 2004)

Schutz's concept of relevance comes into play when looking at the changing typifications of white South Africans' economic responsibility. While it was economically and politically expedient for white people to 'pay' for black homelands in order to create a safe enclave for themselves in Africa, they were prepared to make the sacrifices. Now that their interests have become less important to a black government, it has become less relevant to support it economically. For a white person it has become more important to work out one's own salvation:

> That white Afrikaans-speaking men are the most self-satisfied group after ten years of affirmative action goes without saying for well-meaning Afrikaners' integrity and ability to survive when they are left on their own by an openly hostile and discriminatory government. (Erasmus 15 June 2004)

In this regard it is appropriate to emphasise the pragmatic aspect of Schutz's phenomenology: typifications are effective only insofar as they are relevant to the continued existence and survival of a group. It would therefore be safe to assume that the typification of white guardianship has become obsolete, no longer relevant to the survival of the Afrikaner in the new South Africa. Whereas letter-writers in 1990–1992 wrote about the hardships black South Africans must have suffered under apartheid and that white people should learn an African language, this sentiment seems to have disappeared by 2004. The initial outreach to the Other was not without an agenda, and again Schutz's concept of relevance becomes pertinent: in 1990 whites were afraid that if they were not prepared to learn an African language, their apathy could lead to 'communicative suicide' (Mocke 1991). By 2004 letter-writers refer to the lack of a social conscience among all South Africans:

> Each and every man and woman in South Africa should have a social conscience which forces him/her to either donate money or their free time to an organisation that is trying to make this country a better place. (Landman 2004)

> White Afrikaans-speaking South Africans now only [have] a social responsibility (if they so choose) to help build the country to the extent that it will safeguard their continued existence as a minority group. (Belangstellende in Gauteng 2004)

Broadly speaking, it seems that Afrikaners can still be separated into three groups. The first group's social stock of knowledge still rests on pre-1990 typifications. Although their typifications are not necessarily represented in *Beeld*'s letters column, there are enough references to them by the second type of Afrikaner to warrant attention. This is how the 'new' Afrikaner refers to the 'old' Afrikaner, thereby also typifying the Self:

> O my dear, what on earth is going in the Afrikaner psyche? Is this still the 'groan of the ox wagon' singing in my ears?...After all, the time has long arrived to move away from the eighteen hundreds and realise that we find ourselves in a multicultural society which is far larger than only the Afrikaner...But for all those die-hard *Groot Trek*-zealots (apparently there are tons and tons of you) who are struggling to adapt in a new South Africa (get the hint, Dan), there is still a chance to take part in a similar happening: The big *trek* to Orania! (Meintjies 2004)

The third kind of Afrikaner is lying low. This is someone who supports the new South Africa, admits the injustices of the past, and is morally aware enough of his precarious position *not* to want to draw any attention to himself. This type of Afrikaner will be discussed in the next section.

In summary, the typification of the Other from 1940 to 2004 is presented in Table 12.5.

Table 12.5 Typification of the Other: 1940–2004

Before 1990	1990–1992	2004
White guardianship	Black thanklessness	White taxpayer
	Blacks cannot govern	Black government incapable
	Blacks are also human beings	Blacks are also human beings
White superiority	White superiority	White superiority
Darkest Africa	Darkest Africa	Blacks hate whites
	Moral decay	Corruption, moral decay
Western Christian power against godless powers of dark Africa	Total onslaught	Total onslaught
	Antichrist	Evil (cannot be trusted)
Protection of the white man's interest in Africa	A home for future generations?	A threatened minority should look after itself
Apartheid	Stay apart	Insurmountable differences

Typification of the Self

It has already been shown how a previously accepted way of thinking has become increasingly irrelevant in a new historical and cultural situation. In the analysis of *Beeld*'s letters column, the changes in the Afrikaner's typification of the Self become even more evident. See Tables 12.6 and 12.7.

Table 12.6 Typification of the Self (1990–1992)

Old Afrikaner	New Afrikaner	New SA nationalism
Unreasonable, uninformed, intolerant	Afrikaners have to stand together	New SA nationalism (first a Christian and then an Afrikaner)
Living in a dream-world	Afrikaners are a nation with a proud history	Skin colour not the criterion
Misuse of the Bible to justify apartheid	Whites have a calling in Africa	New values and norms
Violence/war unrealistic	Struggle for Afrikaans	Reverse discrimination is a repetition of the past
Dragging the Afrikaner's name through the mud	Afrikaners should throw open the doors	
Not representative of the average Afrikaner	Own schools are racist – have to search for new models	

Old Afrikaner	New Afrikaner	New SA nationalism
Fears are understandable	Free from the burden of apartheid	
Grievances are justified		
At least civilised mass action		
Worried about the alienation of the right		

Table 12.7 Typification of the Self (2004)

Old Afrikaner	New Afrikaner/New SA nationalism?
Loud minority	Multicultural society
Going to suffer in the new South Africa (relax and laugh a little)	Proud of culture and language
	Modern
	Aware of the injustices of the past
Living in the past	Prepared to work for the new South Africa
Always moaning	Afrikaans has to be expanded (otherwise it will not survive)
Diehards, stubborn	Reconciliation between blacks and well-meaning Afrikaners
	Conditions for the new South Africa (mutual respect and acceptance, protection of minorities)
	Should insist on rights
	Blatant disregard of Afrikaans
	Tired of political correctness of new Afrikaners
	Afrikaans is again the victim of political opportunism (in the name of apartheid)
	Struggle for language rights for Afrikaans is going to anger others

The debate between the old and the new Afrikaner manifested especially in letter-writers' criticism of the right-wing Conservative Party (CP). In February 1991 then state president De Klerk described the difference between the old and the new Afrikaner when he responded to right-wing criticism that the government was selling out the Afrikaner:

The CP speaks on behalf of part of the Afrikaner people, on behalf of the part caught up in the laager of fear and of prejudice…that which is caught up in the laager of racism and bravado. I speak on behalf of that part of the Afrikaner people which has already… joined hands with fellow South Africans who believe in the same values as we do. (quoted in Louw 1994: 39)

Let us look at each of the main elements in the letter-writers' typification of the Self.

TYPIFICATION OF THE AFRIKANER AS CHRISTIAN NATIONALIST

In 1990–1992 the essentially religious nature of the Afrikaners' view of themselves and the rest of the world becomes very clear. It is as if their religion is the central point from which all other understanding originates. The religious foundation of the Afrikaner's nationhood is voiced by a letter-writer's reference to a quote from Treurnicht:

> The message from the church has been adapted in the language, culture, mores and self-image of our *volk*. With us the [Christian] message has thus obtained a particular sound. It has manifested in our nationhood and on the other hand the healthy concept of nationhood was taken up into the life of the church. Christianity does not hang in the air. (Meiring 1990)

A further mutation of this typification is the description of the Afrikaner as the chosen people: Afrikaners have, like the Israelites of old, wandered from God's way and brought all of this on themselves. They should first restore their relationship with God before they will be prosperous again: 'If whites do not realise that their pride has already brought them to a fall, then they and South Africa will be condemned for time and eternity' (Badenhorst 1990) and 'God will only listen to white Afrikaners and have mercy for them if they confess their guilt' (Jasper 1992).

At the same time there is a strong motivation among letter-writers that their religion and Afrikaner nationalism should be separated, and that Afrikaners should find new insight into what it means to be a true Christian. In other words, being a good Christian means more than being a loyal Afrikaner: 'Many believe the fellow man that God's Word orders us to love are people with the same language, education, colour and politics. If that differs, then the commandment doesn't apply' (Du Plessis 1990). Only when it has become relevant again for the survival of the Afrikaner in 1990 do letter-writers campaign for a clear separation between church and state and urge that the church not be misused by the NP for political purposes (Ek Vra 1991; Engelbrecht 1990; Van Loggerenberg 1991).

The church's confession of the sin of apartheid is another controversial topic among letter-writers in 1990–1992. On the one hand, the church is praised for its confession of guilt: it sets an example for others to follow, the confession is evidence of God's work in the heart of the church and the church should grasp this opportunity for the sake of the new South Africa. On the other hand, the church is accused of spiritual bankruptcy and is seen as a servile and inferior church kneeling in front of Marxism; the Afrikaner has nothing to be ashamed of. Making this typification even more complicated and contested is the clear admission among some letter-writers of what apartheid has done to the other population groups in the country. Letter-writers are quite clear about the fact that the Afrikaner's religion was a selfish religion and that the ideology of apartheid was implemented to further white interests only: 'Are black people also humans?...One man may not dare do to another human what the [apartheid] laws did to them [blacks]' (Pohl 1990) and 'If we learnt one thing from apartheid, then it is that separate amenities like hospitals and schools...benefited the ruling group' (M du Toit 1990).

Letter-writers are extremely annoyed by the right wing's misuse of the Bible to justify its politics. Again, there is a motivated attempt by letter-writers to separate their religion from Afrikaner character:

> Dr Treurnicht mustn't think he will go to 'a better heaven' just because his skin is white. (T van Rensburg 1990)
>
> Anyway, as it would become a proper super-Afrikaner, the AWB-commandant knows his Bible. He can explain exactly, according to the Word, why coloureds are not really people. (Emmes 1991)
>
> The deliberate humiliation and derogation of other races by Dr Treurnicht is so un-Christianlike that it will drive any Christian to shame. (Besin voor dit te laat is 1990)

Letter-writers are very aware of the fact that they have nowhere else to go and that they should become involved with rebuilding the country to everyone's benefit: 'The Afrikaner has no other home' (Uijs 1990) and 'Come, let all South Africans stand together to make South Africa a better country' (Botha 1992).

By 2004 one hardly finds the words 'religion' and 'Afrikaner' in the same sentence. While letter-writers are still writing about religion in general, they are mainly concerned with the debate about the 'new reformation' (with no significant political undertones and thus not included in the sample). It is argued here that Afrikaners in the new South Africa have managed to separate their religion from their Afrikaner character (in a political sense), therefore making the typification of Afrikaner Christian nationalism irrelevant. In other words, while letter-writers in 1990–1992 still debated the concept of their Afrikaner character and Christianity, it simply wasn't an issue any more in 2004, thus rendering the typification irrelevant.

TYPIFICATION OF THE NEW AFRIKANER

In the terminology of letter-writers in 1990–1992, the new Afrikaner is someone whose skin colour is not indicative of his character, with decent manners and a courteous and respectful attitude towards others: 'Rather give me a South Africa where my behaviour, and not my skin colour, will be indicative of my character' (Inbors 1990). Of course this new Afrikaner is also described as high and mighty: 'Especially under Afrikaners there exists a sickening guilt complex about apartheid. The converted Afrikaners are trying to lightly whip away the apartheid dust from their shoulders. They are standing all high and mighty apart from the system' (LP Strydom 1991). Even in 2004 this type of new Afrikaner is described as toadyish, brimming over with political correctness: 'It seems to me as if toadyism under the Afrikaners has become endemic' (L Steyn 2004) and 'This Afrikaner-toadyism is breaking my heart…Just look at the former leader of the NNP now!' (De Villiers 2004).

The most significant references are those to the former state president De Klerk and to the leader of the CP, Treurnicht. De Klerk is described by letter-writers as brave and sincere, a statesman and Christian, with the courage of a lion. South Africans can be proud of De Klerk and his calm and friendly conduct; he has courage and nerve; he acts with Christian charity and righteousness. He is humble, a fighter with perseverance. It is as if De Klerk has become the personification of Afrikaner character, while the CP leader is experienced as everything that the new Afrikaner is not.

The right-wingers are described as naive and impudent, intolerant and racist, highly emotional and hysterical. They are extremists living in a pre-1994 dream-world; they are unrealistic and hold double standards; they are anti-Semitic, arrogant, self-important and intolerant: 'I am extremely concerned about those barbeque-ing people whose skin colour is their only qualification to decide about the future of this country' (GJ Steyn 1990).

Amid these negative and derogatory statements is a concern about the growing alienation of the right-wingers. While they are still described by some letter-writers as bitter-enders and unwavering, there is some sympathy with their cause. They are 'our own people' with legitimate fears and shouldn't be taken so seriously. By 2004 there is hardly any sympathy for the hardline right-wingers: 'When I refer here to the Afrikaner, I'm excluding the small group of die-hard wreckers who are still longing after apartheid. It is this loud little group on horseback fuelling our problems even further' (Erasmus 25 June 2004).

The new, sophisticated and urbanised Afrikaner of 1990–1992 is not interested in the CP's civil war. By 2004 the prospect of civil war as a possible solution has become completely irrelevant to the new Afrikaner. Even in 1990–1992 the new Afrikaner is uncomfortable with the racism and superiority of the right-wingers.

In 1990–1992 letter-writers describe themselves as part of Africa and South Africa, with a positive attitude towards the future and a willingness to become part of rebuilding the country. In 2004 letter-writers describe themselves as part of a multicultural society, aware of the injustices of the past and prepared to work for the new South Africa. Letter-writers are proud of their language and culture: 'I, as a white, middle-aged Afrikaans-speaking man [am] as proud as any other South African of my country and the transformation that has taken place over the past ten years' (P Steyn 2004). It seems as if the new Afrikaner of 2004 has made peace with his new Afrikaner character. There are, however, still a few conditions for the new South Africa: the protection of minorities and mutual acceptance and respect. Afrikaners should remain on guard against any infringements of their rights (especially with regard to language rights and affirmative action).

The foregoing discussion makes clear that a previously accepted way of thinking has become irrelevant due to a changing historical context. New circumstances demanded new recipes – or rather, because of changing historical circumstances, typifications that were previously not regarded as relevant to the survival of the group have now become relevant exactly because they can help ensure the survival of the group. The question remains, however, to what extent the new Afrikaners have adjusted the core of their typifications of the Self and the Other.

EMANCIPATION FROM THE STIGMA OF APARTHEID

Extremely significant is how letter-writers in 1990–1992 write about their emancipation from the burden of apartheid, the myth of the total onslaught and the ideology of Afrikaner nationalism. It is as if the release of Nelson

Mandela literally freed them from the psychological chains of apartheid: 'When Mr Mandela was released from prison, many white South Africans felt free' (E Venter 1990).

Letter-writers are aware of the fact that apartheid was an unfair policy and describe apartheid as a sin that has to be confessed: 'Can Afrikaners stand in front of God with a pure conscience after apartheid?' (Venter 1991). Letter-writers describe De Klerk and the NP as a messiah freeing the Afrikaner from the sins of apartheid:

> Every true Christian can thank the Lord every day that He ordained a man like FW de Klerk to lead South Africa at such a critical time in our history. (Du Plessis 1991)

> Now one morning, during quiet time, I suddenly realised that South Africa's State President, this brave man, is putting himself on the altar for the sake of his patriotism. He is busy answering the call of our beloved country: 'We shall live, we shall die, we for you South Africa.' Is there a greater love than that? (Van Heusen 1991)

However, there also exists a strong sense of bitterness about the futility of a wrongful and cruel ideology and the fact that the children will now have to pay for the sins of the fathers. Letter-writers write about the fact that historically there was no other option, that apartheid was not that bad and did a lot to develop this part of Africa. In 2004 there is hardly a trace of any concept of guilt. There is still an acknowledgement that the past was wrong, but in the same breath it is asked for how long the children will have to pay for their fathers' sins (especially in terms of affirmative action). Emotions range from acceptance to bitterness and resentment:

> Affirmative action is a part of our lives at the workplace, whether we like it or not. (Ontevrede, maar verstaan 2004)

> This morning I am only a middle-aged man without a career and with only the military as background...A soldier used up and spit out by a system for which I worked hundreds of hours overtime without remuneration out of loyalty and patriotism. Suddenly nobody can tell me this morning why I am suddenly so bitter. (Kolonel Broekloos 2004)

A HOME FOR FUTURE GENERATIONS?

The way letter-writers describe their experience of traditional Afrikaner political parties such as the NP and the CP gives significant insight into their definition of the Self. For over 40 years the NP was synonymous with the Afrikaner character. By 1990 this typification was under serious threat, and by 2004 it became irrelevant.

As mentioned previously, an important goal of apartheid was to ensure once and for all the future of white people and their offspring in South Africa. By the 1980s most Afrikaners began to question the feasibility of this solution. In 1990–1992 letter-writers virulently attack right-wing parties such as the CP and its inability to come up with a workable plan for the future survival of Afrikaners. To the contrary, right-wing parties are actually jeopardising Afrikaner survival by their racist remarks and outmoded policies: 'How can whites place the very complicated problematics of South Africa in the hands of Dr Treurnicht?' (Lidmaat 1992) and 'If Dr Treurnicht continues on his present way, he may reduce the chances of whites to survive here to a round zero' (Von Wielligh 1990).

The most vehement criticism is aimed against the CP as representative of an outmoded and irrelevant ideology: 'To turn back the clock is an absurdity and impracticable' (Realis 1991). Afrikaners are now forced to look beyond the horizons of their existing social stock of knowledge for new recipes to manage their survival in the new South Africa. Those letter-writers who regard the NP as the best party to ensure the future of white people are more concerned about the fact that the NP might lose the election against the CP than about the possibility of a black majority government: 'The Nats should plan their strategy against a dirty onslaught from the CP' (Richard 1990). Letter-writers in 1990–1992 are quite sure that De Klerk is at the helm, that he caught the ANC unawares and that he is smarter than the ANC: 'The State President's announcement caught the ANC and related organisations off guard' (Botha 1990). It is clear that the new generation of Afrikaners represented by these letter-writers is prepared to discard the idea of self-governance in favour of a negotiated settlement with the other population groups in South Africa. However, it is less clear whether these letter-writers are fully prepared for a black majority government based on universal suffrage. In 1990–1992 the NP is still regarded as the typical father figure, giving equal representation to all the population groups. This version of reality was acceptable as long as the NP stayed in control. With Schutz's concept of relevance in the background, it can be argued that letter-writers support the reform process not so much out of moral considerations, but rather as the only way to survive. Letter-writers are very aware of the fact that reform is more or less the only viable option: 'Pres FW de Klerk could have continued blindly on this road of confrontation to the grave of the white man in this beautiful country of ours' (Meyer 1990).

Supporting the above argument are the concerns of letter-writers that De Klerk should be more forceful with the ANC, or that the NP is hoisting with its own petard and that white people are the 'dupes' of the new South Africa. Closer to the core is the perception that De Klerk has sold out the Afrikaners, giving away piece by piece the land their forefathers spilled their blood for. The NP does not have a plan for the future: 'I only realise now how naive I was to have always believed that the NP is a party that will fight to the death for the interests of the white South African' (Ontnugterde Nasionalis 1992).

The realists among the letter-writers write that the NP will never be able to escape from its apartheid history. The party will either have to disband or change its name if it wants any credibility in the new South Africa: 'The biggest joke is that some members of the NP still believe that they will be able to win an election in a new multi-racial SA' (Jansen van Rensburg 1992). By 2004 the NP is described as powerless and insignificant: 'The NP is in the claws of the ANC. It cannot even write proper Afrikaans anymore' (Pakendorf 2004).

In conclusion

By 2004 it is clear from the letters that there are still mainly two types of Afrikaners. Letter-writers moan about the right-wingers and urge that these people should either leave the country or go live in Orania. Those sitting comfortably overseas should also please keep their comments to themselves: 'What is he scared for? He lives in Australia – he is safe there, isn't he? Here we are positive and we build the country, even when reports are published about the discrimination in service fees' (Barlow 2004).

These descriptions resemble the typification of the old Afrikaner even before 1990. By 2004 there are thus bits and pieces of the old Afrikaner remaining in the social stock of knowledge. In the same vein, the typification of the Self in the new South Africa is representative of the enlightened Afrikaner as envisioned before 1990. The new Afrikaners of 1990–1992 are a nation with a proud history, free from the burden of apartheid and with a definitive break between their Afrikaner character and their religion. These new Afrikaners are prepared to work with others for the new South Africa.

However, apart from the above there is no radical questioning of what it means to be an Afrikaner. Previously in this chapter the question was asked whether the new Afrikaners are going to develop an aversion to their Afrikaner character and whether this character has a moral right to survive (Louw 1958: 63). It seems as if the letter-writers managed to free themselves from this decision by separating Afrikaner character and religion. Afrikaner Christian nationalism was inherently evil and unacceptable. Then De Klerk came and sacrificed himself and Afrikaner power in order to free the Afrikaner of the sin of apartheid. De Klerk went through the 'dark night of the soul' and a new nation was born. In 2004 the new Afrikaners, free from the burden of apartheid, are a minority group in a multicultural society, proud of their language and culture, aware of the injustices of the past and prepared to work for the new South Africa.

The new Afrikaner is, however, not without a shadow: underlying the struggle for the acknowledgement of Afrikaans is the realisation that the language struggle is still used by many as a pretext for the continuation of apartheid. When a government department uses poor Afrikaans in an advertisement, it is seen as indicative of the black government's incompetence and the lowering of standards. And while the letter-writers spend a lot of time redefining the Self, the same cannot be said of their redefinition of the Other.

The essence

Afrikaans letter-writers to *Beeld* have managed to negotiate for themselves a reasonably acceptable place in the new South Africa. While they have seriously revisited their Afrikaner character, it is doubtful whether any fundamental revision of their perception of the Other has taken place.

Letter-writers in 2004 are very aware of the fact that they have to look after themselves (because the government is not going to do it) and that the white taxpayer is actually keeping the country going. The absurdities of the new South Africa are typical of the incompetence of a black government; in any event, the bubble is soon going to burst. Opposition parties are powerless in the face of a totalitarian and communist ANC-led government out to destroy Afrikaans and everything associated with it. There are irreconcilable differences between the West and Africa.

According to Van Jaarsveld (1985: 14), white fear of black domination and miscegenation have been built into their world-view like a self-protection mechanism. This fundamental aspect will remain an essential part of the world-view of Afrikaners as long as they are the minority in black Africa. Any revision of the Afrikaner's typification of the Other is obviously so fundamental that few Afrikaners are able to discard the existing recipe. It is thus easier for most Afrikaners to adjust their social stock of knowledge to handle the new South Africa as the need arises.

It is also possible that very few Afrikaners have been put in a position where they have had to make a fundamental readjustment. According to Schutz (1962/1973: 212, 226), work is the overwhelming reality for many individuals in their everyday lives. Only the working self is fully interested in life and 'awake' – and, according to Schutz, that is the state in which the process of understanding should begin. Wide-awake people concentrate on that part of the world which is pragmatically relevant to them, and those relevancies will determine the form and content of their conscience. It is posed here that while letter-writers to *Beeld* had to readjust their daily behaviour in order to adapt to the changing realities of the new South Africa, this has not necessarily implied a radical revision of the essence of their typification of the Other – namely, that of inherent racial inferiority.

One can ask, however, what the critics expect from the Afrikaner. According to Giliomee (1991: 120), there has been no fundamental change in the basic thought patterns of white South Africans. This is confirmed by Du Plessis (1997: 15) when he says that there is something seriously wrong with the moral conscience and psyche of the Afrikaner establishment: there is a 'moral vacuum' and a lack of 'a respectable ethos of self criticism' among especially Afrikaner institutions such as the church. What, however, would be regarded as a fundamental revision in the thought patterns of the Afrikaner? In September 2006 the former minister of police, Adriaan Vlok, stunned South Africa and the world when he publicly washed the feet of some of his victims. Reaction ranged from outrage and cynicism to deep-seated gratitude for this symbolic gesture from a former NP minister (Anon. 2006: 2; Jackson 2006). In more mundane terms, one could say the ideal would be individuals who are mature enough not to fall back on stereotypes in their recognition of the Other, individuals who are prepared to grasp the uniqueness of every individual they meet – and who withhold that second-hand and trite opinion when they do not know the Other.

However, it is not without reason that Schutz calls typifications the lifeblood of the everyday world. It is much easier to function amid those general truths commonly accepted by 'everyone'. Is the critical and informed individual thus only an ideal to strive for, or is it possible that such a critical disposition could become part of the social stock of knowledge? Du Toit writes thus about the Afrikaner's concept of guilt:

> For a confession of guilt to have meaning, it should not come too easy. It has to be earned. It should have consequences. What we confess and admit [has] implications for the past as well as for the future. (Du Toit 1991: 47)

Notes

1   The other three Afrikaans newspapers are *Volksblad* (Free State), *Die Burger* (Western Cape) and *Oosterlig* (Eastern Cape).

2   Born in Austria, Schutz obtained a doctorate in law from Vienna University in 1923. In 1939 he fled the Nazi occupation and went to the United States, where he joined the New School for Social Research in 1943. His most important work, *The Phenomenology of the Social World* (1932), was translated into English only in 1967. His essays are available in three volumes of *Collected Papers* (1962, 1964, 1966). Only after his death did his work have a real influence on American thought.

3   Schutz was influenced by William James, Henri Bergson, Max Weber and in particular Edmund Husserl (Altheide 1977).

4   Four well-known Afrikaner academics went to study in Germany: Nico Diederichs, Geoff Cronjé, Piet Meyer and Hendrik Verwoerd (Sparks 1995: 163).

5   All quotations from Afrikaans letters appearing in this chapter have been translated into English by the author.

6   For more information about the third of six language movements, see HJ Pieterse, 'Alternatiewe Afrikaans: 'n historiese oorsig en tipologie' in *Suid-Afrikaanse Tydskrif vir Taalkunde* 26 (November 1995): 133–162.

7   In Afrikaans 'kreatiewe voortbestaan'.

References

Books and journal articles

Allport G (1958) *The nature of prejudice: A modern perspective*. Garden City, NY: Doubleday

Altheide DL (1977) The sociology of Alfred Schutz. In JD Douglas and JM Johnson (eds) *Existential sociology*. Cambridge: Cambridge University Press

Anon. (2006) Kerk moet SA se 'Boetmanne' help. *Beeld*, 9 September

Berger PL & Luckmann T (1967) *The social construction of reality: A treatise on the sociology of knowledge*. New York: Doubleday

Bosch B (2000) Ethnicity markers in Afrikaans. *International Journal of Social Linguistics* 144: 51–68

Cattell K (2000) Die konstrukie van Afrikaner-nasionalisme, met spesifieke verwysing na NP van Wyk Louw. *Stilet* 12(2): 135–152

Coetzee JM (1991) The mind of apartheid: Geoffrey Cronjé (1907–). *Social Dynamics* 17(1): 1–35

Creswell JW (1998) *Qualitative inquiry and research design: Choosing among five traditions*. Thousand Oaks, CA: Sage Publications

Cronjé G (1945) *'n Tuiste vir die nageslag: Die blywende oplossing van Suid-Afrika se rassevraagstukke*. Stellenbosch: Pro Ecclesia-Drukkery

Cronjé G, Nicol W & Groenewald EP (1947) *Regverdige rasse-apartheid*. Stellenbosch: Christen Studente Vereeniging Boekhandel

Degenaar J (2000) Die spanning tussen voortbestaan en geregtigheid. *South African Journal of Philosophy* 19(4): 307–320

De Klerk WJ (1984) *Die tweede (r)evolusie*. Johannesburg: Jonathan Ball Publishers

De Klerk WJ (2000) *Afrikaners: Kroes, kras, kordaat*. Cape Town: Human and Rousseau

Diederichs N (1936) *Nasionalisme as lewensbeskouing en sy verhouding tot internasionalisme*. Bloemfontein: Nasionale Pers

Du Plessis LM (1997) Afrikanernegatiwiteit oor die WVK: Viva Rip van Winkel? *Woord en Daad* 360 (Winter): 14–17

Du Toit A (1983) *Die sondes van die vaders: 'n Poging tot die verkenning van die posisie van die Afrikaner-intellektueel in die komende legitimiteitskrisis van die Afrikaner-nasionalisme en die apartheidsorde*. Cape Town: Rubicon-Pers

Du Toit A (1991) Was alles dus maar net 'n ligte mistykie? *Die Suid-Afrikaan* 32 (April–May): 45–47

Du Toit JD (Totius) (1944) Die Godsdienstige grondslag van ons rassebeleid. *Inspan* (December): 7–17

Fourie PJ (1991) Media, mites, metafore en die kommunikasie van apartheid. *Communicatio* 17(1): 2–6

Garfinkel H (1967) *Studies in ethnomethodology*. Englewood Cliffs, NJ: Prentice Hall

Giliomee H (1991) Changing everything (except the way we think). *Leadership South Africa* 3(3): 125

Giliomee H (2003) *The Afrikaners: Biography of a people*. Cape Town: Tafelberg

Goffman E (1959) *The presentation of self in everyday life.* Garden City, NY: Doubleday

Jackson N (2006) Ek het gestruikel en geval. *Beeld,* 3 September

Jansen N (1989) *Philosophy of mass communication research.* Johannesburg: Juta

Jansen N (1991) Implikasies van die keuse van 'n teoretiese benadering vir beslissings oor navorsingsontwerp. *Communicatio* 17(2): 34–40

Jansen N & Steinberg S (1991) *Theoretical approaches to mass communication research.* Johannesburg: Juta

Kenney H (1991) *Power, pride and prejudice: The years of Afrikaner Nationalist rule in South Africa.* Johannesburg: Jonathan Ball Publishers

Kriel M (1997) Taal en sedes: Die nasionalistiese en religieus-morele waardes onderliggend aan taalpurisme. *Suid-Afrikaanse Tydskrif vir Linguistiek* 1997 15(3): 75–85

Lauer Q (1965) *Edmund Husserl: Phenomenology and the crisis of philosophy.* New York: Harper and Row

Louw C (2000) Boetman is die bliksem in. 'Baie jammer, ek is genoeg verneuk, en boonop gatvol.' *Beeld,* 5 May

Louw NP van Wyk (1958) *Liberale nasionalisme.* Johannesburg: Nasionale Boekhandel

Louw PE (1994) Shifting patterns of political discourse in the new South Africa. *Communicatio* 20(1): 26–43

Mervis J (1989) *The fourth estate: A newspaper story.* Johannesburg: Jonathan Ball Publishers

Moustakas C (1994) *Phenomenological research methods.* Thousand Oaks, CA: Sage Publications

Mouton A (2002) *Voorloper: Die lewe van Schalk Pienaar.* Cape Town: Tafelberg

Muller CFJ (1990) *Sonop in die suide: Geboorte en groei van die Nasionale Pers – 1915–1948.* Cape Town: Nasionale Boekhandel

Munroe WA (1995) Revisiting tradition, reconstructing identity? Afrikaner nationalism and political transition in South Africa. *Politikon* 22(2): 5–33

Nash A (2000) The new politics of Afrikaans. *South African Journal of Philosophy* 19(4): 340–364

Natanson M (ed. and trans.) (1973) *The problem of social reality* (4th edition). Vol. 1 of *Alfred Schutz: Collected Papers.* The Hague: Martinus Nijhoff

Nicol W (1947) 'n Grootse roeping. In G Cronjé, W Cronje & EP Groenewald *Regverdige rasse-apartheid.* Stellenbosch: Christen Studente Vereeniging Boekhandel

Olivier G (ed.) (1985) *Praat met die ANC.* Emmarentia: Taurus

Owen K (1985) Well, we all live in cloud-cuckoo-land. *Sunday Times,* 18 August

Pauw J (1997) *Into the heart of darkness: Confessions of apartheid's assassins.* Johannesburg: Jonathan Ball Publishers

Pelzer AN (ed.) (1966) *Verwoerd speaks: Speeches, 1948–1966.* Johannesburg: APB Publishers

Pienaar S (1974/1984) *Beeld 1974–1984 gedenkbylae.* 14 September 1984

Rickman HP (ed.) (1961) *Meaning in history: W Dilthey's thoughts on history and society.* London: George Allen and Unwin

Scholtz JJJ (1992) Deurbraak na die Noorde. In WD Beukes (ed.) *Oor grense heen: Op pad na 'n nasionale pers. 1948–1990.* Cape Town: Nasionale Boekhandel

Schutz A (1962/1973) *The problem of social reality* (4th edition). Vol. 1 of *Collected papers,* ed. and trans. M Natanson. The Hague: Martinus Nijhoff

Schutz A (1964/1976) *Studies in social theory.* Vol. 2 of *Collected papers.* The Hague: Martinus Nijhoff

Schutz A (1970) *Reflections on the problem of relevance.* New Haven: Yale University Press

Schutz A & Luckmann T (1974) *The structures of the life-world.* Trans. RM Zaner and HT Engelhardt, Jr. London: Heinemann

Slabbert F van Zyl (1999) *Afrikaner Afrikaan.* Cape Town: Tafelberg

Sparks A (1995) *The mind of South Africa: The story of the rise and fall of apartheid.* London: Mandarin

Thompson L (1985) *The political mythology of apartheid.* New Haven, CT: Yale University Press

Van Deventer H (1998) *Kroniek van 'n koerantman: 'n Persoonlike perspektief op die jare ná 80.* Welgemoed: Tarlehoet BK

Van Jaarsveld FA (1985) Die Afrikanerdom: 'n Histories-vertraagde volk – weg en selfbegrip. *Historia* 2(31): 6–32

Van Niekerk A (2000) Afrikanerskap: Ten slotte, of opnuut? Nabetragting van André du Toit se 'Die Sondes van die Vaders'. *South African Journal of Philosophy* 19(4): 365–385

Webb V & Kriel M (2000) Afrikaans and Afrikaner nationalism. *International Journal of Social Linguistics* 144: 19–49

Beeld letters

Anti-Mandela (1990) Herken hom vir wat hy is. 7 June

Badenhorst D (1990) Vertroue in God nodig. 22 June

Barlow (2004) Nie te sê die diskriminasie is rassisme. 8 October

Bekommerd (1990) Is dit die nuwe Suid-Afrika? Lesers sê swartes verdring blankes van die strande af. 12 January

Belangstellende in Gauteng (2004) Gee koerante aan skole in Noordwes. 18 June

Besin voor dit te laat is (1990) Swartmense het rede om te kla. 2 May

Besorg (1990) Versterk polisie-hande. 1 September

Bester S (2004) Ontspan, Fredericka, jy't dit nodig. 25 March

Botha AH (1992) Sinloos om na oplossings te soek en nie te beding. 3 April

Botha DF (1990) Nog net APT moet oor. 9 March

Brand JE (1992) Grondwet is 'n verleentheid! 25 March

Brand JE (1992) Slagoffers van gewetenlose tiran. 11 September

Crous T (1990) Mandela ken nie Afrikaner-mag. 7 June

De Bruyn DJ (1991) Daagliks ongeloofwaardiger. 7 August

De Klerk B (2004) Mediese toestande sal land nog soos swart griep tref. 7 February

De Kock MJ (2004) VF + hou meer van ANC as van DA. 23 August

De Lange C (2004) Naamsveranderings mors geld, ontken geskiedenis. 14 June

De Villiers PH (2004) Ontstellend baie Afrikaners is kruipers. 30 October

Du Plessis DP (1990) KP praat van minderheid. 27 February

Du Plessis DP (1991) Dáárom betaal swartes nie soveel belasting nie. 12 July

Du Plessis F (2004) Hanteer eerder oorsaak van rowers wat so moor. 18 November

Du Preez PH (2004) NNP kan nie so maklik net ontbind. 8 June

Du Toit JHC (1990) Dink goed oor nuwe SA. 11 January

Du Toit M (1990) Praat namens hulleself. 6 June

Du Toit Y (2004) Wrede geweld nie weens armoede. 30 November

Ek Vra (1991) Hul moet daarmee rekening hou. 9 March

Emmes LD (1991) Waarvan en van wie is hy eintlik 'kommandant'? 18 March

Engelbrecht B (1990) NG Kerk moet nóú inspring. 15 November

Engelbrecht B (1992) NP se 'voorbokke moet inderdaad begin bid'. 27 June

Erasmus PF (2004) Moenie Afrikaner-Afrikane uitsluit. 15 June

Erasmus PF (2004) Publiseer dringend die taal-struggle. 25 June

EV (1992) Moses se wysheid, Job se geduld. 10 June

Henson L (2004) Dis rassisme – noem dit op sy naam. 2 October

Hugo-Tritter R (2004) Plaas polisie se dapperheid, hartseer op die voorblad. 27 January

Inbors (1990) Gedrag, nie velkleur. 25 October

Jacobs J & Jacobs M (2004) Wie staan pa vir gesteelde motor? 16 April

Jansen van Rensburg PJ (1992) NP ook nie aanvaarbaar as hy eers alles weggegee het. 19 March

Jasper (1992) Hulle het die Here gaan spreek, nie die regering.

Jordaan BJ (1990) Onderhandeling sal nie werk. 27 March

Jordaan R (2004) Vergadering laat busse 2 uur staan. 23 August

Joubert H (1991) Sal die ouers dit kan bekostig? 28 June

Kemp JJ (1992) Wêreld se erkenning nie gesoek. 8 January

Kolonel Broekloos (2004) Weermag spoeg my uit ná jare diens. 4 November

Kuhn K (2004) Gaan transformasie nie 40 j. verduur. 12 November

Landman R (2004) Tronke nie net die regering se taak. 5 July

Levinson S (2004) Mbeki op ontdekkingsreis in eie land. 26 March

Lidmaat (1992) KP-leier is fanatiek oor sy ideologie. 16 March

Lotz FJ (1992) Sterker anderkant onder die KP. 3 March

Lotz FJ (1992) Bisho wys kommuniste heers. 15 September

Lucas T (2004) Dié voorblad sal lank by my spook. 30 July

Maré GS (1990) Geen manna in die nuwe SA. 29 May

Meintjies J (2004) Doen iets beters, Afrikaner, as mompel oor toeka se tyd. 26 February

Meiring PG (1990) Laat hulle meer hoor. 30 November

Meyer EJ (1990) FW het oog op toekoms. 30 March

Mocke E (1991) Kommunikatiewe 'selfmoord'. 13 March

Ontevrede, maar verstaan (2004) Wit sportmanne benadeel nes sakelui. 27 October

Ontnugterde Nasionalis (1992) NP besig om duisende blankes te vervreem. 27 October

Oosthuizen N (2004) Is moord tans hoër as Olimpiese peil? 21 July

Pakendorf M (2004) NNP sleep sy vlerk in die modder. 26 February

Patriot (1990) In ou stryd was dit wit teen wit. 10 March

Piet Patriot (1990) 'n Stemlose minderheid. 10 February

Pohl N (1990) Waar was Treurnicht? 18 December

Realis (1991) Sanksies, boikotte dan nog erger. 10 December

Richard D (1990) Betaal die KP in eie munt terug. 8 October

Saunders C (2004) Niks niks NP nóg vis, nóg vlees. 9 June

Steyn GJ (1990) Tot hiertoe en nie verder. 4 December

Steyn JML (1990) Velkleur beskerm hulle. 23 October

Steyn L (2004) Herdink eer aan kommunis Fischer. 2 October
Steyn P (2004) Net regering kan dié vrese besweer. 10 March
Strydom AG (1991) In wese en liggaam dieselfde? 14 March
Strydom LP (1991) ANC moet steeds wys hy wil eerlik onderhandel. 17 September
Transformaat (2004) Wie is rede vir transformasie vandag? 11 November
Uijs MJ (1990) Afrikaner het nou kans. 12 April
Vaderlander (1991) Die mense is belastingvoos en miljarde rande vloei. 17 August
Van der Merwe GS (1991) Naidoo, vakbonde moet eers hul rekenings betaal. 21 October
Van der Merwe PJ (1990) Varkkop: Nuwe soort terreur? 8 April
Van Dyk F & Coetsee E (2004) Skokkende advertensie dui op swak onderwys. 24 September
Van Eeden G (1992) Nuwe denke is hier noodsaaklik. 12 May
Van Heusen K (1991) SP plaas sy alles op die altaar. 26 June
Van Loggerenberg NJ (1991) Die sinode in partypolitieke kryt is sonde. 31 October
Van Oostrum LJ (2004) Konflik aangestook deur regering. 8 December
Van Rensburg E (2004) Kyk feite om Karabo-dood in oog. 17 February
Van Rensburg K (1990) Treurnicht sal gou moet vlug. 25 June
Van Rensburg T (1990) Dr T. is 'n 'stoute oom'. 12 April
Van Tonder WM (1992) Teë vir tirades van ANC. 2 July
Van Zijl JJ (2004) Foeitog, Dr Nkomo, wat is fout? 17 February
Venter E (1990) Watter opofferings? 5 July
Venter JA (1990) Dié leiers praat nie net. 7 April
Venter JA (1991) Het vermoorde dan nie ook die reg om te lewe? 6 September
Vister PJ (2004) Haiti maak ons nie bang nie, Dirk. 13 March
Von Wielligh CM (1990) Het Treurnicht 'n mandaat? 5 October

Interview and personal communications

Boshoff G (1992) Letters editor of *Beeld*. Interview, Johannesburg, 2 June
Kruger P (2002) Political correspondent and later editor of *Beeld*. Personal communication, 5 December
Kühn W (2003) Editor-in-chief of *Beeld*. Personal communication, 27 March

13 Foreign policy, identity and the media: Contestation over Zimbabwe

Anita Howarth

Introduction

The central contention in this chapter is that state identities and foreign policy can be mutually constitutive or mutually destructive, that constructions of identity can underpin policy frameworks and that the operationalisation or application of these to particular situations can reconstitute state identities. Thus, there is a dialectical interaction between processes of identity construction and foreign-policy construction. These are structured around processes of circulation and legitimation in which the media play a key role as political actors in their own right, able to construct their own counter-discourses or counter-identifications to those presented by the government. Mbeki's strategy of 'quiet diplomacy' towards Zimbabwe highlights how this works in practice as well as the implications of a dissonance between foreign-policy principles and practice for constructions of state identity. This dissonance makes legitimation of policy less likely and undermines the credibility of the country's 'moral stature'.

Overview

Since the 1990s, there has been within the study of international relations a growing interest in the relationship between the construction of foreign policy and of identity.[1] Firstly, both use similar linguistic devices of 'us' and 'them' to construct foreign policy and to build identities. Secondly, identities are meanings emerging out of relationships (Louw 2005) used to construct a sense of 'self' in individuals and communities (Frueh 2003); foreign policies are meanings on how to manage particular types of relationships between particular types of communities associated with the state (Dessler 1999; Weaver 1994). The construction of state identities and the construction of foreign policy can therefore be mutually constitutive or mutually destructive.

State identities are the primary interest in foreign-policy analyses.[2] This focus on the national state[3] as a unit of analysis is based on the contention that, despite globalisation, states have retained primary responsibility for the security of their countries, and citizens still look to the governments of these states to protect them from external threats (Hill 2003), partly through the management of diplomatic relations with other states.[4] This state–citizen, state–state interplay embeds foreign policy in domestic political contexts and in international contexts within which a state has to operate, which facilitate and constrain its ability to do so, but within which it also has to seek legitimation from its domestic constituencies and from other states.

Constructions of state identity influence the construction of foreign policy. Conversely, how a state operates, manages and justifies its domestic and international relationships, as well as how effective it is perceived to be in attaining its policy objectives, influences the reconstruction of state identities (see Campbell 1998, 2001), how these identities are perceived by insiders and outsiders, and whether both foreign policy and state identities are legitimated or validated. Processes of legitimation are linked to processes of identification which draw on common values, beliefs and ideologies (Bloom 1992; Habermas 1974) as well as on shared experiences, similar histories and common legacies (Louw 2005). Who is or is not identified with is constructed around binary discourses of 'us' and 'them'.

In national states with 'imagined political communities'[5] processes of legitimation require mechanisms for a wider circulation of meanings. In Western democracies, the media serve as the 'main storytelling vehicle' and this enables them to play a key role in the construction of mass identities (Louw 2005). State identities are not mass identities – they are too narrowly focused on the apparatus, behaviour, discourse and actors of the state – but the operation of democracy requires a significant or an influential proportion of the electorate to identify with and legitimate state identities and policies (Bloom 1992). Here the media can play a major role. In countries such as South Africa with high levels of illiteracy and a relatively small public sphere (Jacobs 2003; Louw 2005) the media are unlikely to be primary circulators of meaning as they are in Western democracies, but they can still play a significant circulatory role for three reasons. Firstly, studies of elections in Africa have shown how potentially and disproportionately influential a media-consuming urban middle class can be on politics (see, for instance, Temin & Smith 2002). Secondly, other studies suggest that even in Western democracies foreign news usually remains the preserve and interest of these middle classes – public elites with relatively high levels of education and civic engagement (Cohen 1963; O'Heffernan 2000; Robinson 2001, 2002) – and thus far there is little to suggest that in Africa foreign news might have a different readership profile. Thirdly, some permeation of foreign news from these urban elites to the 'masses' may be possible particularly through civil society organisations such as trade unions or activist groups whose memberships may be more socio-economically diverse. Thus, a relatively small public sphere may restrict the scale of circulation possible but does not preclude the need for at least some circulation, some identification and some legitimation of the constructions of state identities and foreign policy. Failure to secure legitimation undermines the credibility of democratic states and the associated identities they have sought to construct, so a crisis of legitimation can also be a crisis of identification (see Habermas 1974: 91).

South Africa's foreign policy towards Zimbabwe presents an interesting case study of how these dialectical processes of construction and reconstruction, circulation, identification and legitimation might work in practice. State identity has been carefully crafted by political leaders out of constructions of the past and around a powerful, unique narrative of the successful transformation to post-apartheid society. This has been circulated, perpetuated and legitimated in part by the media but also by Nelson Mandela and Thabo Mbeki, who have 'sought to invigorate the conduct of international affairs with reference to South Africa's unique transition and moral stature' (Alden & Le Pere 2003: 283). Thus, the construction and circulation of a particular type of state identity has been used to construct the principles and paradigms of a foreign-policy framework and to legitimate it by reference to the past. But the ability to sustain a particular construction depends on practical implementation of policy to actual situations. When operationalisation of policy diverges from the principles embedded in the framework, a dissonance ensues that may extend beyond foreign policy to the constructions of state identity used in the formulation of the framework. This chapter contends that Mbeki's policy of '"quiet diplomacy" despite state repression and abrogation of the rule of law in Zimbabwe' (Nathan 2005: 367) may have undermined the carefully constructed 'moral stature' of state identity, damaged the credibility of Mbeki and contributed to a crisis of legitimation as civil society organisations, including the media, constructed alternative identifications and counter-discourses to those used by the South African state.

These points will be explored in more detail in this chapter, which will:
- outline a constructivist approach to foreign policy and state identity and indicate how these two might be considered mutually constitutive and complementary;
- outline the principles and paradigms underpinning South Africa's foreign policy, link these to the construction of a particular type of state identity and detail the evolution of Mbeki's policy towards Zimbabwe;
- outline processes of circulation and media–state contestation, looking in particular at the media and its role in society and divergences in framing of policy on Zimbabwe; and
- conclude with a brief discussion on whether the foreign-policy approach towards Zimbabwe may represent a crisis of legitimation and a crisis of identification.

Constructed foreign policy and state identity

Processes of identification are constructed around categorisations of 'domestic' and 'foreign', 'us' and 'them'. These linguistic devices provide a major mechanism for the construction of categories of identity which are constructed and challenged between groups (see Billig 1995; Yumul & Ozkirimli 2000). They are also one of the primary methods by which the parameters of foreign policy are constructed, negotiated and contested. On the one hand, 'foreign' can be interpreted in a narrow sense that draws the boundaries at the territorial borders of the national state, limits the ability of states to encroach on the sovereignty of another state (Hill 2003: 236) and enables political leaders to justify non-interventionist foreign policies (DiPrizio 2002). On the other hand, it can also be interpreted much more broadly to include symbolic boundaries constructed out of similar histories, shared experiences and common legacies. Here, foreign policy transcends territorial borders, engenders 'boundary-producing' discourses (Campbell 1998: 69) and provides rhetoric to justify humanitarian intervention in another sovereign state (DiPrizio 2002; Livingston 1997; Livingston & Todd 1995).

A constructivist approach not only draws attention to the linguistic devices identity and foreign policy share, but also highlights a number of common features.[6] Both:
- are constructed discursively and interpretatively in a continuous process;
- are relational in that they construct, interpret, structure and seek to manage intra- and inter-group relations;

- facilitate inclusion or identification with some and exclusion or alienation of others, and thereby give rise to simultaneous centripetal and centrifugal, cohesive and divisive forces;
- are contextualised in local specificities which comprise past histories and shared experiences, present legacies and common problems, and so provide a temporal continuity between past, present and future;
- are in constant flux as contexts change and new conditions present themselves, and thus paradoxically comprise continuity and change;
- are complex, multiple and overlapping, and are therefore potentially contradictory and dissonant at the same time; and
- require constant legitimation in that 'if the interests inherent in identification are not met, then the social system is not legitimated' (Bloom 1992: 48; Habermas 1974).

While foreign policy and identity may share similar characteristics, they differ in their priorities and functions – although this is more a matter of emphasis than absolutes – and this enables them to be complementary. So, on the one hand, the primary function of identity construction is to build cohesiveness in communities; on the other hand, the primary function of foreign policy is to defend the national state by managing relationships with entities beyond its territorial borders. On the one hand, binary discourses are primarily used to categorise identities; on the other hand, they primarily set the parameters of and provide coherence for foreign policy. On the one hand, identities primarily entail a moral and social responsibility for members of the community; on the other hand, foreign policy adds to these a legal responsibility.

However, not only are state identities and foreign policy potentially complementary, they can also be mutually constitutive or mutually destructive – they can serve cohesion or they can serve division. So, for instance, threats posed to the state may be manufactured, potential or actual. Depending on how they are conceptualised and articulated in foreign policy, they can engender cohesiveness through perceptions of a common threat or enemy and so help in the construction of identity (see Keen 1986). Or they can engender divisions if there is contestation over who or what constitutes 'the enemy', or whether enemies should be recategorised as 'friends' or 'allies'. Whether they generate cohesion or division depends on processes of identification – that is, on the extent of consensus or contestation around who constitutes 'us' and 'them'.

South Africa: foreign policy, identity and Zimbabwe

To recap, this chapter contends that state identities and foreign policy can be mutually constitutive or destructive; that constructions of identity form the basis of the principles and paradigms underpinning foreign-policy frameworks; and that operationalisation or application of these to actual situations can reconstitute state identities. These processes of construction and reconstruction need – at least in democracies – to be legitimated. This requires circulation beyond a narrow circle of policy elites and it requires identification – an acceptance of the state's categorising of 'us' and 'them', 'domestic' and 'foreign'– by key civil society actors, including the media. States may fail to secure legitimation for their constructions if there is contestation over where and how boundary-producing discourses are constructed, who is categorised as 'us' and 'them', whether a minimalist or maximalist interpretation of 'foreign' should predominate, and therefore what policy is considered appropriate and consistent with a constructed state identity.

In South Africa, the construction of a particular type of state identity associated with the transition from apartheid has formed the basis of the principles and paradigms of a foreign-policy framework. Conversely, Mbeki's strategy of 'quiet diplomacy' towards Zimbabwe may be reconstituting state identity. His public statements of support for Mugabe have created the appearance of identification with a regime associated with violations of human rights, law and media freedom and therefore antithetical to the state identity Mbeki has sought to create in South Africa. This creates a cognitive dissonance between Mbeki's publicly stated beliefs and his actions, between a particular construction of state identity and the application of foreign policy to specific situations. This dissonance opens up fractures and these fractures facilitate wider contestation over the application of policy. In particular, contestations centre on who is identified as 'us', who is identified as 'them' and to what extent existing policy adequately represents the existing constructions of state identity. In essence, dissonance between principle and practice, between identifications and counter-identifications makes legitimation of policy less likely and may ultimately undermine constructions of state identity.

State identity, principles and paradigms of Mbeki's foreign policy

Political leaders have used three key components in attempting to construct a post-apartheid state identity. Firstly, the perceived success of a unique 'carefully crafted transition' has infused the South African state with a certain 'moral stature' (Alden & Le Pere 2003: 283) in the 'international community' (see also Gumede 2005; Jacobs 2003) and vis-à-vis many of its African neighbours. Secondly, there is South Africa's 'presumed status as one of the de facto leaders of the African continent' (Alden & Le Pere 2003: 283; Bischoff 2003). This combines the country's 'moral stature', its relative economic strength and perceptions of the moral characters of Mandela and Mbeki. But this is at times challenged by South Africa's sub-imperialist history of economic, political and military interference in neighbouring states, which has made many in Africa suspicious of any attempts by Mandela or Mbeki to take a leadership role (Gumede 2005; Nathan 2005). Thirdly, there is the global dimension and questions about where South Africa locates itself – in Africa or in a quasi-Western space (see Alden & Le Pere 2003). Nathan (2005) suggests the Mandela-era ambiguity over this has been resolved by Mbeki's attempts to clearly locate the country within Africa and pursue an Africanist agenda.

These constructions of state identity – of what political leaders perceive the South African state to be and what they want it to be – have influenced constructions of Mbeki's foreign-policy framework, principles and strategies. Such is the 'hold of this...unique transformation [from apartheid] that it continues to exert influence over the shape and conduct of foreign policy' (Alden & Le Pere 2003: 283). The manifestation of this influence is evident in Nathan's (2005) analysis of Mbeki's Strategic Plan for foreign policy (Department of Foreign Affairs 2004). He identifies five principles underpinning Mbeki's policy framework: the promotion of human rights and democracy; justice and international law in international relations; international peace and conflict resolution; promotion of interests of Africa; and economic development (Nathan 2005: 362). These principles have emerged from the liberation struggle and negotiated settlement – as well as, I suggest, out of conceptions of a particular type of state identity. They give the policy framework coherence (Nathan 2005: 362) rather than ambiguity (see Bischoff 2003), render it idealistic (Nathan 2005) rather than largely pragmatic (see Spence 2004). But the application of policy to actual situations has at times diverged from the principles – divergences Nathan (2005) conceptualises in terms of inconsistencies at the strategic rather than policy level. These inconsistencies, he argues, stem from the three paradigms underlying Mbeki's outlook: democratic, Africanist and anti-imperialist. 'The Africanist and anti-imperialist paradigms... are seldom if ever in conflict with each other, but both are occasionally in conflict with the democratic paradigm.' On these occasions – as with Zimbabwe – it is the democratic paradigm that 'gives way' (Nathan 2005: 362).

This framework and the underlying paradigms need to be applied to actual situations and this requires policy strategies. Mbeki's preferred approach is reflected in his preference for conflict resolution, for persuasion and negotiation and for multilateralism (Alden & Le Pere 2003; Gumede 2005) as a 'primary goal and primary strategy' (Nathan 2005: 364). This is consistent with the country's negotiated settlement, pluralist politics, certain constructions of state identity and the 'emphasis in African state politics on unity and solidarity' (Nathan 2005: 364–365). But if the strategy fails to secure policy objectives, there needs to be sufficient flexibility to allow for a tougher strategy; failure to adapt risks weakening a stated commitment to human rights and democracy and undermining the credibility of the state. These strategies and the problems with them have been particularised in Mbeki's policy of 'quiet diplomacy' towards Mugabe. For Mbeki, '"quiet diplomacy" means abstaining from a public rebuke of Mugabe while telling him privately over a cup of tea that some people are a little annoyed with him' (Gumede 2005: 183). In practice, it has meant an active discouragement of public criticism of Mugabe; statements of support for his attempts to address the 'colonial legacy'; attempts to build a broad African front to put pressure on him; the constructing of an aid package that would fund lawful redistribution of land (Alden & Le Pere 2003; Gumede 2005; Nathan 2005); and publicly blaming Britain for failing to deliver on its promises of financial aid to fund land redistribution, thereby exacerbating the conflict.[7] The approach is intended to achieve two main objectives vis-à-vis Zimbabwe: the peaceful resolution of conflict and the redistribution of land through legal means (Gumede 2005).

The failure to achieve these objectives and Mbeki's refusal to publicly criticise Mugabe's continued human-rights abuses, repression of opposition and abrogation of the rule of law have created a dissonance between South Africa's declared commitment to democracy and respect for human rights and its actions, between the policy framework's emphasis on 'human security' and Mbeki's apparent greater concern with 'regime security than with the rights and dignity of Zimbabwean people' (Nathan 2005: 367–368). As Zimbabwean society further polarised and Mbeki's policy strategy solidified around public statements of identification with Mugabe's struggles with 'colonial legacies' and criticisms of the former colonial power,[8] the South African leader was increasingly perceived by the media to have compromised his beliefs in democracy, law and human rights.[9]

This public identification was facilitated in part by Mugabe's framing of the Zimbabwean crisis in terms of land, race, the legacy of colonialism and anti-imperialism – similar problems which beset South Africa (Lahiff & Cousins 2001) and issues which Mbeki feels strongly about (Nathan 2005). In contrast, Zimbabwe's opposition party, the Movement for Democratic Change (MDC), first sought support from Mbeki in its fight against suppression of opposition and repression of the media. When this was not forthcoming, they turned to South Africa's largely white business community and this enabled Mugabe – and possibly also Mbeki – to categorise them as allies of the former colonial power (Gumede 2005) and Britain as reviving its imperialist intentions.

This was deliberately misleading. The MDC comprises a broad-based alliance including black and white workers, former war veterans and human-rights activists. For the first time in Zimbabwe's post-independence history, 'an opposition party had succeeded in creating a genuinely national movement' and it therefore 'represented a real threat to the ruling party' (Human Rights Watch 2002), especially in the context of dwindling support for Mugabe (Gumede 2005). One of the MDC's key election promises was 'people-driven land reform' (Human Rights Watch 2002) and, given Mugabe's failure to redistribute land during his 20 years in power, this resonated powerfully.[10] The response of the Zimbabwean leader was to align his ZANU-PF party with an activist group of war veterans who had been pushing for land redistribution for years and to announce a 'fast-track' programme to redress imbalances in land ownership. This effectively sanctioned a land grab by war veterans; bypassed the law; and was either enforced with the assistance of the army, or saw the Zimbabwean military actively arm the war veterans, effectively making the latter the private militia of Mugabe in the run-up to the tightest post-liberation election. In seven months, 2 706 farms totalling 6 million acres were listed for compulsory acquisition. The process was disorderly and at times violent. Intimidation was levelled at white owners, but most of the victims were black farm workers and their families. Under the masquerade of addressing the 'legacy of colonialism' and redistributing land, Mugabe was able to use the war veteran militias to further repress the MDC and opposition to his regime (Gumede 2005; Human Rights Watch 2002).

Mugabe's framing of the conflict in terms of race, the legacy of colonialism and anti-imperialism resonated throughout the continent. As Tanzanian president Benjamin Mkapa put it, '[T]o us Africans land is much more than a factor of production, we are spiritually anchored in the lands of our ancestors. Now that we are in power, we cannot run away from our historical duty to set right these historical wrongs and injustices.'[11] Other African leaders were able to identity with Mugabe's 'land problem' for three reasons. Firstly, most African countries have similar histories and overlapping collective memories of state-led dispossession and the deliberate undermining/impoverishment of black peasantry forced into subsistence farming. Secondly, these histories and memories gave rise to common discourses of 'stolen' land, racism, injustice and repression which different liberation struggles articulated in the rhetoric of 'land rights for the people' and restitution of 'stolen lands'. Thirdly, these histories, memories and discourses are concretised in the present with the continuance of 'racially skewed distribution of land' (Lahiff & Cousins 2001). By 2000, white South Africans owned 69 per cent of the land. By 1999, 11 million hectares of Zimbabwe's richest land was still in the hands of about 4 500 (mainly white) farmers; by 2000 only 50 per cent of the targeted 8 million hectares had been redistributed. Mugabe used these factors to argue that the land grab was part of an anti-imperialist agenda and any opposition to the illegality of it was part of an imperialist agenda (Gumede 2005).

This particular framing made it possible for Mbeki to extend his identification with these elements into statements of public solidarity with Mugabe; to draw attention to the discrepancies in media focus on 12 white farmers killed in Zimbabwe and their ignoring of the millions killed in Rwanda, Somalia and the DRC (Gumede 2005); and to ignore Mugabe's cynical use of land issues to suppress opposition and to overlook the wider human-rights abuses occurring across the border. Not surprisingly, then, the international community and the South African media perceived this as a personal identification with Mugabe; the price Mbeki paid was to see his 'grand blueprint for an African Renaissance...thoroughly discredited through his handling of the Zimbabwe situation' (Gumede 2005: 194).

But as Gumede points out, '[T]he biggest irony was that Mbeki's reputation for sheltering Mugabe was entirely misplaced. There never was any personal or political affinity between the two men...Mbeki felt contempt for the ailing octogenarian...Mugabe in turn views Mbeki as a young upstart' (Gumede 2005: 186). In addition, 'relations between ANC and ZANU-PF had always been tense even during the struggle for liberation' (Gumede 2005: 187). This private alienation, however, was obscured by the public appearance of identification; but at a certain level appearances or perceptions can create a reality of their own, and this appears to have been the case as Mbeki has continually struggled to justify his policy approach to Zimbabwe.

Process of circulation: media–state contestation

THE MEDIA AND ITS ROLE IN SOCIETY

This chapter has already suggested that constructions of state identity and foreign policy require legitimation and this in turn needs circulation and identification. This gives the media a dual role as significant circulators of foreign news and as political actors in their own right (Jacobs 2003). This position of potential power means it is important to understand the nature of the South African media, the nature of the society within which they operate and normative perceptions of the media's role in that society.

Firstly, the past 10 years have seen a diversification of print media; a shift towards more racially diverse staff; and an adaptation of media content to reflect the changing nature, demands and opportunities of a post-apartheid society (Wasserman 2006). This restructuring has been heavily influenced by globalism[12] with its emphasis on liberal democracy, free markets and individual rights (see Jacobs 2003; Steenveld 2004; Wasserman 2006), which translated into a political economy of the post-apartheid media that constitutionally guaranteed media freedom from state intervention in content and in ownership. The market was liberalised, legal restrictions on the media were lifted or curtailed, and the media were positioned as an industry with commercial concerns operating in a capitalist society. Globalism also translated into an ethical framework based on neo-liberal conceptions of press freedom, public interest and the classic 'watchdog' function of the media (Wasserman 2006).

Secondly, the nature of the society influences how the media operate. The transition years have witnessed a sizeable exodus of white South Africans and a rapid expansion of the black elite; continued high levels of poverty, unemployment and illiteracy; as well as limited property ownership. So, there is an absence of some of the key conditions for the emergence of an archetypal Habermasian public sphere in which private individuals who are property owners come together in a public space to rationally debate issues of common interest, circulate their discourses in journals to a mass audience and exert pressure on the government (Calhoun 1992; Habermas 1974). But this does not mean there is no public sphere – clearly there is one, albeit more reduced in scale than would be ideal in a democracy. Even so, it does consist of a racially diverse elite of predominantly middle classes able to conduct rational debate about foreign policy. It is this public sphere that constitutes a key part of the media audience. However, the media are not 'a neutral conduit for…information' (Jacobs 2003: 44); they do not reflect or report reality but construct it. These constructions are influenced by the political economy of the industry and the individual media outlet as well as the normative frameworks under which they operate. A 'free media' able to provide counter-discourses to the government, the value-laden nature of their discourses, their roles as significant circulators of foreign news and identity constructions as well as legitimators of government policy – all combine to render the media key political actors even when operating within a public sphere limited in scale and normative democratic validity.

Thirdly, perceptions of the role of the media are influenced by normative frameworks, and media–government conflicts about the role of the media in post-apartheid South Africa may be indicative of tensions between 'different value systems' (Wasserman 2006: 75). On the one hand, the media have been informed by 'western ideas about media freedom, democracy and responsibility' (Wasserman 2006: 75) and by a neo-liberalist framing of the post-apartheid structure which stresses the 'uncompromising autonomy of the individual' (Comaroff & Comaroff 1997: 3). On the other hand, the government appears to be moving towards a 'nationalist discourse intent on the recovery of African values and identities linked to the material transformation of the industry' (Wasserman 2006: 75) with an emphasis on group rights and solidarities. These divergent value systems have been articulated in discourses on Zimbabwe.

MBEKI'S FOREIGN-POLICY SPEECHES AND MEDIA TEXTS

A discourse analysis of Mbeki's speeches on Zimbabwe (see Mbeki 2000, 2003a, 2003b) and articles in the *Mail & Guardian* between January 1999 and December 2001 reveal four divergences in how they framed the growing crisis across the border; whom or what they identified with; how they did this; and whom or what they blamed for the situation.

Firstly, the proximity framing of Mbeki draws on similar histories and similar struggles, personal and collective memories, indebtedness to his neighbour, and common 'colonial legacies' of land distribution to contend with. The proximity framing of the *Mail & Guardian* draws on risk perceptions and 'national interest', which is thought to have been compromised by Mbeki's foreign policy. Suffering and abuse of Zimbabweans is subordinated to this national interest. This interest is defined in terms of lost inward investment, destabilised currency markets and a loss of business confidence; concern about the growing number of Zimbabwean refugees and South Africa's ability to absorb these; as well as fears of 'Zimbabwean-style land invasions' taking place south of the border (see *Mail & Guardian [M&G]*, Barrell 2000a; Editorial 2000; McGreal 2000b).

Secondly, the race framing of Mbeki focuses on continued patterns of white ownership of land; the failure of the white power, Britain, to 'honour past pledges'; and the continued 'legacy of colonialism'. The race framing of the *Mail & Guardian* focuses on land-ownership patterns, but presents references to racism as political opportunism of Mugabe and a tactic on his part to obscure abuses and injustices (see *M&G*, McGreal 2000a).

Thirdly, the insider–outsider framing of Mbeki identifies with Mugabe's attempts to tackle the 'colonial legacies' and stresses their common histories in the liberation struggle while ignoring the opposition in Zimbabwe and Mugabe's repression of it. On the one hand, Mbeki uses maximalist interpretations of 'foreign' to construct symbolic boundaries between 'them' as the former colonial power and 'us' as the ones struggling with the legacies of imperialism. On the other hand, he resorts to miminalist interpretations when stressing that Zimbabwe is a 'sovereign' state and so direct intervention in its affairs would be unacceptable (Gumede 2005). In contrast, the insider–outsider framing of the *Mail & Guardian* is more consistently minimalist. While sympathetic to the plight of the Zimbabweans and contending Mbeki should take 'firm action' against Mugabe, this is seen as necessary to protect South Africa's interests from the fallout of the deepening crisis across the border. In other words, the South Africans are categorised as 'us' and the Zimbabweans as 'them', posing a risk to the national interest.

Fourthly, the culpability framing of Mbeki links civil unrest to unresolved land issues, Britain's intransigence on funding and the problem of tackling the colonial legacy. The culpability framing of the *Mail & Guardian* links the deepening crisis to the brutal, illegal and irresponsible actions of Mugabe; he is also seen as the most significant obstacle to land redistribution.

The presentation of alternative framings of proximity, racism, culpability and insider–outsider forms the basis of the *Mail & Guardian*'s critique of Mbeki's foreign policy. His quiet diplomacy is criticised in terms of tone, approach and efficacy, and for the absence of a 'definitive stand' and the avoidance of taking a 'public stand' on land invasions and human-rights abuses.

Such diametrically opposed framing of the escalating crisis in Zimbabwe by the media and Mbeki stems in part from divergent interpretations of 'foreign', different categorisations of 'them' and 'us', and therefore different points of identification and different attributions of blame. As problems escalated in Zimbabwe, the media became more strident in its criticism of Mbeki's 'quiet diplomacy'. So much so that in February 2001, Essop Pahad, minister in the Presidency, said that the South African government was a victim of systematic hostility from a media unrepresentative of the majority tendency in the country. On a number of other occasions, Mbeki has criticised the media for its racial, capitalist bias and its failure to support endeavours to transform the country (see Wasserman 2006).

At the same time, Mbeki sought to repair his relations with the domestic and international media. The government started to 'repackage' Mbeki after a:

> series of public gaffes...that have tarnished his image at home and abroad... As opinion polls showed Mbeki's image...nosedive, his handlers finally took the hint and began a charm offensive... Mbeki has incurred international outrage by...failing to condemn the violent land invasions in neighbouring Zimbabwe. (*M&G*, Sayagues 2000f)

But it was left to Desmond Tutu to spell out that political marketing could not repair the damage to Mbeki and South Africa's reputation caused by the dissonance between constructions of state identity, the principles of foreign policy and its application:

> What has been happening in Zimbabwe is totally unacceptable and reprehensible, and we ought to say so. The credibility of our democracy demands this. If we are seemingly indifferent to human rights in a neighbouring country, what is to stop us one day being indifferent to them in our own?[13]

While the media's framing of the Zimbabwean situation – in particular its preoccupation with the destabilising economic implications for South Africa – does appear to reflect the neo-liberal nature of its political economy, it was disingenuous to single out the media given the criticism levelled at 'quiet diplomacy' by COSATU, the SACP, Mandela and Tutu (see Gumede 2005; Nathan 2005).

The responses of other political and civil society actors

One of the key functions of identity construction is to build cohesion in a designated community. While the construction of a state identity around South Africa's transformation to a post-apartheid society may have the potential to be inclusive, the extent to which this has been sustained over time is debatable. This chapter has already suggested that Mbeki's strategy of 'quiet diplomacy' towards Zimbabwe may be reconstituting state identity. The policy approach; the public identification with a regime associated with violations of human rights, law and media freedom; the ensuing cognitive dissonance between policy application and constructed state identity – these have opened up fractures out of which has emerged wider societal contestation over who is identified with.

While the media have been a major source of counter-discourses and counter-identifications in relation to Mugabe's Zimbabwe, it is Mbeki's partners in the triple alliance of the ANC, COSATU and the SACP that have been 'Mbeki's harshest critics on Zimbabwe' (Gumede 2005: 162). The opposition of COSATU and the SACP needs to be understood partly in terms of the context of frustration at the post-apartheid hegemony of neo-liberal economic policies (Greenberg 2004; Gumede 2005); partly within the context of post-liberation politics in the region in which a 'new generation of political activists has emerged, often in opposition to ruling political parties or former liberation movements' (Freeman 2005: 164); and partly in terms of counter-identifications and counter-interpretations of what was happening north of the Limpopo.

Firstly, the post-apartheid hegemony which has witnessed the adoption of liberal economic principles has meant that most members of the SACP and COSATU have not yet seen any material improvement in their quality of life (see Greenberg 2004; Jacobs 2003). This has fuelled debates within COSATU as to whether its members may not be better served outside the ANC (Gumede 2005). Secondly, the past 10 years have seen the emergence of new activists willing to challenge the hegemony and ideology of the leaders of the former liberation movements. So, COSATU and the SACP have 'identif[ied] strongly' with the MDC, but the South African government 'regards this new wave of political opposition [as] a threat and a challenge' (Freeman 2005: 164). The response of the former liberation movements in the region – the ANC in South Africa, the ZANU-PF in Zimbabwe, the MPLA in Angola, SWAPO in Namibia and FRELIMO in Mozambique – was to join together in October

2000 'to co-ordinate strategies to rejuvenate their image and to counter the challenge of emergent political forces' (Freeman 2005: 164). The goal was to:

> remind people of the glory of past struggles against colonial and white minority-rule and to discredit political parties...human rights groups, legal foundations and the broader forces of civil society as new manifestations of the forces of colonialism and white minority-rule against which the liberation movement had fought – "stooges" of Western financial concerns or "agents" for American and British governments. (Freeman 2005: 166)

As Freeman notes, '"the new form of politics" envisaged by Mbeki is deeply protective of the status quo and profoundly conservative' (2005: 167). At issue may well be a struggle over what constitutes an Africanist discourse, agenda and identity as well as whether this can and should be at odds with democracy and human rights.

This conflict is arguably articulated in counter-identifications and counter-interpretations of what was happening north of the Limpopo. So, for instance, at COSATU's 2000 May Day rally, held in the presence of Mbeki, Willie Madisha 'attacked Mugabe's oppression of workers and civil society and endorsed the complaint of Zimbabwe's trade unionists "that black farm workers were suffering massive hardship as a result of intimidation" by the war veterans' (Freeman 2005: 190). Thus, while Mbeki sought to support and publicly identify with Mugabe, COSATU chose the MDC – not surprisingly, given the latter's inclusion of trade unionists in its membership profile.

The SACP has been equally critical of the policy of 'quiet diplomacy' and has repeatedly challenged a key plank of Mbeki's identification with Mugabe – that is, the framing of the crisis in terms of addressing the colonial legacy of racially skewed land ownership. As the SACP website notes:

> [T]he hastily launched land reform programme was less about land reform, and more about seeking to consolidate the ZANU-PF apparatus and its electoral basis...ZANU-PF is less and less a liberation movement confidently fostering a progressive hegemony in its own country and in the region, and more and more a repressive machine focused narrowly on holding on to power.[14]

These divisions reach beyond COSATU and the SACP into the senior leadership of the ANC. Africanists such as Nkosazana Dlamini-Zuma and KwaZulu-Natal

ANC leader Dumisani Makhaye remained 'unshaken in support for ZANU-PF' (Gumede 2005: 190). But Defence Minister Mosiuoa Lekota called for South Africa to publicly condemn what was happening north of the Limpopo and slammed quiet diplomacy as ineffective; Mbeki demanded he withdraw his comments, but he refused. It has been older, well-respected leaders such as Desmond Tutu and Nelson Mandela who have articulated deep disquiet about the moral contradictions between South Africa's policy towards Zimbabwe and its internal stance on democracy and human rights. The fear of the old guard is that silence about abuses in neighbouring states today may translate into silence about abuses in South Africa tomorrow (see earlier quotation by Desmond Tutu).

Conclusion

The construction of identity around the post-apartheid transition and the founding of a policy framework on this may have been mutually constitutive, but the response of civil society actors such as the media and trade unions to Mbeki's 'quiet diplomacy' illustrates the extent to which state identities and foreign policy can be mutually destructive. The counter-discourses highlight the difficulty of securing legitimation where there is no consensus over identifications. But this still leaves unanswered the question of where the middle-class consumers of media texts on foreign policy positioned themselves. As of yet, there appears to be no systematic attempt to gather empirical data on public perceptions, attitudes or opinions on South Africa's foreign policy. Clearly, there is an urgent need for this if we are to better understand the dialectical processes of circulation and legitimation of policy and identity constructions.

Notes

1   For psychological perspectives structured around 'enemy image', see Keen (1986); for social identification theory, see Tajfel (1982) and Bloom (1992); for nationalism theory, see Anderson (1991); for antinomic constructions, see Connolly (1991); for post-structuralist approaches, see Campbell (1998); and for a critical overview of the field of identity and international relations, see Frueh (2003).

2   State identities are constructed around the apparatus, behaviour, discourse and actors of the state as well as perceptions of it. National identities are constructed out of notions of the 'nation' – that is, a more amorphous 'mass' than the particularised state.

3   The 'nation state' in international relations literature implies that nation 'precedes the reality' of or is 'co-terminous with the state' (Campbell 1998: 11). This notion has been

challenged, firstly by Anderson's argument that the nation is an 'imagined political community' (1991: 6) and nationalism a construct of the state in pursuit of legitimacy. Secondly, Tilly (1990) notes that few national states – including Britain and the USA – have ever had an alignment of territorial sovereignty with an a priori identification, whether it be religion, culture, etc. Campbell uses the term 'national states' to refer to entities that 'do not possess pre-discursive, stable identities', are 'never finished as entities' and so are in 'permanent need of reproduction' (Campbell 1998: 11).

4 Both defence policy and foreign policy are concerned with the security of the state; the former draws on military power and intelligence, while the latter is restricted to diplomatic resources. In some countries, such as the USA, and in the apartheid state, the two departments work closely with the military, often having a major say in foreign policy. In the post-apartheid state, the military has been given a much-reduced role, especially under Mbeki, whose political style is to seek mediation and negotiation.

5 Anderson conceptualises the nation as an 'imagined political community – and imagined as both inherently limited and sovereign'. It is 'imagined' because 'members of even the smallest nation will never know most of their fellow-members...yet in the mind of each lives the image of their communion'. It is 'limited' because 'even the largest of them...has finite, if elastic, boundaries, beyond which lie other nations'. It is sovereign in that the nation replaced 'divinely ordained' and 'dynastic' with 'pluralistic' and 'freedom'. And it is a 'community' because 'regardless of the actual inequality and exploitation that might prevail in each, the nation is always conceived as a deep, horizontal comradeship' (Anderson 1991: 6).

6 For constructivist perspectives on foreign policy, see Weaver (1994) and Dessler (1999).

7 'Mbeki, who has been under intense international pressure to repudiate Mugabe's handling of a...grab...said the crisis arose from the failure to implement a 1998 agreement with Britain to correct the skewed post-colonial distribution of land' (Sayagues 2000d).

8 '[B]oth of our countries...shared the same trenches in the common struggle for freedom, [so] it is natural that we must now work together to build on the victory of the anti-colonial and anti-racist struggle...overcoming the legacy of colonialism and apartheid...Both of our countries, which experienced extensive land dispossession of the indigenous majority by those who colonised our countries, are confronted by the challenge to address this colonial legacy' (Mbeki 2000).

9 'By colluding with Mugabe to pretend land hunger and British obduracy are at the root of Zimbabwe's problems, the regional leaders have solved nothing...When it was launched a few years ago with much fanfare we were told Pretoria's new human rights-based foreign policy would provide a road map for the region. It now seems to have become stuck in

a cul-de-sac. By declining to identify the rule of law and democratic governance as the foundation stones of Southern Africa's future growth, and by pretending land is the big issue when Mugabe's abuse of power has brought this once prosperous nation to its knees, Mbeki has not only let down Zimbabwe's democratic movement, he has missed an opportunity to establish abiding principles for the region's evolution' (Barrell 2000a).

10   Robert Mugabe's ZANU-PF was elected on a platform of post-liberation promises including the redistribution of land, but his ability to deliver this was constrained by 'sunset clauses' in the peace agreement that ended the war and protected white patterns of land ownership. In an attempt to help address land grievances, Britain provided £44 million in a 'land resettlement grant' that originally ran from 1980 to 1996, but had been largely spent by 1988 (Human Rights Watch 2002), with most of the best land going to those close to Mugabe. When the sunset clauses ended in 1990, Mugabe changed the constitution to allow compulsory purchase, restricted the size of farms and imposed a land tax to hasten redistribution. Despite these measures, the pace of redistribution slowed from 3.5 million hectares in the 1980s to 1 million hectares in the 1990s (Human Rights Watch 2002).

11   Reuters, 'African leaders slam West on democracy', 16 August 2004.

12   Steger distinguishes between globalisation and globalism. The former refers to political, economic, cultural and ideological processes of global convergence. Within these processes there are multiple and competing 'ideologically charged narratives', norms, values and meanings that further power and shape identity. But these alternatives are unable to compete with the dominance of globalism, 'an ideology that endows the concept of globalization with neo-liberal values and meanings' (Steger 2004: 11). Essentially, globalism is a neo-liberal hegemony that naturalises and atomises more generalised discourses on free markets, human rights and democracy into a particular framing that renders the autonomy of the individual sacrosanct.

13   Peter Fabricius, 'Tutu slams SA stance on Zimbabwe', *Pretoria News*, 16 December 2003.

14   Accessed 3 November 2004, www.sacp.org.za

References

Alden C & Le Pere G (2003) *South Africa's post-apartheid foreign policy: From reconciliation to revival?* Adelphi Paper No. 362. London: Oxford University Press

Anderson B (1991) *Imagined communities: Reflections on the origins and spread of nationalism* (2nd edition). London: Verso

Billig M (1995) *Banal nationalism.* London: Sage Publications

Bischoff P-H (2003) External and domestic sources of foreign policy amibiguity: South African foreign policy and the projections of pluralist middle power. *Politikon* 27(1): 183–201

Bloom D (1992) *Personal identity, national identity and international relations.* Cambridge, MA: Cambridge University Press

Calhoun C (ed.) (1992) *Habermas and the public sphere.* Cambridge, MA: MIT Press

Campbell D (1998) *Writing security: United States foreign policy and the politics of identity.* Minneapolis: University of Minnesota Press

Campbell D (2001) *Apartheid cartography: Identity, territory and co-existence in Bosnia.* Briefing Paper No. 22. Sturminster Newton: Corner House

Cohen BC (1963) *The press and foreign policy.* Princeton, NJ: Princeton University Press

Comaroff JL & Comaroff J (1997) *Of revelation and revolution.* Vol. 2, *The dialectics of modernity of a South African frontier.* Chicago: University of Chicago Press

Connolly WE (1991) *Identity/difference: Democratic negotiations of political paradox.* Ithaca and London: Cornell University Press

Department of Foreign Affairs (2004) *Strategic plan.* Accessed 13 March 2006, www.dfa.gov.za

Dessler D (1999) Constructivism within a positivist social science. *Review of International Studies* 25(1): 123–137

DiPrizio RC (2002) *Armed humanitarians: US interventions from northern Iraq to Kosovo.* Baltimore, MD: Johns Hopkins University Press

Freeman L (2005) South Africa's Zimbabwe policy: Unravelling the contradictions. *Journal of Contemporary African Studies* 23(2): 147–172

Frueh J (2003) *Political identity and social change: The remaking of the South African social order.* New York: State University of New York

Greenberg S (2004) *The landless people's movement and the failure of post-apartheid land reform.* Durban: Centre for Civil Society

Gumede WM (2005) *Thabo Mbeki and the battle for the soul of the ANC.* London: Zed Books

Habermas J (1974) On social identity. *Telos* 19 (Spring)

Hill C (2003) *The changing politics of foreign policy.* Basingstoke: Palgrave

Human Rights Watch (2002) *World report.* New York: Human Rights Watch

Jacobs S (2003) Reading politics, reading media. In H Wasserman and S Jacobs (eds) *Shifting selves.* Cape Town: Kwela Books

Keen S (1986) *Faces of the enemy: Reflections on the hostile imagination.* New York: Harper and Row

Lahiff E & Cousins B (2001) The land crisis in Zimbabwe viewed from south of the Limpopo. *Journal of Agrarian Change* 1(4): 652–666

Livingston S (1997) *Clarifying the CNN effect: An examination of media effects according to type of military intervention.* Harvard Research Paper R-18. Joan Shorenstein Barone Centre on the Press, Politics and Public Policy. Cambridge, MA: Harvard University

Livingston S & Todd E (1995) Humanitarian crisis and US foreign policy. *Political Communication* 12: 413–429

Louw E (2005) *The media and political process.* London: Sage Publications

Mbeki T (2000) Speech at the opening of the Zimbabwe Trade Fair, 5 May. Accessed 14 February 2006, http://www.anc.org.za/ancdocs/history/mbeki/2000/tm0505.html

Mbeki T (2003a) A new era for Africa in a globalizing world. Speech presented to UNESCO, Paris, 19 November. Accessed 14 February 2006, http://www.anc.org.za/ancdocs/history/mbeki/2003/tm1119.html

Mbeki T (2003b) The people of Zimbabwe must decide their own future: Letter from the president. *ANC Today* 3(18): 9–15

Nathan L (2005) Consistency and inconsistencies in South African foreign policy. *International Affairs* 81(2): 361–372

O'Heffernan P (2000) Mass media roles in foreign policy. In D Graber (ed.) *Media power in politics.* Washington, DC: Congressional Quarterly

Robinson P (2001) Theorizing the influence of media on world politics: Models of media influence on foreign policy. *European Journal of Communication* 16(4): 523–544

Robinson P (2002) *The CNN effect: The myth of news, foreign policy and intervention.* London: Routledge

Spence J (2004) South Africa's foreign policy: Vision and reality. In E Sidiropoulos (ed.) *Apartheid past, renaissance future: South Africa's foreign policy, 1994–2004.* Johannesburg: South African Institute for International Relations

Steenveld L (2004) Transforming the media: A cultural approach. *Critical Arts* 18(1): 92–115

Steger MB (ed.) (2004) *Rethinking globalism.* Lanham, MD: Rowman and Littlefield

Tajfel H (1982) Social psychology of intergroup relations. *Annual Review of Psychology* 33: 1–39

Temin J & Smith DA (2002) Media matters: Evaluating the role of the media in Ghana's 2000 elections. *African Affairs* 101(405): 585–605

Tilly C (ed.) (1990) *Coercion, capital and European states.* Oxford and Cambridge, MA: Basil Blackwell

Wasserman H (2006) Globalized values and postcolonial responses: South African perspectives on normative media ethics. *International Communication Gazette* 68(1): 71–91

Weaver O (1994) Resisting the temptation of post foreign policy analysis. In W Carlsnaes and S Smith (eds) *European foreign policy: The EC and changing perspectives in Europe*. London: Sage Publications

Yumul A & Ozkirimli U (2000) Reproducing the nation: 'Banal nationalism' in the Turkish press. *Media, Culture and Society* 22: 787–804

Mail & Guardian

Barrell H (2000a) Mbeki jets to Harare as Zim crisis mounts. 21–27 April, pp. 4–5

Barrell H (2000b) Another round in Mbeki's diplomatic offensive. 28 April – 4 May, p. 5

Barrell H (2000c) Tell us what's going on, Thabo. 28 April – 4 May, p. 27

Editorial (2000) Build bridges with all Zim parties. 23–29 June, p. 30

Kamemba C (2000) How do we keep power from the mentally unfit? 28 April – 4 May, p. 29

McGreal C (2000a) If they can take the land from the whites, they can take it from me. 21–27 April, p. 4

McGreal C (2000b) Land seizures: Mugabe means it. 11–17 August, p. 31

Sayagues M (2000a) Zim's mobs get licence to intimidate. 28 April – 4 May, pp. 4–5

Sayagues M (2000b) Commercial farmers' union opens its chequebook to buy peace in Zim…while black workers suffer. 19–25 May, pp. 4–5

Sayagues M (2000c) Dr 'Hitler' Hunzvi's torture room. 19–25 May, pp. 4–5

Sayagues M (2000d) Harare for sale. 19–25 May, p. 4

Sayagues M (2000e) The end of an era in Zimbabwe politics? 23–29 June, p. 10

Sayagues M (2000f) No coherent land reform plan in Zim. 10–16 November, p. 15

Wetherell I (2000) Something to shout about. 28 April – 4 May, pp. 28–29

Zimbabwe goes to the polls (2000) 23–29 June, p. 31

14 Masculine ideals in post-apartheid South Africa: The rise of men's glossies

Stella Viljoen

> Products of media culture provide materials out of which we forge our very identities; our sense of selfhood; our notion of what it means to be male or female; our sense of class, of ethnicity and race, of nationality, of sexuality; and of 'us' and 'them'.
>
> M Durham and D Kellner, *Media and Cultural Studies*

In 1979 Joe Dubbert adopted Betty Friedan's famous conceptualisation of sexual difference in order to expose what he termed the 'masculine mystique'. Since then theorists have used the concept of ideal masculinity to translate the popular feminist notion of the feminine ideal into masculinity studies (Connell 1987, 1995; Dubbert 1979; Segal 1990). In doing so, these students of gender effectively communicated the idea that men too were subject to the homogenising machinations of the media and popular politics and that it was time to focus the attention of radical feminist practice on the construction of masculine identity. It thus became evident to students of 'masculine' and 'feminine' types alike that the ascendancy of certain types of masculinity is sustained through the creation of a masculine ideal. Not unlike the feminine ideal, its masculine counterpart was perceived to be a dominant construction of manhood against which other forms of male identity are calculated and evaluated.

In this chapter I briefly chronicle the rise of the five men's lifestyle magazines[1] that emerged in post-apartheid South Africa and situate them within the theoretical discourse surrounding masculinity. In doing so, I consider the various vernacular masculine ideals presented by each magazine as indicative of the nuanced yet homogenising aspirational tropes available to men in this strain of the South African media. A central tenet that emerges from Robert

Morrell's significant collection *Changing Men in Southern Africa* is the idea that 'there is no one typical South African man' but rather many diverse masculinities (Morrell 2001: 33). Following this suggestion, the research undertaken here is underpinned by a twofold concern: firstly, that of globalised media values streaming into the post-apartheid economy, and secondly, the extent to which these values were modified differentially to target Anglo, Afrikaner and black professionals. Two primary methodologies are followed in this chapter. The first is a narrative documentation of the circumstances that gave rise to each magazine. This narrative contextualisation is considered to be important because '[m]edia stories provide the symbols, myths and resources through which we constitute a common culture and through the appropriation of which we insert ourselves into this culture' (Durhan & Kellner 2001: 1). The second is a socio-semiotic analysis of the masculine ideal seemingly presented by each magazine. While the magazines vary in cultural scope and circulation, the same attention and amount of space are devoted to each. Through this largely equalising study, the dominant and marginalised vernacular masculinities are thus juxtaposed in order to subvert the hegemonies normally inherent in a comparative analysis of this kind (which typically preferences the more mainstream publications over the publications with lower circulation figures).

If the conceptions of culture, identity and gender are treated here as more static than they are in reality, it is not in order to undermine the tenuous stuff of each of these occurrences but rather for the sake of communicative clarity. In discussing masculinity at all, we are 'doing gender' in a culturally particular way. It is, after all, necessary for culture, identity and gender to be in conversation with each other as they are with the ever-changing South African landscape. For masculinity, like culture, is an ongoing multifaceted project that involves constant interaction between the individual and society. Masculinity as identity is, in other words, deemed here as both relational and personal. It is therefore dependent on the active choices made by an individual as well as being connected to various societal institutions, such as the men's lifestyle press which may, for instance, serve to construct consumption-driven or 'profitable' masculinities. In the following section, the theoretical notion of the masculine ideal is briefly teased out as a backdrop to the publishing narrative that follows. Thereafter, the South African context in general, as well as the localised debate surrounding each magazine in particular, is sketched.

Masculine ideal

Social analysts such as George Mosse (1996) have traced the history of the modern ideal of masculinity in psychological as well as physical terms, commenting that this dualistic ideal is both a positive stereotype and a social function. Mosse interprets the Western masculine ideal as the blend of middle-class, Christian norms – honesty, strength, courage and self-control – and an ideal of the male physique drawn from classical Greek philosophy and art (and the subsequent theories of eighteenth-century art historian Joachim Winckelmann). Mosse dates the origin of this Western myth as more or less between the latter part of the eighteenth century and the first half of the nineteenth. This process of gender rearticulation occurred alongside the rise of bourgeois society and slowly cemented the correlation between physical beauty and moral fortitude with the image of the male body itself, becoming the ascendant code of manhood.

By the late nineteenth century, this ideal type was not only materialised in a popular preoccupation with body-conscious sports like gymnastics but also militarised so that the modern masculine ideal was typified by a 'Greek' physique, sober character and unwavering nationalism. In spite of the emergence of various *fin de siècle* counter-masculinities (as well as the opposing forces presented by socialism, feminism and the avant-garde), the normative Western masculine ideal remained steadfast, gaining a great deal of momentum from European and American wartime rhetoric of honour, sacrifice and patriotism maintained by the media and psychological Zeitgeist (Mosse 1996: 107). Mosse deems this Ego Ideal to be a binding and directing force in modern Western history because of its ability to reconcile order and progress in the unifying image of the male. In the gendered trope of historical imagination, the ideal male thus symbolises a healthy, well-ordered society.

However, the question of the masculine ideal is not only a political concern but is also intimately connected to the construction of gender and gender ideals in society (meaning families, places of work and other sites where identity is shaped). This means that the existence of masculine ideals – or worse still, a single, dominant masculine ideal – implies that certain masculinities are better than others, leading to the marginalising of individual character traits in favour of the model features of the prevailing masculine ideal. Furthermore, feminist historians such as Linda Nochlin (1991), Sherry Ortner (1974) and Griselda Pollock (1988) are quick to point out the problematic manner in which gender ideals reduce male- and female-ness to the binaries of subject/ object, active/passive and culture/nature. This binary reading of gender typically implies that the gender of an individual is not secure but measured on a continuum according to its compliance with these criteria, thus leading to the notion of 'gendered behaviour' or the 'performativity' of gender (Butler 1990: 136). Judith Butler contends that acts, gestures and enactments are performative in the sense that 'the essence of identity that they otherwise purport to express are *fabrications* manufactured and sustained through corporeal signs and other discursive means' (1990: 136; italics in original). Through the analysis of ideal masculinities in men's lifestyle magazines it is suggested that performative behaviour (Butler 1990, 2004) is as powerful in a represented format as it is in 'real life' and, thus, that gendered tropes of all persuasions are performative.

The presupposition that there is a masculine ideal in contemporary Western society is an interesting assumption against which to sketch the history of the men's lifestyle press in South Africa. Mosse (1996) treats ideal masculinity as both historically amorphous as well as fairly contained in its morphology. This conceptualisation of gender as being simultaneously flexible and fixed is useful to this study because of the varying strains of vernacular masculinity that emerge from the sundry men's lifestyle magazines in South Africa. The ideal masculinities presented by these magazines are diverse and yet involve a measure of horizontal identification or commonality. The normative construction of a masculine ideal across all of the magazines is thus as important as the particular nuances presented by each title.

Two strains of thought or variations on the theme of ideal masculinity particularly impact the study of men's lifestyle magazines in South Africa. Firstly, research surrounding new masculinity or metrosexuality is an important leitmotif throughout various investigations of men's lifestyle magazines because of the way these magazines challenge the traditional Western assumptions about physical and psychological self-interest being the exclusive right of women. Originating in Britain in 1994 with the utterances of social commentator Mark Simpson, the term 'metrosexuality' refers to the disposition of modern, urbane men who embrace the dandified accoutrement of self-beautification. Simpson (2004) describes the metrosexual as:

> a young man with money to spend, living in or within easy reach of a metropolis – because that's where all the best shops, clubs, gyms and hairdressers are. He might be officially gay, straight

or bisexual, but this is utterly immaterial because he has clearly taken himself as his own love object and pleasure as his sexual preference.

Metrosexuality has subsequently become a part of the aspirational syntax of men's lifestyle magazines that aim to procure the support of high-end advertisers, and in doing so endorse the connection between masculinity and consumption. This phenomenon is not overtly present in all the South African men's lifestyle magazines, but seems to be an important signifier in the redefining of masculine identity in this context, particularly considering the fact that 'modern forms of consumption privilege certain public masculinities as the subject of the look' (Nixon 1996: 70).

Secondly, the set of theories established in the 1990s, collectively addressing what is known as 'masculinity in crisis', infuses much of the research concerning why men read men's lifestyle magazines, and thus implicitly informs this chapter. Roughly following the time that men's lifestyle magazines were reaching new circulation highs in the United States, such social theorists and popular writers as Robert Bly (1990), Anthony Clare (2000), Rosalind Coward (1999), Roger Horrocks (1994) and John MacInnes (1998, 2001) theorised various views of masculinity as pathological, defeated or collectively 'confused'.[2] Their assumptions were based on the analyses of statistics relating to crime perpetrated by men, depression and suicide which seemed to indicate that overwhelming numbers of men were engaged in violent or self-destructive behaviour. Stephen Frosh, Ann Phoenix and Rob Patman argue that if this crisis does exist it is anchored in a variety of societal phenomena, including:

> the collapse of traditional men's work, the growth of a technological culture which cannot be 'passed on' in any recognisable way between the generations, the rise of feminist consciousness amongst women, and, more abstractly, challenges to the dominance of the forms of rationality with which masculinity has been identified, at least in the West. (2002)

In 2000, following on the research by Roger Horrocks (1994), clinical psychologist Anthony Clare published his influential social text *On Men: Masculinity in Crisis*, in which he proposed that American men were, as he put it, 'in serious trouble' (Clare 2000: dust jacket).[3] The umbrella phrase for the cooperative theories that culminated in Clare's popularised thesis is 'masculinity in crisis', and the body of knowledge concerning a crisis in Western masculinity is today well developed if not uncontested.[4] Nevertheless, the phrase is useful in exploring global and local trends in the delineation of contemporary masculinities. While not the subject of this investigation, 'masculinity in crisis' forms a subtle backdrop to the proposed analysis since it is assumed that the failure to fulfil a particular masculine ideal on a personal level may result in a crisis of identity (Reid & Walker 2005: 10).

A number of local nuances colour the study of various masculine ideals within the South African context. In particular, the idea of masculinity in crisis takes on a local flavour in the struggle for individual and corporate identity that ostensibly followed the first democratic elections in South Africa (demonstrating that there are as many different experiences of crisis as there are different experiences of ideal masculinity). In the American and British contexts, the emergence of (oftentimes metrosexually orientated) men's lifestyle magazines in the 1980s seems to have been one way in which the media responded to the so-called crisis in masculinity. Men's lifestyle magazines in these contexts presented men with self-affirming, consumption-driven short cuts to their masculinity that cemented the various aspects of (new?) manhood. But, given the melting pot of idiosyncrasies that defined the South African context, the question of whether South African men would be ready for the kind of 'answers' provided by the more media-savvy developed world remained.

The inception of five men's lifestyle magazines in South Africa

In the United Kingdom in the mid-1980s, when publishers considered introducing a men's lifestyle magazine into the otherwise fairly stodgy British market, they were met with a fair amount of scepticism. Media theorists and marketers raised concerns about the consumption habits of the 'typical British male', frequently invoking truisms relating to men as tricky and elusive media consumers who would be unwilling to pay for a glossy magazine (Nixon 1996: 129). Amid growing contention around the potential failure of a British men's lifestyle title, media practitioner Simon Marquis added his perhaps essentialist comment that such a publication was doomed to fail because:

> [w]hile women become 'friends' with their magazines there is an inbuilt resistance to the idea of a magazine that makes public and shares ideas about being a man. To men it is an unacceptable

contradiction. Self-consciousness is permissible, even attractive, in women; it is perceived as weak and unmanly in a man. (Nixon 1996: 129)

As it turned out, these sentiments were unfounded. Nick Logan's *Arena*, published by Wagadon and targeted at a market defined as style leaders and innovators, first appeared in 1986, while the more conservative first British edition of *Gentleman's Quarterly* (*GQ*), published by Condé Nast, appeared in 1988. The success of these two magazines in the United Kingdom indicated that the British market was indeed ready for the new kind of masculine consumption sceptics had warned against. More or less a decade later, the same debate was taking place against the backdrop of the embryonic new South Africa. The apartheid oligarchy had come to an end, a democratically elected government was in place, sanctions were lifted and the stage was set for new media entities to capitalise on the newfangled enthusiasm of a people seeking to redefine themselves.

Up to this point there were no men's lifestyle magazines in South Africa, but there were a number of so-called soft-porn magazines. Most notable among these was *Scope*, a local magazine roughly modelled on Hugh Hefner's American soft-porn magazine *Playboy*, founded in 1953. Like *Playboy*, *Scope* combined objectifying imagery of women with fairly 'serious' (critical and informative) articles, features and interviews on current events. The images of women in such magazines were censored during the apartheid years (with obligatory stars covering the nipples), but the content often went unnoticed and in this way these magazines seemed to occasionally serve as a platform for subversive or iconoclastic social commentary. While not the focus of this chapter, it is interesting to note that coinciding with the crossover to democracy were the dramatic circulation losses and eventual demise of once highly successful soft-porn magazines such as *Scope*.[5] The reasons for this may include the influx of international pornographic titles, the inception of local men's lifestyle magazines and the seeming flux in the articulation of masculine identity within the new cultural climate.

In South Africa at the time, the *global* crisis or flux in the self-articulation of masculinity was compounded by the socio-political changes brought about by the first democratically elected government. The 1996 Constitution and Bill of Rights represents masculine identity in such a way that makes clear the extent to which this identity draws from but also breaks with the past. Liz Walker defines the constitutional masculine ideal simply as a man 'who is non-violent, a good father and husband, employed and able to provide for his family' (Walker 2005: 164). Yet she argues that the transition in gender and power relations embodied in the Constitution has exacerbated a crisis in masculinity. She stresses the fact that different men respond to this crisis in different ways: '[w]hile "constitutional sexuality" seems to have shut some doors for men by shrinking the "patriarchal divide" (at least at the level of legislation), it has simultaneously opened up spaces and created opportunities for men to construct new masculinities' (Walker 2005: 161).

The implementation of a national mandate on employment equity in 1994 also (rightly) brought with it far-reaching shifts in the socio-economic demographics of the country. Affirmative action, implemented in virtually all spheres of industry, has meant that women and professionals of diverse races have gained access (or increased access) to financial and social power while white men have been subject to large-scale retrenchment and omission from the job market. In both cases this fundamental shift in social status necessarily implies a rearticulation of the power relations involved in the societal delineation of gender, race and ethnicity, whether corporately or individually. As is to be expected in any new democracy, the identity crisis of the South African nation was followed by the ripple effect of multiple crises related to the delineation of self or selves in this new, post-apartheid 'imagined community'. The South African context may, in other words, present a new, hybrid slant on the old theme of masculinity in crisis or flux.[6] As in the case of the network of ideas surrounding new masculinity, the theme of masculinity in flux permeates the story of the five men's lifestyle magazines currently available in South Africa as the economic valorisations of a period of wider social change.

Because of sanctions imposed on the apartheid market, South Africa was late in arriving at the fiscal trends that emerged in the Western global economies during the 1970s and 1980s. This meant that the increased globalisation of production, the establishment of new forms of flexible manufacturing (differentiated goods for segmented consumer markets) and the so-called just-in-time process of production that characterised other international markets during the 1970s and 1980s only really manifested in the South African economy in the mid-1990s, after the fall of apartheid. Since these trends were already well established elsewhere in the global sector, it didn't take long for manufacturing processes in South Africa to become increasingly marketing-led with a tighter integration of the stages from production to point of sale. Each stage in the production process of diverse endeavours became linked with design, distribution and retail, and 'flexible specialisation' (as seen in the manufacturing of local designer-clothing lines such as Hilton Weiner and Jenni Button) replaced the old post-Fordist models. Against this backdrop of tailor-made marketing schemes a preference surfaced for subcontracting based on innovation through cooperation and knowledge sharing between firms.

In this vein, the scene was set for men's lifestyle magazines and the profitable partnerships these would forge with the kinds of international designer brands seeking to make an entrance into the virgin territory of South Africa. In addition to the cold cash cow that men's lifestyle magazines promised to become, the discourse of enterprise that marked this new economic playing field gave political direction to these strategies of economic development. It therefore comes as no surprise that the first magazine to enter the South African market would do so not only in tandem with a number of key global brands but in the name of a redeeming moral virtue – namely, to bring health to a situation marred by the maladies of the past.

Men's Health

The past decade of research into male well-being in the Western world is marked by the consistent finding that the high mortality rate for men is not simply related to their biology (Courtenay 2000; Helgeson 1995; Waldron 2000). The fact that in the United States, men, on average, die more than six years younger than women has been attributed by studies such as that conducted by Will Courtenay (2000) and Vicki Helgeson (1995) to harmful behavioural factors such as smoking, poor diet and excessive consumption of alcohol (as well as more taboo phenomena such as the increased rate of eating disorders among men). What makes Helgeson's study interesting is the correlation drawn between these practices and masculine identity, claiming that 'a sizeable portion of men's excess mortality is linked to... men's roles, and gendered patterns of socialization'. In post-apartheid South Africa this pathological reading of male health is further tainted by negative political connotations, ideologically associated with (white) men. Masculine identity in South Africa is affected by the political shift from a patriarchal regime of oppression to a system that attempts to represent and valorise the disenfranchised. In effect, white men have become the subsequent poster children for a past of infamous hostility and domination. The global interest in male well-being and the health of a corporate male self-image is thus a valid concern in the current South African climate.

As if responding to the awareness surrounding male health sparked by the local crisis in masculinity, Media24 (a division of the South African media conglomerate Naspers) launched *Men's Health South Africa* in 1997, more or less following the format of its American predecessor. *Men's Health*, published by Rodale Press, began in the United States in 1987 as an annual before becoming a quarterly and then a bimonthly magazine focused on 'health, fitness, stress, sex and nutrition' (Spira 2003: 1). After having succeeded in the United States (and later Europe – 36 editions are now available worldwide) for a decade, becoming the men's lifestyle magazine with the largest worldwide circulation (*Men's Health* magazine 2006; Stibbe 2004), *Men's Health* finally entered the local market, proving that even in South Africa health was no longer a purely female concern. Paul Kerton was the first editor, and the magazine entered South Africa in order to fill the gap in the market for a magazine that addressed men on their health (Richter 2006, interview).

The American *Men's Health* brand was built on the classical idealisation of the male body and seemingly on the platitude that a healthy body equals a healthy mind. As was the case internationally, the local covers formed an integral component of this brand strategy, with black-and-white photographs of brawny, smiling men personifying Winckelmann and Pater's articulation of ideal beauty as 'rest in motion' (see Mosse 1996 for an explanation of Winckelmann and Pater's theory). At the time, *Men's Health* was almost exclusively concerned with exactly what the title suggests: men's health and fitness. The image of a buff male torso seemed a fitting espousal of the magazine's philosophy and cunningly differentiated the magazine from the laddish thrust of other men's lifestyle magazines set to appear on the scene. It also included more fashion features than its overseas predecessors. Elsewhere in the world, *Men's Health* entered a market chock-full of men's lifestyle magazines and accordingly positioned itself as health and fitness orientated. In South Africa, it was the first magazine of its kind and thus Kerton decided to capitalise on the absence of men's fashion magazines by means of the above-mentioned strategies.

After 2000, *Men's Health* had to diversify its interests to compete with the local editions of *For Him Magazine (FHM)* and *GQ*. In order to rival the titillating inflection of *FHM* and *GQ*, the current *Men's Health* includes more features centred on sexual knowledge as well as more sexualised images of women. Furthermore, in a cunning attempt to procure the interest of more male (and female) readers, the magazine launched a do-it-yourself supplement for pragmatic metromen entitled *Men's Health Living* in 2006. Nevertheless, the content of the original magazine is primarily centred on fitness with divisions such as 'Health', 'Nutrition' and 'Fitness' and features such as '100 Age Erasers' (*Men's Health* December 2003: 164) fondly recalling eighteenth-century hygiene movements and, perhaps, the American nostalgia for a puritan past.

The masculine ideal presented by *Men's Health* is thus a fairly conservative reading of masculinity that places emphasis on the physical health and strength of men as a metaphor for general well-being. This ideal affirms Connell's notion that true masculinity is 'almost always thought to proceed from men's bodies' since 'bodies are seen as sharing in social agency, in generating and shaping courses of social conduct' (1995: 45, 54). In the burgeoning new South Africa, a context sorely in need of assurance in terms of its well-being, *Men's Health* capitalised (and continues to capitalise) on Mosse's (1996) notion of the (bodily) masculine ideal as indicative of a healthy society.

Appropriate to this analogy between bodily health and the health of a culture, Arran Stibbe (2004: 34) argues that the American edition of *Men's Health* is steeped in traditional or dominant masculine ideology (that naturalises male power) and fails to challenge the discourse of hegemonic masculinity in the interest of real health, meaning holistic health that is sensitive to differing personality and body types. In Stibbe's view, *Men's Health* emphasises a one-dimensional view of masculinity in which men are portrayed as physically and emotionally in control. With relation to the South African edition too, Stibbe's critique calls into question the extent to which the magazine favours hegemonic masculinity or so-called health over the actual psychosexual well-being of its readers, presuming that actual, individualised health could not be reduced to the kind of singular, collective ideology maintained by *Men's Health* in South Africa. Since the magazine entered South Africa in tandem with a number of luxury American brands,[7] it was clear from the outset that the image of masculine well-being would be clothed in consumerism, thereby undermining any counter-cultural view of masculinity as independent of mainstream consumption.

Whether the magazine actually cultivates healthy readers or even stimulates any kind of diverse discourse on what this might mean, it has certainly garnered a healthy circulation. With the readership defined as 'affluent,…sophisticated, upscale males' (average age 31; Living Standards Measure [LSM] 8+; 74 per cent male and 26 per cent female [Richter 2006, interview]), the current readership of the magazine is 814 000 (All Media and Products Survey [AMPS] February–

June 2007), making it the primary competitor of FHM (readership 726 000; AMPS February–June 2007). (In 2005 FHM was worth an annualised R40.7 million compared to Men's Health's R23.3 million.[8])

FHM, along with GQ, only entered the South African race for the attention of male consumers in 2000. The international best-seller Maxim also launched a local title in 2000 but folded before the end of the year. The South African editions of FHM and GQ were launched in the same month with December/January editions of both magazines hitting the shelves in the consumer mayhem surrounding the millennium. FHM was published by UpperCase Media (UCM; a joint venture between Media24 and British publishing giant EMAP – UCM also publishes the tabloid Heat), while multinational publishing conglomerate Condé Nast founded GQ South Africa. Where Men's Health was the burgeoning platform for targeting the broader South African male consumer market, FHM and GQ established more niche platforms from which to target men who consider themselves to be happily laddish or aspiringly sophisticated, respectively.

FHM

The differences between FHM and GQ in South Africa are perhaps larger than they may appear at first glance. For instance, both employ glamorous women in provocative, come-hither poses on the all-important covers. On closer inspection, however, there are marked differences. These differences are closely related to the brand strategy on which each magazine is built: where GQ is built on lofty tones and wishful thinking, FHM, like its British antecedent, seems to shun all forms of aspirational rhetoric in favour of outright laddishness.

Founded by Chris Astridge in the United Kingdom, For Him (as the magazine was initially entitled) was at first disseminated through high-street men's fashion outlets, expanding to newsagents as a quarterly by 1987. While the magazine was at this point primarily concerned with fashion, this was to change when James Brown's Loaded entered the British market. With its sensual, no-nonsense content and photographs, Loaded set the tone for the lad-mag genre and, along with later titles such as GQ and Esquire, compelled For Him to harden its editorial approach. In 1994 the magazine, published by the consumer media division of EMAP, introduced a 'sports supplement', went monthly and changed its name to FHM. (Soon after, the magazine went international; currently 27 editions are published per month.)

The first editor of *FHM* South Africa was marketing man Neil Bierbaum, who more or less followed a toned-down version of the international *FHM* recipe, meaning that the South African edition of the magazine also employed sports trivia, a locker-room dialect and a plethora of objectifying images of already famous women (primarily models, actresses and musicians) in order to lure a young male readership and eventually become 'the most successful men's lifestyle magazine in South Africa' (Cooper 2006, interview). Inspired by the now-defunct but widely read *Scope*, UCM publisher Kim Brown proffers that '[y]ou have to give the market something they want' (Derby 2006). The readership is LSM 7+, AMPS age 28, of which 30 per cent are women (although the majority of the female readers do not purchase the magazine but read it second-hand) (Cooper 2006, interview). Describing the average reader, the 2006 *FHM* editor Brendan Cooper sketches him as an everyman who likes to 'sit on the couch, drink beer with his mates and talk kak' (Cooper 2006, interview).

Former *Directions*[9] and *SL* editor, Cooper took over from Bierbaum in September 2002, and with him came a number of subtle editorial changes. According to Cooper (2006, interview), he firstly improved the design of the magazine so that it became a more direct read with easier access points. Competing for the attention of readers (who on average are about five years younger than the *Men's Health* and *GQ* readers) is an increasingly abstruse endeavour, and since iPods, satellite television and an assortment of other publications are in the running for male attention, Cooper deemed it important to guide the reader so that each feature speaks for itself. Thus the design and layout are now more direct, with fixed features like 'Reporter' and 'Sex Confidential' sporting new hard-to-miss banners.

Secondly, the new editor endorsed the down-to-earth tone of the magazine by including more South African colloquialisms such as 'kief', 'ouks', 'miff' and 'jislike'. With the subtitle to the magazine being 'It's a guy thing', Cooper continued to employ the editorial mantra 'sexy, funny, useful, relevant' but did so with a decidedly local flavour. In retrospect this was a smart and fortuitous move, considering the looming threat of an Afrikaans men's lifestyle magazine entering the South African market, now realised in Wilhelm du Plessis and Mike de Villiers's new title *Manwees*, launched in June 2006.

What further differentiates the magazine from its competitors is its unabashed sense of plebeian self. Cooper disdains the aspirational quality of *GQ* that dares to prescribe to men which kind of suits they should don, the women they should date or the cars they should drive. Rather than add more consumer pressure to their media-savvy audience with 'must-have' features, the magazine thrives on reader-driven stock inserts like the popular 'Homegrown Honeys' competition that features countless South African beauties and the 'Grossest Pics Ever' mainstay, which more or less speaks for itself.

The masculine ideal presented by the South African issue of *FHM* is thus a twofold construct: firstly, the sense of laddish, naughty-but-niceness the magazine espouses, and secondly, the feminine ideal so overtly maintained throughout the magazine. Here too the object seems to be good, 'innocent' fun, since the women are scantily clad but almost never naked. Cooper (2006, interview) is clear on the fact that South African men are a pretty conservative bunch and as such do not take kindly to 'nipples or swearing'. Though stocked to the brim with semi-naked, pouting, big-haired, big-chested women, there are thus no nipples or curses to be found on the pages of the South African *FHM*.

In other words, while the magazine is quite guilty of the usual charges held against top-shelf magazines (the objectifying of women, stereotyping of male sexuality and dumbing down of male interests), it nevertheless appears as a refreshingly honest take on a particular kind of masculine identity and therefore seems quite at peace with its own hegemony. Perhaps the most perceptible area of psychosocial concern is the fact that increasing numbers of women read the magazine, presumably for the same reason that men ostensibly read *Cosmopolitan*: in order to better understand the opposite sex. If this is indeed the reason the magazine has such a wide female readership, then it can emphatically be said that the view of both men and women that readers will find there is two-dimensional at best and grossly stereotypical at worst.

GQ

The oldest of the aforementioned magazines, *Gentlemen's Quarterly* was launched in the United States in 1931 as *Apparel Arts*, a fashion quarterly for men. The title of the magazine changed to *GQ* in 1957, and although it became a monthly magazine in the 1970s it was still primarily concentrated on fashion and attracted a large gay readership. In 1983 the then editor, Art Cooper, introduced articles and features of a more global scope, aligning the magazine with the men's lifestyle genre and a larger heterosexual (and metrosexual) readership.

In the first issue of the South African edition, editor Daniel Ford (2000:14) commented: 'This is it then. At last, a classy, intelligent magazine for South

African men.' As a motive for purchasing the magazine he added, '[O]nce you're looking great, real style is about how you choose to live. And which magazine you read' (*GQ South Africa* Millennium issue 2000: 14). Not unlike *Playboy* in the 1950s in America, which catered to the needs of the more educated, sophisticated, middle-class male (Dubbert 1979: 268), *Gentlemen's Quarterly South Africa* was founded in order to capitalise on the increasing consciousness about style, urbanity and 'new masculinity' or metrosexuality amid upwardly mobile South African men after the first democratic elections in 1994.

Unlike *FHM*, *GQ* is built on the fundamental assumption that its readers are aspiring to more in life and see the magazine as a shorthand means of achieving the information needed to attain their social goals. Where Cooper (2006, interview) describes the average *FHM* reader as 'cheeky and full of shit… not on the fast track to becoming the next CEO', the *GQ* reader appears, as far as can be discerned from the magazine's content and articles, to be something of a modern-day *flâneur*. The *GQ* readership demographic is LSM 7+, 'urban males, aged 18 to 45 with post matric qualifications [and a fairly high income]' (*GQ South Africa Psychographics Package* 2002).

GQ differentiates itself from *FHM* by creating a brand that encapsulates 'class' and sexualised display. For instance, it fluently couples saucy pin-ups with upmarket advertisements (Mercedes, Tag Heur, Armani), and in so doing sexualises materialism. Subtle references to the genteel customs of old (hunting and hand-tailored suits) are employed to remind readers that gentlemen are their demographic, thus encouraging aspirational branding and dressing up sexist stereotypes in a classy savoir faire. On paging through features on everything from boardroom to bedroom etiquette (and the two are frequently coupled), it becomes apparent that *GQ* is a 'how-to' guide on personal branding. Today gentility depends not on birthright but on personal branding, and *GQ* enables its readers to brand themselves more favourably. The masculine ideal presented by *GQ* is defined more by its many biographical features on Fortune 500 celebrities, rigorously chronicling their rise to fame, than by the equally prevalent features on sex or the latest South African models.

Where *FHM* runs the now-famous competition to gauge who their readers consider to be the sexiest women in the world, *GQ*, to its credit, used to publish an annual calendar that included the sexy renderings of a number of local and international artists (the calendar was stopped due to advertisers' discomfort with the pin-up connotation associated with a calendar of virtually naked women). In this way, *GQ* teases the boundary between art and pornography, but never quite sustains the kind of real discourse or intellectual substance that would lend it subversive or artistic credibility. Instead the magazine seems to create a sense of chauvinist exclusivity and clubbish camaraderie by enforcing a limited definition of masculinity based on sexual conquest, high-flying corporate culture and extreme sports. Sleek and modern design, a cognitive and discrete tone, celebrity journalists and mostly subtle humour create a sense of dignified responsibility and maturity. But while the background image of a Jeep may be replaced with that of a Jaguar, the indulgent display of women as sexualised visual pleasure and the cop-out consumer-driven tone is not so different from that found in *FHM*.

The real difference between these two magazines seems to be their readership figures. With a current readership of 319 000 (AMPS February–June 2007), *GQ* is no threat to *FHM* and is deemed by some to be something of a failure in the South African magazine industry.[10] However, under the influence of the current editor, Craig Tyson, the magazine has returned to a monthly publication schedule (with an additional three issues of *GQ Cars* being published every year), having lapsed to a bimonthly status for a short period. At R31.95, *FHM* is the most expensive men's lifestyle magazine in South Africa and makes most of its money from off-the-shelf sales, giving *FHM* the highest retail sales value (RSV) in the country.[11] *GQ*, on the other hand, generates more income from advertising than from magazine sales and has been known to adapt its content in order to accommodate the sensibilities of its upmarket advertisers. Thus, *GQ* seems to represent quite neatly the kind of magazines which Nixon (1996) describes as being founded in order to provide a platform from which advertisers can access a particular niche audience.

Apparently in a bid to rectify the vast gap in readership figures between *GQ* and *FHM*, Tyson decided to realign the magazine in 2006 with the core values of style, entertainment and sophistication. While the ostensible objective was to make the design or format easier for the reader to follow (Tyson 2006, interview), one cannot help but feel that the result is a raunchier, more laddish *GQ*. While it is easy to understand the temptation to mimic the *FHM* formula, one cannot help but wonder whether Tyson is not sabotaging the only claim to differentiation he had. Either way, it is currently quite difficult to tell the difference between *FHM* and *GQ* from the covers and this, after all, is a powerful persuader in determining those all-important news-stand buys. Commenting on the magazine's current status as the butt-end of men's press jokes, Tyson (2006, interview) notes that, as a sophisticated read, GQ does not follow the 'tits-and-bums' approach to publishing and is therefore not aiming to reach the mass market. But Tyson's glib response belies his apparent denial regarding the similarity between the covers of FHM and GQ, a fact that may be indicative of the horizontal identification between the three mainstream men's lifestyle magazines.

For instance, *Men's Health*, *FHM* and *GQ* all boast that roughly a third of their readers are black, yet, true to the homogenising influence of the men's lifestyle magazine format, not one of these titles addresses its readers as multiracial, includes features on multiculturalism or even provides a representative sample of 'black' subjects and models. Instead, *Men's Health*, *FHM* and *GQ* present a narrow view of the South African population that in its lack of political substance and tonal diversity recalls a pre-1994 picture of masculinity. In this picture, to be 'mainstream' means to be white and middle class, as if this is the dominant demographic in the South African social structure. Perhaps the problem lies in the fact that the magazines are not upfront about their target market but pretend to be speaking to the affluent male population as a whole, when they are, in fact, more racially exclusive than this. In contrast to the mainstream men's lifestyle magazines that address a white audience without ever calling them this, the more fringe magazines like *Maksiman* and *BL!NK* seem more honest in their deliberate exclusivity.

Maksiman

The first Afrikaans men's lifestyle magazine was founded in 2001 by Carpe Diem Media under the title *Maksiman* (literally 'Maximan'). Not only was this a departure from the traditional use of English as the communicator of globalising new masculinity but, as editor Hennie Stander points out, the magazine was also the first Christian men's lifestyle magazine in South Africa (De Wet 2005). The magazine was thus created in order to reach a sector of the market that was not being specifically targeted by other magazines – namely, Christian Afrikaans-speaking men – and as such, its competitors, according to Stander, are imported magazines like *New Man* and not the local titles (De Wet 2005). The target market and demographics of readership is thus 30+ (the exact LSM of the magazine is not defined by the editorial team but presumably falls around 7+ [Briers 2006, interview]).

Feminist writers Susan Faludi (1999) and Mary Stewart van Leeuwen (1990, 1993, 1998, 2002) have theorised the conceptualisation of masculinities within religious contexts such as the Promise Keepers movement in the United States, but the South African situation is naturally nuanced in a localised way. The construction of masculinity within the Afrikaans-speaking 'Christian' community, for instance, is emphatically informed by the theologies of the Dutch Reformed Church, which is, historically, the dominant religious persuasion of Afrikaners. The magazine does not, however, make overt reference to the Dutch Reformed tradition or to any other denomination for that matter. It seems to avoid contentious doctrinal or theological issues in favour of lifestyle-orientated features and articles that attempt to provide answers (albeit fairly obvious ones) to questions such as how to be a good husband or father ('Jou vrou' and 'Jou kinders' are regular features) and whether the Christian masculine ideal includes ambition or a hunger for success ('Soete droom wereld', *Maksiman* November/December 2005: 22–24).

Not only is the masculine ideal presented by this magazine more tentative than that extolled by *Men's Health*, *FHM* and *GQ*, meaning that it is not quite so boldly maintained as the norm for all self-respecting men, but this version of masculinity includes the relationship to significant others. The secular, mainstream men's lifestyle magazines discussed previously all employ the silent but emphatic omission of almost all references to wives and children, preferring instead to depict their subjects and readers as eternally uncommitted. Through the construction of this simulacral male fantasy world,[12] sans wives and children, the magazines presumably facilitate the guilt-free perusal of the many inviting women libidinously represented on their pages. In a similar vein, mention is seldom made of the love interests of women quixotically featured in men's lifestyle magazines. In her seminal essay *To be Two*, analytical feminist Luce Irigaray muses that where women almost always privilege the 'relationship between two', men typically prefer a 'relationship between one and the many', between the I-masculine subject and others: people, society, understood as *them* and not as *you*' (2001: 17; italics in original). Although this is a simplistic generalisation, Irigaray's point is perhaps useful in explaining the abundance of women all represented as available within the context of a magazine such as *FHM* and the need for men to likewise be represented as unattached. In contrast to this trope of eternal and thriving bachelorhood favoured by *Men's Health*, *FHM* and *GQ*, *Maksiman* seems to consciously draw the attention of its readers to their partners and to cultivate a culture of accountable responsibility.

The sense of anti-escapist rhetoric employed by *Maksiman* (including the aforementioned articles on cultivating a healthy family life) coincides with the brotherly tone of Christian men's movements internationally. Writers like Faludi (1999), Stewert van Leeuwen (1990, 1993, 1998, 2002) and the pop-psychology best-selling author John Eldridge (2001) have interpreted the notion of masculinity in crisis within the Christian context and found that Christian men also suffer from an often severe sense of collective confusion regarding their identities and what it means to be a man in the modern-day context and church. Thus, a Christian men's magazine in some way answers to the general rhetoric of *Christian* masculinity in crisis in much the same way that *Men's Health*, for instance, responds to the widespread readings of secular masculine behaviour as unhealthy.

Maksiman's editorial team do not seem to consciously engage with the crisis or flux that may or may not be plaguing their readers, nor are the articles that pretend to deal with such issues aggressive or 'serious' enough to provide genuinely fruitful answers. For the most part, the magazine follows the light, entertaining tone employed by the majority of mainstream lifestyle magazines and thus may leave a reader truly seeking answers to the stereotypical masculinities available to him in the marketplace quite unsatisfied. It may be a conscious decision on the part of the magazine's editorial team to give their readers a space where they can relax and find a refuge from serious questions, but if this is the case then one cannot help but wonder whether this approach coincides with the apparently Christian philosophy of *Maksiman*. Perhaps because of this confused brand identity – it's neither a theological nor a populist magazine – this bimonthly publication has a circulation of only 20 000 (Briers 2006, interview).

Moreover, *Maksiman* is no longer the only Afrikaans men's lifestyle magazine. The first issue of *Manwees* appeared on South African shelves on 28 June 2006 with an initial print run of 30 000. Edited by former *De Kat* editor Wilhelm du Plessis and published jointly by Du Plessis and Mike de Villiers, the magazine embodies Naspers mogul Koos Becker's sentiment that people have the desire to read in their kitchen language. According to Du Plessis:

> South Africa has needed a men's magazine that caters for the needs of Afrikaans men between 25 and 45 for quite some time...That's why we believe it is such a relevant publication – Afrikaans men have long been overlooked and that is why we will be offering them a quality product in their own language that will keep them informed, entertained and hopefully enthralled.[13]

Manwees was launched, perhaps strategically, at a time when Afrikaans-speaking South Africans seemed ready to put up a fight for the right to go about their business in Afrikaans (whether in universities or in more informal sectors). Comments Du Plessis: 'We want the magazine to be a reflection of how Afrikaans as a language is blossoming in magazines, in music, on radio and on television. It is no longer a deadly sin to be Afrikaans-speaking and old stereotypical connotations of the language and her speakers are thankfully dying a long overdue death!' (*Being a man...in Afrikaans* 2006). Clearly this magazine and its editors are not backing away from the politicised contention surrounding the language but rather are capitalising on it. Whether because of the inception of *Manwees* or because of the confused purpose of *Maksiman*, the latter magazine effectively closed its doors in 2006. According to the editor, the magazine may still appear from time to time as a supplement to the Christian women's magazine, *Finesse*, but is no longer economically viable on its own.

BL!NK

The latecomer of the five, the first edition of *BL!NK* was launched in October 2004 by Orlyfunt Holdings as an upmarket magazine aimed at young black males. Here too, the South African context provides its own narratological twists, as *BL!NK* was launched (against much political disputation) with a R3.5 million loan from the National Empowerment Fund (NEF) as a black empowerment project (Loxton 2005).[14] The magazine was the brainchild of BL!NK Lifestyle Trading chief executive officer Vuyo Radebe, but in its infancy was edited by 28-year-old Simphiwe Mpye. According to Mpye, 'most men's issues in S[outh] A[frica] are not universal, they are race specific' which is why the magazine aims to 'paint a new face for the black man' who is still frequently associated with 'abuse and desertion' (McCloy 2005).

In discussing the initial objectives of the magazine, Mpye (2006, interview) tenders that the primary incentive behind the founding of *BL!NK* was:

> to show the rest of the country that the affluent black male has not only emerged, but will, given time, increasingly be the backbone of [the South African] economy...we had also realised and wanted to show this man to be about much more than soccer, BMWs and bling. We wanted to show that he was also passionate, compassionate, intelligent, worldly, sensitive, politically aware, discerning, etc.

Mpye thus defines *BL!NK*'s target market (and its masculine ideal) as 'a thinking man who [is] every bit an [*sic*] African as he is worldly...[A man who is] well read, he challenges outmoded perspectives and is not afraid to stand alone in his conviction. Of course he just so happens to be tasteful and confident' (McCloy 2005). In other words, *BL!NK* both articulates the emergent identity held by black professionals as assertive confidence (a reflection of new power relations in society) and presents itself as a defence against charges of this new class being made up of 'affirmatives'. With the demographic being described in more idealistic terms than simply age 25–35, LSM 7+ and predominantly black, Mpye (2006, interview) is not afraid to classify himself as a *BL!NK* man, even now that he has left the magazine to pursue other areas of the media industry (and been replaced by Thami Masemola).

Thus, the political alignment of the magazine with progressive and enlightened views of black masculinity that attempt to arrogate hegemonic representations of black men raises the issue of *black* post-apartheid masculinity in crisis. Australian socio-psychological pundit and feminist Lyn Segal (1990: 168–204) has examined the stereotypical rendering of black masculinity from the perspective of white masculinity.[15] Segal postulates that behind the social construction of 'subordinated masculinity' one finds more evidence of the 'conflict and chaos at the heart of the dominant ideal of masculinity' (1990: 169). In lieu of her research and other investigations like it (Bertelsen 1998; Hunter & Davis 1994; Nyquist 1983) that emphasise the competitive aspect of diverse masculinities, one is struck by the earnest differences between *BL!NK* and the other men's lifestyle magazines available in South Africa. For instance, Segal highlights the manner in which black masculinity is viewed and sketched through the eyes of white masculinity (as well as in contrast to it) as not really about men at all – 'a child rather than an adult, a body not a mind' (1990: 169).

In addition to this colonialist reading are the many contemporary interpretations of black masculinity as pathological, leading to implicit associations with domestic violence and crime (Gray 1995). In South Africa, such negative associations can in part be traced to the era of apartheid when black male youths in urban areas were typically represented as inherently violent, disturbed and irrational mobs, thus allowing the state to justify the brutal actions of the South African Defence Force (Mtebule 2001: 5). In response to this demonising representation (particularly in the national media) the tendency arose for young black men to identify the then masculine ideal with the collective struggle of liberation politics (Carter 1991). This comrade identity provided young black men with the hope of being regarded as 'men' and thus the possibility of extraditing themselves from a system that reduced black men to the status of 'boys' (Mtebule 2001: 5). But it also led to conformity and undermined individual responsibility, self-criticism and differences of opinion (Ramphele 1992). Nkhensani Mtebule (2001) points out that between the late 1970s and late 1980s young black men were thus fighting a double war: to be recognised as equals and as individual men.

This stereotype makes evident the need for radically new representations of black South African masculinity that leave room for individual idiosyncrasies. The typical masculinities available to young black men today fall into a number of diverse but intertwined categories. Three contemporary types, identified by Mtebule (2001: 9), seem pertinent to the construction of a collective consciousness that may appeal to the BL!NK market. It should be noted that, although useful in detailing the BL!NK readership, these types are themselves constructions that border on being stereotypical. The types identified by Mtebule (2001: 9) are the 'amagents', the 'Y generation' and the 'ama-bourgeoisie'. Taken from the word 'gentlemen', the amagents are the contemporary version of the *bo-tsotsi* subculture prevalent in Soweto between the 1950s and 1970s. The amagents are regarded as comprising black, urban (township) men who make a living out of organised crime and have a notable taste for 'flashy cars, materialism and beautiful women as defining possessions of "the man"' (Mtebule 2001: 9). Named after the popular black radio station and magazine (and the international generational term), the Y generation have of late been berated by the African National Congress for being politically and academically apathetic, being more concerned with kwaito and street parties than with the manner in which they can contribute to local politics (Mtebule 2001: 9). Finally, and perhaps most significantly, ama-bourgeoisie is the colloquial term for the black middle class that spearheaded the exodus from the townships to the suburbs where they epitomise the highly charged divide between the black haves and have-nots. None of these types form the sole readership of BL!NK, but by constituting in some small way the collective understanding of black masculinity in South Africa they do feed the discourse regarding masculinity evident in the magazine.

Antithetical to the simplistically negative aforementioned versions of black masculinity (past and present), BL!NK, unlike the other men's lifestyle titles, emphasises the cognitive prowess and ethical ideology of its readers.[16] In reference to the localised stereotypes of upwardly mobile black South Africans,

Mpye boldly remarks, '[I]f you are not in touch with yourself and you find validation in your material possessions, then you are not a BL!NK man' (McCloy 2005). Through such didactic proclamations, the tone of BL!NK recalls the political cadence of black philosophers such as Aime Cesaire, Steven Biko, Frantz Fanon and Malcom X, who through their racially conscious pedagogy emphasised the possibility for taking ownership of the processes that govern identity in the wake of an oppressive ideological system.

With thoughtful, critical features on black South African intellectuals ('A love letter to black intellectuals', BL!NK March 2006: 56–59), seditious African artists ('The subversive palette', BL!NK March 2006: 64–65) and articles that honestly grapple with responsible black identity ('Modern male identity', BL!NK March 2006: 14–16) forming the mainstay of the magazine, BL!NK successfully challenges the haggard stereotypes not only about black masculinity, but about manhood in general. It would therefore appear as though black male identity is differentiated from white male identity within BL!NK through an emphasis on political responsibility that underscores the Afrocentric nature of the magazine. If there is any criticism to be expressed in terms of the masculine ideal presented by the magazine, it is that it still paints a fairly monolithic portrait of black masculinity. Through the absence of homosexual voices, for instance, the magazine naturalises the othering of homosexuality within the black community, drawing into question the possibility of representing the complex, hybrid and fluid nature of gender within a men's lifestyle magazine. Similarly, the multicultural nature of South Africa is rarely recognised, with the content generally glossing over the issues related to ethnic diversities in South Africa. Addressing ethnic stereotypes and tensions or even just difference seems vital to the project of realistic discourse in the South African context. Having said that, the women featured in the magazine are represented with individual poise and personhood and, since they are rarely featured in scant clothing, there is none of the 'body fascism' (Nead 1992) that seems to underpin the editorial style of men's lifestyle magazines as a genre. Indeed, Mpye (2006, interview) cites one of the goals of the magazine at its inception as 'bridg[ing] the divide between the sexes', an ideal sorely amiss in BL!NK's competitors.

Commenting on this niche magazine, FHM editor Brendan Cooper (2006, interview) noted that, in his opinion, the magazine is a little ahead of its time, that the black market is not yet ready for what the magazine offers. Indeed, BL!NK challenges the expected formulae of a men's lifestyle magazine by pushing the content beyond the usual rhetoric of sex, sport and financial success. The fact that it presents its readers with content that is more than just 'sexy, funny, useful, relevant' may explain why, as a monthly, *BL!NK* had a total circulation of only 35 000 and also closed its doors in 2007.

Conclusion

This chapter has attempted to sketch the rise of five men's lifestyle magazines that emerged in South Africa in the wave of the post-1994 consumer fervour. Toward this end each magazine was analysed in order to determine something of the philosophy that differentiates it from or identifies it with the other men's lifestyle titles available in South Africa and to determine the extent to which it reflects the different pockets of masculine identity found in the South African media. In each case the niche objectives, demographics of the readership, identity crises potentially faced by this target market as well as the editorial tone of the magazine were juxtaposed with the masculine ideal the magazine seems to extol. The investigation of the masculinities represented by the South African men's lifestyle magazines was informed by the underlying assumption that all of these magazines present a simplified and two-dimensional masculine ideal. This assumption may lead to the further conjecture that the genre of men's lifestyle magazines, whether targeted at any culturally specific readership, is fundamentally concerned with the commodification and simplification of masculinity to an aspirational type, but this is certainly a generalisation and (as in the case of *BL!NK*) there may be exceptions.

A number of general conclusions emerged out of this study. The first is that, while a target market does seem to have emerged that marketers and media owners can conceptualise in non-racial (cosmopolitan or metrosexual?) terms – meaning that this identity attracts white, black (including coloured) and Indian readers – the dominant target market of the mainstream men's lifestyle magazines is an affluent white South African male. For while the dominant South African discourse of nation building would like to conceptualise the existence of a hybrid or non-racial identity, the financially successful men's lifestyle magazines (*Men's Health*, *FHM* and *GQ*) all present their masculine ideal, albeit on a subtextual level, as white. This white masculine ideal does not on any level resist the discourse of a unified South African maleness, but neither does it engage with what a unified identity might mean or 'look like'. It does not necessarily draw on the old pre-1994 patriarchal identity, but replaces this trope with yet another, that of the globalised, cosmopolitan, non-racialised (but white) male.

The second, analogous summation that emerges from this study is that in spite of the more or less 'mixed' demographics of the mainstream men's lifestyle magazines (*Men's Health, FHM* and *GQ* have a black readership of between 20 and 30 per cent) and the commercial formulation of a unified target market (in advertising, for instance), there nevertheless seem to be identifiable white-Anglo, Afrikaner and black male identities that magazines still appeal to, a fact underscored by the emergence of *BL!NK* and *Maksiman*. On the other hand, the financial failure of both of these magazines does seem to indicate that South African men still prefer to buy into a globalised and two-dimensional image of masculinity in the form of mainstream men's lifestyle magazines, as opposed to a more authentic, vernacular image of masculinity.

The third conclusion is that while the various magazines under discussion in this chapter each present a nuanced slant on ideal masculine identity, a definite masculine ideal is evident in each. *Men's Health* places emphasis on holistic well-being, *FHM* on laddish good fun and self-acceptance and *GQ* on the aspirational effort of (especially stylistic or fashion-conscious) self-actualisation. *Maksiman* is a magazine that attempted to reconcile ideal masculinity with a Christian world-view, and *BL!NK* ostensibly challenged negative stereotypes surrounding black masculinity with an ethical and socially responsible black masculine ideal. In other words, each responds to a particular aspect of the South African crisis in masculinity, whether this crisis is real or chimerical. Having said that, not all South African men read one of the men's lifestyle magazines available, perhaps indicating that there are men who do not identify with any of the masculine ideals available in these magazines.

Stephen Whitehead (2002: 45–46) has pointed out that studying gender or masculinity in the South African context is a doubly charged endeavour because of the history of racial inequality that defines this country. The resultant political correctness endemic to the so-called new South Africa (1994–2000) further complicates any analysis that attempts to foreground stereotypical trends in gender construction within the public domain. In his comprehensive analysis of masculinity and the study thereof, entitled *Men and Masculinities: Key Themes and New Directions*, Whitehead (2002: 46) underscores the importance of treating masculinity as an entity situated on the threshold between the personal and the political.

As if to echo Whitehead's sentiments, the South African government in July 2006 introduced new regulations to the Films and Publications Act of 1996, making it an offence to sell pornographic publications like *Hustler*, *Loslyf* and *Playboy* at garages, local cafes or magazine stores. It is thought that this restriction may inadvertently influence the content of men's lifestyle magazines, which will fall within the ambit of the law if the articles in a particular magazine are deemed to border on pornography rather than sex education (Naidu 2006). It is as yet unclear the extent to which this restriction will be enforced and, thus, the extent of the influence it will have on men's lifestyle magazines, but it again highlights the fluctuation that exists within the public sector regarding sexuality and the representation thereof.

The fact that masculinity is in flux in South Africa may mean that men are more susceptible to the homogenising influence of men's lifestyle magazines, but it also means that the role that these magazines may play in articulating vernacular identities is amplified. It is unclear how wide the gap is between how identity is constructed in media representations and 'lived reality'. What is apparent is that shifting power relations after 1994 have contributed to untidy disjunctures marking the field of gender studies in contemporary South Africa. Finally, if '[masculinity is a] vexed term, variously inflected, multiply defined, not limited to straightforward descriptions of maleness', as Maurice Berger, Brian Wallis and Simon Watson (1995: 2) have asserted, then South Africa with its unique cultural inflections is fertile ground for the analysis of the many masculine ideals that form part of the fabric of the new and not-so-new South Africa.

Notes

1 The phrase 'men's lifestyle magazine' is used to refer to glossy magazines targeted at men. The phrase is essentially interchangeable with the phrase 'men's general interest magazine' or what feminists Andrea Dworkin and Cathrine A MacKinnon (1988) termed 'glossy men's magazines' (while these magazines may be fairly objectifying of women, they are not legally speaking classified as pornography). The phrase 'men's lifestyle magazine' is employed in this chapter because it seems to be preferred by the editors of the magazines in question (Cooper 2006, interview).

2 Later theorists have continued this theme. See Malin (2005) and Piner (2001).

3 Clare posed two primary questions. First, he asked whether 'phallic man, authoritative, dominant, assertive – man in control not merely of himself but of woman – was starting to die'. Second, he asked whether 'a new man [would] emerge phoenix like in his place or whether man himself [would] become largely redundant' (Clare 2000: 9).

4 The fissures in this collective taxonomy have been highlighted by, among others, Rosalind Gill (2005), James Heartfield (2002) and Stephen Whitehead and Frank

Barret (2001), who question whether this is a valid social phenomenon or something of a moral dread invented by those who consider feminism to be threatening to a social system that preferences male power.

5   *Scope* in fact rebranded itself in 1995 as a men's lifestyle magazine, but without the pin-up, centrefold-style imagery that had been its mainstay, the magazine folded in 1996.

6   'Crisis' is perhaps too strong a word to describe the changes taking place in the delineation of gender in South Africa. The term 'flux' is probably a more accurate and less dramatic indication of the local situation. The term 'crisis' is, nevertheless, still used in this study to call into question the body of research that falls within it.

7   Kerton reportedly approached a number of global luxury brands in order to ensure that they would be entering post-apartheid South Africa, thereby procuring important advertisers for *Men's Health* as well as establishing a symbiotic branding strategy between *Men's Health* and certain luxury brands.

8   See *FHM International on South Africa* (2006). Accessed 29 June 2006, http://www.fhm-international.com/news?num=48

9   Emerging in 1994 (from a water sports magazine), *Directions* was in fact the first South African men's lifestyle magazine. It built its brand identity on the British *FHM*, but with the inception of the local *FHM* the copycat magazine folded in April 2000.

10 It should be noted that unlike *GQ*, both *Men's Health* (published by the Naspers affiliate Touchline Media) and *FHM* have the financial backing of Naspers, the largest media conglomerate in South Africa. *FHM*, for instance, only turned a profit three years after its inception, meaning that it relied on the heavy investment of UCM, also affiliated with Naspers (Spira 2003).

11 RSV gauges a magazine's cover price multiplied by its frequency and its news-stand circulation. *Men's Health* and *GQ* rank 11th and 44th in terms of RSV (Derby 2006).

12 Creating an artificial milieu within the magazine is a strategy employed by most men's magazines. One of *Playboy*'s advertising directors, Howard Lederer, explained in 1967 that the magazine deliberately 'takes the reader into a kind of dream world. We create a euphoria and we want nothing to spoil it. We don't want a reader to come suddenly on an ad that says he has bad breath. We don't want him to be reminded of the fact, though it may be true, that he is going bald' (Dubbert 1979: 268).

13 *Being a man…in Afrikaans* (2006). Accessed 22 June 2006, http://biz-community.com/Article/196/39/10209

14 The resultant contention around *BL!NK* culminated with the NEF coming under fire in Parliament when Ben Turok, an ANC member of Parliament, stated that he thought it was unacceptable that the NEF had granted the loan to a magazine which contains 'nothing but disgusting pornographic pictures and articles' (Loxton 2005).

15 Segal's (1990) analysis is useful to this research because of the manner in which she foregrounds the reality of different races existing alongside one another. It should be noted, however, that, as Graeme Reid and Liz Walker have argued, '[t]he study of sexuality in Africa has been shaped by [the] false dichotomy between "us" and "them"' (2005: 3) and Segal's perspective occasionally promotes this polarity.

16 Although clearly a different project, BL!NK does seem to draw from older black magazines such as *Tribute* in its appropriation of a socially ethical tone.

References

Berger M, Wallis B & Watson S (eds) (1995) *Constructing masculinity*. London: Routledge

Bertelsen E (1998) Ads and amnesia: Black advertising in the new South Africa. In C Coetzee and S Nuttall (eds) *Negotiating the past*, pp. 221–241. Cape Town: Oxford University Press

Bly R (1990) *Iron John: A book about men*. New York: Addison-Wesley

Butler J (1990) *Gender trouble: Feminism and the subversion of identity*. New York: Routledge

Butler J (2004) *Undoing gender*. New York: Routledge

Carter CE (1991) *Comrades and community: Politics and construction of hegemony in Alexandra township*. Johannesburg: University of the Witwatersrand

Clare A (2000) *On men: Masculinity in crisis*. London: Chatto and Windus

Connell RW (1987) *Gender and power: Society, the person and sexual politics*. Cambridge: Polity

Connell RW (1995) *Masculinities*. Berkeley: University of California Press

Courtenay W (2000) Constructions of masculinity and their influence on men's well-being: A theory of gender and health. *Social Science and Medicine* 50(1): 385–401

Coward R (1999) *Sacred cows: Is feminism relevant to the new millennium?* London: Harper Collins

Derby R (2006) *South Africa: Glitzy Heat, sexy FHM blaze trail in magazine market*. Accessed 12 April 2006, http://allafrica.com/stories/200604070246.html

De Wet P (2005) *Outside the laager*. Mail & Guardian Online. Accessed 4 July 2005, http://www.themedia.co.za/article.aspx?articleid=243793&area=/media_insightfeatures/

Dubbert JL (1979) *A man's place: Masculinity in transition*. Upper Saddle River, NJ: Prentice-Hall

Durham MG & Kellner D (2001) *Media and cultural studies: Keyworks*. Malden, MA: Blackwell

Dworkin A & MacKinnon CA (1988) *Pornography and civil rights: A new day for women's equality.* Minneapolis, MN: Organisation Against Pornography

Eldridge J (2001) *Wild at heart: Discovering the secret of a man's soul.* Nashville, TN: Thomas Nelson

Faludi S (1999) *Stiffed: The betrayal of the modern man.* London: Chatto and Windus

Ford D (2000) Editor's letter. *GQ South Africa* (December/January): 14

Frosh S, Phoenix A & Patman R (2002) *Young masculinities.* Basingstoke: Palgrave

Gill R (2005) *Rethinking masculinity: Men and their bodies.* Accessed 20 June 2005, http://www.fathom.com/course/21701720/session5.html

GQ South Africa Psychographics Package (2002) Cape Town: Condé Nast

Gray H (1995) *Watching race: Television and the struggle for blackness.* Minneapolis: University of Minnesota Press

Heartfield J (2002) *There is no masculinity crisis.* Accessed 26 June 2006, http://www.genders.org/g35/g35_heartfield.html

Helgeson V (1995) Masculinity, men's roles and coronary heart disease. In D Sabo and F Gordon (eds) *Men's health and illness: Gender, power and the body*, pp. 68–104. London: Sage Publications

Horrocks R (1994) *Masculinity in crisis: Myths, fantasies and realities.* London: Macmillan

Hunter AG & Davis JE (1994) Hidden voices of black men: The meaning, structure, and complexity of manhood. *Journal of Black Studies* 25(1): 20–40

Irigaray L (2001) *To be two.* Trans. MM Rhodes and MF Cocito-Monoc. New York: Routledge

Loxton L (2005) Turok outraged by R3.5m Blink loan. *Business Report.* Accessed 27 June 2005, http://www.busrep.co.za/general/print_article.php?fArticleId=2436820&fSectionId...htm

MacInnes J (1998) *The end of masculinity: The confusion of sexual genesis and sexual difference in modern society.* Buckingham: Open University Press

MacInnes J (2001) The crisis of masculinity and the politics of identity. In SM Whitehead and FJ Barret (eds) *The masculinities reader*, pp. 311–329. Cambridge: Polity

Malin BJ (2005) *American masculinity under Clinton: Popular media and the nineties 'crisis of masculinity'.* New York: Peter Lang

McCloy M (2005) Brotha's blink. [AU: Should this be *BL!NK?*] Accessed 27 June 2005, http://www.rage.co.za/issue43/nubrosblink.htm

Men's Health (2006) Accessed 19 May 2006, http://en.wikipedia.org/wiki/Men's Health (magazine)

Morrell R (ed.) (2001) *Changing men in southern Africa*. London: Zed Books

Mosse GL (1996) *The image of man: The creation of modern masculinity*. Oxford: Oxford University Press

Mtebule N (2001) Masculinity at the margins: Researching young black urban masculinities in the post-apartheid era. In *The burden of race? 'Whiteness and blackness' in modern South Africa*, pp. 1–13. Johannesburg: History Workshop and Wits Institute for Social and Economic Research

Naidu E (2006) Porn restrictions aim 'to protect children'. Accessed 12 April 2006, http://www.iol.co.za/general/news/newsprint.php?art_id=vn20060408

Nead L (1992) *The female nude: Art, obscenity and sexuality*. London: Routledge

Nixon S (1996) *Hard looks, masculinities, spectatorship and contemporary consumption*. New York: University of California Press and St Martin's Press

Nochlin L (ed.) (1991) *The politics of vision: Essays on nineteenth-century art and society*. London: Thames and Hudson

Nyquist T (1983) *African middle-class elite*. Grahamstown: Rhodes University

Ortner SB (1974) Is female to male as nature is to culture? In MZ Rosaldo and L Lamphere (eds) *Woman, culture, and society*. Stanford, CA: Stanford University Press

Piner WF (2001) *The gender of racial politics and violence in America: Lynching, prison rape, and the crisis of masculinity*. New York: Peter Lang

Pollock G (1988) *Vision and difference: Femininity, feminism and histories of art*. London: Routledge

Ramphele M (1992) Social disintegration in the black community. In D Everett and E Sisulu (eds) *Black youth in crisis*, pp. 10–29. Cape Town: Ravan Press

Reid G & Walker L (eds) (2005) *Men behaving differently*. Cape Town: Double Storey

Segal L (1990) *Slow motion: Changing masculinities, changing men*. London: Virago

Simpson M (2004) *MetroDaddy speaks*. Accessed 19 June 2006, http://www.marksimpson.com/pages/journalism/metrodaddyspeaks.html

Spira T (2003) *What men want*. Accessed 9 October 2006, http:www.themedia.co.za/article.aspx?articleid=31000&area=/media_insightfeatures

Stewart van Leeuwen M (1990) *Gender and grace: Love, work and parenting in a changing world*. Downers Grove, IL: Intervarsity

Stewart van Leeuwen M (ed.) (1993) *After Eden: Facing the challenge of gender reconciliation*. Grand Rapids, MI: William B. Eerdmans

Stewart van Leeuwen M (1998) Promise keepers and proof-text poker. *Sojourners* 27(1): 16–21

Stewart van Leeuwen M (2002) *My brother's keeper: What the social sciences do (and don't) tell us about masculinity*. Downers Grove, IL: Intervarsity

Stibbe A (2004) Health and the social construction of masculinity in *Men's Health* magazine. *Men and Masculinities* 7(1): 31–51

Waldron I (2000) Trends in gender differences in mortality: Relationships to changing gender differences in behaviour and other causal factors. In E Annandale and K Hunt (eds) *Gender inequalities in health*, pp. 150–181. Buckingham: Open University Press

Walker L (2005) Negotiating the boundaries of masculinity in post-apartheid South Africa. In G Reid and L Walker (eds) *Men behaving differently*, pp. 161–182. Cape Town: Double Storey

Whitehead SM (2002) *Men and masculinities: Key themes and new directions*. Cambridge: Polity

Whitehead SM and Barret FJ (2001) The sociology of masculinity. In SM Whitehead and FJ Barret (eds) *The masculinities reader*, pp. 1–26. Cambridge: Polity

Interviews

Briers A (2006) Financial manager at *Maksiman*. Telephonic interview, 30 June

Cooper B (2006) Editor of *FHM*. Interview, Johannesburg, 31 May

Mpye S (2006) Former editor of *BL!NK*. Electronic interview, 14 June

Richter K (2006) Managing editor of *Men's Health*. Telephonic interview, 30 June

Tyson C (2006) Editor of *GQ South Africa*. Interview, Cape Town, 25 August

15 Tsotsis, Coconuts and Wiggers: Black masculinity and contemporary South African media

Jane Stadler

This chapter explores representations of race, class and gender and addresses the cultural politics of difference expressed in language, youth media and popular culture. It questions how the international media affect conceptions of black masculinity in South Africa by contrasting cinematic representations of African Americans and black Africans in the films *Shaft* (Singleton 2000) and *Hijack Stories* (Schmitz 2001), and relating the findings to issues of class and subjectivity in *Tsotsi* (Hood 2005). I argue that globalisation is contributing to the hybridisation of identities and, while South African media are influenced by what has been termed the 'cultural imperialism' of Hollywood, Hollywood itself incorporates and recuperates elements of the 'oral tradition' and 'resistance vernacular' present in African kwaito, hip-hop and rap music. Additionally, South African media appropriate and rework messages about black identities in innovative and knowing ways, leading to the emergence of terminology and texts that both acknowledge and resist the homogenising influences of globalisation and racial assimilation.

In order to analyse racial stereotypes and identity hybridisation, I begin by contrasting the representation of black masculinity in *Shaft* with those in the South African films *Hijack Stories* and *Tsotsi*, which have analogous settings and some interesting parallels, and which raise issues about the relationship between race and class. In the course of investigating whether mainstream American stereotypes of black masculinity are being reproduced in South African media, I move on to discuss the emergence of two hybrid identities known as Coconuts and Wiggers, which incorporate but also challenge assumptions about race, class and culture. 'Coconut' is a term used to describe a person who is black on the outside but white on the inside.[1] The white centre of the coconut seed is a metaphor for a black person who has internalised 'white culture' or 'white values'.[2] 'Wigger' has become a popular term for a

343

'wannabe negro', a white person who is 'black underneath'.[3] I use intertextual analysis to extend the discussion of contemporary black masculinity in feature films to explore the emergence of these hybrid identities within South African popular culture, considering street slang, music and advertising.

Shaft and the 'tough guise'

In a thought-provoking article titled 'He is a "Bad Mother*$%@!#": *Shaft* and Contemporary Black Masculinity', Matthew Henry (2002) argues that *Shaft* typifies a particular trend in representations of blackness that he terms the 'tough guise' of masculinity.[4] This trend sees black men in mainstream American media linked to crime, violence and 'gangsta' rap:

> A particular type of black masculinity – one defined mainly by an urban aesthetic, a nihilistic attitude, and an aggressive posturing – has made its way into the cultural mainstream... This image of masculinity has developed mainly as a result of the commodification of hip-hop culture and the ubiquity of rap music...it is the result of the popularity of the urban 'gangsta.' (Henry 2002: 114)

Henry contends that one way for black men to compensate for the 'perceived loss of power, potency or manhood' that arises from the experience of poverty and racism is to define their identity in terms of 'rampant materialism, fatalistic attitudes, physical strength, and the acquisition of respect through violence' (Henry 2002: 116).[5] In his analysis of *Shaft*, Henry argues that 'Singleton's film asks viewers to support unquestioningly the hypermasculinization of the character, to accept the sexualized nature of the violence, and to advocate a patriarchal mindset that equates masculinity with violence' (Henry 2002: 116).

The stereotype that Henry discusses is just one of many representations of black masculinity, but the prevalence and popularity of the 'tough guise' has given it heightened significance.[6] Much of the research into black stereotypes has focused attention on African Americans. The relevance to African cultures, where demographics, history, socio-political contexts and patterns of media production and consumption differ substantially, has not been ascertained.

A scene from *Shaft* offers a clear example of the dark, violent stereotype of black masculinity that Henry describes. As he attempts to obtain information to convict a racist murderer, John Shaft (played by Samuel L Jackson) is asked by Terry, his informant, to 'take care of' Malik, a black drug dealer who is recruiting her young son. While Terry looks on in approval, Shaft verbally and physically brutalises Malik in front of his gang and extracts a promise to leave her son alone. The sound of rap music fills the street, and in Malik's low-slung jeans, red cap and slouching figure we recognise the 'urban gangsta' that Henry critiques. Shaft's actions are endorsed as a white policeman drives by, sees what is going on and gives Shaft the nod. Viewers are invited to vicariously participate in the violence by being aligned with Shaft's viewpoint, and to perceive it as justified when the police sanction it.

The 'tough-guise' stereotype presents a cause for concern if it is the prevailing image of masculinity that black youths identify with. Underlying Henry's argument is the idea that identity is performative, and that black audience members are being taught to adopt the 'tough guise' that is projected on screen, ultimately harming themselves and one another. Since John Shaft is a sexy, authoritative character who is involved in situations that may resonate with the life experiences of African Americans, he is likely to have an influence on their behaviour and ideals. While urban life is very different for young black South Africans, they are still more likely to identify with Shaft than with white, middle-class characters.

The fact that the aggression is 'black-on-black' violence is also significant, especially in a film where interracial violence figures strongly and has significant legal ramifications. Speaking of the representation of black-on-black violence in 'hood movies', Denzin writes: 'In pitting dark skin against dark skin, they posited acculturation to white goals' (Denzin 2002: 6). According to Denzin (2002: 115), hood movies glorify violence, represent it as a black problem and become metaphors of black culture that lead to stigma and stereotyping. At the same time they reinforce perceptions among middle-class audiences that their attitude towards black people is correct (Denzin 2002: 116). This function of the representation of black-on-black violence is not restricted to cinematic fictions – it also pervades the news and has parallels outside the USA. As Jo-Ellen Fair and Robert Astroff (1991) have pointed out, the representation of black-on-black violence in the South African media (and subsequently abroad) was used to shift responsibility for apartheid-era violence from the white government onto the black population, concealing the government's complicity in the violence while justifying its own use of force. Black people were represented as ungovernable savages who fought among themselves rather than directing their energies into peaceful political action. This eroded the credibility of the anti-apartheid struggle. One could say that the cinematic representation of violence among black gang members fulfils a similar function, undermining the social criticism offered by rap music and deflecting attention from the social problems that give rise to gangs and drugs.

Tsotsi

Tsotsi, which won the 2006 Academy Award for Best Foreign Language Film, touches base with several of the key elements of *Shaft* outlined in Henry's work, including music, characterisation and disturbing scenes of black-on-black violence. In his epilogue to Athol Fugard's novel of the same title, Stephen Gray writes that '[i]n *Tsotsi* we have a white man's vision of the black ghetto' (Fugard 1980: 168). While *Tsotsi* is not an instance of self-representation by blacks of blacks, it is a nuanced and compassionate vision that has been interpreted with integrity and skill by another white South African, Gavin Hood, and his multicultural cast and crew. Fugard's *Tsotsi* was written and set in Soweto around 1959, but when adapted for the screen by Gavin Hood the pass laws, security police and forced evictions of the era were updated to reflect the concerns characterising South Africa 10 years after the transition to democracy. In Fugard's novel, Tsotsi saw his mother abducted in the night during a political raid, whereas the young Tsotsi in Hood's film loses his mother to AIDS (signified by her wasted, bedridden state, the fear of contagion expressed by those around her, and the omnipresent billboards stating 'We are all affected by HIV/AIDS'). In many respects the film is a very faithful adaptation of the novel, and the alterations I discuss here are raised as interesting in terms of social change (or the lack thereof), rather than as criticisms of either text.

One significant departure from the novel that does reflect changing social conditions is that the film offers broader representations of class. In the film the baby that Tsotsi attempts to care for is the child of an affluent black couple, accidentally abducted when Tsotsi hijacks the mother's luxurious silver BMW, whereas in the novel the baby is given to Tsotsi by a poor, terrified young black woman carrying her child furtively through the night in a shoebox. The baby's privileged parents, with their wine cellar and their expensive house decorated with tribal fabrics and African artefacts, are representative of the changing cultural composition of South Africa in which:

> African professionals, skilled workers and entrepreneurs benefited from the collapse of apartheid, making them the most upwardly mobile 'race' group. As a result, South Africa is currently witnessing the emergence of differentiated class structure among the African population, which includes a strong middle-class and professional stratum and a tiny economic elite. (Strelitz 2004: 630)

Like *Shaft*, *Tsotsi* depicts the ultra-violent 'tough guise' of black masculinity, embodied in the figure of the urban gangsta (the term 'tsotsi' means gangster or thug) and embellished with the familiar sounds of rap-style music and new extremes of black-on-black violence. What distinguishes *Tsotsi* from *Shaft* is the compelling use of subjective imagery, allowing the audience greater insight and empathy into characters that Fugard eloquently describes as being 'sick… from life' (1980: 152). As in the novel, Tsotsi (the gang leader, played by Presley Chweneyagae) is haunted by repressed memories of his traumatic childhood that begin to surface when Boston (Mothusi Magano), a fellow gang member, tries to figure out what made Tsotsi so coldly vicious and questions him about his past. Tsotsi summarily beats Boston to a pulp and flees the scene to avoid confronting the painful memories.

Though it does communicate what Tsotsi feels and thinks, Fugard's novel is not written as a first-person narrative, nor is Hood's film shot entirely with subjective camera. The film skilfully deploys shot-reverse-shot sequences to offer diverse perspectives on the action, and there are many moments in the film when the camera locates the audience in screen space directly inside Tsotsi's point of view, focusing our attention on what the criminal sees and hears as he stalks his targets so that, like the scene when Shaft beats Malik, the audience is caught between the experience of being a predator and being prey. The use of a richly layered soundscape with city noises and the pumping beat of the musical score (performed by popular South African musicians including Zola – a.k.a. Bonginkosi Dlamini – who also plays Fela, a rival gangster in the film) work in counterpoint with subjective and non-diegetic sounds such as the haunting melody of a woman humming and the ominous warning sound like a rattlesnake's tail which add emotional depth to the images. Even more powerful are the moments of bleak, grey, bleached-out subjective imagery from Tsotsi's memory, shot at a low level approximating the eye level of Tsotsi as a young boy watching as his mother sickens and his beloved dog is crippled. These emotively charged techniques denaturalise the 'tough-guise' stereotype, adding levels of complexity and compelling close spectatorial identification, and they encourage the audience to develop a significant investment in Tsotsi's plight and in his future possibilities.

Discussing his decisions as a director, Gavin Hood states:

> The challenge in this film was to draw the audience into the world of a very marginal, anti-social character and have them empathize with him so we shot most close-ups with eye-lines very tight to camera. I wanted to create a real sense of intimacy between audience and actor; to allow the audience to look almost directly into the actor's eyes...I hope that the audience will feel, in the quieter moments of the film, a profound intimacy with and between the characters. It was my intention that, by the end of the film, the audience would find that they have developed a genuine empathy for characters whose lives may in reality be very different from their own. (Hood 2006)

Where Fugard's Tsotsi dies tragically after coming to terms with his traumatic past and finding compassion for his fellow human beings, Hood allows Tsotsi to live and gives him the chance to repent and reform. Tsotsi's chance for a happy ending may be slim as he enters South Africa's notoriously rough penal system at the end of the film; nevertheless, the resolution ultimately reinforces the redemptive representation of black masculinity depicted in the novel and lends it a more hopeful spin in keeping with the potential and opportunities emerging in the new democracy.

As remakes and adaptations, both *Shaft* and *Tsotsi* reveal the extent to which current understandings of identity are shaped by the representations, narratives and stereotypes of the past, and by the need to reclaim and rewrite history, bringing to light images of black masculinity that were often absent, marginalised or distorted at the time. In contrast, *Hijack Stories* was from the outset written and set in contemporary South Africa and is concerned with current events and identities rather than with reworking past representations. Because of this, *Hijack Stories* arguably offers more interesting insights into black masculinity in 'the new South Africa'.

Hijack Stories

In comparing *Shaft* and *Tsotsi* to *Hijack Stories*, we see that several of the stereotypical characteristics associated with representations of black masculinity are present, but there are also noteworthy differences. Like *Tsotsi*, *Hijack Stories* is set in Soweto, a black South African township that is the cultural equivalent of the ghetto or the hood. *Hijack Stories* self-consciously borrows from the stereotype Hollywood projects, but it also questions and reworks it. While the black protagonist Sox (Tony Kgoroge) is an outsider in Soweto and can be characterised as a Coconut, the white director Oliver Schmitz could be described as something of a Wigger due to his affinity with black culture. According to the film critic Derek Malcolm, Schmitz is 'one of the few Africaans [sic] directors who has the trust of the black community in South Africa' (Malcolm 2001). Furthermore, research by Keyan Tomaselli reports on responses by South African audiences in the 1990s to Schmitz's earlier film *Mapantsula*, with black respondents indicating that the 'authentic, painful portrayal of township conditions and recognisable characters' could well have been made by a black director (1993: 72).

As a youngster, Sox lived in Soweto and Zama (Rapulana Seiphemo) was his childhood friend. Sox's family left the township and made the transition to the middle class, while Zama became a gangster. When we meet Sox at the beginning of the film, he has evidently received a good education and is at home in the affluent suburb of Rosebank, where he has a pretty white girlfriend and a career as a television presenter. Derisively called 'Mr Rainbow Nation', he habitually speaks English and has been assimilated into white culture. He wants to play a bad-ass gangsta in a television series, but he acts 'too white' in the audition and is advised to head to the township to learn to act like a real gangster. In the process he gets drawn into a world of violence and criminality, but he also reconnects with his roots.

A key scene from *Hijack Stories* shows Sox hanging around Zama's gang, hoping that participant observation will improve his chances of landing the role of gangster. The beat of hip-hop and kwaito music is persistent in the background, thumping from car stereos and kerb-side radios. When Sox sees the police approaching, he hurries away, wary of getting into real trouble and jeopardising his career. We witness Zama bribing the police to ignore his gang's criminal activities, securing the same kind of endorsement that we saw when Shaft 'got the nod' from the white policeman. Again, it is suggested that the police are willing to overlook crime and violence as long as it is contained in black neighbourhoods.

In his attempt to evade police attention Sox runs into Grace, a township girl with whom he becomes entangled (while still involved with his white girlfriend). 'Don't test me, city boy,' she says, telling him he must decide who he is and who he wants to be with, rather than keeping a foot in 'white culture' and a foot in Soweto. Sox is driving away from Grace's house when Zama abruptly drags him from the car and throws him to the ground, threatening him with a gun. Zama looms large in the frame, his eyes masked by the dark glasses that guard his expression throughout the film. He looks down on Sox cowering in the dirt at his feet and asks, 'After it is over, what do you remember?' Sox's red hat, terrified submission and inability to recall anything coherently presents a striking parallel with the scene in which Shaft intimidates Malik. Sox replies, 'I see the gun, just the gun.' 'Exactly,' says Zama. Moments later, Sox asks Zama where he and his gang learned to hijack cars at gunpoint. They joke that they learned in 'boarding school', a slang term for jail that plays on class assumptions about criminality. Then Zama admits, 'Nah, from the movies. Mostly action stuff, Sylvester Stallone.' 'Movies! You guys are shitting me,' Sox retorts. 'You learned from white actors? What about black actors? I'm talking about Wesley Snipes. You have to use nigger psychology. I thought you brothers were radical.' Having challenged their claim to authenticity, Sox demonstrates his own skill as a method actor, intimidating Zama by thrusting a gun at his temple as the film moves into menacing slow motion. Despite the 'aggressive posturing' in the scene, it is *sending up* the concept of the 'acquisition of respect through violence' (Henry 2002: 116) that characterises representations of gang subculture. Zama and Sox are actually forming a bond and learning from one another, and the film itself is launching a critique of 'cultural colonisation' that both acknowledges and challenges Hollywood's influence on black culture and identity.

In their influential article 'Colonialism, Racism and Representation', Robert Stam and Louise Spence consider how film positions spectators in relation to screen characters, stating that 'image scale and duration are intricately related to the respect afforded to a character and the potential for audience sympathy, understanding and identification' (Stam & Spence 1983: 17). The authors go on to argue that the mechanisms of cinematic identification amount to political tools that can subtly articulate discourses of race and colonialism. Films can literally make us see the world from a patriarchal or racist perspective by telling the story from a certain point of view. In *Hijack Stories* we are primarily invited to identify with Sox, but by the end we are also in sympathy with Zama, and any clear distinction between hero and villain has been undermined. This is a political move for which Schmitz has been criticised. Critics claim that the film glorifies gangsterism, reinforcing the stereotype that black townships are populated with 'career criminals whose lives revolve around drink, sex and crime' (Majola 2003). This point has some validity but, taken together, character development, plot, cinematography and other elements in *Hijack Stories* acknowledge the reality of violence in the townships while undermining stereotypes.

It is not only through visual images that the audience is positioned and the tendency to engage with or judge screen characters is manipulated. This also occurs through the use of language and music. Unlike *Tsotsi*, which is filmed for the sake of authenticity almost entirely in 'tsotsi-taal' (South African township slang), to an outsider *Hijack Stories* seems richly multilingual. It reflects the linguistic diversity of South Africa, a land with 12 national languages, including sign language, where code switching is common in everyday life and in media texts. The characters in *Hijack Stories* communicate in fluent English mixed liberally with Zulu and Afrikaans. The absence of subtitles in local prints suggests that the audience is or should be multilingual (as most South Africans are) and places the onus of understanding on the listener. This gives *Hijack Stories* an aura of authenticity and undermines the assumption of English dominance.

However, there is a residue of what Stam and Spence would term 'linguistic colonialism' beneath this multilingual veneer. The characters in *Hijack Stories* often speak English in locations and situations where black people would normally communicate in their home language. For instance, gangsters would usually only speak English if whites were present and would not be likely to address gang members in English while in Soweto. In *Hijack Stories*, the implied spectator is therefore positioned as an outsider, a white observer of black culture.[7] While this mode of address is not intentionally Eurocentric, it arises from our alignment with the storytellers: Sox, the Coconut, and Schmitz, the Wigger. The prevalence of English in *Hijack Stories* may also reflect an economic compromise in which a desire for authenticity was balanced against the recognition that the majority of audience members both locally and internationally understand English. All told, the linguistic character of the movie offers further evidence of the cross-cultural hybridisation of identity, and of the incomplete breakdown of the hierarchical opposition of black and white.

The use of music in *Hijack Stories* also expresses a sense of cultural identity and sends a political message. Gibson Boloka writes that music, as a product of popular culture, 'is a vehicle for identity construction' (2003: 103–104), while other authors contend that '[t]he culture of hip-hop has become the nexus from which youth (particularly lower income Black youngsters) can create their values, define their selfhood, and express their heightened consciousness of violence and its implications' (Richardson & Scott 2002: 185). Black African youths report that they listen to rap and hip-hop music, whether it is performed by local or foreign musicians, because it reflects their experience and connects with their sense of identity; for instance, the violence in American gangsta rap relates to violence in townships like Soweto (Strelitz 2004: 633–634).

Gangsta rap music is tightly linked to the stereotype of the tough African American male that Henry identifies in *Shaft*. Although the association between such music and the urban gangsta is also evident in African cinema, in *Hijack Stories* and *Tsotsi* one can discern distinctive local variations on the 'global' or American stereotype. The soundtracks of these films feature local hip-hop artists such as Prophets of da City along with a rap variant called kwaito performed by popular musicians like Mandoza and Zola. Kwaito is a generic hybrid that incorporates hip-hop with African rhythms, instruments and language.[8] Writing of how 'glocal' subcultures derived from the transnational musical idiom of rap emerge from global media flows, Tony Mitchell states:

> The assertion of the local in hip hop cultures outside the United States also represents a form of contestation of the importance of the local and regional dialect as a 'resistance vernacular' in opposition to a perceived U.S. cultural imperialism in rap and hip hop. (Mitchell 2000: 41)

With regard to the use of local dialects in *Hijack Stories* and its soundtrack, the use of local and indigenous languages can be understood to be 'an act of cultural resistance and preservation of ethnic autonomy' (Mitchell 2000: 52–53). Musicians act as modern versions of the African *griot* or bard, providing 'a way for youth to voice their dissatisfaction with society employing the heritage of the Black oral tradition' (Richardson & Scott 2002: 178). Thus, through its soundscape as much as through its storyline, *Hijack Stories* articulates a challenge to the dominant media culture and responds to global media flows with its own form of hybridisation and 'glocalisation', reclaiming elements of the African oral tradition that have been commercialised in gangsta rap.

Globalisation

According to Larry Strelitz, black South Africans favour 'black' programming and identify more with black protagonists, but the opportunities provided for identification in global media texts are limited and often stereotypical (see Strelitz 2002). As John Gabriel points out in his book *Whitewash* (1998), the globalisation of communication has effects that impact directly on understandings and experiences of racial identity. In a positive sense, globalisation has the potential to break down perceptions that national identity is homogeneous, and it can lead to opportunities for expression by and recognition of diasporic communities and marginalised ethnic groups (Gabriel 1998: 3). However, the media can also perpetuate stereotypes, widen the digital divide, or be used for exploitation and control in ways that discriminate on racial grounds (Gabriel 1998: 12–13).

Many Africans are painfully aware of the impact of globalisation and colonisation on traditional cultures, often through direct experience. Two conflicting discourses of globalisation have infiltrated popular culture and mainstream advertising in South Africa. One, associated with the work of Marshall McLuhan (1987) and Benedict Anderson (1991), is the concept of the global village as an imagined multicultural community in which everyone is interconnected by the media. Here globalisation is linked to a utopian vision of shared understanding and the transcendence of difference, as global citizens use the media to find unity in diversity. This discourse of globalisation is one that transnational corporations like Microsoft and Siemens have capitalised on in advertising campaigns representing global unity in a montage of images featuring traditional cultures and people of all colours and creeds smiling as they surf the Internet and send digital photos and messages across the globe using their mobile phones. The other, more dystopian discourse of globalisation is linked to the work of Herbert Schiller (1998) and is disseminated via subversive youth culture channels and the anti-globalisation movement (notably, Naomi Klein's *No Logo* [2000], and the media activism of 'culture jammers' who parody and rework commercial images). Schiller (1998: 5) argues that global media flows and monopolies of ownership bring the threat of cultural imperialism and the loss of cultural diversity. Hence the process of globalisation has, according to Schiller, contributed to the appropriation, commodification and destruction of traditional cultures via the intrusion of and dependence on Western value systems, particularly the ideology of consumerism. Not surprisingly, given the history of colonisation, the cultural imperialism thesis is the main thread that has been incorporated into the media in Africa.

Wiggers

The figure of the Wigger has been playfully incorporated into the branding strategy of Sprite, a popular brand of 'junk food' that trades in black identity. Sprite, owned by Coca-Cola, is a brand that has endeavoured to corner the black market and to become synonymous with hip-hop. It has done this through the commodification of black subculture via the sponsorship of music events (like MTV's Total Request Live), and by creating a brand identity that is associated with the subversive elements of youth culture, particularly the visible trappings of hip-hop and the knowing, postmodern cynicism about advertising that is expressed in the practice of culture jamming. One advertisement (screened on South African television in 2004) features an excellent example of the Wigger identity. In it, Sprite 'disses' whites who 'wanna be' negroes and who try to appropriate the 'cool' façade of black subculture by buying hip-hop music and clothing and imitating the way black youths dress, rap and move. Four white guys drive a convertible through deserted urban streets and car parks, their heads moving like synchronised pigeons in time to the beat of the music they are rapping to: 'rolling through the hood/up to no good'. A nonchalant group of young black men watch the white guys go by with their low-slung trousers literally falling off their hips and dragging around their ankles. They exchange knowing glances and they laugh at the Wiggers. The tag line 'See through it' references Sprite's difference from cola soft drinks. At the same time it acknowledges that black teens are the inimitable authorities on their own subculture. They are smart enough to see through impostors, to see through those who seek to appropriate and commodify elements of their identity for the sake of status or profit. Indeed, they can see through and laugh at Sprite's own advertising ploys. In this self-reflexive move Sprite cleverly co-opts dissent. It appropriates the anti globalisation rhetoric of brand parody as it has done in previous ad campaigns using the sports star Grant Hill to tell teens that they don't need celebrities to tell them what soft drinks they want, just so the brand can increase its profit margin.

Coconuts

Instead of seeing a clear dichotomy in which white is pitted against black, an idealised version of assimilation, or a vision of racial harmony in the 'rainbow nation' as might be expected in a country with a history of troubled race relations, we see the South African film, television and music industries awash with images of hybrid identities that are not wholly black or white.[9] What is emerging in popular culture – including advertising, lyrics, movies and the everyday vernacular of young people – are ways of naming and labelling that both acknowledge and resist racial integration and assimilation to white commercial culture. Notions of authenticity, cultural purity, and entrenched perceptions of the alignment between race and class are being challenged in contemporary cultural texts.

Channel O, a digital satellite television (DSTV) channel offered by the pay-TV company MultiChoice Africa, has incorporated popular terminology that references black identity and the impact of globalisation in its marketing campaigns. This channel addresses a young, upwardly mobile, predominantly black audience with advertising strategies that demonstrate an awareness of the discourse of cultural imperialism. The advertisements feature coconuts that do not have white centres: they are chocolate all the way through. In other words, Channel O represents itself as actively resisting domination by foreign media products that feature and address white people. The caption beside the chocolate-centred coconut reads, 'Channel O. Uncolonized: Get back to black', meaning that watching the black-oriented programming will enable the black audience to avoid the internalisation of white culture. Because Channel O is an expensive satellite service rather than being free-to-air, it is likely that its well-to-do audience members are (or are in danger of becoming labelled) Coconuts. In this instance the media is encouraging black viewers to return to their roots, and to value their own identities and cultures.

Despite McLuhan and Schiller's predictions, South African media texts like the Channel O advertisements (and *Hijack Stories*, as we shall see below) suggest that the globalisation of communication has not led to straightforward American dominance or to global harmony. It has resulted in a complex process of adaptation, appropriation, hybridisation and mutual incorporation of different cultural texts and traditions as the media spread different cultures around the globe. Ironically, South Africa has been accused of its own form of cultural imperialism due to the exportation of media throughout southern Africa, partly via DSTV's Channel O. Power relations of domination and dependency certainly do exist and the economic benefits of globalisation are unequally distributed, but the exchange of culture through the media is not one-way, nor is it entirely positive or negative, as the following analysis of cinematic representations of race, class and gender indicates.

Assimilation

Thus far the figures of the Coconut and the Wigger have been considered in terms of the hybridisation of identity, but further analysis is required to deliberate the extent to which screen characters who look black but act white signify assimilation to white culture. Some actors, such as Danny Glover as Murtaugh in *Lethal Weapon*, play roles in which their skin colour is irrelevant to the character's identity, culture or circumstance. In such cases the character could easily be white without altering the essence of the film. These roles can be played by actors of any colour as they are not about the specificity of black experience. Avoiding casting blacks in negatively stereotyped roles gives the appearance that mainstream films are becoming more inclusive and progressive. However, Denzin argues that this serves an assimilationist agenda and renders blackness unnoticeable, celebrating only the characteristics that support white middle-class values (Denzin 2002: 6). In the process of assimilation, black culture and identity merges with white, shedding distinctive markers of culture, religion, language and clothing (see Stam & Spence 1983: 9, 16). For this reason, Denzin speaks of black actors playing white roles as a practice that devalues racial and ethnic difference and constructs a cultural narrative that privileges 'full assimilation into the American racial order as the proper end-point for all minority group members' (2002: 6).

When Denzin says, 'Glover as Murtaugh is a black man who is not black. He is a black man who is white. Like Michael Jordan, he enacts a racially neutered identity...a black version of a white cultural model' (Denzin 2002: 100), he could equally well be referring to Kgoroge's character Sox in *Hijack Stories*. While Denzin is not wrong to suggest that 'the dream of integration' that such characters embody may be a form of 'ideological whitewash' (Denzin 2002: 60), I am not convinced that he is right to pose such a strong criticism. His critique picks up on the negative connotations that the term 'Coconut' carries, but viewing middle-class black individuals in this way risks reinforcing an oppositional form of thought in which the working-class 'tough guise' exemplified by Zama and Shaft represents authentic black identity and anything else entails selling out and assimilating into white culture. It seems unjust to call black men who don't conform to the stereotype 'white' or 'neutered' or 'sell-outs'. Such a stance runs the risk of maintaining existing power relations by suggesting an essentialist approach in which identity is indelibly marked by the colour of one's skin. Making upwardly mobile black persons (and versatile black actors) feel guilty about 'betraying their roots' may conceal an agenda that 'keeps them in their place'. In certain contexts, the term 'Coconut' can in fact carry positive connotations. It contrasts authenticity with superficial appearances, necessitating an understanding of identity that is more than 'skin-deep', and is influenced by culture.

The terms 'Coconut' and 'Wigger' signal that ethnic identity does not correspond directly to skin colour, but they also suggest a contested relationship between race and class. Philippa Gates claims that positioning black characters in a white role or context in order to make them easier for white audiences to identify with displaces the issue of race onto class: 'identification on the level of values, profession, or lifestyle is bound up in the discourse of class and becomes an important issue in the representation of black masculinity' (Gates 2004: 26). Gates argues that Hollywood predominantly represents middle-class, consumerist, American characters, thereby exoticising and 'othering' the working class:

> By placing black characters within white mainstream definitions of middle-class values, lifestyle, and profession, they are made more familiar, identifiable, and 'unthreatening'…White hegemonic power, thus, occupies the middle class and defines it as the ideal to which to aspire. The middle class then becomes a space that cannot be redefined with specificity for black culture and meaning for the 'other'; instead it can align the 'other' with the mainstream. (Gates 2004: 27)

This issue of the relationship between class and race is a complex one, and it gets to the heart of the rift in identity that labels like Coconut and Wigger have come to fill.

Stereotypes

Stereotypes organise expectations about the roles, characteristics and abilities of people in various social categories. Although stereotypes work with generalisations, they are useful as tools for cultural analysis. Henry's thought-provoking paper is essentially a critique of a negative stereotype that has been presented as something worth aspiring to. Both *Shaft* and *Hijack Stories* have attracted criticism from reviewers because they employ stereotyped representations of the 'tough guise' of black masculinity, contributing to the perception that black neighbourhoods and townships are populated with gun-toting, dope-dealing, car-thieving criminals. *Tsotsi* opts instead for a redemptive narrative and an anti-violence message, but it still works with the association between working-class black culture and criminality. Given these complexities, the function of stereotypes and their relationship to identification and identity formation among audience members warrant further discussion.

Denzin notes that one of the side effects of the global reach of the film industry is its ability to disseminate negative and inaccurate stereotypes of various ethnic identities to audiences around the world (Denzin 2002: 5). Negative stereotypes and under-representation in the media can lead to alienation. If the cost of taking pride in one's identity entails a rejection of the values and norms of the dominant group, it can foster antisocial behaviour, divisiveness or fragmentation in the community (see Huntemann & Morgan 2001: 317). This is not to suggest that the media should only represent positive images. 'Positive' images, as we have seen in the discussion of black actors playing middle-class characters, are *relative* to individual and cultural value systems. It is open to debate whether Samuel L Jackson embodies a 'negative' stereotype of black masculinity, a harmless escapist fantasy or an image of empowered masculinity. Similarly, Tony Kgoroge may be interpreted as a 'positive' image of a successful black African, or as assimilationist 'ideological whitewashing'.

Hybridity, performativity and social change

Hijack Stories critiques the idea that authentic black identity is embodied by the 'tough guise' projected in Hollywood movies. The film specifically comments on the process of role modelling and 'acting a part' based on media representations and the stereotypes that pervade popular culture. The final scene complicates notions of identity and authenticity, essentialism and performativity and invites spectators to engage with these issues in the process of identifying with the screen characters.

In the film's denouement Sox, having entered the criminal underworld, takes a bullet escaping from the police. Zama pays to have him transferred from the inadequate township clinic to a good 'white' hospital; then he literally takes Sox's place and successfully auditions for the role of TV gangster. On one level the narrative punishes Sox and rewards Zama because he is better able to play the role of 'tough guy', thereby substantiating Henry's claim that black masculinity is essentially performative. It seems that passing, dissembling and wearing masks is core to black identity and the 'tough-guise' stereotype is the ultimate performance signifying 'successful' black masculinity, as suggested by Denzin (2002: 81) and Henry (2002: 114). However, the resolution of *Hijack Stories* points to the underlying bond of solidarity that the protagonists discover, despite superficial differences of class and culture. Both Sox and Zama have, like all of us, been playing parts that were scripted for them by the circumstances of their lives and by the examples provided by their role models. These 'roles' and 'scripts' make them seem more different than they really are. Instead of materialism, vengeance and the use of black violence to combat white racism, as we see in *Shaft*, *Hijack Stories*, like *Tsotsi*, leaves us with a tentative sense of brotherhood and altruism that transcends class, ethnicity and culture.

Coconuts and Wiggers, as represented in films like *Hijack Stories* and in advertisements targeting black consumers, are alternatives to the 'toughguise' stereotype. They are middle terms that represent an uneasy synthesis of black and white, providing polysemic metaphors for contested identities. The reference to global brands of junk food signals a sophisticated awareness of the commodification of identity and the commercialisation of black subcultures, making a snide swipe at globalisation and cultural imperialism. While the Wigger comes under fire for 'buying into' black culture through the processes of appropriation and exploitation, the Coconut is accused of 'selling out' and assimilating. This suggests that there is no neutral space between pitch black and pure white. However, I have argued that these are not the only plausible interpretations. The terms also imply that skin colour does not define a person's 'inner' identity or essence. The terms 'Coconut' and 'Wigger' are evolving as they are taken up in different cultural forms and embodied in new ways by individuals. They should not necessarily be read as figures of assimilation and appropriation. The terms function as metaphors for hybrid multicultural identities, not a monoculture devoid of diversity. Sympathetic, playful representations of Coconuts and Wiggers may indicate increasing acceptance of complex multilayered identities that traverse race and class barriers, providing a stimulus for social change that equals the strong bonds of spectatorial understanding and cross-cultural identification formed in response to *Tsotsi's* compelling use of subjective sound and imagery. While there is still a pressing need to create positive black role models without sacrificing realism, reproducing conservative ideologies or promoting an assimilationist agenda, images of Coconuts and Wiggers and multidimensional black characters, however problematic, do represent a move towards the recognition of diversity and social mobility.

Notes

1   The terms 'Oreo' and 'Buppie' (black yuppie) can be used interchangeably with 'Coconut' in some contexts.

2   The terms 'black culture' and 'white culture' are neither homogenous nor unproblematic. There are significant cultural differences between members of the black Xhosa-speaking community and the coloured Afrikaans-speaking community, and between white Afrikaans speakers and white English speakers. 'Whiteness' as critiqued in Richard Dyer's (1997) research is not the focus of this chapter, nor do I wish to suggest that black South Africans represent all persons of colour. This chapter is concerned with the representation of heterogeneous identities within social groups. 'Black' is a multivalent political term that encompasses black Africans such as Zulu and Xhosa people, as well as Indians and so-called coloureds. Reflecting on the use of the term 'coloured' to describe hybrid racial identities, Zimitri Erasmus writes: 'coloured identities are not about "race mixture". Attempts to define these identities in terms of mixture buy into notions of "race purity" that can be traced to nineteenth-century European eugenicists. Since cultural formations involve borrowing from various cultural forms, and thus all identities could be seen as culturally hybrid, it should not be difficult to conceive of coloured identities as such, rather than in terms of "race mixture" or "miscegenation". They are cultural formations born of appropriation, dispossession and translation in the colonial encounter' (Erasmus 2001: 18).

3   Topdeck, a candy bar with a layer of white chocolate topping darker chocolate underneath, is another term for Wigger.

4   Matthew Henry's article (2002) offers an insightful analysis of the relationship between the original *Shaft* (directed by Gordon Parks, 1971) and Singleton's remake in 2000. In order to avoid repeating material that is already well theorised, this chapter does not address the earlier film and its sequels (which were not widely available to South African audiences), not does it cover the genre of blaxploitation.

5   The prevalence of the 'tough guise' of black masculinity in the media has also been noted by Tricia Rose (1994) and Norman Denzin (2002), among others. In Denzin's words, 'In the popular media black (and brown) youths are symbolically defined as threats to the social order…Their seemingly senseless rage and violence are directly connected to rap and hip hop culture' (Denzin 2002: 48).

6   To an extent the 'tough-guise' stereotype functions as the central term against which other representations are interpreted. For instance the film *Drum* (Maseko 2004), based on actual events and the history of the South African magazine by the same name, actively undercuts the 'tough-guise' stereotype, replacing it with an idealised representation of articulate and politically conscious black masculinity located nostalgically in a golden era of multicultural diversity in Sophiatown in the late 1950s. The film reveals the influence

of American popular culture that characterised the era as much as it does the present day through the use of music and *mise en scène*, and by casting Taye Diggs in the lead role as the heroic journalist 'Mr Drum' Nxumalo, making no move to conceal his American accent, his burnished muscles or the compromises entailed by the film's foreign finance base.

7   I am grateful to my research assistant Steve Werner for raising this point. The audience's linguistic position as outsiders is particularly noticeable in the scene in which Grace berates Sox and then translates what she said, repeating it in English for his benefit and for the audience.

8   Kwaito developed 'in response to the political, social and economic transition South Africa undertook since 1990. Kwaito represented the coming together of a number of South African musical genres (bubblegum, mbaqanga, township jazz, Afro-pop, among others) and Western genres (e.g. rhythm and blues, house, hip hop, jungle, and drum'n'bass). The word "kwaito" was Afrikaans slang derived from the word "kwaai", meaning wild or angry' (Boloka 2003: 99).

9   For example, see Steyn (2001), Roome (1997), Badsha (2003), Battersby (2003) and Haupt (2001) for analyses of race, culture and hybrid identities in the music industry.

References

Anderson B (1991) *Imagined communities: Reflections on the origins and spread of nationalism* (2nd edition). London: Verso

Badsha F (2003) Old skool rules/new skool breaks: Negotiating identities in the Cape hip-hop scene. In H Wasserman and S Jacobs (eds) *Shifting selves: Post-apartheid essays on mass media, culture and identity*, pp. 131–143. Cape Town: Kwela Books

Battersby J (2003) 'Sometimes it feels like I'm not black enough': Recast(e)ing coloured through South African hip-hop as a postcolonial text. In H Wasserman and S Jacobs (eds) *Shifting selves: Post-apartheid essays on mass media, culture and identity*, pp. 109–129. Cape Town: Kwela Books

Boloka G (2003) Cultural studies and the transformation of the music industry: Some reflections on kwaito. In H Wasserman and S Jacobs (eds) *Shifting selves: Post-apartheid essays on mass media, culture and identity*, pp. 97–107. Cape Town: Kwela Books

Denzin N (2002) *Reading race*. London: Sage Publications

Dyer R (1997) *White*. New York: Routledge

Erasmus Z (2001) Introduction: Re-imagining coloured identities in post-apartheid South Africa. In Z Erasmus (ed.) *Coloured by history, shaped by place: New perspectives on coloured identities in Cape Town*. Cape Town: Kwela Books and SA History Online

Fair J-E & Astroff R (1991) Constructing race and violence: US news coverage and the signifying practices of apartheid. *Journal of Communication* 41(4): 58–74

Fugard A (1980) *Tsotsi*. London: Rex Collings

Gabriel J (1998) *Whitewash: Racialized politics and the media*. New York: Routledge

Gates P (2004) Always a partner in crime: Black masculinity in the Hollywood detective film. *Journal of Popular Film and Television* 32(1): 20–30

Haupt A (2001) Black thing: Hip-hop nationalism, 'race' and gender in Prophets of da City and Brasse vannie Kaap. In Z Erasmus (ed.) *Coloured by history, shaped by place: New perspectives on coloured identities in Cape Town*, pp. 173–191. Cape Town: Kwela Books and SA History Online

Henry M (2002) He is a 'bad mother*$%@!#': Shaft and contemporary black masculinity. *Journal of Popular Film and Television* 30(2): 114–119

Hood G (dir.) (2005) *Tsotsi*. Momentum Pictures

Hood G (2006) *Tsotsi* official website. Accessed 25 July 2006, www.tsotsi.com

Huntemann N & Morgan M (2001) Mass media and identity development. In D Singer and J Singer (eds) *Handbook of children and the media*, pp. 309–321. Thousand Oaks, CA: Sage Publications

Klein N (2000) *No logo*. London: HarperCollins

Majola B (2003) *Role reversal in* Hijack stories. Accessed 6 May 2003, http://www.southafrica.info/what_happening/arts_entertainment/hijackmovie.htm

Malcolm D (2001) *Hijack stories* (film review) in the *Guardian*. Accessed 15 May 2003, http://film.guardian.co.uk/cannes2001/storynav/0,7677,491363,00.html

Maseko Z (dir.) (2004) *Drum*. Armada Pictures International

McLuhan M (1987) *Understanding media: The extensions of man*. London: Ark

Mitchell T (2000) Doin' damage in my native language: The use of 'resistance vernaculars' in hip hop in France, Italy, and Aotearoa/New Zealand. *Popular Music and Society* 24(3): 41–54

Richardson JW & Scott KA (2002) Rap music and its violent progeny: America's culture of violence in context. *Journal of Negro Education* 71(3): 175–192

Roome D (1997) Transformation and reconciliation: 'Simunye', a flexible model. *Critical Arts* 11 (1–2): 66–94

Rose T (1994) *Black noise: Rap music and black culture in contemporary America*. Hanover, NH: Wesleyan University Press

Schiller H (1998) American pop culture sweeps the world. In R Dickson, R Harindranath and O Linne (eds) *Approaches to audiences*, pp. 2–14. London: Arnold

Schmitz O (dir.) (2001) *Hijack stories*. BSkyB, British Screen, Deutsche Bank

Singleton J (dir.) (2000) *Shaft*. Paramount Pictures

Stam R & Spence L (1983) Colonialism, racism and representation: An introduction. *Screen* 24(2): 3–20

Steyn M (2001) *Whiteness just isn't what it used to be: White identity in a changing South Africa.* Albany: State University of New York Press

Strelitz L (2002) Media consumption and identity formation: The case of the 'homeland' viewers. *Media, Culture and Society* 24(5): 459–480

Strelitz L (2004) Against cultural essentialism: Media reception among South African youth. *Media, Culture and Society* 26(5): 625–641

Tomaselli K (1993) Colouring it in: Films in 'black' or 'white' – reassessing authorship. *Critical Arts* 7(1): 61–77

16 The media and the Zuma/Zulu culture: An Afrocentric perspective

Simphiwe Sesanti

In 2005, following the dismissal from his position as South Africa's deputy president, Jacob Zuma was charged with corruption. The state alleged that he had entered into an agreement with a French company that would give him R500 000 in exchange for protection against the government's arms-deal investigation and to buy further 'help' from Zuma (*The Star* 2006b). Towards the end of 2005, Zuma was slapped with another charge, this time for allegedly raping the daughter of an African National Congress (ANC) comrade and family friend.

The corruption and rape trials of Jacob Zuma ushered in a great deal of focus on African culture as a result of statements made by observers and Jacob Zuma himself. Among the claims made by observers was that the reason that some people showed sympathy for Zuma amid the allegations of corruption had to do with what the Zulus call *ukusizelana* – 'empathy' or 'mutual help'. Explaining this concept, Protas Madlala, an independent analyst, said that to the 'typical Western person, the African person must look very stupid supporting a man charged with corruption. But it's exactly this traditionalism that has been overlooked. Africans look at the bigger picture, not because they condone corruption, but because they weigh other things in balance' (*Mail & Guardian* 2005b). Arguing along similar lines that issues involving Africans must be seen not from the Eurocentric view but from an Afrocentric angle, Dr Mathole Motshekga, an advocate of the high court and a cultural activist, noted that Zuma, in invoking 'Zulu culture', was 'completely correct [to base his argument on culture] because South Africa interprets human rights through Europeanised views[;] that's why there is a problem' (*Mail & Guardian* 2006d). Further, Motshekga insisted that Zuma was correct because the cultures of citizens play an important role in informing the society about its own cultural and moral values, pointing out that human rights 'don't fall from heaven but are products of this world and need to be observed through it' (*Mail & Guardian* 2006d). This chapter examines the manner in which the media have dealt particularly with Zuma's rape case, with special reference to his claims that his conduct was partly influenced by Zulu culture. I argue that while both Madlala and Motshekga are correct in saying that African issues need to be weighed on the basis of Afrocentricity, the Zuma cases have exposed how culture can be misappropriated and misused in the cause of selfish interests. It is not the purpose of this chapter to say whether Zuma was guilty or innocent. That is for the courts to decide, and they have pronounced themselves. The focus of this chapter is on the cultural claims and how the media have dealt with these claims. My approach is first to outline the role of the media in multicultural societies. Recognising that sometimes the 'universal' or general theories tend to fail the 'particular', I then bring in Afrocentric perspectives, linking them to the role of the media. But because many people either do not know or misunderstand and misinterpret what Afrocentricity stands for, I explain what it is, trace its historical foundations and indicate how it is linked to the role of the media.

The role of the media in multicultural environments

In multicultural societies, the media should serve as the screens on which diverse images can be projected for all to see (Croteau & Hoynes 2001). They are expected to reflect on the range of creative visions and ideas that constitute a society's vibrant cultures (Croteau & Hoynes 2001). The media should enrich public life by promoting the notion that public dialogue matters, and by providing spaces where people can both see parts of their own experiences and be exposed to ideas, experiences and cultures that they do not encounter in their day-to-day lives (Croteau & Hoynes 2001: 28). What all this means is that, as Fuller observed (in Kovach & Rosenstiel 2003: 143), the media need to reflect their communities deeply, failing which they will not succeed in meeting these expectations. That is, if the media do not challenge their community's values and preconceptions, they will lose respect of their community by failing to provide the honesty that the media are expected to offer.

While the foregoing describes a desirable state of affairs, years of colonialism in South Africa have made this a difficult task. Africans' cultural values, except in distorted and limited forms, have not found space in the South African media. In terms of content, as Fourie (2002) points out, the mainstream media have catered mainly for the white population's Western history, culture and economic and political interests. It is as a result of this tendency and against this background that Afrocentricity emerged in scholarship.

Afrocentric perspectives

Asante (1998: xii–xiii) defines Afrocentricity as a moral as well as an intellectual location that posits Africans as subjects rather than as objects of human history and that establishes a perfectly valid and scientific basis for the explanation of African historical experiences. Afrocentricity places African ideals at the centre of any analysis that involves African culture and behaviour (Asante 1998: 2). Among the criticisms levelled against Afrocentricity is the charge that it is a yearning for a fantasised, idealised past of racial grandeur, a romanticisation of Africa and a preoccupation with an imagined way of life (Gerald 1995). It has been charged – in the African American context – that Afrocentricity seeks to make Africa for African Americans what Europe is for white Americans. This criticism comes against assertions such as those of Keto that the 'Africa-centred perspective of history rests on the premise that it is valid to posit Africa as a geographical and cultural starting base in the study of peoples of African descent' (Obeyade 1990).

The charge that Afrocentricity is a yearning for a fantasised, idealised past of racial grandeur and that Afrocentrists tend to romanticise Africa is strongly rejected by Afrocentrists. In refuting the allegation, Williams pointed out that in researching African history, Afrocentrists 'wanted to know the whole truth, good and bad. For it would be a continuing degradation of the African people if we simply destroyed the present system of racial lies embedded in world literature only to replace it with glorified fiction based more on wishful thinking than on the labours of historical research' (Williams 1987: 19). Therefore, Afrocentricity is not a glorification of pigmentology or, more specifically, blackness, as critics have made it out to be, but rather a theory rooted in the history, culture and world-view of Africans (Okafor 1993). Afrocentricity is a rigorous intellectual exercise, and one becomes a theorist by training and study, not merely by wearing a Kente cloth or dashiki, for instance, even though the wearing of such is aesthetically pleasing (Bekerie 1994). As a response to Eurocentric hegemony, Afrocentricity demands that African culture must be treated as original, unique and distinct (Hoskins 1992).

While it is true that Afrocentrists seek to make Africa a point of reference just like Eurocentrists make Europe a point of reference, the reasons are not the same. Historically, Europe has imposed itself upon the rest of the world, both physically and intellectually. In ideological terms, Rodney has observed that 'Europe has assumed the power to make decisions within the international trading system' – an excellent illustration of that being the fact that 'the so-called international law which governed the conduct of nations on the high seas was nothing else but European law. Africans did not participate in its making, and in many instances, African people were simply the victims, for the law recognised them only as transportable merchandise' (Rodney 1982: 77). While the Eurocentric paradigm has often assumed a hegemonic universal character, and European culture has placed itself at the centre of the social structure, becoming the reference point or the yardstick by which every culture is defined, the Afrocentric perspective seeks to liberate African studies from the Eurocentric monopoly on scholarship, and thus to assert a world-view through which Africa can be studied objectively (Obeyade 1990). Afrocentric scholars emphasise that it is not the aim of Afrocentricity to replace Eurocentrism as a universal perspective; rather, Afrocentricity recognises the validity of other non-hegemonic perspectives, strongly insisting that hegemonic or alleged universal tendencies, regardless of their source, are unacceptable (Bekerie 1994; Obeyade 1990). The forces that brought about liberation fought for the destruction of every form of injustice and for concrete changes in black people's lives.

In his book *Beyond the Miracle: Inside the New South Africa*, Sparks notes that, on seeing South African president Thabo Mbeki and Zimbabwean president Robert Mugabe smiling and holding hands on a CNN newscast, he 'cringed' as the 'sickening scene appeared on screen again and again over the following days and weeks' (Sparks 2003: 268). In explaining his reaction, Sparks observes that even though he knew that it was culturally acceptable for African men to hold hands, he could not understand how 'Mbeki with his British education and understanding of the Western world' could allow 'this impression of smiling support for Mugabe's outrageous action to be broadcast globally' (2003: 268).

In response to Sparks's assertion, it is appropriate to raise the question of why Sparks was so preoccupied with Mbeki's 'British education and sophisticated understanding of the West'. Why did Mbeki's African cultural practice of holding hands with Mugabe weigh less as compared to Mbeki's understanding of the Western world? The answer to this question is not difficult to understand, and that is because to a very great extent issues in the world are judged and measured against the standards of Europeans. Afrocentricity rejects this tendency. Afrocentricity calls for the placement of African people in the centre and a mode of thought and action in which the centrality of African interests, values and perspectives predominates (Asante 2003: 2). It seeks to uncover and use codes, paradigms, symbols, motifs, myths and circles of discussion that reinforce the centrality of African ideas and values as a valid frame of reference for acquiring and examining data (Winters 1994).

While journalism is a universal profession with many common principles and values that are shared worldwide, Kasoma (1994: 9) argues in line with Afrocentricity that African journalists must look to their own moral philosophy for those principles and values that will elevate African journalism. This is because every society is characterised by social values and it is these values that predispose journalists to act in a certain manner under certain conditions (Kasoma 1994: xvii). As things stand, what is required of African journalists by Kasoma is very difficult to achieve. As Mokegwu (2005) points out, a cursory look at the different curricula of various media programmes on the African continent gives the impression that many African institutions are striving to produce clones of American or Western journalists in many parts of Africa. It is significant to note that the journalism values that Europeans and Americans brought to Africa were embedded in their cultural history and traditions (Kasoma 1994: 29). One such value was not to violate individual rights, meaning that the individual, rather than society, carried more importance.

Kasoma (1994: 19) observes that to a great extent the postcolonial period in Africa has been marked by syndromes of 'do what the authorities tell you and behave like Western journalists'. As an alternative to this approach, Kasoma (1994: xvii) recommends that African culture should set the boundaries of what the media can do and with what effects. In line with this alternative, Mphahlele (2005: 331) notes that the role of black journalists is to help develop an African consciousness, or African ways of perceiving which expand to the outer reaches of the world from a position of self-knowledge. Afrocentricity advances the need to look at Africa's cultures and history from their own centres or locations (Bekerie 1994).

On the issue of 'African culture', I have come across a number of academics who have argued that there is no single 'African culture' to speak about but many 'African cultures'. Advocates of this argument say that to suggest the existence of 'African culture' implies that Africans are a homogeneous lot. In responding to this position, Afrocentrists have offered different answers. In insisting on the use of the term 'African culture', Williams (1987: 161) says that he is referring to those 'things which are characteristically African, practically universal among them from one end of the continent to the other and which thereby indicated an ancient common culture in a common center of Black Civilization'. This is said with full cognisance of the fact that among Africans, some practices are 'peculiar to one or more tribes'. But other Afrocentrists have rejected outright what is referred to as 'tribal culture'. Mphahlele (2002: 87) states: 'We on the other hand never recognized tribal culture. We believe in African culture that cuts across artificial boundaries. African culture has roots going down several centuries deep...At the deepest spiritual level African culture unifies the whole continent.' Though recognising the diversity existent in African culture, Davidson (1994: 18) has noted that the 'socializing process in Africa suggests an underlying unity of culture'. This chapter is based on the approach advanced by Williams and Davidson in relation to the issue of African culture.

Remarking on the status of African culture, Nyamnjoh (2005: 3) observes that African world-views and cultural values are doubly excluded: first, by the ideology of hierarchies of cultures, and second, by cultural industries more interested in profits than in the promotion of creative diversity and cultural plurality. The Afrocentric approach seeks to do away with this. Afrocentricity recognises Kupe's (2003) argument that the media in Africa should endeavour to create and circulate the broadest possible range of images of African cultures, lifestyles and aspirations that affirm African ways of life and the humanity of Africans as part of the global family of human beings. This is because, as Wilcox (1977: ii) correctly observes, the press as an institution should reflect and gauge the entire social and political structure of a nation, and in many ways the press is a barometer of a nation's values and socio-economic life. Kareithi's (2005: 14) observation that the African press should train future journalists to emphasise stories of interest to their community of audiences, rather than to those that promote the financial interests of the institutions for which the journalists work, is in line with the Afrocentrists' view of the role of the black press.

The need to use African culture as a reference point in the development of democracy in South Africa is best captured by Nhlapho (2000: 137), who has noted that if a 'culture of rights' is to take root in South Africa – and in a sustainable fashion – the association of human rights with Western thought and world-views is not helpful for the general populace. In order for black journalists to be able to promote democracy effectively in South Africa, they have to show an acknowledgement and understanding of African culture, failing which they will lose credibility. Similarly, in assessing the progress or lack of democracy in this country, black journalists need to demonstrate an understanding not just of African culture, but of the history of Africans along with the values that informed their march to progress before and after European colonialism. In noting the inseparability of history and culture, Cabral (1979: 141) states: 'Culture is simultaneously the fruit of a people's history and a determinant of history, by the positive or negative influence it exerts on the evolution of relations between man and his environment and among men or human groups within a society, as well as between different societies.' Nhlapho (2000: 143) correctly observes that with the 'possible exception of a few scholars to whom a deep understanding of African value system seems important, much of the condemnation appears to come from people with little real understanding of African culture, and sadly, with no intention of attaining such understanding'.

Ukusizelana – empathy/mutual help

In further explaining the concept of *ukusizelana*, Mike Zuma, who at the time of speaking to the *Mail & Guardian* was a guest at a cocktail party organised by the Friends of the Jacob Zuma Trust, noted that in the 'Zulu tradition, if my neighbour is in financial trouble I will give him a cow that he can milk to feed himself and his family…I can't look at another suffering, knowing that I have much to give. As Zulus, we trust you until you stab us in the back' (*Mail & Guardian* 2005b). The practice of *ukusizelana* is not an exclusively Zulu practice but an African practice. In isiXhosa it is known as *inqoma*; in seTswana it is called *mafisa*. In fact, Africans believe that, as they say in Nguni languages (isiXhosa and isiZulu), *umntu/umuntu akalahlwa* – you don't abandon a human being when the going is tough for him or her. You embrace a person. But that is not the same as declaring a person innocent, as the supporters of Zuma have done – to the extent of accusing others of political conspiracy. Zuma stood accused of stealing from the state. The use of African culture by Zuma supporters has been rather selective. In line with the Africans' code of conduct there is a common African saying to the effect that 'it is far better to beg than to steal' (Mutwa 1998: 632). Moreover, as Mutwa points out, when an African turns criminal he does so as a direct challenge to constitutional authority or society in general. *Ukusizelana* or *inqoma* is not, as Zuma supporters have made it out to appear, to turn a blind eye to a wrong done or alleged.

The 'father–daughter relationship' claim

Hegel once commented that among Africans 'moral sentiments are weak, or more strictly, non-existent' (Magubane 1999: 24–25). Much literature has since emerged to refute Hegel's claims. But in November 2005, some may have felt that Hegel had been vindicated when claims of rape were made by a 31-year-old woman against the ANC deputy president Jacob Zuma. This was especially so when the media mentioned that the woman had a father–daughter relationship with Zuma. Before Zuma confirmed that he did, in fact, have sex with the woman – which he claimed was consensual – the complainant's mother thought that her daughter was being used against Zuma for political reasons (a conspiracy within the ANC). A family friend who requested anonymity commented thus: 'She is still in a state of shock. She can't believe that her child has been used for political reasons. Zuma is like a father to her daughter. How can someone rape his own daughter?' (*Mail & Guardian* 2005a). How, indeed, could a father rape his own daughter? In his defence in court, Zuma said that it was 'very wrong to say that there was a father–daughter relationship. There was never such a relationship' (*The Herald* 2006). Zuma made this claim despite the fact that he and the complainant's father had a comradely relationship (*Sowetan* 2006b). In delivering the verdict:

> the judge rejected the woman's claim that she and Zuma had a father–daughter relationship – which the state suggested explained why she "froze" during the alleged rape. The judge pointed out that Zuma had testified that he did not even call his own daughter "daughter" and had never referred to his accuser that way. He found further support for Zuma's version in the fact that he had not seen the complainant for 14 years since they became acquainted in the late 1990s. What was more, Zuma's children did not know her. (*The Star* 2006c)

The media's engagement with African cultural issues

Judge Willem van der Merwe can be forgiven for not understanding culturally determined social relations among Africans. In the first place, the fact that Zuma did not refer to his own daughter as 'daughter' did not make her any less his daughter. In African culture (this includes Zulu culture), you refer to men or women who are of the same age as your parents or older as 'fathers' or 'mothers' (*baba/mama* in isiZulu). This is especially so in the case of friends that are close to one's parents. It was in this context that both the complainant and her mother regarded Zuma as a father to the complainant. In African culture one does not have to know an older person to refer to him or her as 'father' or 'mother'. Such respect is automatically expected. In this regard, black African journalists failed to educate the public. Failure on the part of black African journalists to deal with this African cultural aspect emboldened Zuma's brother, Michael Zuma, to declare: 'In Zulu culture, one does not go around referring to all elders as uncles because an uncle has to be one's mother's brother' (*The Star* 2006a). While it may be conceded that, as Michael claimed, in African culture people do not randomly refer to men as uncles, it is true that in a relationship where a man and a woman's families are so close, to the extent of regarding each other as one family, the offspring of such men and women refer to the adults involved as 'uncle' or 'aunt'. The relationship does not have to be biological to qualify for such status. Furthermore, although Michael might not be aware of this, Jacob Zuma certainly knows that in exile, children were taught to refer to their parents' male comrades as 'uncles'. This practice aimed at strengthening bonds and forging close relationships among South Africans who found themselves away from home. This historical context was sadly very absent in the media.

Aware that those who presided over the trial were ignorant of African culture, Zuma took full advantage of the situation: 'I accept that learned counsel might not know Zulu customs and traditions…and it happens in our custom, even if you don't know a girl…she can be dropped at home and you have to pay lobola…you have to' (*Sowetan* 2006a). It was with this knowledge of white ignorance of African culture that Zuma, in explaining why he had condomless sex, could boldly state that 'in Zulu culture, you don't just leave a woman in that situation, because if you do then she will even have you arrested and say that you are a rapist' (*The Herald* 2006). But thanks to the *Mail & Guardian*, Zuma did not get away with his false claims. The *Mail & Guardian* travelled to Nkandla, Zuma's village in KwaZulu-Natal, and found that Zuma's claims had nothing to do with Zulu culture. A 'prominent Zulu cultural activist who preferred to remain anonymous' noted: 'What Jacob Zuma and the complainant did is not Zulu culture. Zulu culture tells us to respect each other and I don't think JZ showed any respect to the complainant nor to himself. At this point Zulu culture failed, but Zuma culture conquered' (*Mail & Guardian* 2006d). Mbongeni Biyela, an Inkatha Freedom Party supporter who expressed a liking for Zuma, whom he likened to Jesus, and who believed that Zuma 'is a victim of a plot driven by a perceived Xhosa faction within the African

National Congress', disputed Zuma's Zulu cultural claim: 'I don't think that's Zulu culture, I think it is more Zuma culture' (*Mail & Guardian* 2006a).

Zuma's Zulu cultural claims have revealed that it is not only white people who are unaware of African culture, but Africans as well. Commenting on Zuma's Zulu cultural claims, Professor Silawu Ngubane of the University of KwaZulu-Natal remarked: 'Our culture is not written and there are no books that we can go back to for reference on such issues. JZ's statement on Zulu culture is new to me. I'm not aware of such a thing in Zulu culture' (*Mail & Guardian* 2006d). Professor Ngubane may not be aware of written books that deal with African culture, but there are such books, one of them being Credo Mutwa's *Indaba, My Children*: 'In Zululand, all adulterers, perverts and rapists were given an ant-death. This simply consisted of opening an anthill and the condemned man was spread naked over it with his hands and feet pegged to the ground and honey spread on his belly' (Mutwa 1998: 631). Except for the *Citizen*'s editorial, I have not come across a single newspaper that pointed out that Zuma's having sex with the complainant was adulterous. The *Citizen* correctly noted:

> Although Judge van der Merwe was forthright in his condemnation of Zuma having sex with someone so young, not his regular partner and who is HIV+, no mention was made that Zuma is married. This was not within the judge's ambit, but we wonder whether the women and men who celebrated the acquittal would condone immorality in their own relationships. (*Citizen* 2006).

In Zulu culture, adultery was punishable by ant-death, and for Zuma to have a sexual relationship with his accuser was, as the *Citizen* pointed out, adulterous.

Zuma's reference to Zulu culture as opposed to African culture was very calculated. First, it was a subtle ban on non-Zulus from commenting on the issue since they would be reluctant to speak about what they do not know. Second, it was meant to appeal to the sentiments of his ethnic group for sympathy and solidarity. Similarly, Zuma refused to condemn his supporters who wore a T-shirt emblazoned with '100% Zulu Boy' (*Special Assignment* interview, 10 May 2006), so as not to alienate his ethnic base. Media reports are awash with comments from Zulu-speaking Africans to the effect that 'We Zulus want him to take the chair when Mbeki leaves and we feel the Xhosas don't want that' (*Mail & Guardian* 2006b). Others have claimed that the 'ANC was established by Zulus, then the Xhosas took over and now they don't want the Zulus back in the seat' (*Mail & Guardian* 2006c). In the *Special Assignment* interview, Zuma lent credence to this ethnic conspiracy when he said that there were individuals in the ANC who were motivated by ethnicism even though the ANC as an organisation was not tribalistic. The interviewer failed to pursue Zuma to back up his claims on this issue. *Sowetan* columnist Justice Malala noted that when President Thabo Mbeki relieved Zuma of his duties as deputy president, 'many ignored the corruption allegations against Zuma and started a whispering campaign about his dismissal being tribally related' (Malala 2006: 13). Commendably, Malala also pointed out that the 'irony in the allegations about Zuma's so-called mistreatment because he is Zulu is that his greatest support came from unions and ANC formations in the Eastern Cape, which is almost entirely Xhosa. But this fact seems to have gone straight over the heads of those alleging the tribal conspiracy' (2006: 13). The *Sowetan*'s political editor, Ido Lekota, did well on this issue in calling on Zuma to 'stand up and be counted as a leader who will not allow his supporters to fan the fires of ethnicity or undermine the constitution' (Lekota 2006). It must be conceded that Zuma did voice objection to those who burnt his rape complainant's picture and swore at Mbeki, but he fell short of criticising ANC Youth League spokesperson Zizi Kodwa for calling the vice-chancellors of the University of Cape Town and the University of South Africa, Professor Njabulo Ndebele and Prof Barney Pityana, respectively, 'witches' only because they dared question Zuma's conduct. Calling Kodwa to order was the real test for Zuma, and he failed it. That is because calling ordinary masses to order is easy, but calling his main backers to order would have required courage, and in this regard Zuma lacked it.

Referring to people as 'witches' (*abathakathi* in isiZulu and isiXhosa) has serious implications in African culture. A witch is an evil person. In the past people associated with witches met violent deaths. It took Moshoeshoe (Sotho king) and Shaka (Zulu king) to stop the killing of those associated with witchcraft in African communities (Du Preez 2003: 17; Kunene 1984: 162–163). At the same time it is a historical fact that when king Dingane of the amaZulu was faced with the menace of colonialist settlers whom he referred to as 'witches', he called for their killing. But even in our own time some people have been cruelly killed mob-justice style on allegations of witchcraft. In using the metaphor of witches when referring to Ndebele and Pityana, Kodwa, deliberately or not, was provoking and inciting violence against these academics for exercising freedom of speech – a constitutional right in South Africa. I did not hear any voice in the media reacting to this misconduct.

Conclusion

This chapter has sought to argue that calls for Africans to be judged on the basis of their own cultural bases are valid. But because of our colonial history, many in the media are ignorant of African culture, and this includes Africans themselves who are media practitioners. As a result of ignorance of African culture, many media practitioners have found themselves ill-prepared to deal with the task of engaging those who seek to invoke culture to justify their actions. But newspapers such as the *Mail & Guardian*, the *Sowetan* and the *Citizen* did very well in helping South Africans differentiate between the real and the imagined, between falsehood and the truth. In the case of the *Mail & Guardian*, the newspaper gave voice to the people of Nkandla, Zuma's village, to verify Zuma's cultural claims. In this regard, the *Mail & Guardian* fulfilled the media's role of acting as a screen on which people who knew little or nothing about Zulu culture could be afforded the opportunity of learning something new. The newspaper enabled its audience to make an informed judgement about Zuma's claims. The *Sowetan* played a big role in disproving claims by some of Zuma's supporters that the Xhosas wanted to destroy Zuma's chances of becoming the ANC president. Black journalists failed, however, in vigorously dealing with the 'father–daughter' relationship between Zuma and the rape complainant from an African cultural perspective. The *Citizen* did well in pointing out that even if Zuma had consensual sex with the rape complainant – as he claimed – it was an immoral act since he was not married to the woman. In this regard, backing from black African journalists from an African cultural perspective was sadly lacking. It was necessary because the *Citizen* could easily be dismissed as moralising from a Christian or Western basis. This chapter has resisted attempts to misappropriate African cultural symbols to the Zulus. This is not the same as delegitimising authentic and specifically 'Zulu' practices. Rather, the effort has been to show that certain practices attributed exclusively to the Zulus are indeed African, and that they should not be misinterpreted and misrepresented. In showing respect for and recognition of Zulu identity, this chapter has also argued against some claims in the name of Zulu culture and history. In order to empower media practitioners, this chapter is adding its voice to those who, like Mokegwu (2005), have argued that the time is ripe for a more vigorous incorporation of intercultural communication in media programmes at institutions of learning.

References

Asante MK (1998) *The Afrocentric idea*. Philadelphia: Temple University Press

Asante MK (2003) *Afrocentricity: The theory of social change*. Chicago: African American Images

Bekerie A (1994) The four corners of a circle: Afrocentricity as a model of synthesis. *Journal of Black Studies* 25(4): 131–149

Cabral A (1979) *Unity and struggle: Speeches and writings*. New York and London: Monthly Review Press

Citizen (2006) Zuma's lack of morality. 10 May

Croteau D & Hoynes W (2001) *The business of media: Corporate media and the public interest*. Thousand Oaks, CA: Pine Forge Press

Davidson B (1994) *The search for Africa: A history in the making*. London: James Currey

Du Preez M (2003) *Pale native: Memories of a renegade reporter*. Cape Town: Zebra Press

Fourie PJ (2002) Rethinking the role of the media in South Africa. *Communicare* 23(1): 17–40

Gerald E (1995) Understanding Afrocentrism: Why blacks dream of a world without whites. *Civilization* 2(4): 31–39

Hoskins LA (1992) Eurocentrism vs Afrocentrism: A geopolitical linkage analysis. *Journal of Black Studies* 23(2): 247–257

Kareithi P (2005) Rethinking the African press: Journalism and the democratic process. In P Kareithi and N Kareithi (eds) *Untold stories: Economics and business journalism in African media*. Johannesburg: Wits University Press

Kasoma PF (ed.) (1994) *Journalism ethics in Africa*. Nairobi: African Council for Communication Education

Kovach B & Rosenstiel T (2003) *The elements of journalism*. London: Atlantic Books

Kunene M (1984) *Emperor Shaka the great: A Zulu epic*. London: Heinemann

Kupe T (2003) Introduction: The role of the media in building democratic African societies – challenges and opportunities for the African media. In GL Nassanga (ed.) *The East Africa media and globalisation: Defining the public interest*. Kampala: Makere University

Lekota I (2006) Zuma supporters fan fires of ethnicity and disrespect. *Sowetan*, 24 February

Magubane BM (1999) The African Renaissance in historical perspective. In MW Makgoba (ed.) *African Renaissance*. Cape Town: Mafube and Tafelberg

Mail & Guardian (2005a) Cops, NIA, sucked into 'rape' war. 18–24 November

Mail & Guardian (2005b) Riding on Zulu empathy. 18–24 November

Mail & Guardian (2006a) Nkandla: Our fortunes are tied to Msholozi. 7–12 April

Mail & Guardian (2006b) This mama is speaking lies. 24–30 March

Mail & Guardian (2006c) Who are the friends of JZ? 10–16 March

Mail & Guardian (2006d) Zuma culture, not Zulu culture. 7–12 April

Malala J (2006) Slipping tribal masks. *Sowetan*, 13 February

Mokegwu M (2005) African union: Xenophobia as poor intercultural communication. *Ecquid Novi* 26(1): 5–20

Mphahlele E (2002) *E'skia*. Johannesburg and Cape Town: Kwela Books in association with Stainbank and Associates

Mphahlele E (2005) *Es'kia continued*. Johannesburg: Stainbank and Associates

Mutwa C (1998) *Indaba, my children: African tribal history, legends, customs and religious beliefs*. Edinburgh: Payback Press

Nhlapho T (2000) The African customary law of marriage and the rights conundrum. In M Mamdani (ed.) *Beyond rights talk and culture talk*. Claremont: David Philip

Nyamnjoh FB (2005) *Media, belonging and democratization: Africa's media, democracy and the politics of belonging*. London: Zed Books

Obeyade B (1990) African studies and the Afrocentric paradigm: A critique. *Journal of Black Studies* 21(2): 233–238

Okafor V (1993) An Afrocentric critique of Appiah's *In my father's house*. *Journal of Black Studies* 24(2): 196–212

Rodney W (1982) *How Europe underdeveloped Africa*. Washington, DC: Howard University Press

Sowetan (2006a) Cows on standby if lobola needed. 6 April

Sowetan (2006b) I do not have HIV, says Zuma. 5 April

Sparks A (2003) *Beyond the miracle: Inside the new South Africa*. Jeppestown: Jonathan Ball Publishers

The Herald (2006) Rape charges part of a political plot. 4 April

The Star (2006a) Joy and celebration in village where Msholozi was born. 9 May

The Star (2006b) Judge hammers state in Shaik appeal. 27 September

The Star (2006c) Poetic judge paints the true picture. 9 May

Wilcox D (1977) *Mass media in black Africa*. Sandton: Southern African Freedom Foundation

Williams C (1987) *The destruction of black civilization: Great issues of a race from 4500 BC to 2000 AD*. Chicago: Third World Press

Winters CA (1994) Afrocentrism: A valid frame of reference. *Journal of Black Studies* 25(2): 170–190

17 Black masculinity and the tyranny of authenticity in South African popular culture

Adam Haupt

In this chapter I contend that Oliver Schmitz's *Hijack Stories* (2000) and Gavin Hood's Academy Award-winning film *Tsotsi* (2005) provide meaningful insights into the construction of black masculinity in post-apartheid cinema, media and youth culture. A key argument that this chapter advances is that South African cinema and media place a great amount of currency on that version of black masculinity that embodies the heterosexual, streetwise gangster. I explore this idea through a discussion of the both popular and controversial TV drama *Yizo Yizo* and its use of kwaito as a means of accessing its primary audience, township youth. This sets the scene for a discussion of *Tsotsi*'s use of kwaito as a means of authenticating its narrative. It also opens up the possibility of thinking about actor and kwaito star Zola's rise to fame since he first landed the role of the villain Papa Action in *Yizo Yizo 2* in 2001, as well as his presence in *Tsotsi* as the successful gangster Fela and his dominance on the film's kwaito soundtrack. The tendency to privilege specific types of black masculinity is not unique to South Africa and parallels Hollywood representations of African American men as well as the worldwide appeal of gangster rap,[1] which has come to signify the pervasiveness of US cultural imperialism. In this regard, I examine debates about the use of hip-hop in African American cinema to develop key themes or merely for aesthetic purposes. The key issue that is raised here is that the image of the black man as thug/gangster/tsotsi has been commodified to such an extent that the agency of black male subjects/artists to construct their own personal trajectories is somewhat curtailed by market forces.

My analysis of *Hijack Stories*, which Schmitz wrote with poet Lesego Rampolokeng, will reveal that the film provides one with the opportunity to think about the media's role in constructing limited subject-positions for black subjects. This happens via the characters Sox (Tony Kgoroge) and Bra Zama[2]

(Rapulana Seiphemo), who swap roles by the end of the narrative. Sox is an actor who cannot secure the role of Bra Biza, a gangster in a TV drama, because he is no longer connected to his old neighbourhood, Soweto. After securing a privileged education, he now lives in Rosebank and is a continuity presenter for SABC1. Sox is one of SABC1's 'Simunye' presenters, a 'multicultural'/'rainbow' cast that features Camilla Walker, a white presenter who speaks Zulu. According to Sox's uncle, Bra Dan, his mother worked hard to ensure that he had access to an education that would ensure his upward mobility. However, it is this position of class privilege that makes it difficult for him to land the role of Bra Biza, who, one imagines, embodies all of the qualities that his mother had hoped he would never internalise. In Sox's meeting with Bra Zama and his crew at a shebeen, a key theme emerges. The scene starts with a shot of a TV broadcast of Sox and Walker introducing a music video, 'Hey Ta Da', by legendary hip-hop crew Prophets of da City (POC). As the presenters' lead-in ends, Grace (Moshidi Motshegwa) makes fun of Sox:

> **Grace:** [Sings SABC1 pay-off line] Simunye. We are one [laughs at Sox].
> **Joe:** We live in a fucked-up society, you know that?
> **Zama:** So what do you want, Mr Rainbow Nation?
> **Sox:** Come on, man. It's just a job, you know. I'm actually practising for the audition to play Bra Biza. I haven't got the job yet. I just want to study the real…gangster just to make it more convincing.
> **Zama:** Bullshit.
> **Sox:** I just want to base it on the right person.
> **Zama:** You think I'm like Bra Biza?
> **Sox:** It looks like it.
> **Zama:** Bra Biza?
> **Sox:** Ja.
> **Zama:** Bra Biza? On TV?
> [Cut to scene of Bra Biza terrorising a neighbourhood.]
> (Schmitz 2000)

The film commences with a scene from the show for which Sox is auditioning; we see Bra Biza and his crew hijacking a car from a businessman who is also humiliated in the process. Biza's villainous and apparently legendary character does not appear to be very different from the arch-nemesis Papa Action of *Yizo Yizo*, who was played by Ronnie Nyakala in the first series and then by Zola (Bonginkosi Dlamini) in the second series. The role of Papa Action was thus established by the time Zola secured the role, much like the role of Bra Biza already being established by the time Sox endeavours to land the part. The shebeen scene makes it quite apparent that Grace, Zama, Fly and Joe do not buy into SABC1's attempts to sell the ideal of South Africa as a 'rainbow nation' to its viewers. As suggested by a subsequent scene in the car with Zama, Fly and Joe, this ideal is plausible only for more privileged individuals, like Sox, who live in Rosebank. 'Mr Rainbow Nation' is therefore not 'authentic' in the eyes of Zama and his crew – nor in the eyes of a shebeen patron in Grace's street when he chases Sox out of the shebeen yard and down the street. But these characters are not the only ones who demand authenticity. The casting director who is tasked with finding the actor who will play Bra Biza frames Biza in the following manner:

> **Casting dir:** OK, Sox. Here we go. Bra Biza. The meanest gangster who ever lived. He rapes. He kills. He takes no prisoners. I want anger, I want viciousness, I want horror. You ready?
> **Sox:** Aha.
> **Casting dir:** And action.
> **Sox:** [Nothing.]
> (Schmitz 2000)

In short, Sox's experience of class privilege does not allow him to portray this role convincingly. It is his mother's wish for him to escape the unstable social and schooling environments that Zama experienced during the final years of apartheid that now counts against him in post-apartheid South Africa. The thug or tsotsi now appears to have the most currency in the entertainment industry, and this sends Sox into an identity crisis. This also explains why it is Zama who succeeds in landing the role of Biza by the end of the film, thus blurring the boundary between the 'real' and 'reel'.

Hijack Stories raises important insights about the gangster genre that could best be understood in relation to Schmitz's earlier film *Mapantsula*, which he co-wrote with lead actor Thomas Mogotlane. *Mapantsula* tells the story of a self-serving tsotsi, Panic (Mogotlane), who is rather unconcerned with the climate of political protest against the apartheid regime. This changes after he is arrested along with political activists and is expected to betray them in his interrogation sessions. In her discussion of *Mapantsula*, Lesley Marx notes that the gangster occupies an ambiguous position with regard to capitalism and democracy:

[G]angster films bring to the centre those marginalized, exploited and abused by a capitalist system. They expose inequities and the frustration and violence bred by political, social and economic inequality. But their gangster heroes aspire to the goals set by the system: goals of material wealth, political power and sexual control. (Marx 1996: 11)

This ambiguity can also be seen in gangsta rap music, which places an obsession with 'bling' (overt expressions and performances of opulence) at the forefront of its lyrics and music videos. Marx refers to Keyan Tomaselli's claim that *Mapantsula* should not merely be read as a film about 'black exploitation' but should also be seen as a condemnation of capitalism (Marx 1996: 19; Tomaselli 1993: 72). The class divide that marginalised characters such as Panic experience is thus racialised, thanks to the system of apartheid, and *Hijack Stories* continues to explore some of the issues that were raised by *Mapantsula*. In this regard, Schmitz has the following to say about *Hijack Stories*' key thematic concerns:

It's exactly this issue of 'what has changed' and thinking about a new generation that prompted me to look at a story of youth and how they are dealing with issues of identity. Either to hang on to the past and its bad memories and not wanting to or being able to move on, or wanting so badly to put all that in a closet and lock the door, to change your identity completely...that's really what the movie is about. (SA Film 2004)

To some degree this film examines the agency of its key characters and the choices that they make. It is Zama who offers a critique of the class contradictions that persist in South Africa's democratic dispensation. In the scene before Sox's first lesson in being a car thief, he tries to get to the bottom of Zama's life as a criminal:

Sox: So how did you get like a gangster, nê?
Zama: He thinks we are criminals.
Sox: No, man, you're a gangster, right? So what's the problem?
Zama: Do I look like a dirty criminal?...The criminals are the people you live with.
(Schmitz 2000)

Zama's response to Sox's line of questioning reveals that he is at odds with the 'new' South Africa and official attempts to position him either as a happy citizen of the 'rainbow nation' or as a criminal who acts without a clear sense of purpose beyond personal enrichment. His answer implies that he recognises that the systematic race and class injustices experienced under apartheid continue, partly because of the country's adoption of neo-liberal economic policies such as the Growth, Employment and Redistribution strategy (Bond 2001: 41). In a turn of events that confirms Marx's discussions of the ambiguous position occupied by gangsters, Zama leaps at the chance of auditioning for the role of Bra Biza and slipping into Sox's Rosebank life. It is Zama's ability to bring authenticity to the portrayal of Bra Biza that parallels Zola's rise to stardom after he secured the part of Papa Action for the second series of *Yizo Yizo*.

A key element of Zola's success as a musician and actor is his ability to project the image of the authentic gangster/thug/tsotsi. It was this ability that was critical to the success of *Yizo Yizo 2*. Clive Barnett writes that the show 'was developed with the primary aim of generating wide public debate about educational issues, and of changing the attitudes and behaviour of students, teachers and principals, and parents' (2004: 259). One of the show's 'defining characteristics' was therefore its claims to authenticity and believability (Smith 2003: 250). René Smith contends that the 'prevalence of YFM and the local music genre, kwaito, constitutes a deliberate effort on the part of the creators of the series to represent real township life experiences' (2003: 250). Zola's record label, Ghetto Ruff, played a role here, as it released the *Yizo Yizo 2* soundtrack, which features key kwaito artists such as Mandoza, Arthur, Ishmael, Wanda, Thembi Seete and, at this stage, relative newcomer Zola. This sort of approach, which was devised in the first series, paid off because *Yizo Yizo* attracted 1.2 to 2.1 million viewers, making it the most-watched programme on South African TV (Barnett 2004: 259). Smith claims that there was a great deal of reciprocity between the series and the album and that they therefore contributed to each other's success: 'Viewed as a celebration of youth culture, as an incredible asset to black South African youth culture, and as a form of resistance, kwaito thus is an integral part of representations of "real-life" township experience' (Smith 2003: 250). The notions of affirmation and resistance in kwaito are partly to be credited to its use of *scamtho/tsotsitaal*, which largely incorporates non-standard dialects of Zulu, English, Sesotho and Afrikaans. One could argue that *scamtho* functions like the non-standard dialect of Afrikaans, *gamtaal*, as employed by Cape-based rap groups POC and Brasse vannie Kaap (BVK) – and, in recent years, by a host of younger artists such as Jitsvinger, Terror MC, Die Man Van Staal, Marlon Burgess and Berni Amansure (of Godessa).

This dialect of Afrikaans has typically been seen as a marker of 'coloured' identities within apartheid discourse and continues to be seen as such within certain circles. Here, the reference to *gamtaal* points to the biblical story of Ham and is meant to refer to the shame of 'miscegenation'. In an earlier work (Haupt 2001), I argue that POC and BVK employ *gamtaal* (or what POC calls 'ghetto code') to challenge the legacy of apartheid and racism by aligning this dialect with the discourse of Black Consciousness. POC went so far as to include rappers Ishmael and Junior so that the crew could rap in indigenous languages on songs such as 'Zulu Muffin' off *Age of Truth*. Interestingly, Junior later went on to form the kwaito crew Boom Shaka and Ishmael joined kwaito crew Skeem, which was known for affirming black popular cultural history of the 1980s with the hit song 'Waar Was Jy?' Russell Potter's discussion of the subversive potential of non-standards of English in relation to hip-hop creates a sound understanding of the politics of *scamtho* and *gamtaal*:

> On the one hand there are hegemonic vernaculars, such as 'Received Standard English' (the term postcolonial critics use to highlight the arbitrary status of the privileged 'standard' dialect of English); posed against them, appropriating and subverting their claims to 'standardness', are what I would call *resistance vernaculars*, since even to speak these vernaculars is in a crucial sense to make inroads against the established power-lines of speech. (Potter 1995: 57–58)

In the cases of *gamtaal* and *scamtho*, we find that identities that were negated within neocolonial discourses are validated by the appropriation of the very dialects that were negated within these dominant discourses. The subversion of standard dialects of Afrikaans, English, Zulu or Sesotho subverts the power of historically dominant discourses that positioned subjects as marginal and therefore without agency. *Yizo Yizo* thus went some way in validating not merely a music genre and cultural expression, but a range of black identities that were emerging from the ruins of the monolithic discourse of apartheid.

However, despite the series' success at affirming identities and encouraging debates about the key issues that affect the lives of young township youth, an SABC evaluation of *Yizo Yizo* found that it was 'significantly less successful in stimulating discussion around issues of rape and sexual harassment' (Barnett 2004: 263). One can make sense of this finding by considering René Smith's claim that *Yizo Yizo* commodifies violence in its attempts to set up its narrative as 'real' or authentic:

[T]he contradictions of representing gender-based violence in the series lie at the precise moment of representation where violence is commodified in the process of representing the 'real'. In this regard, certain representations of violence within *Yizo Yizo* are substantiated by the dramatic intent of the series (violence as a 'cliffhanger'). (Smith 2003: 261)

Thus, the very narrative conventions of TV dramas, such as cliffhangers, undermine the creators' attempts to present key social concerns in ways that would engage audiences, who would watch the programme in order to be entertained more than out of a sense of obligation to deal critically with key social problems. Despite the success of the series, there is therefore a measure of uncertainty about its success in challenging conservative gender politics. Barnett contends that '*Yizo Yizo* uses a popular television format to build a large audience, but in "leaving" the classroom and by deploying the aesthetics of popular culture it relinquishes a significant degree of control over the communication process in educational broadcasting' (2004: 264). In the end, there is no certain way of ensuring that the show's key objectives have been met and that the work as a whole has been interpreted in ways that facilitate positive social change, especially with regard to gender politics.

The appeal of kwaito in authenticating the TV programme may play a role here, as the music continues to circulate long after the series has come to an end. This positive spin-off for kwaito has also been beneficial to Zola, who managed to build on his initial success with *Yizo Yizo 2* by securing the role of Fela in *Tsotsi* as well as by featuring prominently on the soundtrack that was released by Ghetto Ruff. Ghetto Ruff has done well in capitalising on the film's success by including kwaito music videos in the film's DVD package, by releasing a *Tsotsi* double-disc music CD as well as by releasing a *Tsotsi* music video DVD that includes a bonus audio disc. The kwaito soundtrack is put to good use in *Tsotsi* and does much to set the scene for the development of the film's narrative. The film, based on the novel by playwright Athol Fugard, tells the story of a tsotsi who finds redemption after hijacking a car without realising that he has also stolen a baby in the process. We meet Tsotsi (Presley Chweneyagae) and his crew, Aap (Kenneth Nkosi), Boston (Mothhusi Magano) and Butcher (Zenzo Ngqobe), in the first scene of the film. Aap and Butcher are rolling dice, while Boston looks on as he reads the newspaper and Tsotsi is standing in the door, gazing out of his home in a Soweto informal settlement. Butcher ends the game and asks Tsotsi what they are doing that night. Tsotsi turns in a close-up shot and

Zola's 'Umdlwembe' starts playing. The song continues as they make their way out of Tsotsi's home and down the street past the communal tap where Miriam (Terry Pheto) is queuing for water along with other residents, towards the railway station. As they make their way past the shebeen, a smartly dressed Fela (Zola) and his crew are standing next to his Audi cabriolet. An amused Fela says, 'Hah...the little gangster. You learn to drive yet?' Tsotsi does not reply as they pass Fela's crew except to show Fela the finger. All the while Zola's 'Umdlwembe' is pumping and we cut to an aerial shot of the immediate neighbourhood. It becomes apparent that the plan is to seek out a commuter from the city as he makes his way from work with his pay packet. 'Umdlwembe', which many kwaito fans would recognise from Zola's debut album by the same title, does much to set the scene for the impending train murder and robbery scene:

> Qafutushu kulobumnyama
> Sesiyobona bafana baseZola
> Bamba imoto abone ukuti umzala ufuna amagegeba
> Bheka la phezulu kwamatafula
> Sesi busy siyaxovaxova
> Slender hoza la bheka la ngithi hoza uzosijoina
> Siphete indlela yomlilo hluvum iyashosholoza
> Buddi lam...omunye munye futi ubuza iholo enotywala
> Masifika kuleyo 'ndawo kuzosala amafelokazi
> He kuyoo'kufa intsizwa kuyosala aboguluva masifika kuleyo 'ndawo

> [Out of the darkness
> We are going to meet the boys from Zola
> Steal this car so that he can see that Cuz wants money
> Look what's on top of these tables
> We are busy enjoying ourselves [binge drinking]
> Slender come here come join us
> We have a road of fire [car]
> My friend...another one just asked where is the alcohol
> When we get there the women will be left behind
> Men are going to die but the real thugs will stay behind when we get there].
> (Zola 2005)

The song's narrative does not relate directly to the train scene, but it does convey the idea of dangerous thugs who are about to wreak havoc. It also lays down the priorities of the crew – the 'acquisition' of money, women, wine and a love of violence – thereby making the characters' gender politics quite clear. Unlike *Yizo Yizo*, it is not merely the use of kwaito that authenticates the film in the minds of South African audiences, but also the presence of Zola in the film, albeit in a supporting role, and on the soundtrack. In his own words, in South Africa Zola 'is more famous than the Cullinan Diamond' (Lynskey 2006). He adds: 'And I have no bodyguards. A top celebrity like me can walk into a party and of course I'll sign a few autographs, but there's no trouble' (Lynskey 2006). In fact, it is Zola who features most prominently on the covers of the *Tsotsi* music CD and music video DVD. Viewers are meant to recognise him and remember his role as Papa Action in *Yizo Yizo*; his celebrity status as a kwaito star lends credibility to *Tsotsi*. Many viewers may also remember that he starred in director Zola Maseko's *Drum* (2004) as the Sophiatown tsotsi Slim, who has two memorable scenes in the film. The first takes place when a gangster challenges Slim to a knife fight and he butchers his opponent effortlessly and without much fanfare. The second memorable scene occurs toward the end of the film when Slim stabs protagonist Henry Nxumalo (Taye Diggs) to death, at the behest of apartheid henchman Major Spengler (Greg Mellville-Smith). In fact, one might say that Zola may be well on his way to being typecast as a gangster in his fledgling film career. According to Dorian Lynskey, Zola does not 'mind that most of his screen roles are mobsters' (Lynskey 2006). He rationalises the issue in the following way:

> I've got a chance to portray what I could have been, and kids who know me can say, 'Hey, hold up. He made different decisions, so maybe we can follow him.' I took Zola as a stage name to make a point: I may come from Zola but I am a man apart. (Lynskey 2006)

Zola seems to be employing the sort of logic that Smith describes in her analysis of *Yizo Yizo*. He gets to become a celebrity and role model by creating the image of the authentic thug/tsotsi. As a whole, the introductory sequence in *Tsotsi* is stylishly shot and edited and has the appeal of slick Hollywood gangster films or hip-hop and kwaito videos that focus on what the late gangster rapper Tupac Shakur dubbed 'thug life'.

Tupac Shakur's song 'Bury Me a G', off the album *Thug Life: Volume 1*, offers one example of the ways in which 'thug life' is represented by gangsta rappers. In the song, he describes the life of a thug in a way that appears to be celebratory:

> Thinkin back, reminiscin on my teens
> A young G, gettin paid offa dopefiends
> Fuckin off cash that I made
> Nigga what's the sense of workin hard if you never get to play?
> I'm hustlin, stayin out 'til it's dawn
> And comin home, at 6 o'clock in the mornin
> Hands on my glock, eyes on the prize
> Finger on the trigger when a nigga ride
> Shootin craps, bustin niggaz out the do'
> Pick my money off the flo', God bless the tre-fo'
> Stuck on full, drunk again
> Sippin on gin with a couple of friends (ha ha)
> Say them Thug Life niggaz be like major pimps
> Stickin to the rules wasn't made for sin (beotch!)
> And if I die, let it be
> But when they come for me, bury me a G
>
> [Chorus 2X: 2Pac]
> I ain't got time for bitches
> Gotta keep my mind on my motherfuckin riches
> Even when I die, they won't worry me
> Mama don't cry, bury me a G
> (Shakur 1994; transcription by Original Hip-Hop Lyrics Archive)

'Umdlwembe' and 'Bury Me a G' are similar in that they articulate an obsession with accumulating wealth, drugs and alcohol as well as sexual power. The performance of masculine aggression is a key aspect of both texts, along with an expression of a kill-or-be-killed credo. Another key song on the *Tsotsi* soundtrack, 'Ghetto Scandalous', expresses the same kind of masculine aggression: 'Ghetto scandalous, ghetto scandalous / He lova tata icova sesiya vela / Don't fuck with us buddi lam [Ghetto scandalous, ghetto scandalous / Thugs better take cover cause we are already here / Don't fuck with us, friend]' (Zola 2005). The roles that Zola portrayed in *Yizo Yizo*, *Drum* and *Tsotsi* as well as *Hijack Stories*' reference to Bra Biza speak well to the aggressive and often nihilistic lyrics performed by Shakur in 'Bury Me a G'. The key exception is that Schmitz and Rampolokeng's script actually appears to be commenting on the values that the media privilege in their representations of black men. For many audiences who are already familiar with Zola's work as an actor and musician, Gavin Hood's theme of redemption could be lost as they engage with the film via a different route: the kwaito soundtrack that works well with the film's visual aesthetic and is also meant to authenticate Hood's project. Hood's dramatic intent is thus potentially undermined within certain communities of viewers. The sorts of nihilistic and rhetorically violent music produced by Shakur (and echoed by Zola in 'Umdlwembe' and 'Ghetto Scandalous') have made their way into Hollywood representations of African Americans.

In his essay on John Singleton's remake of *Shaft* (2000), Matthew Henry writes that African American films have used rap and hip-hop for 'aesthetic and thematic purposes' (2002: 114). In essence, it is the 'tough guise' that has a great deal of currency in popular culture (Henry 2002: 116). According to Henry:

> [a] particular type of black masculinity – one defined mainly by an urban aesthetic, nihilistic attitude, and an aggressive posturing – has made its way into the cultural mainstream in the last two decades. Although there are numerous contributing factors, this image of black masculinity has developed largely as a result of the commodification of hip-hop culture and 'videomercials' that sell it. More specifically, it is the result of the popularity of the urban 'gangsta' and his embodiment in the gangsta rap of artists such as Dr. Dre, Ice Cube, Snoop Doggy Dog and Tupac Shakur. (2002: 114)

Bakari Kitwana concurs with this perspective when he argues that nothing 'was more effective at reinforcing the association between nihilism and the new Black culture than the Black gangster films' portrayal of the thugged-out young Black male' (Kitwana 2002: 130). Kitwana contends that this new culture sees 'any remnants of Black consciousness and/or community-centered activism as outdated and out of touch' (Kitwana 2002: 133–134). The belief that the gains of the civil rights movement have not 'secured our inalienable rights' is the key idea that drives this perception of the previous generation (Kitwana 2002: 133). Kitwana's interpretation is interesting in view of the fact that Tupac Shakur's mother, Afeni, was a member of the Black Panthers. However, this may not apply to the dynamics of kwaito in the South African context, where black South Africans constitute the majority. At least in principle, the political gains made by black South Africans differ from those made by African Americans. Still, there may be an overlap in terms of a newer generation of artists' perceptions of the 'struggle' generation. Angela Impey suggests that kwaito's 'materialistic tendencies are towards materialistic, hedonistic, and flighty preoccupations, and groups such as Boom Shaka appeared to unleash amongst young black consumers an explosive desire to disengage from the long years of oppression and protest of the apartheid era' (2001: 45). In a sense, kwaito liberates artists from 1980s protest culture (Impey 2001: 49). It is debatable just how widely this sense of 'liberation' has been felt by artists and music fans. Artists such as Thandiswa and her band Bongo Maffin have produced Afrocentric music and continue to enjoy much support. Thandiswa's debut album *Zabalaza* offers one example of certain post-apartheid artists' continuing engagement in critical social reflection. On the title track of her album, Thandiswa provides the following criticism of the class divide in South Africa:

> I rise early in the morning
> To stand at a street corner
> With my child at my back
> Asking for money
> I walk the dead of the night
> Trying to forget
> Wanting to forget
> All my pain
> This should not be happening
> At my father's house
> Why is it this way
> At my father's house
> For their blood and their tears
> For their struggle and pain
> Cause they gave up their lives for this
> And it makes me want to scream
> When I see things this way
> Come and see what I see every day
> Ooh! Babies going to bed hungry
> Ooh! My peers are dying of AIDS
> Ooh! We sleep in shacks
> At my father's house
> (Thandiswa 2004)

'Zabalaza' speaks to the racialised class disparities that persist in South Africa after apartheid, despite the sacrifices that citizens made to achieve a democratic dispensation. The perspectives that Thandiswa presents in this song resonate well with Oliver Schmitz's questioning of 'what has changed' in post-apartheid South Africa via his film *Hijack Stories*. Therefore, Thandiswa – much like many South African hip-hop artists such as POC, Black Noise, Godessa, BVK, Tumi and the Volume, Hymphatic Thabz, Terror MC and Zubz – offers one example of a new generation of artists who continue to raise some of the same key social or political concerns that were raised in 1980s protest culture. Her work is significant because Bongo Maffin is considered to be one of the pioneer bands – along with Boom Shaka and solo artists such as Arthur, who now owns the key kwaito label 999 – during kwaito's ascendance in the 1990s. If Impey's argument is accepted as true of a very general trend on the kwaito scene, this explains only one dimension of the phenomenon that Henry describes.

Ethne Quinn (2000: 198) offers a description of the 'burden of representation' in African American cultural practice and criticism in order to make sense of gangsta rap's often offensive and abrasive lyrical content. This burden was intense because African Americans have 'achieved the most in the cultural sphere while at the same time being the most relentlessly typecast in dominant image repertoires' (Quinn 2000: 198). The burden of representation took the form of two discourses: the discourse of authenticity demanded that representations should depict black culture as it exists in reality, whereas the second discourse characterised every representation as acts of delegation – black artists and intellectuals were thus expected to accept the burden of speaking for the black community in every instance (Quinn 2000: 198–200). Black artists and critics thus faced a great deal of pressure to always represent black subjects in ways that were considered to be authentic, representative and positive – this makes sense of many hip-hop references to the notion of 'keeping it real' or 'representing', which have been parodied by Sasha Baron Cohen's Ali G persona as well as by Sprite's soft-drink TV advertisements over recent years. Quinn (2000: 201–202) argues that gangsta rappers were aware of this burden of representation. She contends that they employed the discourse of authenticity while also reneging 'on the contract to act as delegates, self-consciously repudiating uplifting images of black life in a gesture of rebellion and dissent' (Quinn 2000: 202). The rebellion that Quinn refers to manifests in the rejection or critique of representations of race found in texts such as the 1980s sitcom *The Cosby Show*, which offers an example of the ways 'positive images of black life could serve neoconservative ends' (Quinn 2000: 200). However, gangsta rap's gesture of refusal to be 'race delegates' only went so far in that 'the discourse came to be redirected toward a heightened investment in "representing" an image of working-class black male youth' (Quinn 2000: 205–206). In the end, these artists found that they 'have been so successful in portraying, manufacturing, and selling ghetto imagery that market demands have channelled black commercial output into certain narrowly defined coordinates' (Quinn 2000: 210) – thanks to the initiative seized by gangsta rappers, the market is now typecasting black artists. Quinn aptly labels this outcome the 'tyranny of authenticity' and recalls Stuart Hall's claim that 'antihegemonic practice can pull in a rightward as well as left direction' (Quinn 2000: 210, 212; Hall 1996: 436; 1992: 30–32).

In his discussion of the aesthetics of rap music, Mtume ya Salaam argues that when 'the profit-oriented major labels entered the rap scene...[the] fertile breeding ground for good rappers disappeared' (1995: 304). Ya Salaam maintains that this '"business first" attitude has contributed to (some would say *created*) what has become the single biggest threat to the continued development of rap music as an art form – the preoccupation by many rappers with sex and violence' (1995: 304). However, this preoccupation has paid off for many gangsta rappers, who have accumulated great wealth as well as viable Hollywood film or television careers. Tupac Shakur, Snoop Doggy Dog, Ice Cube[3] and Ice-T[4] have gone on to star in films such as *Boyz n the Hood, XXX2, Johnny Mnemonic, Starsky and Hutch, Bullet, Gang Related, Juice* and *Gridlock'd*. Interestingly, many of these films which feature a great deal of violence, offer representations of black masculinity that are consistent with Matthew Henry's claims. It is in this sense that very narrow versions of black masculinity secure upward mobility for black male subjects – the notion of 'the tyranny of authenticity' thus functions as a metaphor that signals the power of the mainstream US entertainment industry in creating limited means through which subjects' commercial success or credibility can be obtained. The gatekeeping function of the US industry has a spillover effect beyond its borders in that Hollywood trends are communicated by a range of media, including fashion magazines (such as *Cosmopolitan, Elle* and *Vanity Fair*) as well as celebrity and tabloid titles (such as *Heat, People* and *You*).

Quinn, Ya Salaam and Henry's perspectives on sex, violence, gangsta rap and the construction of black masculinity seem to relate rather well to the work of Zola, which has foregrounded the image of the thug to great effect. Their perspectives also confirm Schmitz's implicit critique of the currency of one version of black masculinity in the post-apartheid media landscape. As my earlier discussion of Quinn, Henry and Kitwana's work on African American youth culture implicitly suggests, the priorities of South African producers and artists seem to be set by mainstream US media corporations. Here, the influence of American popular culture as well as counter-cultures on black South African cultural expression should not be underestimated. Black South African artists' fascination with African American cultural expression dates back to the 1940s (Coplan 1985: 148; Haupt 2001: 175). Dave Coplan contends that only 'a few jazz musicians of the 1940s brought anything identifiably South African to their playing of American swing' (1985: 148). This had much to do with the internalisation of negative colonial assumptions about rural African subjects and, later on, apartheid policies that pushed for 'separate development' (Coplan 1985: 148). Black South African artists' relationship with African American jazz musicians ultimately had a positive effect because this mutual engagement led 'South African jazzmen to re-examine their own indigenous resources' (Coplan 1985: 189). This affirmation of black African identities and cultures took on an added significance with the rise of Black Consciousness (BC) in Africa and in African American communities in the 1970s. Elsewhere, I argue that it is this history that sets the precedent for South African hip-hop artists such as POC looking to BC-oriented hip-hop crews from the US – such as Public Enemy, Afrika Bambaatha or KRS-One – as well as key BC icons such as Malcolm X for inspiration in their anti-apartheid performances (Haupt 2001: 176). However, black urban youth's fondness of African American popular culture and counter-cultures developed within the broader context of the rise of US cultural imperialism. In the years that preceded the decline of apartheid, the SABC shifted from offering just one TV channel to presenting its viewers a choice of three TV channels: TV1, TV2 and TV3. While these channels seemed to be interpellating viewers along the lines of language, race and culture, what is more significant for the purposes of this chapter is that SABC programming made use of a large amount of US content. By the late 1980s, viewers watched a range of shows, such as *Solid Gold, Fame, The Cosby Show, Miami Vice, Wiseguy, Spencer For Hire, A Man Called Hawk, The Tracy Ullman Show, Cheers, Hill Street Blues, Knight Rider* and *Magnum PI*, to name a few. In an informal discussion I had with former POC MC and producer Shaheen Ariefdien, he recalled that a similar pattern was emerging in the time that he spent in the former apartheid homeland Bophuthatswana (with his musician father Issy Ariefdien). The homeland's TV and radio programming offered consumers an impressive range of entertainment that was mostly obtained from the US. His way of making sense of these changes in South Africa, which had introduced TV programming only in the late 1970s, was that the apartheid government was dazzling its citizens with US entertainment while the townships burned; in short, it was offering citizens spectacle as a means of diversion. At the same time, the previously isolated apartheid state was now also giving viewers a glimpse of less-restricted societies abroad as well opening the door to US cultural imperialism.

At this point, I should add that my understanding of cultural imperialism in the context of this chapter steers clear of the sorts of problems identified by Larry Strelitz. Strelitz takes issue with critics of US cultural imperialism who rely on cultural essentialist assumptions. He claims that this 'bi-polar vision pits a culturally destructive and damaging "global" against the "local", with the latter seen as a site of "pristine cultural authenticity"' (Strelitz 2004: 626). The work of Nancy Morris supports Strelitz's critique when she suggests that 'the fear of the dilution of cultural purity' is unfounded because 'identity and the practices and symbols that express it are never pure and "uncorrupted"' (Morris 2002: 280). In this regard, Morris offers the term 'glocalisation' as a means of explaining how local communities continue to possess agency in the face of cultural imperialism. She defines the term as:

> mutual cross-influences, as powerful 'top-down' globalizing forces such as corporate marketing and international political movements are in turn shaped by 'the bottom-up processes of localisation'...MTV provides an example of media glocalization and indigenization. While incorporating multicultural influences into its US programming, it is also responding to viewer resistance to its international approach in Asia and Europe by producing increasingly localized programming for those regions. (Morris 2002: 281)

Local examples of this approach are the decision of US corporations such as Kentucky Fried Chicken (KFC) and McDonald's to include South African characters/stereotypes in their advertisements. These include KFC's 2005 TV commercial in which former rugby star Naas Botha plays the role of a sports commentator (a role that he actually did assume after he retired as a rugby player) who speaks with a Durbanite Indian accent; McDonald's 2005 ice-cream advertisement that features an Indian father and his son playing in the park; as well as a range of Coca-Cola commercials that feature South African scenes and characters. One could also argue that the South African versions of the British quiz show *The Weakest Link* and the American reality TV show *The Apprentice* offer further instances of glocalisation and indigenisation. However, what Morris appears to be describing is the realignment of marketing strategies by global corporate entities to extend or consolidate their revenue streams in local markets; local communities do not necessarily benefit from the accumulation of these corporations' profits and are seen merely as potential consumers for a range of brands and products. In some respects, it is arguable that debates about the protection of national identities and the hybridisation of cultures deflect attention from a paramount concern: capital flight from economies of the southern hemisphere to economic hegemons, such as the US and EU countries. Claims about indigenisation or glocalisation have real value only when local producers control or own the means of production as well as distribution and local economies benefit from such action. The examples that Morris offers fall short in this regard and could be viewed as co-option of marginal identities by mainstream corporate strategies. The production of films and music by marginal South Africans could be offered as instances where Morris's arguments seem plausible. The indigenisation of elements of US hip-hop in South African kwaito and hip-hop could be viewed as one positive case in point – particularly when US cultural production is indigenised or glocalised in order to speak to cultural and political concerns that affect South African citizens on a local and global level. However, the limits of this argument are revealed when kwaito or South African hip-hop employs *scamtho* or *gamtaal*, thereby affirming historically negated black discourses and identities, but then also replicates the kind of problematic gender politics that is to be found in gangsta rap or gangster films.

Smith's concerns about *Yizo Yizo*'s failure to interrogate its own problematic gender politics resurfaces via *Tsotsi*'s use of music as well as the construction of Zola as a celebrity figure, notwithstanding the fact that he also hosts a reality TV show, *Zola 7*, along the lines of e.tv's *Let's Fix It* or Oprah Winfrey's Angel Network. This particular show, which attempts to improve the lives of less-fortunate Zola fans, would perhaps not have been possible had Zola not already achieved celebrity status. To be fair, some of Zola's other songs, such as 'Don't Cry', are critical of black-on-black violence in much the way that *Tsotsi*'s train murder scene offers critical commentary.[5] But the key questions that remain are exactly what version of masculinity guarantees young male subjects success in the realm of popular culture, and who sets the agenda for such subjects' personal trajectories?

Acknowledgements

Thanks to Ade Ed Camngca for transcribing and translating Zola's lyrics as well as for providing interpretive insights into Zola's use of dialects; to Neelika

Jayawardane and Kathleen McDougall for helpful discussions on this topic; and to Jane Stadler for inviting me to conduct lectures on *Hijack Stories* and for pointing me to Matthew Henry's work.

Notes

1   Gangsta rap is one version of hip-hop that embodies gangster values and thematises the aspirations and struggles of gangsters. This version of hip-hop is widely accepted to have taken root on the West Coast of the USA. East Coast hip-hop was born in the East Bronx of New York and has historically been spoken of as the home of 'conscious'/ socially-aware hip-hop that attempts to speak to experiences of racism in the USA. Early hip-hop artists who are credited with the birth of 'conscious' hip-hop include Afrika Bambaatha, Public Enemy and KRS-One. In South Africa hip-hop artists who have been regarded as 'conscious' include Black Noise, Prophets of da City, Brasse vannie Kaap, Tumi and the Volume, Godessa, Zubz and Jitsvinger. See the following texts for information on hip-hop in and outside of the USA:
George, Nelson. *Hip hop America*. New York: Penguin, 1998.
Rose, Tricia. *Black Noise: Rap music and black culture in contemporary America*. Hanover and London: Wesleyan University Press, 1994.
Mitchell, Tony. 'Another Root – Hip-hop outside the USA'. In Tony Mitchell (ed.) *Global noise: Rap and hip-hop outside the USA*. Middletown, CT: Wesleyan University Press, 2001.

2   Bra Zama is named after the TV game show and scratch card Zama Zama. The story of his name becomes an important element of the film's turning point. Zama held up a truck transporting Zama Zama cards and since then there has been much speculation in the neighbourhood about what really happened to the cards.

3   Ice Cube went from performing 'I Wanna Kill Sam' on his album *Death Certificate* in 1991 to playing a US government agent in *XXX2* in 2005. The subject of 'I Wanna Kill Sam' is the US government, personified by Uncle Sam. In fact, the cover art of *Death Certificate* features a body draped in the US flag with Ice Cube in the background. The toe tag reads 'Uncle Sam'; presumably, the title of the album refers to the death certificate of Uncle Sam himself and expresses rage at continued racism at the hands of the state. His recent film venture is thus rather ironic. Specifically, the song opens with a skit that criticises US military recruiting exercises in black working-class neighbourhoods. Ice Cube also starred in the socially conscious film *Boys n the Hood*. However, according to Michael Franti of the rap group Disposable Heroes of Hiphoprisy, Ice Cube starred in a St. Ides beer commercial a week after this film was released on the film circuit (Reed et al. 1992: 154–155).

4   It is also rather ironic to note that Ice-T has gone on to star in the long-running television series *Law and Order*, in which he plays a detective. The series offers narratives

about the US criminal justice system, detailing the work of detectives and forensic examiners as well as that of prosecutors and judges. Ice-T's incendiary song 'Cop Killer' – which narrates the murder of a policeman – was removed from Body Count's debut album in 1992 after a public outcry. The album in its current form opens with 'Smoked Pork', a skit in which Ice-T shoots an abrasive police officer. Much like Ice Cube on *Death Certificate*, *Body Count* expresses its rage against racism in the USA.

5   In the song's music video – which is available off *Zola: The Journey, Part One* (Zola 2005) – Zola plays three characters: a homeless person, a gangster and a bridegroom en route to his wedding. By the end of the video, the gangster stops the bridegroom's car and shoots him as the homeless man looks on helplessly. The music video cuts to black and the following text is displayed: 'We are killing ourselves.' The social comment that Zola offers here resonates well with the train murder scene, which in itself comments on the futility of black-on-black violence.

References

Barnett C (2004) *Yizo Yizo*: Citizenship, commodification and popular culture in South Africa. *Media, Culture and Society* 26(2): 251–271

Bond P (2001) *Against global apartheid: South Africa meets the World Bank, IMF and international finance.* Cape Town: University of Cape Town Press

Coplan DB (1985) *In township tonight! South Africa's black city music and theatre.* London and New York: Longman

Hall S (1992) What is this 'black' in black popular culture? In G Dent (ed.) *Black popular culture.* Seattle: Bay Press

Hall S (1996) Gramsci's relevance for the study of race and ethnicity. In D Morley and K-H Chen (eds) *Stuart Hall: Critical dialogues in cultural studies.* London: Routledge

Haupt A (2001) Black thing: Hip-hop nationalism, 'race' and gender in Prophets of da City and Brasse vannie Kaap. In Z Erasmus (ed.) *Coloured by history, shaped by place: New perspectives on coloured identities in Cape Town.* Cape Town: Kwela Books and SA History Online

Henry M (2002) He is a 'bad mother*$%@!#': *Shaft* and contemporary black masculinity. *Journal of Popular Film and Television* 30(2): 114–119

Hood G (dir.) (2005) *Tsotsi.* Johannesburg: Tsotsi Films

Impey A (2001) Resurrecting the flesh? Reflections on women in kwaito. *Agenda* 49: 44–50

Kitwana B (2002) *The hip hop generation: Young blacks and the crisis in African-American culture.* New York: Basic Civitas Books

Lynskey D (2006) 'I saw blood on the streets.' *Guardian Unlimited Arts.* Accessed 14 August 2006, http://arts.guardian.co.uk/features/story/0,,1731901,00.html

Marx L (1996) Underworld RSA. *South African Theatre Journal* 10(2): 11–30

Maseko Z (dir.) (2004) *Drum*. Armada Pictures International

Morris N (2002) The myth of unadulterated culture meets the threat of imported media. *Media, Culture and Society* 24(2): 278–289

Potter RA (1995) *Spectacular vernaculars: Hip-hop and the politics of postmodernism*. Albany: State University of New York Press

Quinn E (2000) Black British cultural studies and the rap on gangsta. *Black Music Research Journal* 20(2): 195–216

Reed I, Franti M & Adler B (1992) Hiphoprisy. *Transition* 56: 152–165

SA Film (2004) Oliver Schmitz: Director of *Hijack stories*. *SA film. News and resources for filmmakers*. Accessed 28 July 2006, http://www.safilm.org.za/interviews/interview.php?uid=173

Schmitz O (dir.) (2000) *Hijack stories*. Germany and United Kingdom: Schlemmer Film GmbH and Xenos Pictures

Shakur T (1994) *Thug life: Volume 1*. USA: Interscope Records. Transcriptions obtained from Original Hip-Hop Lyrics Archive, accessed 31 July 2006, www.ohhla.com

Smith R (2003) *Yizo Yizo* and essentialism: Representations of women and gender-based violence in a drama series based on reality. In H Wasserman and S Jacobs (eds) *Shifting selves: Post-apartheid essays on media, culture and identity*. Cape Town: Kwela Books

Strelitz L (2004) Against cultural essentialism: Media reception among South African youth. *Media, Culture and Society* 26(5): 625–641

Thandiswa (2004) *Zabalaza*. Gallo, South Africa

Tomaselli K (1993) Colouring it in: Films in 'black' or 'white' – reassessing authorship. *Critical Arts* 7(1–2): 61–77

Ya Salaam M (1995) The aesthetics of rap. *African American Review* 29(2): 303–315

Zola (2005) *Zola: The journey, part one*. Johannesburg: Ghetto Ruff and Guluva Entertainment

Contributors

Tanja Bosch, a former Fulbright scholar, holds a PhD in mass communication from Ohio University. Her dissertation on community radio and identity in South Africa was awarded the Broadcast Education Association (BEA) Outstanding Dissertation Award. She researches and consults widely on community media, and has worked on projects in Jamaica, Trinidad, India and South Africa. She is currently a lecturer in the Centre for Film and Media Studies at the University of Cape Town.

Wiida Fourie is a lecturer in the Department of Journalism at Tshwane University of Technology in Pretoria, where she lectures in mass communication theory, media ethics, and journalism and trauma. Her chapter is based on her unpublished master's thesis, 'A phenomenological interpretation of the perceptions of letter writers to *Beeld* of the socio-political changes in South Africa (1990 and 2004)', completed in November 2006 with the University of South Africa.

Johannes Froneman is a former journalist and teaches communication studies at North-West University (Potchefstroom campus). He holds a BA, a BA Honours, and a master's degree in journalism (all from the University of Stellenbosch) and a PhD from Potchefstroom University.

Anthea Garman is a senior lecturer in the School of Journalism and Media Studies at Rhodes University in Grahamstown. She is a doctoral fellow in the Constitution of Public Intellectual Life research project in the Graduate School for the Humanities and Social Sciences at the University of the Witwatersrand, where her thesis work focuses on the making and mediation of Antjie Krog as a South African public intellectual.

Ian Glenn is director of the Centre for Film and Media Studies at the University of Cape Town. He has published widely on South African and African literary and cultural studies, and has a particular interest in political communication and in media and the environment. He is working on a study of the French explorer François Le Vaillant, with a focus on Le Vaillant's influence on travel and nature writing.

Adrian Hadland is a chief research specialist in the Democracy and Governance research programme of the Human Sciences Research Council (HSRC). He holds an MLitt from Oxford University and a PhD in film and media studies from the University of Cape Town. Before joining the HSRC, he was the political editor and assistant editor of the *Cape Argus*. He has worked for a number of South African and international news organisations as a political journalist and columnist for more than a dozen years. His areas of research interest include media systems, accountability, democratisation, ethics, community media, government institutions, South Africa's transition, history, culture and heritage.

Adam Haupt is a senior lecturer in the Centre for Film and Media Studies at the University of Cape Town, where he obtained his PhD. He has published on black South African youth culture, global capitalism, technology and intellectual property. Haupt is the author of *Stealing Empire* (HSRC Press 2008). He has worked in the media, mostly as an arts journalist, and taught at the University of the Western Cape, the University of Stellenbosch and the Cape Technikon.

Anita Howarth is currently doing her PhD at the London School of Economics and Political Science on the relationship between media representations and government policy on genetically modified food. She teaches media theory and political communication at Kingston University (London). Her research interests are in political communication and include the role of media in public policy; media representations of foreign policy; media constructions of food scares and environmental scares; as well as the constructions of risk and politicisation of risk in the media. She is also seeking to broaden her research beyond Western dimensions of political communication to include African dimensions. In doing so, she is attempting to draw on perspectives from African theorists, African media and African political actors, thereby providing an alternative to the hegemony of Western media and Western political actors.

Nicola Jones is a senior lecturer in the Media and Cultural Studies Department at the University of KwaZulu-Natal. She has wide experience as a journalist and still works freelance as a specialist writer and regular columnist.

Angie Knaggs is a PhD student at the University of Queensland. She won a Commonwealth Scholarship to study there after completing an MA with distinction at the University of Cape Town's Centre for Film and Media Studies.

Eric Louw is director of Communication Programs in the School of Journalism and Communication, University of Queensland, Brisbane, Australia. His primary area of research is political communication. He has written *The Media* and *Political Process* (Sage Publications 2005); *The Media and Cultural Production* (Sage Publications 2001); *South African Media Policy* (Anthropos 1993); and *The Rise, Fall and Consequences of Apartheid* (Praeger 2004). He also co-edited *The South African Alternative Press* (Anthropos 1991). Another book, *New Voices Over the Air: The Transformation of the South African Broadcasting Corporation in a Changing South Africa* (Hampton Press), is currently in press.

Marguerite J Moritz, a former news producer for NBC, is professor and UNESCO chair in international journalism education at the University of Colorado, Boulder. She was named a Fulbright Senior Scholar in 2002 and has presented her research in more than 17 countries. In 2006 she lectured at universities in Shanghai, Xian and Beijing. In 2004 she was a visiting professor at the Sorbonne and a guest lecturer at UNESCO. Her research looks at professional codes and practices in contemporary news and entertainment media. In particular her work examines the creation and use of still and video images in the digital era, the representations of marginalised groups, and the impact of crisis reporting on journalists and their subjects. In 2005 she received a National Science Foundation grant to conduct research on media coverage of Hurricane Katrina.

Sonja Narunsky-Laden joined the Department of Communication, University of Johannesburg, in 2005 after lecturing in the Department of Poetics and Comparative Literature at Tel Aviv University for many years. Her doctoral research addresses the emergence of a black middle class in South Africa, as represented in and mediated by magazines published for black South African readers. Her current research interests include broader processes of self- and social identity within contexts of socio-cultural change, questions of 'cultural economy', and the ways in which patterns of consumer culture and lifestyle reorganise the broader socio-cultural entities in which they operate. She has published in the fields of New Historicism; consumer culture and women's magazines in Israel; and socio-cultural change through consumerism and how this has impacted on the South African magazine industry and its readerships. She co-edited with Leon de Kock and Louise Bethlehem the award-winning special issue of *Poetics Today* entitled *South Africa in the Global Imaginary*, published in book form by UNISA Press (2004).

Simphiwe Sesanti is a lecturer in the Department of Journalism at the University of Stellenbosch. He has worked as a journalist, writing for South African and international publications in the areas of politics and arts, for more than ten years. He has written an autobiography, *Carry On, African Child* (Vul 'Indlela Publishers 2002).

Jane Stadler is a researcher and lecturer in film and television studies at the University of Queensland, with a PhD from Murdoch University, Australia. Previously she was senior lecturer and convenor of the film studies major at the University of Cape Town. Her research is centrally concerned with media ethics and the relationship between media and identity formation, as well as the role of the media in social change.

Ruth Teer-Tomaselli is currently professor of culture, communication and media studies at the University of KwaZulu-Natal. She holds the UNESCO-Orbicom chair in communication for southern Africa, and is past vice president of the International Association for Media and Communication Research (IAMCR). Her current research interests include the political economy of broadcasting and telecommunications in southern Africa; programme production on television and radio, particularly community radio; and the role of media in development.

Yves Vanderhaeghen, occasional columnist, lecturer and farmer, is deputy editor of *The Witness* newspaper.

Kees van der Waal is a social anthropologist based at Stellenbosch University. His research interests lie in the anthropology of development and in cultural identity politics. His fieldwork was done mostly in Limpopo province while he was working at the University of Johannesburg. Recently he has begun doing research in the Western Cape on organisational complexity in rural development and on the Afrikaans-language debate.

Stella Viljoen teaches history of art and popular culture in the Department of Visual Arts, University of Pretoria. Her field of interest includes the ethical investigation of contemporary visual culture and the politics of gender. Her research is principally centred on the point of intersection between (art historical) 'high culture' and mass culture, particularly within magazine discourse.

Dee Viney works as a lecturer in the Media and Cultural Studies Department at the University of KwaZulu-Natal, and is one of the few academics who have done extensive research into the South African tabloid phenomenon.

CONTRIBUTORS

Herman Wasserman teaches media, communication and cultural studies at the University of Newcastle, United Kingdom, and is associate professor extraordinary in the Department of Journalism, University of Stellenbosch. His research interests include media ethics and social change, media and popular culture, and media constructions of identity. He co-edited *Shifting Selves: Post-Apartheid Essays on Mass Media, Culture and Identity* (Kwela Books 2003). He is editor of the journal *Ecquid Novi: African Journalism Studies.*

Abebe Zegeye, originally from Ethiopia, is a professor of sociology and Primedia chair of holocaust and genocide studies at the University of South Africa. He has taught at universities in Africa, North America and Europe. He has written widely on art, culture and media, as well as on human rights, environmental change and social problems in Africa. He also specialises in identities, both in Africa and elsewhere.